T0399951

Private Policing of Economic Crime

This book discusses private policing conducted by fraud examiners and financial crime specialists when there is suspicion of white-collar crime. The theory of convenience applies to the suspected crime, while the maturity model applies to the conducted investigation.

Private policing of economic crime by fraud examiners in internal investigations is a topic of increasing concern as there is a growing business for law firms and auditing firms to conduct inquiries and reviews when there is suspicion of misconduct, wrongdoing, and crime by white-collar offenders. The key features of this book are the application of a structural model for convenience theory and the application of a maturity model for fraud examinations. The structural model assesses convenience themes for motive, opportunity, and willingness in each case study, while the maturity model assesses the level of private policing maturity in fraud examinations. For the first time, two emerging frameworks to study white-collar offenses and private policing maturity are introduced and applied to a number of cases from Denmark, Iceland, Moldova, the Netherlands, Norway, Sweden, and Switzerland.

This book will be essential to those studying law, business, and criminology, as well as to practicing fraud examiners.

Petter Gottschalk is Professor in the Department of Leadership and Organizational Behavior at BI Norwegian Business School in Oslo, Norway. Dr. Gottschalk has published extensively on knowledge management, intelligence strategy, police investigations, white-collar crime, and fraud examinations.

Private Policing of Economic Crime

Case Studies of Internal Investigations by Fraud Examiners

Petter Gottschalk

LONDON AND NEW YORK

First published 2021
by Routledge
2 Park Square, Milton Park, Abingdon, Oxon OX14 4RN

and by Routledge
52 Vanderbilt Avenue, New York, NY 10017

Routledge is an imprint of the Taylor & Francis Group, an informa business

British Library Cataloguing-in-Publication Data
A catalogue record for this book is available from the British Library

Library of Congress Cataloging-in-Publication Data
Names: Gottschalk, Petter, 1950- author.
Title: Private policing of economic crime: case studies of internal investigations by fraud examiners / Petter Gottschalk.
Description: Milton Park, Abingdon, Oxon; New York, NY: Routledge, 2021. | Includes bibliographical references and index.
Identifiers: LCCN 2020040428 (print) | LCCN 2020040429 (ebook) | ISBN 9780367696252 (hardback) | ISBN 9781003142607 (ebook)
Subjects: LCSH: Fraud. | White collar crimes. | Police, Private. | Commercial crimes. | Business enterprises–Corrupt practices.
Classification: LCC HV6691 .G684 2021 (print) | LCC HV6691 (ebook) | DDC 363.25/963–dc23
LC record available at https://lccn.loc.gov/2020040428
LC ebook record available at https://lccn.loc.gov/2020040429

ISBN: 978-0-367-69625-2 (hbk)
ISBN: 978-1-003-14260-7 (ebk)

Typeset in Galliard
by Deanta Global Publishing Services, Chennai, India

Contents

Introduction

Two decades have soon passed since Schneider (2006) and Williams (2005) emphasized the problematic role of fraud examiners in internal investigations, as examiners conduct private policing of economic crime. In the meantime, the business of fraud examinations has grown substantially in forensic departments in auditing firms and in consulting departments in law firms. Examples of auditing firms include Deloitte (2019, 2020), KPMG (2019, 2020), Kroll (2015, 2017, 2018a, 2018b, 2018c), and PwC (2019a, 2019b). Examples of law firms include Clifford Chance (2020), DLA Piper (2020), Garcia (2019), Kammeradvokaten (2019), Kluge (2019), Sands (2019a, 2019b), and Wiersholm (2019). This book develops all these examples into case studies of private policing of economic crime in terms of internal investigations by fraud examiners.

Private policing is provision of policing services such as investigations and detective work other than by public servants in the normal course of their public duties. The public policing function is typically located in a government body, while private policing in the area of fraud examinations is typically located in auditing firms and law firms. The authority and tools of a policing entity range from full legal authority granted to the office of the public police to no special authority at all beyond that provided by the clients of fraud examinations. However, both need knowledge and awareness of typical human error sources such as confirmation traps, tunnel vision, and social stereotypes are important (Bjerknes and Fahsing, 2018). For example, gender stereotypes distinguishing women and men along traditional thinking can cause investigative errors (Brands and Mehra, 2019).

Beneficiaries can range from everyone, as in the case of public policing, to only those entities that fund policing. Furthermore, "the public police, as an institution of the criminal justice system, inherently possess a punishment or coercion-based mentality propelled by their authority as agents of the criminal law and their capacity to apply state-sanctioned force" (Wood, 2020: 25). In contrast, private policing of economic crime is consulting work where fraud examiners conduct internal investigations to establish facts and advise clients what to do next.

The business of private policing by fraud examiners seems to be growing more rapidly than national and international public police organizations to combat fraud (Wood, 2020: 26):

> Determining the ratios of private agents to public agents is invariability hard to do with much accuracy, but it is clear that private policing entities surpass the latter in sheer numbers and to varying degrees across established democracies and countries in transition.

An example of private policing is the investigation of suspected insurance fraud. Stenström (2018: 478) studied the ways private policing is organized with regard to profitability for insurance firms in Sweden:

> While the literature on private policing has enhanced our understanding of its growth, scope and normative implications, less is known about how "hybrid" policing is conducted to make profit. Informed by 38 qualitative interviews with the seven largest insurance companies in Sweden, the article details how power relations are organized to ensure that the private policing of insurance claims supports and does not pose a threat to profit. Drawing on evidence from the empirical research, a range of issues are discussed, including the relationship between private policing and state power, and the intertwined governance of both claimants and policing actors.

Stenstöm (2018) found that an investigation has to be profitable, which means that a small claim cannot cause a large investigation effort. A relevant example here from the neighboring country Norway is the insurance company Gjensidige, which has a claim against some Hells Angels members. Since Gjensidige believes there are few valuable assets to be retrieved from the Hells Angels members, the insurance firm is not willing to spend resources investigating them. While the perspective of corporate social responsibility might imply that the insurance firm should nevertheless investigate and thus help Norwegian police investigate organized criminals such as Hells Angels, the insurance firm is reluctant to do it (Gottschalk, 2013). The perspective of private policing being profitable is relevant for this book, as a fraud examination effort can be considered an investment, where benefits should exceed costs of the investigation.

The purpose of this book is to study cases of internal investigations by fraud examiners. The book presents a stage model for maturity in private policing and applies the maturity model to each case study. The 14 cases resulted from a search for investigation reports in the spring term 2020, when students in a Norwegian business school had an assignment concerned with evaluation of fraud examinations. The students attended an elective class on leadership and financial crime that focused on white-collar offenders and fraud investigations. While students conducted an in-depth study of one of the fraud examinations, this book reviews all examinations in terms of fraud examination outcome and private policing evaluation.

Client firms who hire investigators tend to keep internal reports by fraud examiners secret. They do not want to disclose the contents to the media or the public in general. Even when there is suspicion of serious economic crime, many clients prefer not to disclose reports to the police (Gottschalk and Tcherni-Buzzeo, 2017). "Typically, corporations tend to take their own measures to resolve instances of fraud without resorting to the police" (King, 2020a: 1). "Corporate clients can effectively choose to sidestep the criminal justice system and not report matters to authorities, propagating debate on the treatment of white-collar criminals compared to others" (King, 2020b: 9).

Therefore, we cannot generalize the extent of fraud examination maturity based on our sample of 14 reports. King (2020a) argues that nine attributes are critical for the corporate investigator's inquiry success: communication, motivation, industry experience, qualifications, police or regulatory experience, business acumen, conceptual thinking, resilience, and rapport building.

Figure 0.1 illustrates the maturity model that we apply in this book. Stages of growth models for maturity levels help to assess and evaluate a variety of phenomena (e.g., Röglinger et al., 2012; Solli-Sæther and Gottschalk, 2015). Stage models predict the development or evolution of investigative maturity from basic performance to superior results (Iannacci et al., 2019: 310):

> They also suggest that this development is progressive (i.e., each successive stage is better than the previous one), stepwise (i.e., each step is a necessary

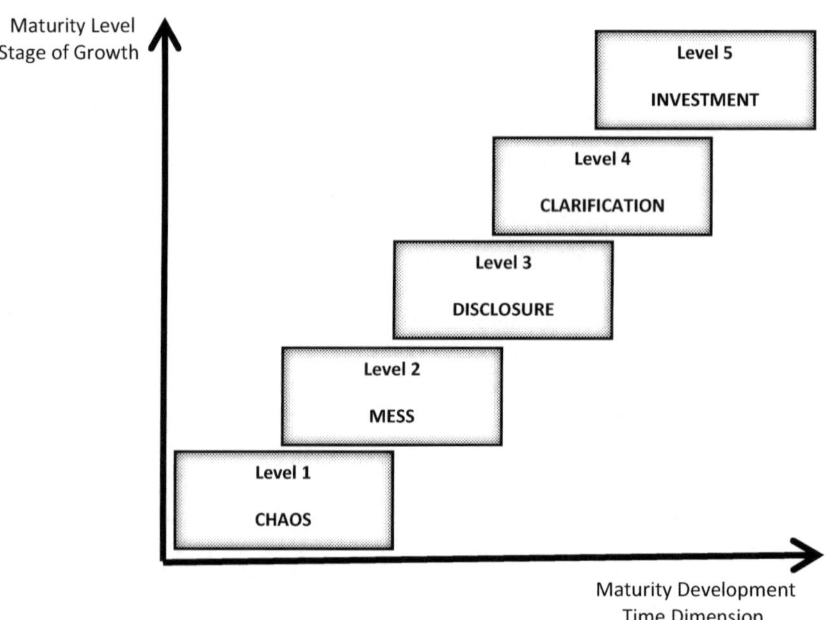

Figure 0.1 Maturity model for internal private investigations with five stages

prerequisite for the following step in the sequence), and prescriptive (i.e., each step must occur in a prescribed order in accordance with a pre-existing plan or vision), thus emphasizing the chain of successful events rather than the mechanisms by which subsequent stages come about.

Here we apply the concept of stages in terms of maturity levels to evaluate private internal investigations (Brooks and Button, 2011; Button and Gee, 2013; Button et al., 2007a, 2007b; King, 2020a, 2020b; Schneider, 2006; Williams, 2005). The purpose is to develop characteristics of investigations at different maturity levels. Based on previous studies of investigation reports (Gottschalk, 2020), we present a five-stage model as illustrated in the figure.

The five maturity levels in the stage model for private policing have the following descriptions:

1. *The investigation was a chaos.* The investigation caused more confusion than before the examination was initiated. The investigation was insufficient, inadequate, surface-oriented, a waste of time, useless, passive, unprofessional, worthless, immature, unacceptable, bad, meaningless, fruitless, awful, and chaotic. The investigation was a failure and a disaster. The investigation lacked results and had no value. Investigators looked where it was easy to find something, rather than searching for relevant information to solve the case. This stage might deserve the label "Waste of Time".
2. *The investigation was a mess.* Nothing came out of the investigation. The investigation was random, amateur, formalities focused, somewhat good, not enough, mainly descriptive, problem-oriented, neutral, unsystematic, inadequate, activity-oriented, shortsighted, fruitless, deviations-oriented, reactive, questions-oriented, and messy. The investigation lacked scrutiny, was a collection of information without analysis, and had too many assumptions that made conclusions invalid. The investigation was superficial and very limited. This stage might deserve the label "Wishful Thinking".
3. *The investigation was a disclosure.* Examiners were successful in identifying and documenting some new facts. The investigation had a clear perspective; it was competence-oriented, average, biased, targeted, systematized, integrated, moderate, indifferent, standard, competent, cause-based, revealing, and disclosure-oriented. The investigation was problem-oriented and limited by the mandate. The investigation was reflective, yet average. This stage might deserve the label "Better Luck Next Time".
4. *The investigation was a clarification.* The investigation was able to reconstruct past events and sequences of events. The investigation was responsible, detailed, conscientious, enough, professional, neutral, unprejudiced, integrated, proactive, preventive, mature, competent, systematic, professional, explorative, immaculate, expedient, truth seeking, facts-based, complete, independent, and clarifying. The investigation added value. The investigation was thorough and worked well. This stage might deserve the label "Time Well Spent".

5. *The investigation was an investment.* The investigation made a valuable contribution to the organization, where investigation benefits exceed investigation costs. The investigation was optimal, innovative, profitable, strategic, extraordinary, outstanding, provident, value-oriented, advanced, learning-focused, valuable, irreversible, truth-based, socially responsible, exceptional, excellent, perfect, exemplary, and a profitable investment. The investigation was a masterpiece and enrichment for the client and society. The investigation was complete and influential. The investigation was strategically a success. This stage might deserve the label "Here's My Money".

Fraud examination strategies influence the level of maturity, where Gottschalk (2020) makes distinctions between five strategies. First, knowledge strategy defines the areas of expertise that fraud examiners must apply to the task of reconstructing past events and sequences of events. Very often, legal knowledge is the dominating expertise applied, while there is a lack of organizational and accounting knowledge in the investigation. Next, information strategy defines sources of information that contribute to reconstructing past events and sequences of events. Very often, formal documents such as minutes of meetings are the dominating source applied, while there is a lack of investigative interviewing and visits to potential crime scenes. Third, value configuration strategy defines the primary activities in the investigation. Very often, the value chain is the dominating configuration, where tasks follow in a sequential manner, while the alternative of the value shop is a more relevant configuration, where tasks follow each other iteratively by returning to earlier tasks. Fourth, systems strategy defines the application of information technology and digitalization in the investigation. Very often, simple search words are used in digital queries that provide few and inconclusive instances of suspicious activities. Finally, methods strategy defines the overall approach and perspectives in the investigation. Very often, fraud examiners conduct interviews in a confrontational rather than cooperation manner. Very often, examiners have a thinking style of systematic analysis rather than the challenge style or the risk style of investigative thinking.

Each case study in this book applies the described model of maturity in private policing. Each case study also applies the structural model of convenience theory, as illustrated in Figure 0.2. The emerging theory of convenience for white-collar crime is concerned with financial possibilities and threats, organizational opportunity to commit and conceal financial crime, as well as personal willingness for deviant behavior.

The research literature on convenience theory is growing (e.g., Braaten and Vaughn, 2019; Chan and Gibbs, 2020; Dearden and Gottschalk, 2020; Gottschalk, 2019; Hansen, 2020; Kireenko et al., 2019; Leasure and Zhang, 2018; Otu and Okon, 2019; Reese and McDougal, 2018; Vasiu and Podgor, 2019).

White-collar offenders commit financial crime during their occupations (Craig, 2019; Craig and Piquero, 2016; Dearden, 2016, 2017, 2019; Jordanoska, 2018; Klenowski et al., 2011; Onna, 2020; Onna and Denkers, 2019). Convenience

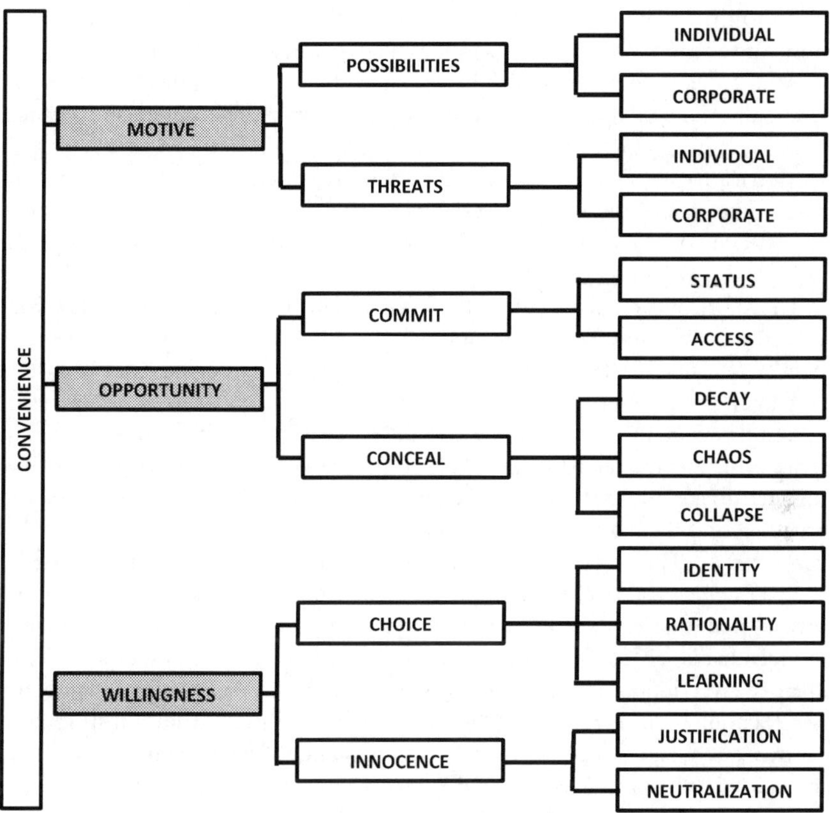

Figure 0.2 Structural model of convenience theory for white-collar crime

theory suggests that the financial motive in white-collar crime is to explore possibilities and avoid threats; the organizational opportunity is to commit as well as conceal crime, while the willingness is deviant behavior by justification and neutralization (Vasiu and Podgor, 2019). The theory of convenience is an integrated and deductive perspective based on the synthesis of individual-level, group-level, and nation-level themes (Chan and Gibbs 2020; Gottschalk, 2019). Convenience theory builds on previous theoretical perspectives on fraud, such as the fraud triangle, the fraud scale, the fraud diamond, the MICE model, and the ABC model (Desai, 2020), as well as general theoretical perspectives on economic crime (Gottschalk, 2019).

Convenience is the state of being able to proceed with something with little effort or difficulty, avoiding pain and strain (Mai and Olsen, 2016). Convenience is savings in time and effort (Farquhar and Rowley, 2009), as well as avoidance of pain and obstacles (Higgins, 1997). Convenience is a relative concept concerned with efficiency in time and effort as well as reduction in pain and solution to problems (Engdahl, 2015). Convenience is an advantage in favor of a specific action to the detriment of alternative actions. White-collar offenders choose the most convenient path to reach their goals (Wikstrom et al., 2018).

White-collar crime results from delinquent behavior by individuals in competent positions (Piquero, 2018). White-collar offenders commit and conceal their crime in a professional setting (Yeok et al., 2020) where they have legitimate access to premises, resources, and systems (Logan et al., 2019). The benefit from white-collar crime might be financial gain, personal adventure, or some other desired outcome (Craig and Piquero, 2017; Jordanoska, 2018; Sutherland, 1939, 1983; Williams et al., 2019).

The figure illustrates the structure of white-collar convenience as derived from the research literature within criminology, sociology, psychology, and management (Gottschalk, 2019). The extent of white-collar crime convenience manifests itself by motive, opportunity, and willingness. The motive is either occupational crime to benefit the individual or corporate crime to benefit the organization because of possibilities or threats (Alalehto, 2020). The ability of white-collar offenders to commit and conceal crime links to their privileged position, the social structure, and their orientation to legitimate and respectable careers (Friedrichs et al., 2018). The personal willingness for deviant behavior manifests itself by offender choice and perceived innocence. The choice of crime can be caused by deviant identity, rational consideration, or learning from others. Social identity is an individual's self-concept as an organizational member (Piening et al., 2020). The perceived innocence at crime manifests itself by justification and neutralization (Schoultz and Flyghed, 2020). Identity, rationality, learning, justification, neutralization, and lack of self-control all contribute to making white-collar crime action a convenient behavior for offenders (Craig and Piquero, 2017; Engdahl, 2015; Holtfreter et al., 2010; Sutherland, 1983; Sykes and Matza, 1957).

In criminology, the conceptualization of deviant behavior is implicitly negative actions that lack conformity to norms (Sykes and Matza, 1957). Deviant behavior typically causes harm to victims. Offenders depart from norms in destructive ways. In our context, deviance is negative departure from norms by white-collar offenders (Gottschalk, 2019, 2020).

In white-collar research, there are different kinds of conception and operationalization of the construct of white-collar crime. Even though Sutherland (1939) coined the term more than eight decades ago, white-collar research remains preoccupied with definition. While many still engage in agitation and dispute about the white-collar crime concept, as exemplified by Galvin (2020), this research simply applies the basic characteristics of the offender, which include status, trust, and access.

White-collar offenders commit economic crime where a great variety of options of financial misconduct is available to them, as illustrated in Figure 0.3. Fraud, theft, manipulation, and corruption are four main categories of financial crime with several subcategories.

Fraud is intentional perversion of the truth for inducing another in reliance upon it to part with some valuable thing belonging to him or to surrender a legal

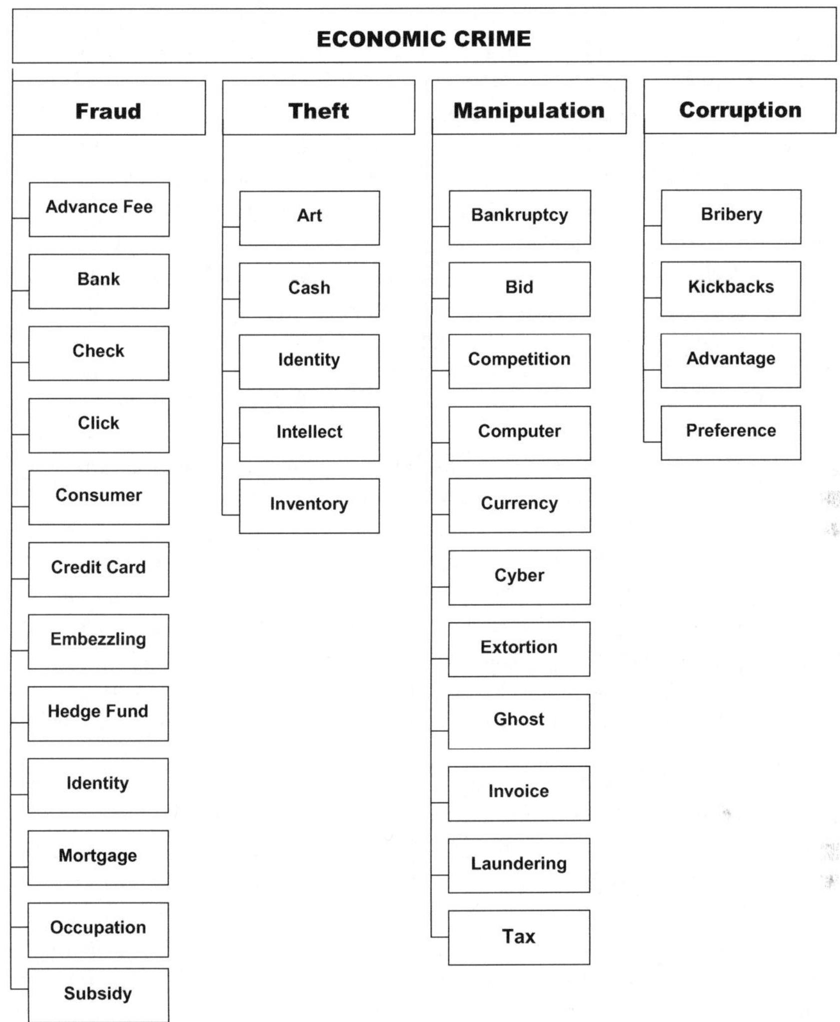

Figure 0.3 Main categories and subcategories of crime

right. Fraud is unlawful and intentional making of a misrepresentation, which causes actual prejudice, or which is potentially prejudicial to another. Bank fraud is a typical example. Bank fraud is a criminal offense of knowingly executing a scheme to defraud a financial institution.

Theft is the illegal taking of property from another person, group, or organization without the victim's consent. For example, identity theft combined with identity fraud is the unlawful use of another's personal identifying information. It involves financial or other personal information stolen with the intent of establishing another person's identity as the thief's own. It occurs when someone uses personally identifying information, like name, social security number and date of birth, government passport number, or credit card number without the owners' permission, to commit economic crime.

Manipulation is a form of cheating where the offender breaks the rules while deliberately leading or allowing others to think the offender respects the rules (Eabrasu, 2020). Manipulation is a means of gaining illegal control or influence over others' activities, tools, and results. For example, bankruptcy crime is criminal acts committed in connection with bankruptcy or liquidation proceedings. A person filing for bankruptcy or a business that has gone into liquidation can hide assets after proceedings start. Thereby, fraudsters can prevent creditors from collecting their valuable belongings. However, most of the criminal acts are typically committed before bankruptcy/liquidation proceedings start, e.g., the debtor has failed to keep accounts or has unlawfully withdrawn money from the business.

Corruption is the giving, requesting, receiving, or accepting of an improper advantage related to a position, office, or an assignment. The improper advantage does not have to relate to a specific action or to not doing this action. It will be enough if the advantage connects to a person's position, office, or assignment. An individual or group is guilty of corruption if they accept money or money's worth for doing something that he is under a duty to do anyway, that he is under a duty not to do, or to exercise a legitimate discretion for improper reason.

Corruption is to destroy or pervert the integrity or fidelity of a person in his discharge of duty, it is to induce to act dishonestly or unfaithfully, it is to make venal, and it is to bribe.

Corruption involves behavior on the part of officials in the public or private sectors, in which they improperly and unlawfully enrich themselves and/or those close to them, or induce others to do so, by misusing the position in which they find themselves. Corruption covers a wide range of illegal activity such as kickbacks, embezzlement, and extortion.

While most case studies in this book are from Norway, there are also other case studies. Switzerland (FIFA World Cup investigated by Garcia), Moldova (Moldovan banks investigated by Kroll), the Netherlands (Oceanteam investigated by Sands), Iceland (Samherji Fishing investigated by Kleinfeld at Al Jazeera), Denmark (Social Security investigated by both PwC and Kammeradvokaten), and Sweden (Swedbank investigated by Clifford Chance) are all present in this book.

The 14 case studies in the first 14 chapters of this book resulted from a search for investigation reports in the spring term 2020, when students in a Norwegian business school had an assignment concerned with evaluation of fraud examinations. Chapters 15 and 16 present slightly different case studies where we also follow what happened after the private policing.

Over the years, this research into private policing of economic crime in terms of case studies of internal inquiries by corporate investigators has resulted in a database with fraud examination reports from all over the world. In Appendix A at the end of this book, a table lists the complete set of reports retrieved so far.

The methodology applied to investigation reports in this book is content analysis (Bell et al., 2018; Braaten and Vaughn, 2019; Saunders et al., 2007). Content analysis is any methodology or procedure that works to identify characteristics within texts attempting to make valid inferences (Krippendorff, 1980; Patrucco et al., 2017). Content analysis assumes that language reflects both how people understand their surroundings and their cognitive processes. Therefore, content analysis makes it possible to identify and determine relevant text in a context (McClelland et al., 2010).

The empirical research design applied in this book is content analysis of investigation reports by fraud examiners. This research design is in the middle of three alternative designs:

1. Interviews with fraud examiners who conduct internal investigations for their clients. This is what King (2020a, 2020b) did. Since his interviewees expressed that they have relevant and comprehensive competence as well as professional working procedures, the research concludes that private policing works well.
2. Content analysis of investigation reports written by fraud examiners. This is the research design applied in this book resulting in a mixed picture regarding the quality of fraud examination work.
3. Interviews with people who have become victims of internal investigations by fraud examiners. An example are whistleblowers who turn into being problematic and then suffer from retaliation and reprisals (Miceli and Near, 2013; Rehg et al., 2009).

As already mentioned, 14 cases resulted from a search for investigation reports in 2020, when students in a Norwegian business school had an assignment concerned with evaluation of fraud examinations. Three hundred students handed in 149 term papers, which means that on average 2 students wrote 1 term paper. They had the choice of one, two, or three students on each paper. Students in Oslo handed in 72 papers, where 33 were about XXL Sports by DLA Piper, 13 about the Navy Logistics by PwC, 10 about Ferde by Kluge and Deloitte, 5 about Oslo Energy Recovery by PwC, and 11 about others. Students in Bergen handed in 29 papers, where 10 were about Ferde by Kluge and Deloitte, 9 about XXL by DLA Piper, 7 about the Navy Logistics by PwC, and 3 about others. Students online handed in 48 papers, where 20 were about the Navy Logistics by PwC, 13 about XXL by DLA Piper, 8 about Ferde Kluge and Deloitte, and 7 about others. Some of the suggestions in student papers are included in this book.

Chapters 1–14 present these cases studies, and Chapters 15 and 16 add two more case studies, Chapter 17 reviews all detected and retrieved private policing reports from different parts of the world that are also listed in Appendix A, and Appendix B only lists reports where a suspect was identified. The review is concerned with cost-benefit analysis, where the issue is whether each investigation is profitable when viewed as an investment by the client firm.

Chapter 17 also reviews conclusions in private policing reports. Surprisingly often, these reports conclude with misconduct but no crime. There is often deviant behavior, there is often wrongdoing, but surprisingly few cases end up in the criminal justice system.

One explanation for the low frequency of public policing in the criminal justice system after private policing is the role of attorneys at work for their clients. When attorneys work as examiners, then they want to be helpful to their clients without causing unnecessary harm to them. When attorneys work as defense lawyers for their clients, then they apply symbolic defense and information control in addition to substance control as introduced in Chapter 18 and discussed in Chapter 19.

Chapter 20 presents the theory of crime signal detection for economic crime, where we return to the issue of low crime detection by fraud examiners from law firms and auditing firms in client organizations.

Private policing of economic crime can take on many forms as illustrated in this book. The case study of internal investigation by fraud examiners in Chapter 21 is concerned with public administration's abuse of power financially to hurt entitled social security recipients and legally to cause incarceration of several social security recipients for alleged fraud. The case study illustrates what the outcome can be when institutions that are supposed to ensure that public authorities do not cause injustices to individuals do not have the competence required to do so and do not react or communicate adequately. In the perspective of convenience theory, blame game, institutional deterioration, and neutralization techniques are some of the convenience themes that can explain the deviant practice in Norwegian social security.

Chapter 22 presents a case study where convenience for criminals mainly derives from lack of digital competence in the victim organization and in police forces. The private policing report illustrates that fraud examners also lack the required knowledge to conduct digital investigations by reconstructing past events and sequences of events, where both actions and actors should be identified.

This book is a monograph with elements of a textbook as several sections of the book can be used for education and training purposes. The research in this book addresses management, consulting, accountancy, auditing, policing, criminology, and sociology. The book does not address law. Therefore, the book does not provide legal frameworks nor identify legal instruments that apply to the countries and cases examined. It does not link cases with the actual court judgments if present in the case. Key criminal offenses referred to in the book are not defined or examined in the light of relevant legal provisions.

Bibliography

Alalehto, T. (2020). Corporate crime: A logical misconception, but with one analytical point, *Journal of Financial Crime*, published online https://doi.org/10.1108/JFC-04-2020-0063.

Bell, E., Bryman, A. and Harley, B. (2018). *Business Research Methods*, 2nd edition, New York: Oxford University Press.

Bjerknes, O.T. and Fahsing, I.A. (2018). *Etterforskning – Prinsipper, Metoder og Praksis (Investigation – Principles, Methods, and Practice)*, Bergen: Fagbokforlaget Publishing House.

Braaten, C.N. and Vaughn, M.S. (2019). Convenience theory of cryptocurrency crime: A content analysis of U.S. federal court decisions, *Deviant Behavior*, published online https://doi.org/10.1080/01639625.2019.1706706.

Brands, R.A. and Mehra, A. (2019). Gender, brokerage, and performance: A construal approach, *Academy of Management Journal*, 62 (1), 196–219.

Brooks, G. and Button, M. (2011). The police and fraud investigation and the case for a nationalized solution in the United Kingdom, *The Police Journal*, 84, 305–319.

Button, M. and Gee, J. (2013). *Countering Fraud for Competitive Advantage – The Professional Approach to Reducing the Last Great Hidden Cost*, Chichester: John Wiley & Sons.

Button, M., Frimpong, K., Smith, G. and Johnston, L. (2007a). Professionalizing counter fraud specialists in the UK: Assessing progress and recommendations for reform, *Crime Prevention and Community Safety*, 9, 92–101.

Button, M., Johnston, L., Frimpong, K. and Smith, G. (2007b). New directions in policing fraud: The emergence of the counter fraud specialists in the United Kingdom, *International Journal of the Sociology of Law*, 35, 192–208.

Chan, F. and Gibbs, C. (2020). Integrated theories of white-collar and corporate crime, in: Rorie, M.L. (editor), *The Handbook of White-Collar Crime*, Hoboken, NJ: Wiley & Sons, chapter 13, pages 191–208.

Clifford Chance (2020). *Report of Investigation on Swedbank*, March 23, Washington, DC: Law Firm Clifford Chance.

Craig, J.M. (2019). Extending situational action theory to white-collar crime, *Deviant Behavior*, 40 (2), 171–186.

Craig, J.M. and Piquero, N.L. (2016). The effects of low self-control and desire-for-control on white-collar offending: A replication, *Deviant Behavior*, 37 (11), 1308–1324.

Craig, J.M. and Piquero, N.L. (2017). Sensational offending: An application of sensation seeking to white-collar and conventional crimes, *Crime & Delinquency*, 63 (11), 1363–1382.

Dearden, T.E. (2016). Trust: The unwritten cost of white-collar crime, *Journal of Financial Crime*, 23 (1), 87–101.

Dearden, T.E. (2017). An assessment of adults' views on white-collar crime, *Journal of Financial Crime*, 24 (2), 309–321.

Dearden, T.E. (2019). How modern psychology can help us understand white-collar criminals, *Journal of Financial Crime*, 26 (1), 61–73.

Dearden, T.E. and Gottschalk, P. (2020). Gender and white-collar crime: Convenience in target selection, *Deviant Behavior*, published online https://doi.org/10.1080/01639625.2020.1756428.

Deloitte (2019). *Lilleakerveien 39 A – Boligbygg Oslo KF Gransking (Lilleaker Road 39 A – Housing Oslo Investigation)*, May, Oslo: Auditing Firm Deloitte.

Deloitte (2020). *Selskapskontroll. Hordaland, Sogn og Fjordane og Rogald Fylkeskommuner: Ferde AS (Company Control.Hordaland, Sogn and Fjordane and Rogaland Municipalities: Ferde Ltd.)*, January, Bergen: Auditing Firm Deloitte.

Desai, N. (2020). Understanding the theoretical underpinnings of corporate fraud, *VIKALPA The Journal for Decision Makers*, 1–7, https://doi.org/10.1177/0256090920917789.

DLA Piper (2020). *Granskingsrapport XXL ASA (Examination Report XXL Ltd.)*, January, Oslo: Law Firm DLA Piper.

Eabrasu, M. (2020). Cheating in business: A metaethical perspective, *Journal of Business Ethics*, 162, 519–532.

Engdahl, O. (2015). White-collar crime and first-time adult-onset offending: Explorations in the concept of negative life events as turning points, *International Journal of Law, Crime and Justice*, 43 (1), 1–16.

Farquhar, J.D. and Rowley, J. (2009). Convenience: A services perspective, *Marketing Theory*, 9 (4), 425–438.

Friedrichs, D.O., Schoultz, I. and Jordanoska, A. (2018). *Edwin H. Sutherland, Routledge Key Thinkers in Criminology*, London: Routledge.

Galvin, M.A. (2020). Substance or semantics? The consequences of definitional ambiguity for white-collar research, *Journal of Research in Crime and Delinquency*, 57 (3), 369–399.

Garcia (2019). *Report on the Inquiry Into the 2018/2019 Fifa World Cup Bidding Process*, Investigatory Chamber, Zürich: FIFA Ethics Committee.

Gottschalk, P. (2013). Limits to Corporate Social Responsibility: The Case of Gjensidige Insurance Company and Hells Angels Motorcycle Club, *Corporate Reputation Review*, 16(3), 177–186.

Gottschalk, P. (2019). *Convenience Triangle in White-Collar Crime – Case Studies of Fraud Examinations*, Cheltenham: Edward Elgar Publishing.

Gottschalk, P. (2020). Private policing of white-collar crime: Case studies of internal investigations by fraud examiners, *Police Practice and Research*, published online https://doi.org/10.1080/15614263.2020.1789461.

Gottschalk, P. and Tcherni-Buzzeo, M. (2017). Reasons for gaps in crime reporting: The case of white-collar criminals investigated by private fraud examiners in Norway, *Deviant Behavior*, 38 (3), 267–281.

Hansen, L.L. (2020). Review of the book "Convenience Triangle in White-Collar Crime: Case Studies of Fraud Examinations", *ChoiceConnect*, 57 (5), Middletown, CT: Association of College and Research Libraries.

Higgins, E.T. (1997). Beyond pleasure and pain, *American Psychologist*, 52, 1280–1300.

Holtfreter, K., Beaver, K.M., Reisig, M.D. and Pratt, T.C. (2010). Low self-control and fraud offending, *Journal of Financial Crime*, 17 (3), 295–307.

Iannacci, F., Seepma, A.P., Blok, C. and Resca, A. (2019). Reappraising maturity models in e-government research: The trajectory-turning point theory, *Journal of Strategic Information Systems*, 28, 310–329.

Jordanoska, A. (2018). The social ecology of white-collar crime: Applying situational action theory to white-collar offending, *Deviant Behavior*, 39 (11), 1427–1449.

Kammeradvokaten (2019). *Ansvarsvurdering Vedrørende Sagen om Svindel med Tilskuddsmidler – Offentlig Rapport (Responsibility Assessment Regarding the Case of Fraud with Benefits Funds – Public Report)*, February 22, Copenhagen: Law Firm Poul Schmith.

King, M. (2020a). What makes a successful corporate investigator – An exploration of private investigators attributes, *Journal of Financial Crime*, published online https://doi.org/10.1108/JFC-02-2020-0019.

King, M. (2020b). Out of obscurity: The contemporary private investigator in Australia, *International Journal of Police Science and Management*, published online https://doi.org/10.1177/1461355720931887.

Kireenko, A.P., Nevzorova, E.N. and Fedotov, D.Y. (2019). Sector-specific characteristics of tax crime in Russia, *Journal of Tax Reform*, 5 (3), 249–264.

Klenowski, P.M., Copes, H. and Mullins, C.W. (2011). Gender, identity, and accounts: How white collar offenders do gender when making sense of their crimes, *Justice Quarterly*, 28 (1), 46–69.

Kluge (2019). *Vurdering av Forhold i Ferde AS (Assessment of Circumstances at Ferde Ltd.)*, December 4, Bergen: Law Firm Kluge.

KPMG (2019). *Rapport Undersøkelse av Varslingssaker Helgelandssykehuset (Report Examination of Whistleblowing Cases Helgeland Hospital)*, October 18, Trondheim: Auditing Firm KPMG.

KPMG (2020). *Rapport Undersøkelse av Varslingssaker – Mandatets del 2 – Helgelandssykehuset (Report Examination of Whistleblowing Cases – the Mandate's Part 2 – Helgeland Hospital)*, January 17, Trondheim: Auditing Firm KPMG.

Krippendorff, K. (1980). *Content Analysis: An Introduction to its Methodology*, Beverly Hills, CA: Sage.

Kroll (2015). *Project Tenor – Scoping Phase, Final Report Prepared for The National Bank of Moldova*, April 2, Nexus Place: Investigation Firm Kroll.

Kroll (2017). *Project Tenor II – Summary Report, Report Prepared for The National Bank of Moldova*, December 20, Nexus Place: Investigation Firm Kroll.

Kroll (2018a). *Project Tenor II – Detailed Report, Report Prepared for The National Bank of Moldova*, March 22, Nexus Place: Investigation Firm Kroll.

Kroll (2018b). *Project Tenor II – Confidential Working Papers – Part I to the Detailed Report: Detailed Tracing Analysis*, Nexus Place: Investigation Firm Kroll.

Kroll (2018c). *Project Tenor II – Confidential Working Papers – Part II: Evidence Packs – Funds Traced to: Ilan Shor, Alexandr Maclovici and Olga Bondarciuc*, Nexus Place: Investigation Firm Kroll.

Leasure, P. and Zhang, G. (2018). "That's how they taught us to do it": Learned deviance and inadequate deterrents in retail banking, *Deviant Behavior*, 39 (5), 603–616.

Logan, M.W., Morgan, M.A., Benson, M.L. and Cullen, F.T. (2019). Coping with imprisonment: Testing the special sensitivity hypothesis for white-collar offenders, *Justice Quarterly*, 36 (2), 225–254.

Mai, H.T.X. and Olsen, S.O. (2016). Consumer participation in self-production: The role of control mechanisms, convenience orientation, and moral obligation, *Journal of Marketing Theory and Practice*, 24 (2), 209–223.

McClelland, P.L., Liang, X. and Barker, V.L. (2010). CEO commitment to the status quo: Replication and extension using content analysis, *Journal of Management*, 36 (5), 1251–1277.

Miceli, M.P. and Near, J.P. (2013). An international comparison of the incidence of public sector whistle-blowing and the prediction of retaliation: Australia, Norway, and the US, *Australian Journal of Public Administration*, 72 (4), 433–446.

Onna, J.H.R. (2020). From the avalance to the game: White-collar offenders on crime, bonds, and morality, *Crime, Law and Social Change*, published online https://doi.org/10.1007/s10611-020-09899-x.

Onna, J.H.R. and Denkers, A.J.M. (2019). Social bonds and white-collar crime: A two-study assessment of informal social controls in white-collar offenders, *Deviant Behavior*, 40 (10), 1206–1225.

Otu, S.E. and Okon, O.N. (2019). Participation in fraud/cheat in the buying and selling of meats without legal metrology: A theoretical and empirical investigation, *Deviant Behavior*, 40 (2), 205–224.

Patrucco, A.S., Luzzini, D. and Ronchi, S. (2017). Research perspectives on public procurement: Content analysis of 14 years of publications in the Journal of Public Procurement, *Journal of Public Procurement*, 16 (2), 229–269.

Piening, E.P., Salge, T.O., Antons, D. and Kreiner, G.E. (2020). Standing together or falling apart? Understanding employees' responses to organizational identity threats, *Academy of Management Review*, 45 (2), 325–351.

Piquero, N.L. (2018). White-collar crime is crime: Victims hurt just the same, *Criminology & Public Policy*, 17 (3), 595–600.

PwC (2019a). *Undersøkelse av Energigjenvinningsetaten i Oslo Kommune (Inquiry into the Energy Recycling Authority at Oslo Municipality)*, October 22, Oslo: Auditing Firm PwC.

PwC (2019b). *Ekstern Undersøgelse af Tilskudsadministrationen 1977-2018 (External Examination of the Benefits Administration 1977–2018)*, February, Oslo: Auditing Firm PwC.

Reese, B. and McDougal, M.K. (2018). Gender, status, and tax offenses, *Deviant Behavior*, 39 (12), 1647–1657.

Rehg, M.T., Miceli, M.P., Near, J.P. and Scotter, J.R.V (2009). Antecedents and outcomes of retaliation against whistleblowers: Gender differences and power relationships, *Organization Science*, 19 (2), 221–240.

Röglinger, M., Pöppelbuss, J. and Becker, J. (2012). Maturity model in business process management, *Business Process Management Journal*, 18 (2), 328–346.

Sands (2019a). *Factual Report: Oceanteam ASA Investigation of Related Party Transactions*, November 4, Oslo: Law Firm Sands.

Sands (2019b). *Report – Legal Review: Oceanteam ASA Investigation of Related Party Transactions*, November 4, Oslo: Law Firm Sands.

Saunders, M., Lewis, P. and Thornhill, A. (2007). *Research Methods for Business Students*, 5th edition, London: Pearson Education.

Schneider, S. (2006). Privatizing economic crime enforcement: Exploring the role of private sector investigative agencies in combating money laundering, *Policing & Society*, 16 (3), 285–312.

Schoultz, I. and Flyghed, J. (2020). Denials and confessions: An analysis of the temporalization of neutralizations of corporate crime, *International Journal of Law, Crime and Justice*, published online https://doi.org/10.1016/j.ijlcj.2020.100389.

Solli-Sæther, H. and Gottschalk, P. (2015). Stages-of-growth in outsourcing, offshoring and backsourcing: Back to the future? *Journal of Computer Information Systems*, 55 (2), 88–94.

Stenström, A. (2018). The private policing of insurance claims: Power, profit and private justice, *British Journal of Criminology*, 58 (2), 478–496.

Sutherland, E.H. (1939). White-collar criminality, *American Sociological Review*, 5 (1), 1–12.

Sutherland, E.H. (1983). *White Collar Crime – The Uncut Version*, New Haven, CT: Yale University Press.

Sykes, G.M. and Matza, D. (1957). Techniques of neutralization: A theory of delinquency, *American Sociological Review*, 22 (6), 664–670.

Vasiu, V.I. and Podgor, E.S. (2019). Organizational opportunity and deviant behavior: Convenience in white-collar crime, in: *Criminal Law and Criminal Justice Books*, July, Rutgers, the State University of New Jersey, www.clcjbooks.rutgers.edu.

Wiersholm (2019). *Presentasjon av Granskingsrapport: Lønns- og Arbeidsvilkår i Caverion med Utvalgte Underleverandører (Presentation of Investigation Report: Wages and Work Conditions at Caverion with Selected Subcontractors)*, November 18, Oslo: Law Firm Wiersholm.

Wikstrom, P.O.H., Mann, R.P. and Hardie, B. (2018). Young people's differential vulnerability to criminogenic exposure: Bridging the gap between people- and place-oriented approaches in the study of crime causation, *European Journal of Criminology*, 15 (1), 10–31.

Williams, J.W. (2005). Reflections on the private versus public policing of economic crime, *British Journal of Criminology*, 45, 316–339.

Williams, M.L., Levi, M., Burnap, P. and Gundur, R.V. (2019). Under the corporate radar: Examining insider business cybercrime victimization through an application of routine activities theory, *Deviant Behavior*, 40 (9), 1119–1131.

Wood, J.D. (2020). Private policing and public health: A neglected relationship, *Journal of Contemporary Criminal Justice*, 36 (1), 19–38.

Yeok, S.G., Ngah, K., Mustapha, J. and Hamid, K.A. (2020). Assessing the efficacy of rehabilitation programs for white-collar criminals: A case study of the northern states of Malaysia, *International Journal of Social Science Research*, 2 (1), 109–123.

1 Caverion services by Wiersholm

Caverion was a subcontractor at a major government construction site in Norway. Management at Caverion faced accusations of white-collar crime in terms of substandard wages and too long working hours for employees from Lithuania who worked at the construction site (Aarseth, 2019):

> Lithuanian workers with illegally low wages were building the National Museum, according to a report. Several Lithuanian workers involved in the development of the new National Museum have salaries far below the general minimum rate, according to a new report. The Lithuanian subcontractor disagrees with the definition of salaries used in the report. According to Statsbygg, it was after random controls in March this year that they suspected possible violations of the regulations for employees on the contract Caverion Norway has at the new National Museum. The Finnish company supplies pipes, ventilation and electric installations to the construction project, and hires workers from its subsidiary in Lithuania. A report from the consulting firm KPMG now concludes that hired workers from Caverion Lithuania had unlawfully low wages.

Statsbygg, the Norwegian government's agency for construction and property affair, hired corporate investigators from law firm Wiersholm (2019) to examine the accusations.

White-collar convenience

Assuming the allegations are correct, we briefly study the alleged white-collar crime by application of convenience theory.

Exploiting the workforce is corporate crime based on possibilities to manipulate foreign workers in Norway. Figure 1.1 illustrates this motive along the axis of motive-possibilities-corporate. Maybe reaching business objectives justified means (Jonnergård et al., 2010), or making as much profit as possible was the only goal (Naylor, 2003).

A lack of organizing created decay that enabled executives to defraud employees. The figure illustrates this opportunity along the axis of opportunity-conceal-decay.

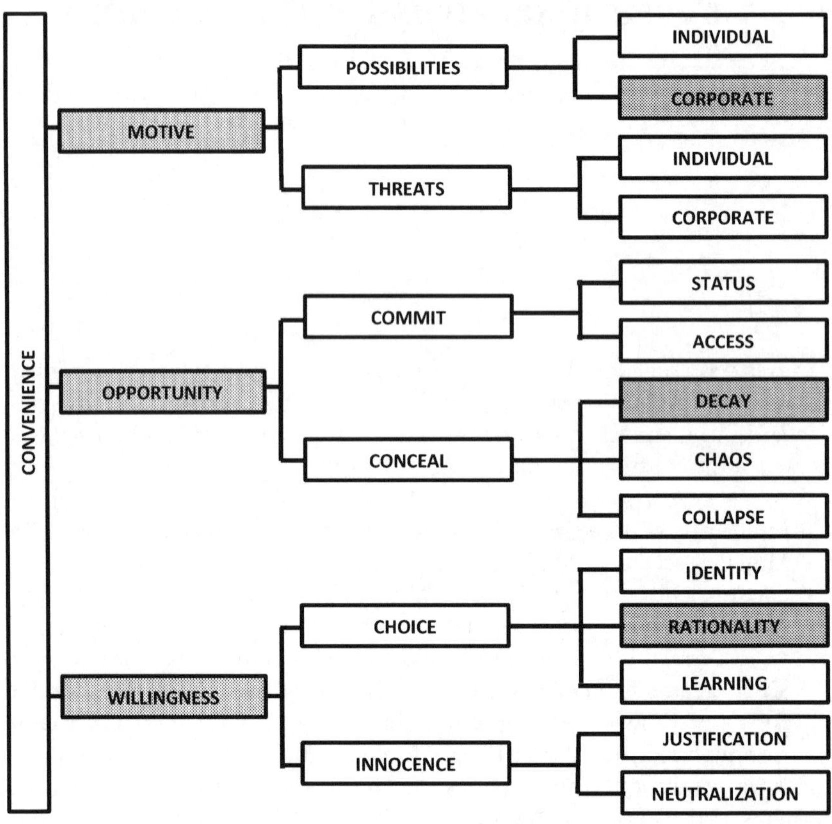

Figure 1.1 Convenience themes in the case of Caverion

Maybe there was a lack of control in principal-agent relationships for the subcontractor (Bosse and Phillips, 2016), or an inability to control because of social disorganization (Hoffmann, 2002).

Finally, in the willingness dimension, it was a rational choice to pay substandard wages and to violate regulations of working hours. The figure illustrates this phenomenon along the axis willingness-choice-rationality. Maybe executives had a perception of benefits from wrongdoing exceeded costs (Pratt and Cullen, 2005), or no perceived deterrence effect seemed present (Comey, 2009).

Fraud examination outcome

In their report of investigation, fraud examiners from law firm Wiersholm (2019) draw the following main conclusions:

1. Caverion is responsible for comprehensive and systematic violations of laws and regulations regarding minimum wages and working conditions in the

Norwegian working environment act. However, the violations do not represent social dumping.
2. Caverion is responsible for violations of agreements in the contract with Statsbygg, which is the Norwegian authority for government buildings.
3. The project management at Statsbygg has done what reasonably were their duty and obligation in monitoring Caverion's activities, including wages paid and working hours practiced.

Fraud examiners nevertheless make the final assessment that the violations of the law are not systematic throughout or very serious in nature. Furthermore, they state that the violations do not represent social dumping, where social dumping is the practice of employers to use cheaper labor than is usually available at their site or in their country.

The knowledge strategy applied to the examination was legal knowledge. Two attorneys conducted the investigation. This knowledge was relevant, as the main task was to examine the extent of conformity to laws and regulations in Norway by the Finnish firm with its Lithuanian workers. The information strategy applied was concerned with documents that related to payments based on hours worked by each employee. While there is an obvious need for documents as evidence of deviance and potential law violations, there was also a need for interviews to understand motives. Therefore, the lawyers conducted 45–50 interviews with relevant persons, including 25 workers on the construction site in Oslo, Norway.

Fraud examiners described their main findings (Wiersholm, 2019: 3):

> The investigation has revealed that several subcontractors who have been working on the construction site, regularly and in different ways have violated obligations to follow Norwegian laws and regulations. It is revealed that Caverion Lithuania is responsible for considerable and serious violations of the working environment act. The violations are mainly related to the rules that regulate working hours and wages in the working environment act and the general coverage act, respectively. Several violations of the working environment act have been detected as they address working hours, overtime and overtime compensation. In addition, there are examples of illegal hiring of a work force. Furthermore, several deviations from standards are detected in labor contracts and lacking registration of working time. We have not performed a complete review of all the incidents related to such violations. Even though the violations in total are both considerable and serious, the foreign workers from Lithuania have nevertheless not been exploited in such a way that it can be characterized as "social dumping".

As part of the investigation, fraud examiners were to assess potential inequality among workers in terms of their working conditions and compensations. The examiners failed in obtaining enough information about experience levels and qualifications among Lithuanian workers. Nevertheless, the examiners concluded that they got the impression that workers were paid fairly.

Fraud examiners ask themselves the following question: How could the illegal activities happen? This is their answer (Wiersholm, 2019: 10):

> The way Wiersholm views the situation, Caverion attempted to correct the deviance at Caverion Lithuania. The magnitude of the problem was, however, never examined or detected in full. In addition, the follow-up of noticed deviance never occurred. In Wiersholm's view, the basic problem was that the situation was not considered sufficiently serious by the Caverion leadership. Caverion's ability and initiative to assess what they noticed in a professional manner was lacking. Wiersholm believes that, based on several interviews and archival evidence, that Caverion for the most part in the project were understaffed.

Private policing evaluation

The fraud examination report by investigators from Wiersholm (2019) deserves a classification of maturity into level 4 in Figure 1.2, as the report contributes to clarification of what went on at the construction site. The private policing report makes clear statements of what was wrong and the extent of misconduct. For example, they identified abuses of working hour regulations in terms of too long working hours, while they at the same time conclude that these violations were not of considerable magnitude. Positive aspects of employment also receive

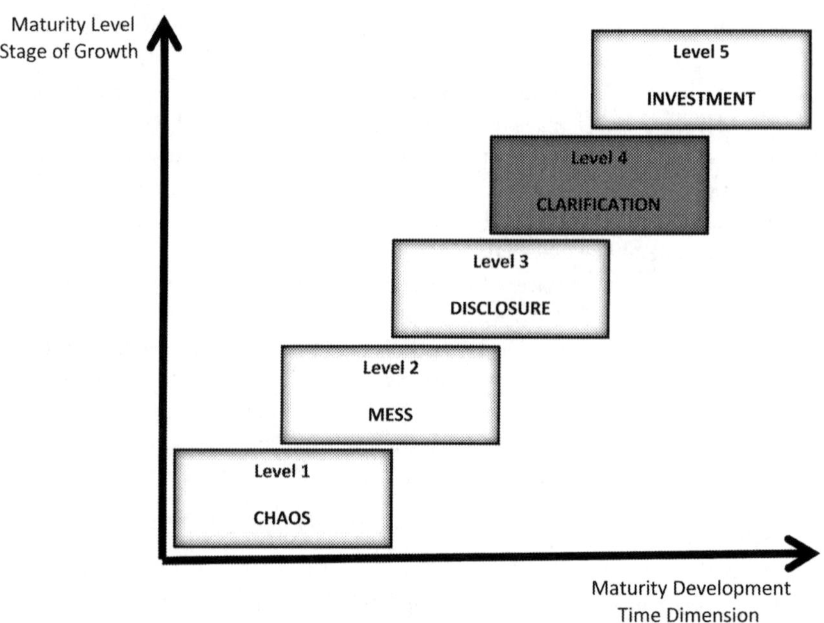

Figure 1.2 Maturity model for internal private investigations applied to Wiersholm

attention, such as acceptable living conditions for workers from abroad and the option of time off to travel home for visits.

The only questionable conclusion relates to the client for the investigation. It was Statsbygg, not Caverion, who hired Wiersholm and paid for their examination. Since Wiersholm reiterates in their report that Statsbygg has done nothing wrong, it seems that it was important to clear the client of any responsibility for the misconduct. The investigators claim in their report that Statsbygg fulfilled all their duties as the contracting agency for constructions, even when it comes to serious aspects related to Lithuania. The investigation reports claim that "given the prevailing circumstances, there were no real sanctions that would have had the desired effect" (Wiersholm, 2019: 8).

An investigation is a reconstruction of events and sequences of events. Not all reconstructions in the current report are satisfactory. The description of activities conducted by Statsbygg in the role of principal leaves many open spaces. A conspiracy perspective would be that Statsbygg is paying for the investigation and thus receives less attention and less blame than they deserve. The report confirms violations of laws and regulations, but there is no mention of the role of Statsbygg. Therefore, examiners have not reconstructed all facts and causes in their report. The report does not only claim that transgression of laws and rules are confirmed, but also that Caverion is solely responsible for the wrongdoing. This has implications for recommendations.

Examiners thus address recommendations solely to Caverion, and nothing concerning Statsbygg. Caverion receive recommendations to improve their control routines, compliance function, organizational structure, and organizational culture. This is fine, but there is no mention of required changes in monitoring systems as applied by Statsbygg. Certainly, there are avenues for improvement in regulatory systems. However, based on the conspiracy assumption, examiners were reluctant to write critically about Statsbygg since they pay law firm Wiersholm for the examination.

An investigation requires assessment based not only on the outcome, but also on the process. The ideal investigation finds all answers in a professional and transparent manner. The protection against self-incrimination, the possibility of contradiction, and written evidence are some important elements. Contradiction means that someone who has a role in the draft report gets the option of commenting on what the report says, and the comment should normally be included in the final report. However, contradiction often takes place in a manner that makes it impossible for a suspect to reflect and present opposing views. For example, examiners request the suspect to come to the law firm, sit in an office, and then only have access to a few sentences or pages on a computer screen. Examiners deny the suspect the reasonable and fair right to take the file or the page home for review. Examiners deny the suspect the reasonable and fair right to confer with anyone else, such as a friend or an attorney. Examiners claim they do it because of the required secrecy, confidentiality, or anonymity of involved persons.

In this line of skepticism, Caverion had many objections to the situational and factual descriptions that should form the basis of the examiner's assessments.

However, Caverion executives were uncertain whether Wiersholm considered the arguments, comments, and objections that the company made before drawing their conclusions. Caverion does not have that impression.

For example, the report contains factual errors in the form of a claim that came from a union representative at Caverion, which evidence has proven wrong. The same applies to the allegations of a lack of existing and relevant routines, according to Caverion executives. Caverion claim they missed the option of contradiction, as they say that if they had read the report in advance of publication, they could have documented that these allegations were not correct. The examined enterprise, Caverion, has thus a bad impression of unfair treatment in the investigation initiated by the enterprise's customer Statsbygg.

Bibliography

Aarseth, T. (2019). Litauiske arbeidere med ulovlig lav lønn var med å bygge Nasjonalmuseet (Lithuanian workers with illegally low wages were engaged in building the National Museum), *Norwegian Union Magazine FriFagbevegelse*, www.frifagbevegelse.no, published October 24.

Bosse, D.A. and Phillips, R.A. (2016). Agency theory and bounded self-interest, *Academy of Management Review*, 41 (2), 276–297.

Comey, J.B. (2009). Go directly to prison: White collar sentencing after the Sarbanes-Oxley act, *Harvard Law Review*, 122, 1728–1749.

Hoffmann, J.P. (2002). A contextual analysis of differential association, social control, and strain theories of delinquency, *Social Forces*, 81 (3), 753–785.

Jonnergård, K., Stafsudd, A. and Elg, U. (2010). Performance evaluations as gender barriers in professional organizations: A study of auditing firms, *Gender, Work and Organization*, 17 (6), 721–747.

Naylor, R.T. (2003). Towards a general theory of profit-driven crimes, *British Journal of Criminology*, 43, 81–101.

Pratt, T.C. and Cullen, F.T. (2005). Assessing macro-level predictors and theories of crime: A meta-analysis, *Crime and Justice*, 32, 373–450.

Wiersholm (2019). *Presentasjon av Granskingsrapport: Lønns- og Arbeidsvilkår i Caverion med Utvalgte Underleverandører (Presentation of Investigation Report: Wages and Work Conditions at Caverion with Selected Subcontractors)*, November 18, Oslo: Law Firm Wiersholm.

2 Ferde toll collection by Kluge

Ferde was a regional toll collection company that, with a mandate from the state, financed new toll road projects and managed toll collection on public roads. Investigative journalist Peter Svaar at the Norwegian public broadcasting NRK accused the chief executive at Ferde, Trond Juvik, of abusing his position to do work for others and to make Ferde buy computer software from a company where Juvik was a major shareholder (Svaar and Venli, 2019). NRK published a story called "The Treasure Hunt" (Svaar, 2019):

> The Bergen toll collection chief enjoyed his million-level salary from the public authority while managing a tax collection system in a province in Congo. NRK can document how Trond Juvik was:
>
> - Working on the tax system during office hours: Ferde boss Trond Juvik worked on the private Congo project during the office hours of the publicly owned toll collection company Ferde, data logging shows.
> - Sitting on the owner side: Juvik had ownership interests in the private company that ran the tax project in Congo. At the same time, he gave two employees in the toll collection company his permission to work on the project.
> - Dealing with the same company: When the Congo project had expensive data system licenses that they could not use, Ferde spent toll money to buy the licenses from the private company.
> - Keeping a central role: Juvik was sitting "on the cash" in the Congo project, according to a central employee. The same firm, from which the toll company bought the computer licenses, ran the project. The toll company chief Juvik himself participated in the trade deal.
>
> NRK has provided the information in this article to Trond Juvik, but he did not want to participate in an interview. Instead, in an email, he states that the company Ferde is under private internal investigation, and that he will not respond while the investigation is ongoing.

The board at Ferde first hired corporate investigators from law firm Kluge (2019) to investigate the accusations. Later, the owners of Ferde hired corporate examiners from audit firm Deloitte (2020) to investigate, which is presented in the following chapter.

White-collar convenience

Assuming the allegations by public broadcaster NRK against CEO Trond Juvik at Ferde are correct (Svaar, 2019; Svaar and Venli, 2019), we briefly study the alleged white-collar crime by application of convenience theory.

Taking advantage of a position for personal gain is occupational crime. Figure 2.1 illustrates this motive along the axis of motive-possibilities-individual. Maybe the motive was to climb the hierarchy of needs for status and success (Maslow, 1943), or realize the American dream of prosperity (Schoepfer and Piquero, 2006), or satisfy the need for acclaim as a narcissist (Chatterjee and Pollock, 2017) as the individual exhibits grandiosity, arrogance, self-absorption,

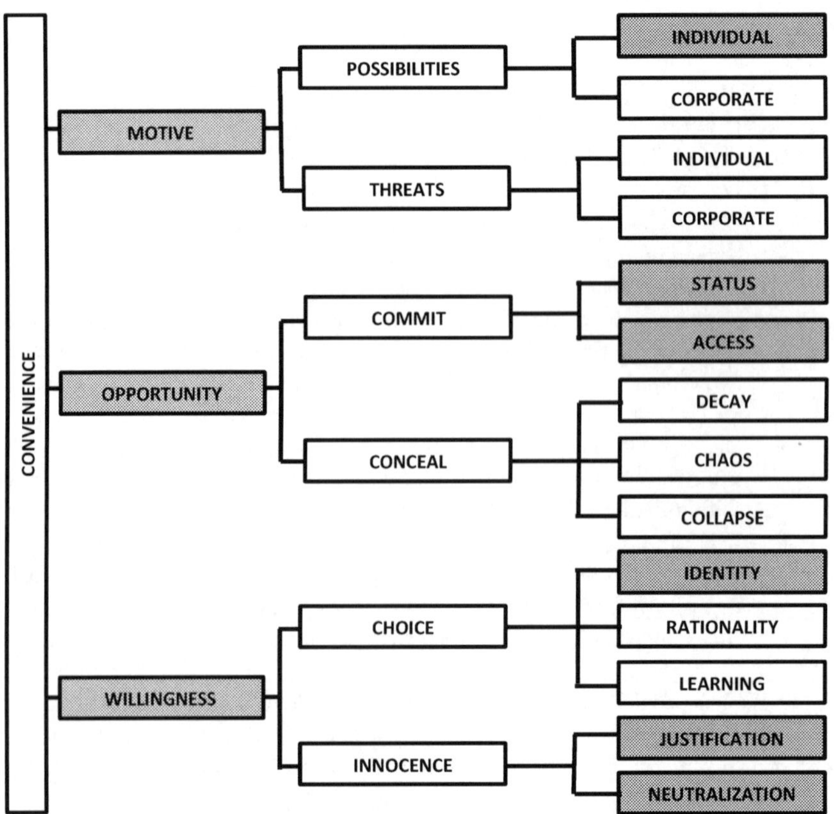

Figure 2.1 Convenience themes in the case of executives at Ferde

and entitlement (Gupta et al., 2019). One aspect of the motive to climb in the hierarchy was the need for acclaim by helping others. BTS Norway, the computer software firm, could avoid bankruptcy if Ferde bought licenses for computer software Allain. The motive is to satisfy the desire to help others as social concern (Agnew, 2014). This motive of helping others moves beyond the assumption of simple self-interest. However, as argued by Paternoster et al. (2018), helping others can be a self-interested, rational action that claims social concern.

Juvik was the CEO at Ferde at the same time as he had ownership interests in BTS Norway, and thus had the opportunity to manage his own working day and carry out any wrongdoing without the board, owners, or employees reacting to it. Juvik had made a good impression on the owners and the board and had built trust with them. Therefore, they found no reason to question Juvik's double role. Together with a few others at Ferde, who also had ownership interests in BTS Norway, as a team, they were able to commit deviant actions together by covering for each other.

This team had worked together for several years, also when the toll company was a private rather than public business. The team could stretch their reins longer than normal, which media coverage of Ferde's Christmas party reflected, where 38 employees had consumed 186 units of alcohol at the expense of the public. Juvik's explanation in the media was that they still had a commercial culture from the private business world.

Taking advantage of personal status and access to resources as a chief executive makes white-collar crime a convenient option in the organizational dimension, as illustrated in Figure 2.1 along the axis opportunity-commit-status and the axis opportunity-commit-access. Status is an individual's social rank within a formal or an informal hierarchy, or the person's relative standing along a valued social dimension. Status is the extent to which an individual is respected and admired by others, and status is the outcome of a subjective assessment process (McClean et al., 2018). High-status individuals enjoy greater respect and deference from, as well as power and influence over, those who are positioned lower in the social hierarchy (Kakkar et al., 2020: 532):

> Status is a property that rests in the eyes of others and is conferred to individuals who are deemed to have a higher rank or social standing in a pecking order based on a mutually valued set of social attributes. Higher social status or rank grants its holder a host of tangible benefits in both professional and personal domains. For instance, high-status actors are sought by groups for advice, are paid higher, receive unsolicited help, and are credited disproportionately in joint tasks. In innumerable ways, our social ecosystem consistently rewards those with high status.

Power is relative control over outcomes through the capacity to withdraw rewards or introduce punishments (Berdahl, 2007). Elite members might be too big to fail and too powerful to jail (Pontell et al., 2014), they can apply the blame game by misleading attribution to others (Eberly et al., 2011), or they can apply offender humor to distract attention from deviant behavior (Yam et al., 2018). Elite members have legitimate access to premises and systems (Benson and Simpson, 2018), they can create opportunities by entrepreneurship (Ramoglou and Tsang, 2016), they have specialized access in routine activity (Cohen and Felson, 1979), and they have access to strategic resources (Adler and Kwon, 2002).

As illustrated in Figure 2.1, the willingness for alleged misconduct seems to derive from identity and justification. The chief executive found his own actions quite acceptable based on his professional identity (Petrocelli et al., 2003), and he felt innocent as his acts were morally justifiable (Schnatterly et al., 2018).

Juvik applies five neutralization techniques in interviews and the investigation report. First, he denies responsibility for any misconduct. He says he had to solve problems that others created in Congo. Responsibility rests with those who initiated the project in Congo. Second, he defends the necessity of misconduct. He says he had to help people in Congo who suffered strain and pain. Third, he condemns those who condemn the misconduct. He claims that NRK has presented several fake news and has been completely unbalanced in their media reports. Fourth, he appeals to higher loyalty as someone had to take charge in the difficult Congo situation. Finally, he presents himself as a victim of unreasonable media coverage over a long period.

Fraud examination outcome

In their report of investigation, fraud examiners from law firm Kluge (2019) draw the following main conclusion: The procurement of software licenses was a violation of guidelines as no competitive bid from alternative vendors had access in the procurement process. Chief executive officer Trond Juvik was not entitled to approve 30 software licenses since he personally benefited from the acquisition. While the procurement in business terms might represent a reasonable contract, the corporate investigators found Juvik's behavior to be misconduct since he had involved himself so actively in the choice of software from a firm where he himself had financial interests (Kluge, 2019: 17):

> Regarding the agreement that the parties entered between Ferde and BTS Appian licenses, it is clear that both Juvik and Bratseth have ownership interests in BTS Norway. Although neither Juvik nor Bratseth have received any personal benefits because of the agreement entered by Ferde, this bond will nevertheless be a circumstance, which is suited to cast doubt concerning the interests that determined the agreement. It was an advantage for BTS Norway that the transfer of licenses to Ferde reduced the company's payment obligations to Appian. This is reinforced by the fact that the initiative to transfer the licenses to Ferde coincides in time with the cancellation of the Congo project at BTS Norway.

In addition to the accusation that Juvik involved himself in the procurement of software, he was also facing an accusation of working part-time for others.

Fraud examiners found evidence that this was the case, but they disagree that it represented misconduct, as the part-time work occurred while organizational changes involved transfer of business activities from one enterprise to the formal establishment of Ferde as a company. Fraud examiners found it justifiable that Juvik in a transition period had different assignments in different companies (Kluge, 2019: 39):

> Trond Juvik has explained to us that, after joining Ferde, he has had some involvement with the Congo project, including board membership at BTS Norway, but not on behalf of Ferde. He has explained that this might be about 20–30 hours of work in total. The work has included an action response to reports that personnel employed by BTS Africa were at risk of death. In this instance, BTS Norway paid thirty thousand kroner to cover the costs of getting the allegedly threatened personnel out of dangerous regions. These payments were made by BTS Norway and have nothing to do with Ferde.

Fraud examiners Thomas Rieber-Mohn and Christian Galtung, both lawyers, claim in the report that it was enough to interview only six persons at Ferde. This contrasts with the large number of documents that they reviewed. The information strategy was thus limited to a few interviews and several documents. The examiners searched for no other information sources. The knowledge strategy was limited to legal knowledge, as both additional examiners, Sunniva Nising Sandvold and Fredrik Aadahl, are lawyers as well.

The investigation addressed a third topic, in addition to private work and software procurement, which was Ferde's practice of leaving the interpretation of license plates of cars that the computer system was unable to interpret, to a company in China. This was a violation of the data protection act concerned with the confidentiality of personal data.

Private policing evaluation

The fraud examination report by investigators from Kluge (2019) might deserve to be assigned to level 4 in Figure 2.2, as the report contributes to clarification of what went on at Ferde in terms of software procurement. However, the issue of working for others and thus being loyal to another employer at the detriment of Ferde lacks clarification in the investigation report. Fraud examiners simply relied on explanations presented by Juvik as the suspect. The investigators ignored several witnesses, who had blown the whistle on Juvik in the media. Of course, the conclusion that no misconduct occurred might be correct and true. Nevertheless, it seems that fraud examiners mainly avoided controversial issues related to the various roles occupied by Juvik over time. Therefore, the fraud examination deserves to end up at level 2 in Figure 2.2, since the investigation report contributes no disclosure in terms of a reconstruction of events and sequences of events.

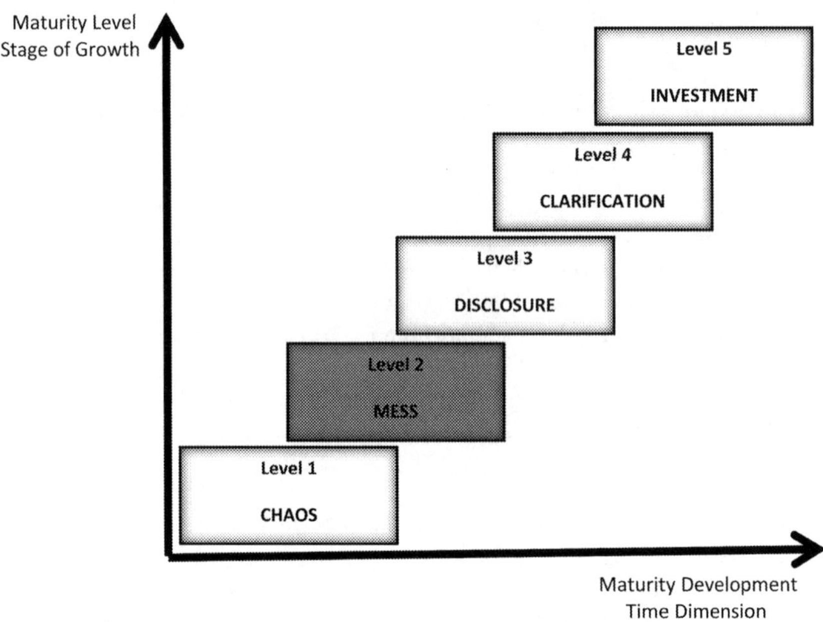

Figure 2.2 Maturity model for internal private investigations applied to Kluge

Kluge was the general legal advisor to Ferde at the time. Their objectivity, impartiality, and independence were thus questionable when they conducted the investigation. Even worse, the integrity and accountability of Kluge is lacking since they were willing to take on this assignment despite being the legal counsel to the company Ferde on a continuous basis. Furthermore, it does not seem at all that Kluge has conducted an objective investigation. On the contrary, this report proves defective and testifies to the fact that Kluge has acted biased and subjective, since the board and the owners avoid any attention in the examination regarding responsibility. Kluge does not come up with more than what people already knew from media coverage. This is typical in client-friendly investigations of scandals, where examiners confirm what has been exposed, while avoiding scandals to grow by more revelations (Gottschalk and Benson, 2020).

For the persons concerned, this examination has had few consequences, since all retained their positions. The law firm Kluge (2019) almost cleans the people involved. CEO Trond Juvik has only received some minor criticism in the report, and he has acknowledged that the criticism is justified. The board almost exalted and excused him, and Juvik continued having the board's confidence. If Kluge had concluded otherwise, Juvik could have lost his position at Ferde. The consequence of such a negative outcome for Juvik could be that Juvik himself would go against his employer who had not facilitated the transition from private to public ownership. Although there has been no consequence for Juvik at work, it has probably been a heavy burden feeling unfairly exposed negatively in the media. For example, he received a death threat. For Johnny Bratseth and others at Ferde, there is no formal consequence either. The report does not even mention Bratseth's wife by name, who was involved as well. Kluge also cleans her company Unitel Bratseth Services of any allegations or accusations. For Paul Magne Nilsen, the chairperson, and the board of directors, the investigation report by Kluge (2019) provides full exemption to the accused individuals. The report does not criticize the board, which believes that the media has been wrong. However, following Kluge's report, questions have been raised about the value of it, and what role the board has had, as well as what significance it has had for the very investigation that Kluge had a dual role as Ferde's law firm.

Marit Husa comments

Marit Husa is in charge of communications at Ferde. She helped business school students to access both the Kluge (2019) report evaluated in this chapter and the Deloitte (2020) report evaluated in the next chapter. After the spring term 2020 was over and the external examiner had graded project reports from students regarding Ferde investigations, the current and next chapters in draft form were emailed to Husa for comments. Her general comment emailed August 12, 2020, was that the description seems biased, and that none of the private policing reports concluded with corruption. In her response, Husa answers her own question: Why did Ferde trade with a company where employees were owners?

> Many of the employees who followed from BT Signaal to Ferde owned shares in BT Signaal before the purchase. The content of BT Signaal that the buyer did not want to include in the transaction, such as services related to parking, was either discontinued, or left with the seller. Among other things, something was left in the seller's subsidiary BTS Norway. The selling shareholders who were employed by the toll company were thus in practice forced to continue owning shares in BTS Norway until the company was wound up. This was known and accepted by the county municipalities that bought BT Signaal.
>
> The acquisition/merger resulted in Ferde taking over all employees and all agreements entered into by the private company. In practice, many of the employees had to continue to own shares in BTS Norway until it was wound up. In order to get a quick start of toll operations after the acquisition and maintain operations, it was necessary to remain in a number of agreements that were transferred to Ferde from the acquisition of BT Signaal.

When Svaar and Venli (2019) are mentioning that Juvik was a major shareholder, Husa comments:

> It was a prerequisite for the acquisition that there should be a business relationship between Ferde and BTS Norway in order to ensure operational

continuity. There was therefore knowledge and acceptance that employees in Ferde had ownership interests in companies outside, with which Ferde had a business relationship.

NRK uses wrong premises as regards Juvik's role, time use and general work capacity. As mentioned, Juvik was not the top manager of the project and had no formal responsibility. The responsibility rested first with the two who resigned, then with the chairman of the board/the board in the absence of the two who had left the ship. The documented incidents show Juvik's time-limited, voluntary and unpaid support for the board with a few activities in what was perceived as a precarious situation. Based on this, claiming that Juvik "managed a tax collection project in Congo" is completely wrong. NRK should also know that a chief executive officer is expected to work much more than a normal working day and has by law not regulated working hours or office hours.

In addition to misinterpreting documentation and using the wrong premises as a basis for the case, the NRK article lacks essential information:

- Omission of the information that Juvik only had read access to the computer system's reporting module is a significant shortcoming.
- The article omits that Juvik as CEO according to the Working Environment Act had no fixed office hours, and that he worked a lot of unpaid overtime.
- The article's premise and headline also seem completely to ignore former board chairman Tor Andersen's comment that Juvik "was not a driving force in any decisions in the project".

In the perspective of convenient motive, Husa comments:

> No Ferde employees have contributed to securing the finances of BTS Norway. BTS Norway was under planned liquidation and the license purchase had no significance for the company's future. Trond Juvik has not received any salary, fees, or indirect dividends from BTS Norway for the years 2017/2018/2019.

The suggestion that BTS Norway could avoid bankruptcy if Ferde bought Allain licenses was wrong, since the company was to be terminated. Furthermore, there is no reason to speculate that any employees did anything illegal.

Husa comments on the Christmas party at Ferde:

> Here it is suggested that former colleagues at BT Signaal arranged the Christmas party?! The Christmas table in December 2017 was planned while BT Signaal was a private, commercial company, and the employees had signed up for the Christmas table before the transition, and the Christmas table was completed immediately after the transition.

Husa comments that investigators ignored several witnesses, who had blown the whistle on Juvik in the media:

> It was not part of the mandate to interview external parties. How to contact anonymous whistleblowers? What whistleblowers is it referred to?

Bibliography

Adler, P.S. and Kwon, S.W. (2002). Social capital: Prospects for a new concept, *Academy of Management Review*, 27 (1), 17–40.

Agnew, R. (2014). Social concern and crime: Moving beyond the assumption of simple self-interest, *Criminology*, 52 (1), 1–32.

Benson, M.L. and Simpson, S.S. (2018). *White-Collar Crime: An Opportunity Perspective*, 3rd Edition, New York: Routledge.

Berdahl, J.L. (2007). Harassment based on sex: Protecting social status in the context of gender hierarchy, *Academy of Management Review*, 32 (2), 641–658.

Chatterjee, A. and Pollock, T.G. (2017). Master of puppets: How narcissistic CEOs construct their professional worlds, *Academy of Management Review*, 42 (4), 703–725.

Cohen, L.E. and Felson, M. (1979). Social change and crime rate trends: A routine activity approach. *American Sociological Review*, 44, 588–608.

Deloitte (2020). *Selskapskontroll. Hordaland, Sogn og Fjordane og Rogald Fylkeskommuner: Ferde AS (Company Control.Hordaland, Sogn and Fjordane and Rogaland Municipalities: Ferde Ltd.)*, January, Bergen: Auditing Firm Deloitte.

Eberly, M.B., Holley, E.C., Johnson, M.D. and Mitchell, T.R. (2011). Beyond internal and external: a dyadic theory of relational attributions, *Academy of Management Review*, 36 (4), 731–753.

Gottschalk, P. and Benson, M.L. (2020). The evolution of corporate accounts of scandals from exposure to investigation, *British Journal of Criminology*, published online https://doi.org/10.1093/bjc/azaa001.

Gupta, A., Nadkarni, S. and Mariam, M. (2019). Dispositional sources of managerial discretion: CEO ideology, CEO personality, and firm strategies, *Administrative Science Quarterly*, 64 (4), 855–893.

Kakkar, H., Sivanathan, N. and Globel, M.S. (2020). Fall from grace: The role of dominance and prestige in punishment of high-status actors, *Academy of Management Journal*, 63 (2), 530–553.

Kluge (2019). *Vurdering av Forhold i Ferde AS (Assessment of Circumstances at Ferde Ltd.)*, December 4, Bergen: Law Firm Kluge.

Maslow, A.H. (1943). A theory of human motivation, *Psychological Review*, 50 (4), 370–396.

McClean, E.J., Martin, S.R., Emich, K.J. and Woodruff, T. (2018). The social consequences of voice: An examination of voice type and gender on status and subsequent leader emergence, *Academy of Management Journal*, 61 (5), 1869–1891.

Paternoster, R., Jaynes, C.M. and Wilson, T. (2018). Rational choice theory and interest in the "fortune of others", *Journal of Research in Crime and Delinquency*, 54 (6), 847–868.

Petrocelli, M., Piquero, A.R. and Smith, M.R. (2003). Conflict theory and racial profiling: An empirical analysis of police traffic stop data, *Journal of Criminal Justice*, 31 (1), 1–11.

Pontell, H.N., Black, W.K. and Geis, G. (2014). Too big to fail, too powerful to jail? On the absence of criminal prosecutions after the 2008 financial meltdown, *Crime, Law and Social Change*, 61 (1), 1–13.

Ramoglou, S. and Tsang, E.W.K. (2016). A realist perspective of entrepreneurship: Opportunities as propensities, *Academy of Management Review*, 41, 410–434.

Schnatterly, K., Gangloff, K.A. and Tuschke, A. (2018). CEO wrongdoing: A review of pressure, opportunity, and rationalization, *Journal of Management*, 44 (6), 2405–2432.

Schoepfer, A. and Piquero, N.L. (2006). Exploring white-collar crime and the American dream: A partial test of institutional anomie theory, *Journal of Criminal Justice*, 34 (3), 227–235.

Svaar, P. (2019). Skattejakten (The Treasure Hunt), *Norwegian Public Broadcasting NRK*, www.nrk.no, published December 1.

Svaar, P. and Venli, V. (2019). Finanstilsynet kritisk til at bomselskapet Ferde skal "granskes" av egen revisor (The Finance Inspection Authority is critical to the toll company Ferde shall be "investigated" by its own auditor), *Norwegian Public Broadcasting NRK*, www.nrk.no, published October 30.

Yam, K.C., Christian, M.S., Wei, W., Liao, Z. and Nai, J. (2018). The mixed blessing of leader sense of humor: Examining costs and benefits, *Academy of Management Journal*, 61 (1), 348–369.

3 Ferde toll collection by Deloitte

While law firm Kluge (2019) investigated allegations that emerged in the media (Svaar, 2019; Svaar and Venli, 2019), with the board at Ferde as the client for the investigation, the municipal owners hired auditing firm Deloitte (2020) to review control mechanisms and audit procedures at Ferde. The review focused on mergers in toll collection that resulted in the establishment of Ferde. The investigation was to determine the extent of professional organizing of employment contracts, management routines, governance structures, accounting practices, board work, organizational structure, and organizational culture.

Auditing firm Deloitte was the permanent auditor at Ferde. Maybe integrity concerns should have prevented Deloitte from taking on this assignment. Like the law firm Kluge, which was the permanent legal advisor at Ferde, Deloitte was the permanent auditing function at Ferde. Both firms were thus in a relationship with the client already. If Ferde really wanted an independent and objective investigation, they would probably ask firms in the auditing and legal business not currently involved with Ferde. If Kluge and Deloitte wanted to protect their integrity and accountability, they would not have taken on such an assignment for a company where they already had work that related to matters in the investigation.

Just like Board Chair Janne Johnsen seemingly ignored such concerns, so did obviously Leiv Olav Sunde, company attorney at Ferde, and Marit Husa, communication executive at Ferde. Just like fraud examiners Thomas Rieber-Mohn and Christian Galtung at Kluge seemingly ignored such concerns, Birthe Bjørkelo at Deloitte took on the assignment despite potential lack of impartiality. Bjørkelo at Deloitte enterprise risk services headed the investigation. It seems strange that Deloitte investigated transactions that they already had approved as auditors.

White-collar convenience

If fraud occurred during and after mergers in toll collection organizations, this section briefly studies the assumed white-collar crime by application of convenience theory.

Many individuals had an opportunity to enrich themselves in the merger process of several toll collection companies, where governance was lacking, partly because politicians rather than board members monitored the companies. The financial motive might be a desire to restore the perception of equity and equality (Leigh et al., 2010), as people in publicly own companies tend to make less money than people do in privately owned companies. In addition, some employees might have perceived uncertainty about their future roles in the merged company, where embezzlement and other forms of financial crime might help remove strain and pain (Langton and Piquero, 2007). Therefore, Figure 3.1 emphasizes both motive-possibilities-individual and motive-threats-individual.

In the transition period from several toll collection units to Ferde as a single collection unit, there was a chaotic situation as indicated in Figure 3.1. There was lack of control in the principal-agent relationships (Bosse and Phillips, 2016), where politicians were principals and employees in transfer were agents. Costs could exceed benefits for potential whistleblowers (Keil et al., 2010), thereby preventing disclosure of potential misconduct.

Differential association by learning from others in the diffusion of misconduct (Mohliver, 2019) might lead to a willingness to choose deviant behavior (Sutherland, 1983). In addition, neutralization in terms of denial of damage and

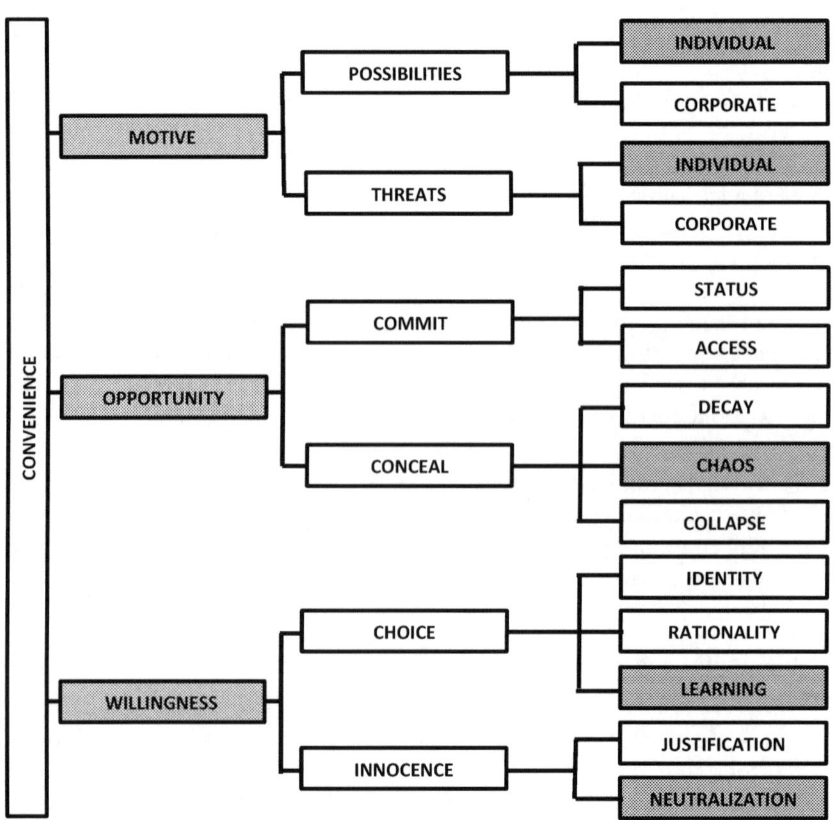

Figure 3.1 Convenience themes in the case of mergers at Ferde

victim might lead to willingness (Sykes and Matza, 1957). Neutralization is also possible because people did not know what rules to follow in the transition from private to public business organization. Both lack of rules and rule complexity in a transition period were problematic. Lehman et al. (2019) suggest that rule complexity often prevents compliance as people struggle to understand what is right and what is wrong.

Fraud examination outcome

Fraud examiners conclude that there were, and still are, shortcomings and holes in the management of financial resources. Processes and routines lack documentation, and roles and responsibilities seem unknown to many people in the Ferde organization. Nobody, including the external auditor, had a professional overview of financial matters at Ferde more than two years after the merger.

However, the outcome of the report is so general in nature that it could apply to several different organizations. For example, the following recommendations for the future are so obvious in the sense that all kinds of organizations might improve by following them (Deloitte, 2020: 7):

- Consider actions to secure a satisfactory continuity when it comes to owner representation in the general assembly and owner meetings
- Establish a unified owner strategy for Ferde
- Establish routines for frequent owner meetings
- Systematically review owner reporting from the company

There are some more specific recommendations, such as to complete labor contracts for all employees, and to develop guidelines for task work outside the company. However, none of these recommendations seem to derive from any reconstruction of past events. Instead, they emerge as general recommendations typically presented in superfluous reviews by auditors.

It comes as no surprise, therefore, that the accused chief executive, Trond Juvik, expresses his satisfaction with the report in an attachment dated January 16, 2020 (Deloitte, 2020: 76):

> Ferde expresses thanks for a thorough and good control of the company. We think that the corporate control provides an excellent picture of the status in the company. We are especially happy that the corporate control in a good manner describes the process of purchasing BT Signal, and what challenges this created for the company. The purchase of BT Signal led to the founding of Ferde as a unified regional toll collection company.

Birthe Bjørkelo and her team at Deloitte (2020) skipped the most important part in any review, which is to reconstruct past events and sequences of events. Reconstruction is a prerequisite for making relevant recommendation in a report of investigation.

Private policing evaluation

The report by Deloitte (2020) seems overwhelmed by general characteristics of issues and challenges at Ferde. Yet evidence of allegations implicit in the negative characterizations is lacking, and most descriptions are impossible to verify to the extent that they could fit most organizations, both successful ones and unsuccessful ones. The report contributes neither to clarification nor to disclosure. Rather, the report is a chaotic reflection on several seemingly selected random and unrelated topics and issues.

Deloitte interviewed 13 persons. The selection of interviewees does not seem to satisfy requirements of relevance, quality, diversity, and knowledge.

The mandate from county authorities as owners of Ferde gives a high degree of freedom to investigate the criticism-worthy situation, as well as other matters that should be relevant in the case. The investigation report provides the county council with findings, assessments, and recommendations, but the mandate did not permit Deloitte to investigate further criticism of the case should they find such paths in their investigation.

The information strategy applied by Deloitte was extremely limited, and so was the knowledge strategy. The configuration strategy was sequential like a value chain rather than iterative like a value shop. Formalism rather than facts dominate the report by Deloitte (2020). Like the result of the Kluge (2019) investigation, the client is seemingly happy with the outcome of the examination by firms that are already in a business relationship with the client (Figure 3.2).

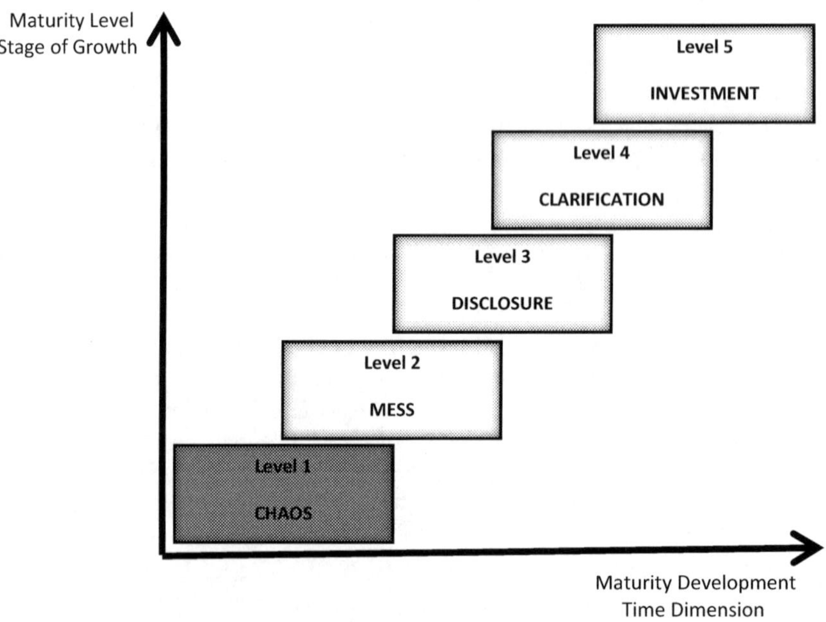

Figure 3.2 Maturity model for internal private investigations applied to Deloitte

Press Complaints Commission

Investigative journalist Peter Svaar at the Norwegian public broadcasting NRK accused the chief executive at Ferde, Trond Juvik, of abusing his position to do work for others and to make Ferde buy computer software from a company where Juvik was a shareholder (Svaar, 2019; Svaar and Venli, 2019). In the fall of 2019, NRK published several stories in news broadcasts on television regarding Ferde, in addition to radio programs and website stories. The media coverage focused mainly on the CEO. Ferde had to investigate the accusations and hired Kluge (2019) and Deloitte (2020). The fraud examiners did not support the allegations presented by NRK.

In February 2020, Ferde decided to complain to the Norwegian Press Complaints Commission regarding NRK's coverage (Ferde, 2020a: 1):

> NRK has covered over a long period the establishment of the toll collection company Ferde. In this context, the public channel has conveyed false and harassing allegations about the company, and the company's CEO. In the media coverage, NRK transgresses both norms for journalistic behavior and publishing rules.

Since fraud examination reports tend to be more favorable to the clients paying for their work than media coverage of the same cases, as documented in this book, it is not obvious who is more trustworthy. NRK formulated and published several allegations against the company Ferde in general, particularly CEO Juvik. Kluge and Deloitte, on the other hand, dispute allegations and explain possible deviance by the transition of Ferde from a privately owned to a publicly owned company.

In this book's perspective of applying convenience theory to suspected wrongdoing and applying a stage model to investigation maturity, the gap between media reports and examination reports is interesting. If NRK is right and examiners are wrong, then the convenience of wrongdoing becomes more likely, while the maturity of investigations in this and the previous chapter declines. On the other hand, if NRK is wrong and examiners are right, then the convenience of wrongdoing becomes less likely, while the maturity of investigations in this and the previous chapter increases.

In the complaint, Ferde refers to "The Treasure Hunt" (Svaar, 2019) by claiming that the image of Trond Juvik presented in the media is fake news (Ferde, 2020a: 2):

> Using images and literary tools, NRK creates the impression that Trond Juvik, before becoming toll collection chief, was the central figure in a tax collection project in Congo. He was not, as NRK also points out at the end of the article.

Norwegian media established the Norwegian Press Complaints Commission (PFU) itself and has no role in the Norwegian criminal justice system. Nevertheless, it causes harm to publishing houses and journalists when they receive negative decisions from the commission. Typically, a verdict from the commission leads to sanctions internally in the affected publishing house after some time.

More important in our context of maturity level for private policing is the discussion and conclusion that the commission presents. Very often, they present a detailed discussion of the allegations and media handling of information generally. For example, there was a whistleblower who contacted NRK but who did not want his/her identity to be disclosed.

However, at the time of writing this book, the verdict from the commission was not ready.

While Ferde sent a complaint to PFU, NRK had already sent their report to a prize-winning competition among investigative journalists. A jury of media people received the report (Svaar and Venli, 2019) together with several other reports from investigative journalism projects. In the 25-page report, journalist Svaar documents their methodology and findings, which were the basis for accusations against key people at Ferde.

The brief review of private policing by Kluge (2019) and Deloitte (2020) resulted in mess and chaos as the levels of maturity in this chapter. However, the client was obviously happy with the reports as Ferde used quotes from the reports in their criticism of NRK to PFU. NRK (2020a: 3) responded by citing other parts of Deloitte's review report:

> The review states that the arrangement with part-time outside job may entail a risk that work will be performed that is not in accordance with the employer's interests and undue role confusion, especially since some of the employees had ownership interests in one of the firms. As there is little evidence of what was approved as outside work, and what work the individual employee has actually performed, it is not possible to ascertain whether the outside work is in accordance with the guiding principles used, for example the board's presuppositions that outside work on BTS Norway's behalf should only concern the termination of ties between companies. The review finds that it is both correct and necessary that the company has started a process of drawing up new employment contracts.

Ferde (2020a) filed their complaint on February 20. NRK (2020a) responded on April 21. Ferde (2020b) commented on the response on May 13, while NRK (2020b) submitted their final comments on June 3. In their comment, Ferde (2020b: 1) wrote:

> In their response, NRK starts by raising a "higher sky". It is recalled that this issue with toll companies is a large and important journalistic project and that one has admirable motives. The project may have started there. But eventually a lot went wrong. Not all public toll companies can be cut over a comb. Serious false accusations against individuals and companies cannot be promoted and unethical working methods cannot be used to confirm

> hypotheses developed in an atmosphere of uncritical tunnel vision. In their response, NRK admits that they have made mistakes, and they make several concessions. But the question is how deep this goes when they on top of everything nominate the project for the SKUP award.

The SKUP award is a prestigious prize among investigative journalists in Norway. Investigative journalists have detected most of the serious white-collar crime cases that later led to conviction and incarceration of offenders. To receive the award, candidates must submit their work in the form of a methodology report. It is not enough just to submit a varying number of articles or news reports. The report of methods used in the investigative journalism has to describe information sources and procedures used to identify facts and combine those facts into a picture of what happened, how it happened, who did what to make it happen, and why it happened.

In their final comment, NRK (2020b: 1) wrote:

> NRK has not cut all toll companies in Norway over one comb. We have examined the finances of all toll companies, and then concentrated on two companies in our coverage: Fjellinjen and Ferde. At Fjellinjen, the CEO resigned last fall, in agreement with the board. The departure came as a result of an investigation triggered by NRK's journalistic disclosures of money use in violation of adopted guidelines, particularly related to consultancy, travel, events, and catering.
>
> At Ferde, our journalism has so far led to 3 different examinations and reviews, the last of which is still ongoing. NRK has also, through several articles, problematized the integrity and independence of two of these investigations. One of the investigations was carried out by Ferde's own auditor, Deloitte, who thus ended up in a double role, that, among others, the Financial Supervisory Authority of Norway has been critical of.
>
> Another report made by the law firm Kluge was ordered by Ferde's own board, and this report found several violations. The board's own hired investigators concluded, among other things, that Juvik had been incompetent when he purchased computer licenses from the company where he himself had ownership interests, as NRK has revealed. The processing of motorists' personal data was also not in line with the rules when Ferde sent pictures of Norwegian car license plates to a company in China.

PFU is a committee with seven members, out of which two are journalists, two are editors, and three are from the public. It was expected that Ferde's complaint against NRK would be concluded toward the end of 2020.

Bibliography

Bosse, D.A. and Phillips, R.A. (2016). Agency theory and bounded self-interest, *Academy of Management Review*, 41 (2), 276–297.

Deloitte (2020). *Selskapskontroll. Hordaland, Sogn og Fjordane og Rogald Fylkeskommuner: Ferde AS (Company Control.Hordaland, Sogn and Fjordane and Rogaland Municipalities: Ferde Ltd.)*, January, Bergen: Auditing Firm Deloitte.

Ferde (2020a). *Klage til PFU på NRK fra Ferde (Complaint to the Norwegian Press Complaints Commission from Ferde)*, Bergen, www.ferde.no, published February 20.

Ferde (2020b). *PFU-tilsvar i sak 032/20 – Ferde AS mot NRK (PFU Reply in Case 032/20 – Ferde AS Against NRK)*, Bergen, www.ferde.no, published May 13.

Keil, M., Tiwana, A., Sainsbury, R. and Sneha, S. (2010). Toward a theory of whistleblowing intentions: A benefit-cost differential perspective, *Decision Sciences*, 41 (4), 787–812.

Kluge (2019). *Vurdering av Forhold i Ferde AS (Assessment of Circumstances at Ferde Ltd.)*, December 4, Bergen: Law Firm Kluge.

Langton, L. and Piquero, N.L. (2007). Can general strain theory explain white-collar crime? A preliminary investigation of the relationship between strain and select white-collar offenses, *Journal of Criminal Justice*, 35 (1), 1–15.

Lehman, D.W., Cooil, B. and Ramanujam, R. (2019). The effects of rule complexity on organizational noncompliance and remediation: Evidence from restaurant health inspections, *Journal of Management*, 1–33, published online https://doi.org/10.1177/0149206319842262.

Leigh, A.C., Foote, D.A., Clark, W.R. and Lewis, J.L. (2010). Equity sensitivity: A triadic measure and outcome/input perspectives, *Journal of Managerial Issues*, 22 (3), 286–305.

Mohliver, A. (2019). How misconduct spreads: Auditors' role in the diffusion of stock-option backdating, *Administrative Science Quarterly*, 64 (2), 310–336.

NRK (2020a). *PFU-tilsvar i sak 032/20 – Ferde AS mot NRK (PFU Response in Case 032/20 – Ferde Inc. Against NRK)*, Oslo: Norwegian Public Broadcasting NRK, published April 21.

NRK (2020b). *PFU-sak 032/20 – Avsluttende Kommentarer fra NRK (PFU Case 032/20 – Final Comments from NRK)*, Oslo: Norwegian Public Broadcasting NRK, published June 3.

Sutherland, E.H. (1983). *White Collar Crime – The Uncut Version*, New Haven, CT: Yale University Press.

Svaar, P. (2019). Skattejakten (The Treasure Hunt), *Norwegian Public Broadcasting NRK*, www.nrk.no, published December 1.

Svaar, P. and Venli, V. (2019). Finanstilsynet kritisk til at bomselskapet Ferde skal "granskes" av egen revisor (The Finance Inspection Authority is critical to the toll company Ferde shall be "investigated" by its own auditor), *Norwegian Public Broadcasting NRK*, www.nrk.no, published October 30.

Sykes, G.M. and Matza, D. (1957). Techniques of neutralization: A theory of delinquency, *American Sociological Review*, 22 (6), 664–670.

4 FIFA World Cup by Garcia

Media reports have suggested that the reason why FIFA World Cups ended up in Russia in 2018 and in Qatar in 2022 was corruption. Members of the executive committee at FIFA did not only receive bribes from the winning nations Russia and Qatar, but also from losing competitors such as Australia. On December 2, 2010, the executive committee of the international football association FIFA, using an anonymous voting procedure, determined the hosts for the 2018 and 2022 FIFA World Cup tournaments. Allegations of corruption related to the voting process had surfaced even before the final vote that December day in Zürich in Switzerland. Ever since, there have been persistent allegations of misconduct with respect to the selection process. In 2017, British newspaper *The Guardian* reported that a FIFA official allegedly took bribes to back Qatar's 2022 World Cup bid (Laughland, 2017):

> Julio Grondona, a senior vice-president at FIFA and head of the Argentinian football association until his death in 2014, allegedly told the witness, Alejandro Burzaco, an Argentinian sports marketing executive, that he was owed the money in exchange for his vote, which helped Qatar secure the lucrative tournament.

Three years earlier, in 2014, the Garcia report was completed. The Garcia (2014) report was an investigation produced by Michael Garcia and Cornel Borbély into allegations of corruption in world association football. FIFA appointed Garcia and Borbély in 2012 to investigate ethical breaches at FIFA, which is world football's governing body. The two examiners quickly focused on persistent public accusations of bribery in the 2018 and 2022 World Cup bids, which Russia and Qatar, respectively, won in 2010. FIFA kept the Garcia report secret for several years before it leaked to a German newspaper, which caused FIFA subsequently to release the report to the public by FIFA in 2017.

White-collar convenience

Both briber and bribed in a corruption relationship have their financial motives, organizational opportunities, and willingness for deviant behaviors. In Figure 4.1,

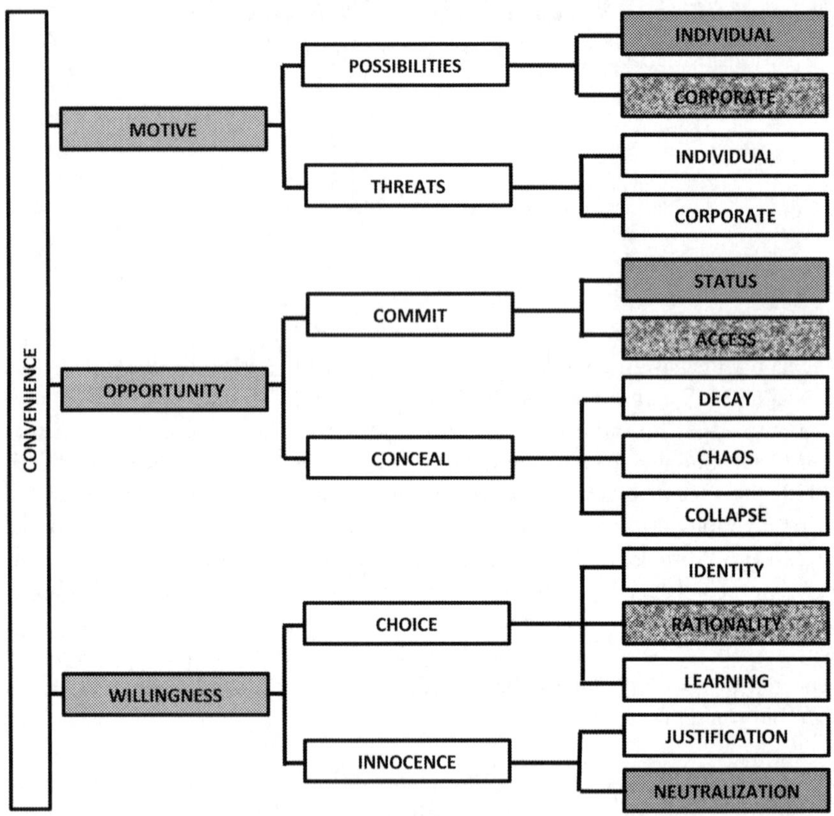

Figure 4.1 Convenience themes in the case of FIFA

illustrations for the briber are with texture, while illustrations for the bribed are in dark gray. The briber has a motive of winning the bid for the World Cup, which leads to prestige for the country. It is a situation where business objectives justify means (Jonnergård et al., 2010).

The bribed committee member can make an extraordinary profit, which is possible because of the position at FIFA (Pontell et al., 2014). The briber has access to resources to bribe members (Benson and Simpson, 2018). It is a rational choice for the briber to get involved in corruption to improve the nation's chance of winning the bid (Pratt and Cullen, 2005). The bribed can neutralize potential feeling of guilt by arguing that his or her vote did not change (Sykes and Matza, 1957).

Fraud examination outcome

From the perspective of evolving accounts as scandals arrive at the attention of stakeholders and the public (Gottschalk and Benson, 2020), the FIFA scandal is a typical example (Hundt and Horsch, 2019; Naheem, 2018). Persistent public accusations of bribery and corruption forced top officials at FIFA to initiate an investigation. Initially, the Swiss Joseph Blatter, president of FIFA since 1998, denied any wrongdoing. However, Blatter had to resign in 2015 when the Swiss attorney general announced criminal proceedings against him regarding criminal mismanagement and misappropriation. Swiss police arrested seven FIFA officials at hotel Baur au Lac in Zürich. FBI in the United States arrested other FIFA officials and charged them with corruption (Viswanatha et al., 2015).

When Garcia and Borbély handed in their investigation report to FIFA in 2014, FIFA officials attempted to keep it secret forever. Hans-Joachim Eckert, the FIFA's head of adjudication on ethical matters, refused to publish the report, citing various legal grounds. Instead of releasing the report of 350 pages, Eckert chose to publish his own 42-page summary late in 2014. Outsiders heavily criticized Eckert's summary in the media as a whitewash, which is like money laundering (Kurum, 2020), where traces of wrongdoing are supposed to disappear after washing and laundering information. Rumors and suspicions concerning FIFA corruption led in 2015 Europe's footballing nations to meet to discuss an alternative location to Russia for the World Cup in 2018 (Wallace, 2015).

Garcia criticized Eckert's summary as materially incomplete. After unsuccessfully appealing FIFA to publish the complete 350-page report, Garcia resigned from the position of chairperson at the investigative branch of FIFA's ethics committee (Roan, 2014). Over the following years, there was much speculation in the media regarding the contents of the report, particularly which aspects Eckert had left out of his summary and Garcia had felt were serious enough to warrant his resignation (Laughland, 2017; Wallace, 2015). In June 2017, the German newspaper *Bild* announced that it had obtained a leaked copy of the report and planned to publish it (Roan, 2014). FIFA released the report on the following day, pre-empting the newspaper coverage. The German Eckert, who had previously been a judge in the regional Munich court, had now to resign from his position as chairperson of the adjudicatory chamber of FIFA (Das, 2017).

The investigation into the bidding by 9 teams from 11 different countries – a process that in its formal phase covered more than a year – required significant commitment of time and resources. The inquiry into the bidding process involved interviewing representatives of each of the bid teams, current and former executive committee members, and FIFA officials (Garcia, 2014: 7):

> In addition, other football officials who were believed to have relevant information were called upon to assist in establishing the facts of the case. Third parties, although not subject to the cooperation requirements of the FCE (FIFA Code of Ethics), were also approached and asked for cooperation.

The fraud examiners conducted in all 75 interviews, either in person with an audio recording for documentation or through written channels such as emails. Fraud examiners traveled to ten countries to conduct interviews, including Australia, England, Italy, Japan, Malaysia, the Netherlands, Oman, Spain, Switzerland, and the United States. Interviewers taped all oral interviews, and the interviewees or their attorneys received copies of the transcripts with an opportunity to propose corrections. The tapes, transcripts, and any comments or additions by witnesses became parts of the investigation record.

The fraud examiners announced early on that they would listen to anyone who believed they had relevant information, and that such information would be duly evaluated (Garcia, 2014: 7):

> It was a message aimed at making public an opportunity to assist for those interested in making this review as complete as possible. Many, including several media outlets, took advantage of that opportunity to provide information helpful in clarifying the facts.

Corruption allegations and accusations were widespread and varied. The media presented some of them, and informants reported some of them directly to the fraud examiners. Still others were uncovered while reviewing the materials collected and produced during the investigation (Garcia, 2014: 8):

> With each issue, and with every witness, the same procedure was followed, namely a process designed to address the significant allegations in as thorough and efficient a manner possible while treating fairly all parties to that process.

The 350-page report of investigation mentions FIFA president Joseph "Sepp" Blatter 81 times. The corporate investigators conclude that Blatter was responsible for mismanagement, but not fraud (Garcia, 2014: 336):

> President Blatter's responsibility for the myriad issues that developed over the course of the bidding process or were uncovered by this inquiry merits consideration. As a preliminary matter, it must be made clear that evidence in the record does not establish a prima facie case that President Blatter violated the FCE. The one concrete allegation against the President, concerning an account purportedly held in his name at a U.S. bank, was demonstrably false. As head of FIFA, however, President Blatter bears some responsibility for a flawed process that engendered deep public skepticism, and for presiding over an Executive Committee whose culture of entitlement contributed too many of the issues this Report identifies.

Fraud examiners argue that Blatter must take responsibility for the failures that occurred on his watch. He made himself accessible on a selective basis, giving the impression that individuals such as Peter Hargitay were insiders afforded preferential treatment, including freedom to speak to high-ranking FIFA officials about inappropriate topics, such as quality of competing bids, in a manner that was not tolerated by others. Hargitay was in the business of lobbying and campaign strategies. He worked as a consultant to several of the 9 bidding teams from 11 different countries.

One of the failures mentioned by the fraud examiners was FIFA payments of $200,000 in bonus to Adamu and Temarii, who FIFA banned as devils of the sport (Garcia, 2014: 338):

> Messrs. Adamu and Temarii were prohibited from voting because they were found, pursuant to FIFA's own internal governance procedures, to have committed misconduct related to the bidding process.

Adamu and Temarii could not anymore attend executive committee meetings at FIFA because they had accepted bribes in the World Cup bidding process. Nevertheless, Blatter allowed the payment of bonuses to all executive committee members, including the two members labeled devils of the sport (Garcia, 2014: 338):

> As the leader of FIFA, responsibility for these failings and for positive steps taken to reform the organization resides with President Blatter.

Initially, the Swiss Sepp Blatter, president of FIFA since 1998, denied any wrongdoing documented in the Garcia report in 2014. However, Blatter had to resign the following year in 2015 when the Swiss attorney general announced criminal proceedings against him regarding criminal mismanagement and misappropriation.

FIFA consists of the following branches: the congress (legislative), the committee (executive), and the secretariat (administrative). Given the importance of the executive committee for international football and given the already terminated committee members Adamu and Temarii, Garcia (2014) discussed the authority of the committee in some detail. The committee is responsible for making decisions regarding allocation of World Cup tournaments. There are 23 members on the committee.

Garcia (2019) attempted to interview several committee members, including former German top football player Franz Beckenbauer. By a letter, dated March 6, 2014, fraud examiners requested Beckenbauer's cooperation in establishing the facts relevant to their inquiry. Specifically, the investigators asked him to provide dates when he would be available to meet for a witness interview. He did not respond until March 24, saying that he was busy and asking for questions in writing. Accordingly, the investigators sent Beckenbauer a letter with 21 questions on April 8. The letter noted Beckenbauer's obligation to cooperate with the investigation. One month later, Beckenbauer replied by asking to have the questions translated from English to German. Accordingly, the investigators sent Beckenbauer a German translation on May 16. A case developed against Beckenbauer for the conduct of failure to cooperate.

Franz Beckenbauer is among several FIFA executive committee members whose behaviors received scrutiny in detail by Garcia (2014). The 350-page report mentions Beckenbauer 149 times, for example, on page 248:

> Qatar bid team members repeatedly denied that Mr. Bin Hammam had a direct relationship to or role on the Qatar bid team. For example, in October 2009, Messrs. Bin Hammam, Beckenbauer and Radmann met with the Emir of Qatar in Doha. According to Mr. Beckenbauer, the purpose of the meeting was to discuss the Qatar bid, and the Emir tried to convince Mr. Beckenbauer of the merits of the Qatar bid. Email correspondence from Mr. Bin Hammam's assistant indicates that Mr. Bin Hammam arranged the meeting with the Emir.

Other executive committee members frequently mentioned by Garcia (2019) as not cooperating with the investigation include Jack Warner (provisional ban and resignation), Ricardo Teixeira (resigned from all football-related activity), and Mohamed Bin Hammam (banned for life from all football-related activity). Chuck Blazer (provisional ban) and Nicholás Leoz (resigned from all football-related activity) received criticism together with some more.

According to the investigation report by Garcia (2014), Mohamed Bin Hammam was an active briber who bribed several FIFA executive committee members. Hammam was a FIFA vice president and held formal positions in the football association in Qatar. On behalf of Qatar as one of the 11 bidders for the FIFA World Cup, Hammam was involved in corruption to enable Qatar to win the bidding competition for the FIFA World Cup in 2022.

Hammam received the ban for life from all football-related activity (Garcia, 2014: 231):

> The Ethics Committee conducted proceedings against Mr. Bin Hammam in 2011 and 2012. Mr. Bin Hammam was interviewed and provided written statements and documents during those and related matters. In a final report submitted with the supporting evidence to the Adjudicatory Chamber and to Mr. Bin Hammam on December 3, 2012 (the "December 2012 Bin Hammam Report"), the Investigatory Chamber concluded that "Mr. Bin Hammam has engaged in a pattern of misconduct" in violation of the FCE. Based on that report, the Adjudicatory Chamber banned Mr. Bin Hammam from football-related activity for life. Mr. Bin Hammam, who had appealed a previous lifetime ban from the Ethics Committee in 2011 to CAS and secured a reversal, did not appeal the December 2012 ban.

In May 2013, a source suggested that the investigation team contact an anonymous whistleblower in Australia. The person was a former member of the Australia 2022 bid team. The person had been the head of corporate and public affairs at Australia 2022. The whistleblower noted during her initial communications with the examiners that providing information might violate nondisclosure or confidentiality obligations that she owed her former employer under the terms of her severance agreement. Accordingly, upon examiners' request, the football federation of Australia provided a release statement. Examiners subsequently interviewed the whistleblower twice, in New York in November 2013 and in Australia in April 2014.

The whistleblower told examiners that Australia 2022 was involved in corruption to win the FIFA 2022 World Cup. For example, Australia 2022 bought an expensive pearl necklace as a gift for the wife of FIFA executive committee member Jack Warner. However, stories from the Australian whistleblower (AW) found no support in evidence from the whistleblower (Garcia, 2014: 59):

> While AW provided some useful information regarding possible issues for the Investigatory Chamber to examine, the evidence – including evidence she provided – often did not support her specific recollections and allegations. For example, the Investigatory Chamber asked about a highly publicized 2009 incident in which Australia 2022 reportedly bought a pearl necklace as a gift for the wife of FIFA Executive Committee member Jack Warner. AW said she sent Australia 2022 Chairman Frank Lowy and CEO Ben Buckley an email at the time expressing concerns that the gift violated bidding rules.

Another whistleblower mentioned in the investigation report was from Qatar. Allegations by an insider on the Qatari bid team emerged soon after Qatar won the rights to host the 2022 World Cup tournament. Accusations of corruption by a former Qatar bid team employee began circulating in the global press almost immediately after Qatar's victory (Garcia, 2014: 250):

> A few days later, President Blatter received a letter from British politician Ivan Lewis – Member of Parliament and Shadow Secretary of State for Culture, Media and Sport – regarding serious allegations which have been made with regard to corruption associated with the bidding process for the 2022 World Cup.

Both FIFA president Blatter and secretary general Valcke denied the allegations by claiming that there was no supportive evidence, and they responded to Lewis that FIFA was not able to intervene. Similarly, fraud examiners ended up not believing the Qatar whistleblower (Gacia, 2014: 272):

> Accordingly, the Investigatory Chamber has not relied on any information or material it received from QW (Qatar whistleblower) in reaching any conclusions in this Report.

In the conclusion section of the Garcia (2014) report, fraud investigators suggest opening formal proceedings against certain individuals on the executive committee of FIFA:

- Angel Maria Llona violated FIFA rules of conduct by intimidating the investigation and interfering with the investigation by threatening to recuse fraud examiners.
- Michel D'Hooghe received a valuable painting from a member of the Russian bidding team.
- Worawi Makudi had a conflict of interest where a large contract with Qatar reached signatures during the bidding process.
- Franz Beckenbauer faced allegations of involving himself with the Australian bid team as he had a conflict of interest.
- Chung Mong-Joon wrote letters to other committee members indicating improper offers or promises of benefits in order to influence the World Cup vote.
- Amos Adamu caused the Qatar bidding team to be the sponsor of an event for his son where the son would personally benefit from the sponsorship.
- Reynald Temarii received more than €300,000 from Bin Hammam for "legal fees" shortly after announcing he would pursue his appeal of the FIFA ethics committee decision to ban Hammam from football.
- Jack Warner requested benefits from the Australian and English bid teams.
- Ricardo Texeira accepted lavish accommodations and other benefits provided to him in Doha, and he arranged contracts for the Brazilian federation's commercial rights.
- Mohamed Bin Hammam paid Temarii more than €300,000 immediately after Temarii's decision to appeal a ban imposed by the FIFA ethics committee.
- Nicholás Leoz requested a substantial personal benefit – namely, a knighthood – from England's bid team.
- Julio Grondona faced allegations of wrongdoing, but he died before the release of the Garcia (2014) report.

Several of the named executive committee members mentioned above faced no accusations of corruption or other kinds of financial misconduct. Instead, they faced accusations of not cooperating with the fraud examiners. This kind of accusation is problematic, since several of the approaches by the investigators seem confrontational rather than cooperative. Therefore, there might have been acceptable reasons why individuals such as Llona and Beckenbauer did not cooperate with the investigators. If Garcia and the other examiners had approached suspects and witnesses in a more professional manner, they might have succeeded in obtaining relevant and complete statements. Therefore, the report gives the impression that investigators rather than informants are to blame when the investigation failed in obtaining statements from relevant persons on the executive committee of FIFA. It seems that the tradition of public prosecutors in the United States of blaming witnesses for not cooperating and then prosecuting witnesses for lack of cooperation as an offense does not transfer into a European context where the courts are quite unfamiliar with such a perspective. For example, Garcia (2014: 333) suggests, "Mr. Beckenbauer's actions in response to the Investigatory Chamber's efforts to seek his assistance are already the subject of formal investigative proceedings".

Private policing evaluation

A review of the investigation report by Garcia (2014) requires evaluation criteria according to the maturity model for private policing in fraud examinations as illustrated in Figure 4.2. We place the FIFA investigation by Garcia (2019) at level 3 of disclosure in the figure. The desire by powerful FIFA people to keep the investigation report secret is evidence of disclosure of misconduct and potential crime that FIFA executives did not want to leak out to governments, the media, and the public in general. The Garcia (2014) report deserves no better evaluation, as there is no real clarification of roles and responsibilities, and there seems to be no learning or other aspects of investment from the report.

Fraud examiners failed in achieving cooperation with important informants. Fraud examiners thus failed probably because they were confrontational rather than cooperative in their attempts to talk to informants. As mentioned above, there might have been acceptable reasons why executive committee members such as Beckenbauer and Llona did not cooperate with the investigators. If Garcia and the other examiners had approached suspects and witnesses in a more professional manner, they might have succeeded in obtaining relevant and complete statements. Based on their failure to interview informants, the Garcia (2014) investigation has similarities with criteria at level 2 in the maturity model in Figure 4.2, as the process of private policing resembled a mess. However, since they succeeded in disclosing new information, the investigation remains at level 3 in the model.

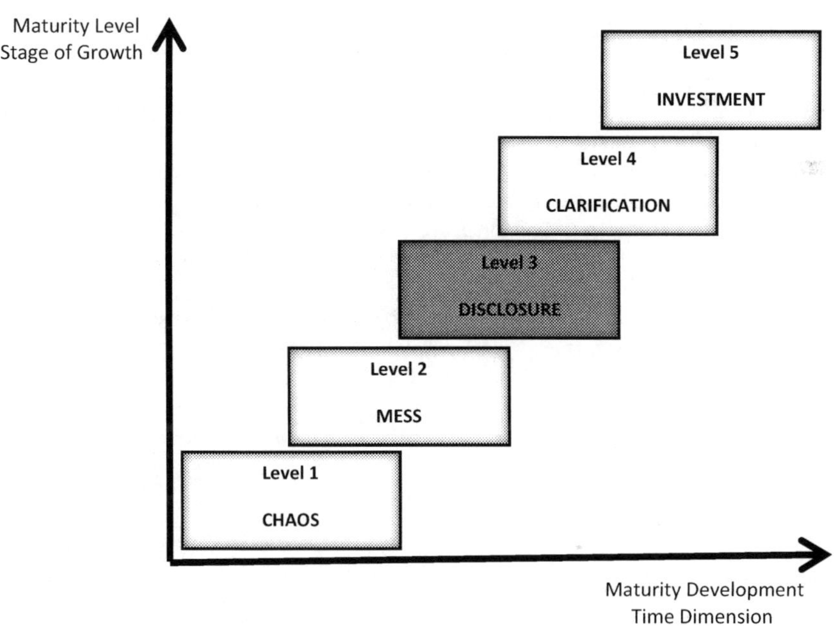

Figure 4.2 Maturity model for internal private investigations applied to Garcia

Bibliography

Benson, M.L. and Simpson, S.S. (2018). *White-Collar Crime: An Opportunity Perspective*, 3rd Edition, New York: Routledge.

Das, A. (2017). Fifa moves to replace ethics committee leaders, *The New York Times*, www.nytimes.com, published May 9.

Garcia (2014). *Report on the Inquiry into the 2018/2019 Fifa World Cup Bidding Process*, Investigatory Chamber, FIFA Ethics Committee, Zürich, Switzerland.

Gottschalk, P. and Benson, M.L. (2020). The evolution of corporate accounts of scandals from exposure to investigation, *British Journal of Criminology*, published online https://doi.org/10.1093/bjc/azaa001.

Hundt, S. and Horsch, A. (2019). Sponsorship of the Fifa world cup, shareholder wealth, and the impact of corruption, *Applied Economics*, 51 (23), 2468–2491.

Jonnergård, K., Stafsudd, A. and Elg, U. (2010). Performance evaluations as gender barriers in professional organizations: A study of auditing firms, *Gender, Work and Organization*, 17 (6), 721–747.

Kurum, E. (2020). RegTech solutions and AML compliance: What future for financial crime? *Journal of Financial Crime*, published online https://doi.org/10.1108/JFC-04-2020-0051.

Laughland, O. (2017). Fifa official took bribes to back Qatar's 2022 world cup bid, court hears, *The Guardian*, www.theguardian.com, published November 15.

Naheem, M.A. (2018). Fifa – highlighting the links between global banking and international money laundering, *Journal of Money Laundering Control*, 21 (4), 498–512.

Pontell, H.N., Black, W.K. and Geis, G. (2014). Too big to fail, too powerful to jail? On the absence of criminal prosecutions after the 2008 financial meltdown, *Crime, Law and Social Change*, 61 (1), 1–13.

Pratt, T.C. and Cullen, F.T. (2005). Assessing macro-level predictors and theories of crime: A meta-analysis, *Crime and Justice*, 32, 373–450.

Roan, D. (2014). Fifa hits new low after Michael Garcia resignation, *BBC*, www.bbc.com, published December 18.

Sykes, G.M. and Matza, D. (1957). Techniques of neutralization: A theory of delinquency, *American Sociological Review*, 22 (6), 664–670.

Viswanatha, A., Robinson, J., Morse, A. and Matthews, C.M. (2015). Fifa rocked as U.S. charges 14 in corruption investigation, *The Wall Street Journal*, www.wsj.com, published May 27.

Wallace, S. (2015). Fifa corruption: Europe plots to stage an 'alternative World Cup' I place of Russia 208, *Independent*, www.independent.co.uk, published June 2.

5 Helgeland hospital by KPMG

This is no typical case of private policing of economic crime. The internal investigation at Helgelandssykehuset (Helgeland Hospital) by KPMG (2019, 2020) was concerned with whistleblowing from union representatives who felt ignored in the process of planning a more efficient hospital structure in a region in Norway. Whistleblowing is the disclosure by organizational members of illegal, immoral, or illegitimate practices under the control of their employers to persons or organizations that may be able to effect action to terminate such practices (Wells et al., 2020). The KPMG investigation is included here, however, because the underlying cause for restructuring was cost savings at hospital operations, and because the underlying cause for lack of involvement in the planning process was the need for a time-saving and thus cost-saving planning phase.

The medical association in Norway made comments on the problems in a letter to the hospital (Legeforeningen, 2019), and the media commented on the case (Budalen and Thonhaugen, 2020). The whistleblower Svein Arne Monsen left the hospital before KPMG conducted their private policing (Wiig and Hansen, 2019):

> Last week, we learned from the media that Svein Arne Monsen had resigned his position as area manager for emergency medicine and surgery at Helgeland Hospital. We are many who have gradually questioned how the process of Helgeland Hospital 2025 has been handled by the management/administration at the hospital. Reading Svein Arne Monsen's rationale for his drastic step confirms that something is rivetingly wrong with the way this work is done. Svein Arne Monsen is known for his integrity and has always put patients' needs at the top of his priority.

This is a quote from a debate in the local media that was quite lively and confrontational. The debate caused hospital management to leave the strategy of labeling the issue an internal staff matter to hiring fraud examiners from KPMG (2019, 2020) to conduct an internal investigation.

White-collar convenience

Here we assume that the allegations against hospital executives are correct. The top executives preferred a planning process ignoring the Norwegian working environment act. The misconduct benefited the organization and thus represented corporate crime.

Figure 5.1 indicates the relevance of the axis of motive-possibilities-corporate as well as the axis motive-threats-corporate. Maybe there was a motive of reaching business objectives that justify means (Jonnergård et al., 2010), or maybe there was a motive of avoiding pain, strain, and uncertainty (Langton and Piquero, 2007).

Top executives in the health region had status and access to resources to implement the planning process for a new hospital structure in the region (Ramoglou and Tsang, 2016). There was a power inequality between the elite and others (Patel and Cooper, 2014). Top executives thus could choose whether to involve union representatives and other key employees in the process, as indicated in

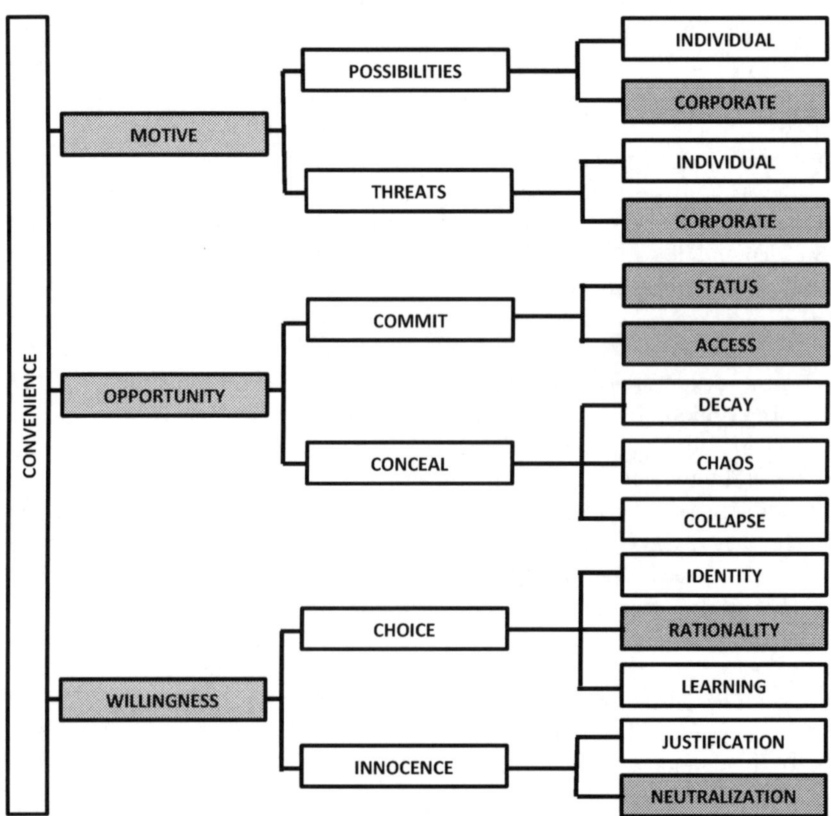

Figure 5.1 Convenience themes in the case of Helgelandssykehuset

the figure. It was a rational choice to ignore and reject participation to speed up the process of planning and constructing new hospitals in the region (Pratt and Cullen, 2005). Top executives could easily claim loyalty to higher authority (Sykes and Matza, 1957) as a relevant neutralization technique.

Fraud examination outcome

In their first report of investigation, fraud examiners from auditing firm KPMG (2019) draw the following main conclusions:

- We have not detected any misconduct in relation to the working environment act
- There are no violations of laws, rules, or generally accepted norms in the process
- Several allegations in the whistleblowing messages seem based on incorrect facts
- Several accusations express disagreement regarding the planning process, including the role of the board and the lack of project groups with participation from union representatives
- The alleged misconduct is partly concerned with the structure of the planning process, which is the job of the chief executive in the health region
- Allegations of abuse of power by two executives lack factual reasoning
- Most of the allegations and accusations emerged late in the process, and too late for management to act upon
- It seems that the complaints occurred because the planning process resulted in a hospital structure, with which the whistleblowers disagree
- Our inquiry does not support an allegation that harassment and retaliation occurred at a budgeting seminar on May 9, 2019

In their second report of investigation, fraud examiners from auditing firm KPMG (2020) draw the following main conclusions regarding the whistleblowing:

- KPMG's assessment is that there was no prior internal notice and that there was no factual basis for whistleblowing to the public. Furthermore, there was no factual basis for the allegations of critical circumstances.
- KPMG's assessment is that there has been no prior internal whistleblowing. Neither the letter from the unit directors nor the whistleblower's dialogue with the CEO prior to the notification satisfies requirements for whistleblowing.
- The notification received an assessment based on the hospital's whistleblowing routine. It follows from the Working Environment Act that it will always be justifiable to notify in accordance with the notification routines. Harassment is a condition that normally triggers notification obligations for employees.

Fraud examiners from KPMG conducted 24 interviews. They reviewed documents from the planning process.

Private policing evaluation

It seems that KPMG (2019, 2020) in their internal investigation at Helgelandssykehuset have done a thorough examination by reviewing documents and interviewing several stakeholders. They have contributed to clarification at level 4 in the maturity model in Figure 5.2. They failed in reaching the top level 5 of investment, since the benefit of solving and closing the dispute did not occur in the aftermath of publishing their report. Union leaders, key personnel, and other stakeholders continued to criticize the planning process in the media (Budalen and Thonhaugen, 2020). Therefore, the benefits of the investigation did probably not exceed the costs of the investigation, and the investigation was thus no profitable investment.

The Norwegian medical association criticized the investigation while it was still going on, where they focused on the whistleblower Svein Arne Monsen (Legeforeningen, 2019):

> As far as we understand, Monsen was not given the opportunity to review the report before it was handed over to the employer. Therefore, he also did not have access to the defense of the contents of the report, which appears to be a significant weakness. Through a submission to the whistleblowers, KPMG would have revealed several errors and strengthened the factual bases

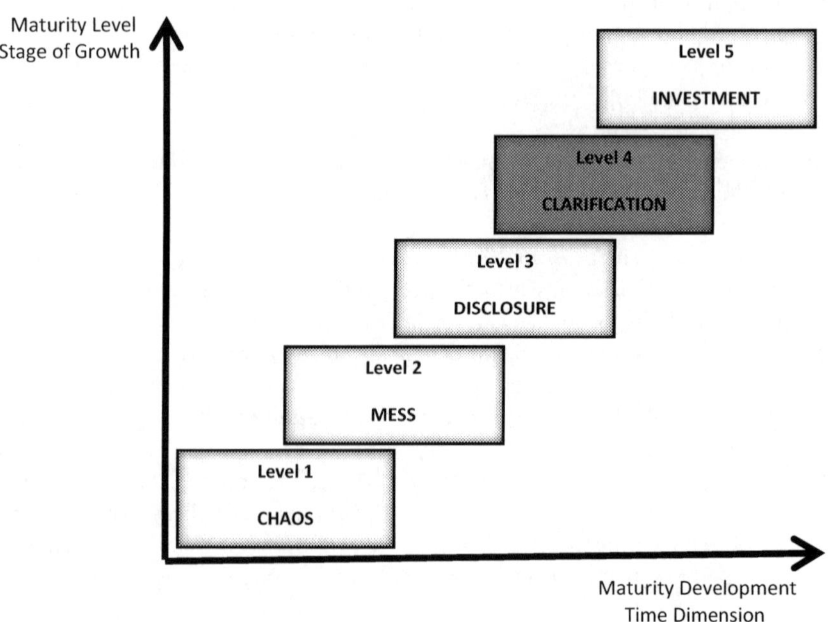

Figure 5.2 Maturity model for internal private investigations applied to KPMG

> for their assessments. It appears that KPMG now will assess the accuracy and soundness of the whistleblowing based on the findings in the first report. Since Monsen has not been given the opportunity to comment on the findings in the report, the process appears to be very little justifiable. Monsen finds it necessary to provide feedback to the issues in the report where he disagrees, as he has not been given the opportunity in the past, and KPMG is now to make an assessment of the reasonableness of the notification based on the judgements in the report.

Rather than confirming misconduct and potential white-collar crime, fraud examiners from KPMG (2019, 2020) have produced a convincing report that documents the false nature of allegations and accusations.

Bibliography

Budalen, A. and Thonhaugen, M. (2020). 20 sykehusansatte på Helgeland får sterk kritikk: -Varselet hadde stort skadepotensial (20 hospital employees at Helgeland get strong criticism: -The whistleblowing had large damage potential), *Norwegian Public Broadcasting NRK*, www.nrk.no, published February 18.

Jonnergård, K., Stafsudd, A. and Elg, U. (2010). Performance evaluations as gender barriers in professional organizations: A study of auditing firms, *Gender, Work and Organization*, 17 (6), 721–747.

KPMG (2019). *Rapport Undersøkelse av Varslingssaker Helgelandssykehuset (Report Examination of Whistleblowing Cases Helgeland Hospital)*, October 18, Trondheim: Auditing Firm KPMG.

KPMG (2020). *Rapport Undersøkelse av Varslingssaker – Mandatets del 2 – Helgelandssykehuset (Report Examination of Whistleblowing Cases – the Mandate's Part 2 – Helgeland Hospital)*, January 17, Trondheim: Auditing Firm KPMG.

Langton, L. and Piquero, N.L. (2007). Can general strain theory explain white-collar crime? A preliminary investigation of the relationship between strain and select white-collar offenses, *Journal of Criminal Justice*, 35 (1), 1–15.

Legeforeningen (2019). *Ang. KPMGs Faktaundersøkelse (Regarding KPMG's Fact Finding)*, letter from Den Norske Legeforening (The Norwegian Medical Association) to Helgelandssykehuset (The Helgeland Hospital) in Mo i Rana in Norway, dated December 12.

Patel, P.C. and Cooper, D. (2014). Structural power equality between family and nonfamily TMT members and theperformance of family firms, *Academy of Management Journal*, 57 (6), 1624–1649.

Pratt, T.C. and Cullen, F.T. (2005). Assessing macro-level predictors and theories of crime: A meta-analysis, *Crime and Justice*, 32, 373–450.

Ramoglou, S. and Tsang, E.W.K. (2016). A realist perspective of entrepreneurship: Opportunities as propensities, *Academy of Management Review*, 41, 410–434.

Sykes, G.M. and Matza, D. (1957). Techniques of neutralization: A theory of delinquency, *American Sociological Review*, 22 (6), 664–670.

Wells, J.B., Minor, K.I., Lambert, E.G., and Reeves, A. (2020). An exploratory study of possible correlates of individual whistleblowing propensity among sworn staff in a city jail, *Criminal Justice Policy Review*, 1–29, published online https://doi.org/10.1177/0887403420919478.

Wiig, H.B. and Hansen, B.H. (2019). Svein Arne Monsens oppsigelse: - En ønsket avgang av ledelsen? (Svein Arne Monsen's resignation: - A desired departure by the management?), *Local Norwegian Newspaper Helgelendingen*, www.helg.no, published April 20.

6 Moldova banks by Kroll

This case study is concerned with an internal investigation by fraud examiners in Moldova banks that the National Bank of Moldova (NBM) initiated. On January 28, 2015, the NBM engaged forensics firm Kroll (2015) to conduct a scoping phase of investigation into certain transactions involving Banca de Economii, Banca Sociala, and BC Unibank in Moldova. The Republic of Moldova is a landlocked country in Eastern Europa, bordered by Romania and Ukraine. Kroll is a UK-based firm that conducts investigations.

The *New York Times* reported in October 2015 that Moldova

> was rocked this year by the discovery that $1 billion had fraudulently siphoned from Moldova's banking system over a period of years, a huge amount for an impoverished country whose entire economic output is only about $8 billion a year
>
> (Nechepurenko, 2015).

Financial Times reported in January 2016 that "until the fraud came to light last year, Moldova was considered a rare success in the EU's campaign to build bridges to post-Soviet states".

In 2017, Kroll (2017) was again working for the National Bank of Moldova (NBM) to evidence what caused the three Moldovan banks to collapse, to understand who perpetrated and benefited from the fraud and to support criminal and/or civil proceedings to recover the misappropriated funds. One billion dollars had disappeared from the banks in a coordinated effort. Ilan Shor, a 28-year-old Moldovan business executive and the mayor of Orhei organized the swindle. Shor was chairperson of the board of Banca de Economii.

The Times of Israel reported in 2019 that Ilan Shor was sentenced to 7.5 years for fraud and money laundering (Iordachescu and Rodina, 2019; Liphshiz, 2019). Kroll's (2015) scoping phase report found evidence that suggested that Ilan Shor and companies and individuals affiliated with him (the "Shor Group") played an integral role in coordinating the illegal financial transactions. Kroll (2017) developed further evidence of Shor's involvement leading to his conviction.

The Guardian reported in 2015 that Grant Thornton, the UK-based accountancy firm with local offices in many countries, was the auditor for the three

Moldovan banks through which the money was embezzled and spirited out of the country in complex financial transactions. Investigators accused auditing firm Grant Thornton of negligence and incompetence after $1 billion disappeared out of Moldova, a sum equivalent to 15% of the country's gross national product (Rosca, 2015).

White-collar convenience

Assuming the allegations are correct, we briefly study the alleged white-collar crime by application of convenience theory. The motive was both individual and corporate gain based on possibilities to commit bank fraud, as illustrated in Figure 6.1. Probably, involved individuals wanted to climb the hierarchy of needs for status and success (Maslow, 1943) and realize the American dream of prosperity (Schoepfer and Piquero, 2006). In addition, they wanted their businesses to make as much profit as possible (Naylor, 2003) and reach business objectives that justify means (Jonnergård et al., 2010).

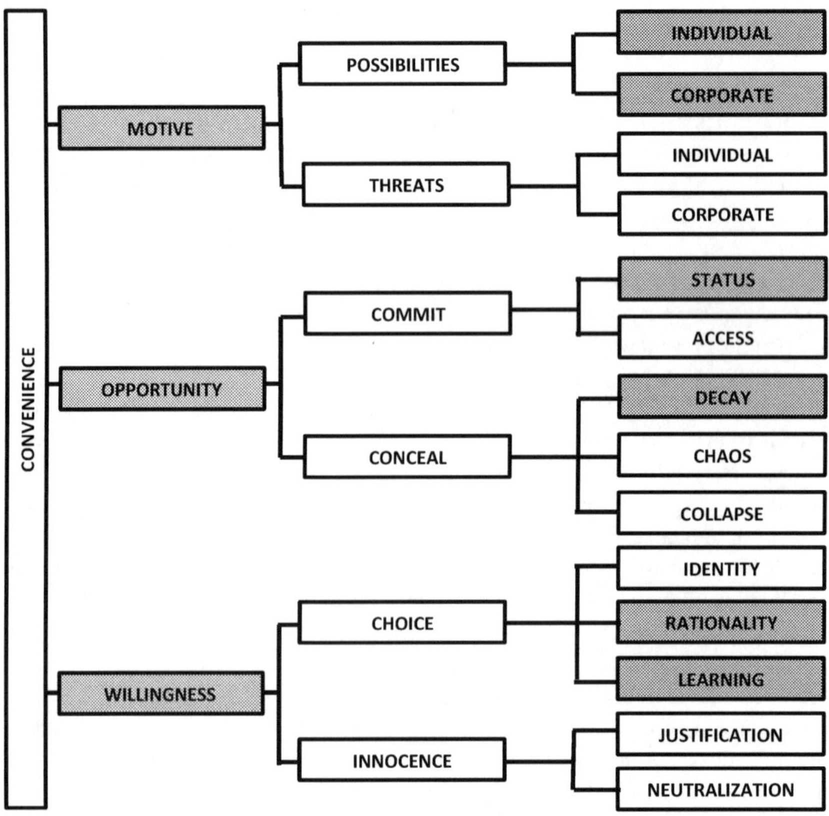

Figure 6.1 Convenience themes in the case of Moldovan banks

In the opportunity dimension of convenience theory, Moldovan banks obviously lacked guardianship, control mechanisms, and professional audit functions. There was decay by institutional deterioration (Rodriguez et al., 2005), inability to control because of social disorganization (Hoffmann, 2002), and misrepresentation in accounting (Qiu and Slezak, 2019) – in addition to the status of the offenders in the elite (Pontell et al., 2014).

Elite members in Moldova involved in the bank fraud did it on purpose as a rational choice where perceptions of benefits exceed costs (Pratt and Cullen, 2005). There was probably a behavioral reinforcement of deviance over time (Benartzi et al., 2017), and offenders learned from each other by differential association (Sutherland, 1983). A collectivist value orientation emerged among offenders (Bussmann et al., 2018), where they perceived no deterrence effect (Comey, 2009).

Fraud examination outcome

The mandate for the investigation was to reconstruct events and sequences of events to provide insights into financial irregularities, the main suspect parties, and the roles and responsibilities. In particular, investigators should identify events leading to the collapse of the three banks and identify the beneficiary of the funds that had disappeared from these three banks. The main source of information was NBM.

Fraud examiners from Kroll reviewed transactions from 2012 to 2014 in the three Moldovan banks. The banks were consecutively subject to significant shareholder changes, which had the effect of transferring ownership to a series of apparently unconnected individuals and entities. Each bank entered a series of transactions resulting in such a significant deterioration in each of their balance sheets that they no longer were viable as going concerns. It was bankruptcy in 2014 in all the three banks that triggered the fraud examination.

Fraud examiners established that important bank files were missing. They did not believe the story told to them that someone had stolen and burned down a car with bank files (Kroll, 2015: 67):

> The order was communicated to relevant department heads and 12 sacks of files were transferred to Birca's office. Iurie Buruiana, head of BEM's department for management, collection, and technical protection, was tasked with procuring a vehicle to transport the files to the archive. A vehicle was provided at 7 pm on 26 November by Klassica Force SRL, a security which BEM staff has stated is controlled by Ilan Shor. The sacks were loaded into the vehicle by the driver under the supervision of Iurie Buriana. As it was late, the driver stated that the documents would be transported to the archive the following day, on the 27th, and the vehicle would be held in a secure garage overnight. The following day, Klassica Force SRL informed BEM that the vehicle had been stolen and found burned out, a fact confirmed by a Moldovan police report issued on 1 December 2014.

Fraud examiners suggested the following events leading to the collapse of the banks. First, between January and November 2014, exposure of companies deemed directly and indirectly linked to Ilan Shor increased by MDL 3 billion to almost MDL 8 billion. The fact that almost all this exposure was concentrated in the three banks cannot be a coincidence. Funding of this explosive loan activity was largely through interbank deposits between the banks.

Second, transactions within each of the three banks had an appearance of lending to related parties to each of them, where the explosive lending activity developed its own dynamics.

Third, such a significant level of interrelated lending with three, apparently independent banks would have required a significant level of coordination. Significant connectivity between the shareholders of each of the banks as well as the number of common management changes between the banks could explain the coordination.

Fourth, such extended and interrelated funding and loan activity within and between the three banks culminated in a series of events in November 2014, which indicate that this was no longer sustainable. Most of the lending seemed like a routinized activity, facilitated by interbank deposits from Moldovan and Russian banks. Analysis of loan transactions reflects a clear pattern of lending within each bank, finding repayment by loans issued to entities in another bank, via the passing of funds through Russian banks, Latvian bank accounts, and UK limited partnerships.

Fifth, a series of highly unusual events took place on November 28, 2014, at the same time as new loans flowed out of banks, which were further indicative of efforts to extract the maximum value of funds possible from the banks before they collapsed.

Finally, as quoted above, Moldovan police destroyed evidence and reported the loss on December 1.

The mandate for the second investigation was to evidence what caused the three Moldovan banks to collapse, to understand who perpetrated and benefited from the fraud, and to support criminal and civil proceedings to recover the misappropriated funds. Fraud examiners from Kroll (2017: 11) start their executive summary with the following sentences:

> Our investigation to date has identified contemporaneous and independent documentary evidence that indicates that the Three Moldovan Banks were subjected to a large, coordinated fraud, which took place over at least three years, and intensified in 2014, ultimately resulting in their collapse.

Fraud examiners investigated suspected fraud that involved the issuing of hundreds of loans to seemingly cooperating companies. They found some evidence that the loan funds ended up a laundering mechanism in Latvia. Afterward, most of the money returned to Moldova to repay existing loans and to allow the continuation of lending, while at least US$600 million disappeared to other destinations.

> Contemporaneous documents suggest the involvement in the suspected fraud of a large group of Moldovan companies working in concert, linked to Mr. Ilan Shor ("Mr. Shor") (the "Shor Group").

Kroll (2017: 57) addresses the identification of beneficiaries as perpetrators:

> A proportion of the fund flows which have been traced to date have revealed a number of individuals who appear to have either been part of the administration of the suspected fraudulent activity, or to have obtained some benefit from the outflow of the funds. This benefit was identified partly through the flow of funds to companies with known affiliations to individuals.

Fraud examiners did not want to disclose names or provide more evidence in their report (Kroll, 2017: 57):

> As stated in the introduction to this report, in order to protect due process with regards to ongoing or future civil or criminal procedures, it is important that the apparent beneficiaries are kept confidential except in cases, which can contribute to any ongoing procedures. Details will be provided to the relevant authorities under separate cover.

Ilan Shor was a businessperson and politician. He served as mayor of the Moldovan city of Orhei from 2015 to 2019. He owned several Moldovan businesses, and he was chairperson of the board of the savings bank Banca de Economii. One billion dollars had disappeared from that bank and two other banks. Shor organized the fraud. Kroll (2015, 2017, 2018a, 2018b, 2018c) developed evidence of Shor's involvement leading to his conviction. In 2017, he was sentenced to 7.5 years in prison for fraud and money laundering (Iordachescu and Rodina, 2019; Liphshiz, 2019). Two years later, no criminal justice system had still not incarcerated him, as Moldova sought "arrest of convicted oligarch Ilan Shor" in 2019 (Necsutu, 2019).

Shor was born in Tel Aviv in Israel in 1987 as the son of Miron and Maria Shor, Moldovan Jews who had moved to Israel in the late 1970s. The family returned to Moldova in 1990. The wedding of Jasmin and Ilan Shor took place in September 2011 and became perhaps the most luxurious in the entire history of Moldova. Not only celebrities, but also politicians and businesspeople attended the wedding.

Kroll (2015) mentions Ilan Shor and his business Shor Group 163 times in the 84-page report, and 128 times by Kroll (2017) in the 58-page report. In their first report labeled scoping phase report, Kroll (2015) states:

> Based on information available to date, several factors suggest that Ilan Shor and individuals associated with him played an integral role in coordinating this activity, suggesting that he was one of, if not the only beneficiary (Page 9).
>
> Most of the Moldovan national shareholders are political figures of varying degrees of seniority (Page 19).
>
> During 2014, the value of loans issued by Moldovan banks to Shor Group companies increased by approximately 65% (Page 42).
>
> Where did the money go? A full forensic trace is required, in order to establish the ultimate beneficiaries of the MDL 8 billion in exposure of Shor Group companies as at 31 October 2014 and how this developed over time (Page 71).
>
> Priority next steps: Check if there had been devices brought into the bank after the acquisition by Mr. Shor and if yes, if these devices had been removed again later (Page 81).

In their second report, Kroll (2017) focuses less on the individual Ilan Shor and more on his companies:

> The transactions to which these Shor Group entities were party to appear to have ultimately contributed to the collapse of the banks at the end of 2014 (Page 7).
>
> Contemporaneous documents suggest the involvement in the suspected fraud of a large group of Moldovan companies working in concert, linked to Mr. Ilan Shor (Page 11).

Ilan Shor was still a free man in 2019. “Moldova has issued an arrest warrant for the businessman convicted in 2017 over the so-called ‘grand theft’ from the banking system – but remained at liberty and is thought to have left the country” (Necsutu, 2019).

Private policing evaluation

In their second report, Kroll (2017: 20) admits that they failed in interviewing the main suspect Ilan Shor, and they failed in obtaining a verifiable statement from him, which is an obvious shortcoming of the investigation:

> Kroll was made aware of the existence of a statement that has been uploaded onto the internet, which purports to be Mr. Shor’s statement to the Public Prosecutor, providing an explanation for some of the events that took place within the Three Moldovan Banks. Kroll has not been provided with an official copy of Mr. Shor’s statement and has not had the opportunity to meet with Mr. Shor. As such we are not at this stage in a position to confirm the authenticity of the document and do not comment on its content within this report.

The quoted statement seems arrogant and ignoring criminal justice, where everyone is innocent until proven guilty. Furthermore, fraud examiners should have listened to and respected statements from a suspect, since everyone is innocent until proven guilty, and not ignored as seems to be the case by fraud examiners from Kroll. Therefore, we consider their two investigations far from perfect. A professional crime investigation is about not only what you find out, but also how you did it, and how you treated suspects and witnesses in the process.

Fraud examiners relied too heavily on information from NBM, especially in the first investigation (Kroll, 2015: 7):

> In conducting this preliminary scoping phase of investigation, Kroll has relied upon information and analysis conducted by NBM, in order to assess the basis of their findings to date, and concerns raised.

Nevertheless, we place the Kroll (2015, 2017, 2018a, b, c) reports at the clarification level 4 in the maturity model in Figure 6.2.

The overall structure of Kroll reports is acceptable, despite the incredible scope of the case. Wordings in their reports are both clear and placed into context. Investigators are visualizing various examples of how offenders carried out the irregular transaction flow, and how the foreign banks became victims in the loan carousel. This is a complement to the wording of the text.

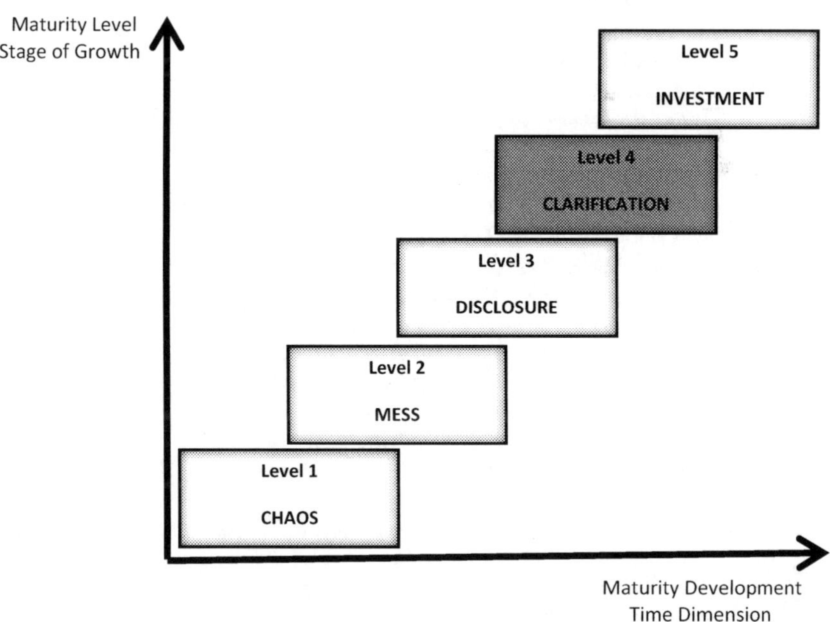

Figure 6.2 Maturity model for internal private investigations applied to Kroll

The mandate for the review is not present initially in the report, which is a weakness. It seems that the investigation had no set framework and thus could change direction during the examination period, depending on what findings Kroll made so far in the inquiry.

After completion of the investigation report, it is the responsibility of the prosecution in Modova to follow up examination results. Kroll submitted a detailed tracking analysis in parts labeled I and II and Kroll helped the national bank in Moldova to establish contact with authorities in other countries to support the continued process of returning embezzled funds.

Bibliography

Benartzi, S., Beshears, J., Milkman, K.L., Sunstein, C.R., Thaler, R.H., Shankar, M., Tucker-Ray, W., Congdon, W.J. and Galing, S. (2017). Should governments invest more in nudging? *Psychological Science*, 28 (8), 1041–1055.

Bussmann, K.D., Niemeczek, A. and Vockrodt, M. (2018). Company culture and prevention of corruption in Germany, China and Russia, *European Journal of Criminology*, 15 (3), 255–277.

Comey, J.B. (2009). Go directly to prison: White collar sentencing after the Sarbanes-Oxley act, *Harvard Law Review*, 122, 1728–1749.

Hoffmann, J.P. (2002). A contextual analysis of differential association, social control, and strain theories of delinquency, *Social Forces*, 81 (3), 753–785.

Iordachescu, I. and Rodina, M. (2019). Israeli-born convicted fraudster on track for seat in Moldovan parliament, *The Times of Israel*, www.timesofisrael.com, published February 20.

Jonnergård, K., Stafsudd, A. and Elg, U. (2010). Performance evaluations as gender barriers in professional organizations: A study of auditing firms, *Gender, Work and Organization*, 17 /6), 721–747.

Kroll (2015). *Project Tenor – Scoping Phase, Final Report Prepared for The National Bank of Moldova*, April 2, Nexus Place: Investigation Firm Kroll.

Kroll (2017). *Project Tenor II – Summary Report, Report Prepared for The National Bank of Moldova*, December 20, Nexus Place: Investigation Firm Kroll.

Kroll (2018a). *Project Tenor II – Detailed Report, Report Prepared for The National Bank of Moldova*, March 22, Nexus Place: Investigation Firm Kroll.

Kroll (2018b). *Project Tenor II – Confidential Working Papers – Part I to the Detailed Report: Detailed Tracing Analysis*, Nexus Place: Investigation Firm Kroll.

Kroll (2018c). *Project Tenor II – Confidential Working Papers – Part II: Evidence Packs – Funds Traced to: Ilan Shor, Alexandr Maclovici and Olga Bondarciuc*, Nexus Place: Investigation Firm Kroll.

Liphshiz, C. (2019). Moldova Jews bear anti-semitic brunt as corrupt lawmaker flees, maybe to Israel, *The Times of Israel*, www.thetimesofisrael.com, published August 30.

Maslow, A.H. (1943). A theory of human motivation, *Psychological Review*, 50 (4), 370–396.

Naylor, R.T. (2003). Towards a general theory of profit-driven crimes, *British Journal of Criminology*, 43, 81–101.

Nechepurenko, I. (2015). Moldova parliament dismisses government amid bank scandal, *The New York Times*, www.nytimes.com, published October 29.

Necsutu, M. (2019). Moldova seeks arrest of convicted oligarch Ilan Shor, *BalkanInsight*, www.balkaninsight.com, published July 26.

Pontell, H.N., Black, W.K. and Geis, G. (2014). Too big to fail, too powerful to jail? On the absence of criminal prosecutions after the 2008 financial meltdown, *Crime, Law and Social Change*, 61 (1), 1–13.

Pratt, T.C. and Cullen, F.T. (2005). Assessing macro-level predictors and theories of crime: A meta-analysis, *Crime and Justice*, 32, 373–450.

Qiu, B. and Slezak, S.L. (2019). The equilibrium relationships between performance-based pay, performance, and the commission and detection of fraudulent misreporting, *The Accounting Review*, 94 (2), 325–356.

Rodriguez, P., Uhlenbruck, K. and Eden, L. (2005). Government corruption and the entry strategies of multinationals, *Academy of Management Review*, 30 (2), 383–396.

Rosca, M. (2015). Vanishing act: How global auditor failed to spot theft of 15% of Moldova's wealth, *The Guardian*, www.theguardian.com, published July 1.

Schoepfer, A. and Piquero, N.L. (2006). Exploring white-collar crime and the American dream: A partial test of institutional anomie theory, *Journal of Criminal Justice*, 34 (3), 227–235.

Sutherland, E.H. (1983). *White Collar Crime – The Uncut Version*, New Haven, CT: Yale University Press.

7 Oceanteam services by Sands

The background for this private policing of suspected economic crime in terms of an internal investigation by fraud examiners is slightly different from most other cases presented in this book, where the organizations themselves initiated investigations. In 2016, one of the minority shareholders, Roger Nymo, in the corporation Oceanteam (OT) requested an investigation in accordance with chapter 5 of the Norwegian Public Limited Liability Companies Act. Bergen District Court ruled in favor of the demand from the minority shareholder. The board at Oceanteam appealed the ruling. Nevertheless, in 2018, Gulating Court of Appeal ruled in accordance with the Bergen District Court ruling (Riisnæs, 2018). Subsequently, lawyer and partner Nicolai Skridshol at the law firm Sands in Norway received an invitation from Bergen District Court to carry out the investigation. The courts stated the mandate for the assignment given to Sands (2019a: 10) in their rulings dated February 20, 2018, and March 23, 2018, respectively:

> The investigation of Oceanteam ASA shall cover the period between 1 January 2013 and 31 December 2017, comprising the following main parts:
>
> 1. Mapping of the facts, including: a) Review and mapping of related transactions and agreements between Oceanteam ASA and Haico Halbesma (CEO), Hessel Halbesma (Chairman of the Board) and members of the Board, and between its related parties and Oceanteam ASA, which are referred to in audit reports, annual accounts and auditor's communication with the management of Oceanteam ASA. b) Investigations and verification of whether there are further possible related party transactions or agreements other than those mentioned in audit reports, annual accounts, and the auditor's communication with the management of Oceanteam ASA. c) Mapping of travels and other forms of remuneration to Haico Halbesma (CEO), Hessel Halbesma (Chairman of The Board) and Board Members that Oceanteam ASA has covered.
> 2. Legal assessments of the facts, including assessment of whether the mapped transactions violate the provisions of the Public Limited Liability Companies Act on related transactions.

The corporation Oceanteam was in the business of providing support for offshore contractors all over the world through its fleet of large offshore vessels and its expertise in marine equipment, cable logistics, and design engineering. Haico Halbesma, chief executive officer, Hessel Halbesma, chairperson of the board, as well as three board members faced accusations of fraud against Oceanteam.

White-collar convenience

Assuming the accusations are correct, we briefly study the alleged white-collar crime by application of convenience theory. The chief executive and board members were obviously greedy. Greed implies that offenders are never satisfied, as they always want additional personal financial gain for themselves, independent of the level of wealth they have achieved already (Goldstraw-White, 2012). In the opportunity dimension of convenience theory, the chief executive and board members had high status and convenient access to resources to commit misconduct and crime (Benson and Simpson, 2018; Cohen and Felson, 1979).

In the dimension of willingness for deviant behavior, it seems that the two Halbesmas suffered from narcissistic identification with the organization. Narcissistic identification is a special type of narcissism, where the offender sees little or no difference between self and the corporation. The company money is personal money that can be spent whatever way the narcissist prefers (Galvin et al., 2015). While narcissistic grandiosity and admiration belong to the motivational dimension of convenience theory, narcissistic empathy deficit belongs to the willingness dimension of convenience theory where the offender possesses a sense of entitlement (Nichol, 2019). The narcissistic offender shows unreasonable expectations to receive and obtain preferential treatments (Zvi and Elaad, 2018). Figure 7.1 illustrates narcissistic identification along the axis willingness-choice-identity.

Fraud examination outcome

Sands (2019a) found that in general, fraud examiners observed an extensive lack of control of invoices and timesheets from executives and board members. Relevant functions had not controlled board members' timesheets, and the same applied to the CEO. For example, in 2015, Hessel Halbesma invoiced 3,600 additional hours of a total of EUR 1,080,000. Travel bills and other remunerations were extremely high. For example, Hessel Halbesma had travel expenses of EUR 333,000 in 2013 (Sands, 2019a: 9):

> In our review of Hessel Halbesma's travel bills, several expenses classified as company expenses, appear highly questionable with regards to being associated with OT's daily operations, for example purchases of clothing, numerous toll road passing, travels to places where OT has no operations (e.g. Verbier, San Remo), helicopter rental expenses in Monaco and dining

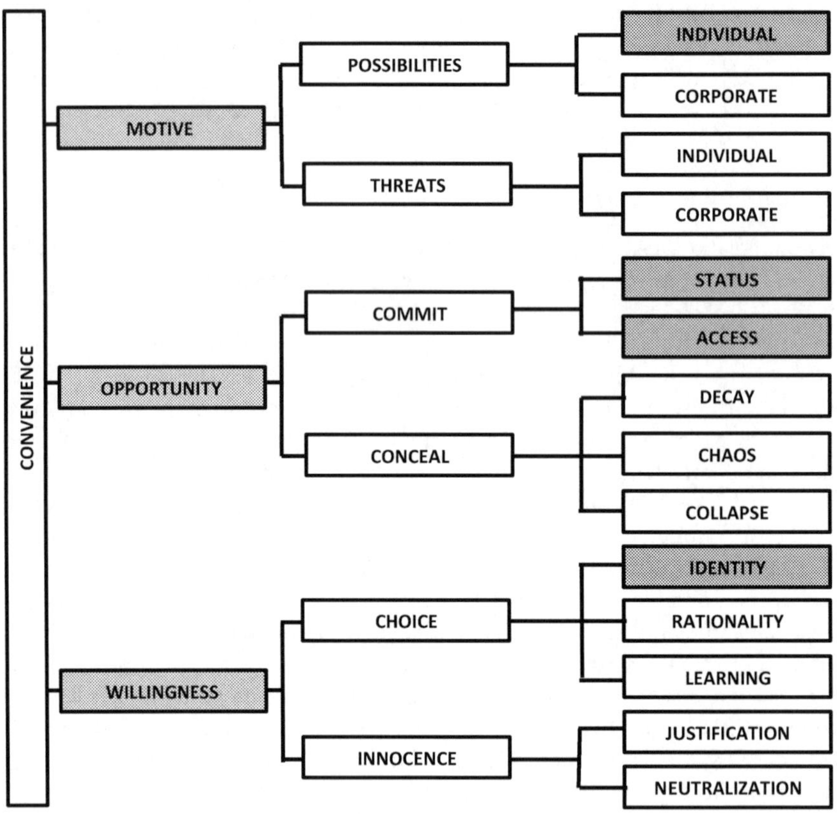

Figure 7.1 Convenience themes in the case of Oceanteam

> expenses with no information about participants, the purpose of the meal or the relation to OT's operations.

Fraud examiners drew similar conclusions regarding Haico Halbesma's travel bills, where several expenses appeared unrelated to Oceanteam's business. Art purchases, sponsorship of a Mexican artist, boat purchase in Monaco, and a personal legal dispute are some of the additional examples presented in the report by Sands (2019a).

Fraud examiners conclude in their report on related party transactions such as fees, salaries, and incentives, travels, and remunerations. Other relevant findings and transactions include art purchases (Sands, 2019a: 176):

> We have been informed that Halbesmas allegedly bought art paid by OT (Oceanteam) for private use. However, OT states that they possessed and are still in possession of the art, and that the purchases are registered in B.V. …

> It therefore remains unclear whether OT is in possession of all art specified in the financial account.

It seems surprising that fraud examiners were unable to conclude on this issue. Similarly, fraud examiners failed in concluding whether boat purchases in Monaco and sponsorship of Mexican artist were corporate expenditures or private expenditures paid by the corporation. Yet another example of lacking conclusion is Halbesmas' legal dispute with another party, which Oceanteam paid for (Sands, 2019a: 180):

> Through interviews, we have received various information about what and who this dispute concerns. Both Haico Halbesma and OT's corporate counsel describe the legal matter and the parties involved imprecisely in their interviews and not correctly compared with the legal documents.

The final issue in the factual report is the nomination and remuneration committee. Minority shareholders Storm Capital and Otterley Group had requested such a committee to be established. Over a long period, the shareholders followed up on the matter, but such a committee was never established. Again, fraud examiners failed to conclude on the matter.

An interesting approach applied by the fraud examiners was to distinguish in their report between a factual review (Sands, 2019a) and a legal review (2019b). The legal review was required in the mandate as quoted above. Fraud examiner Skridshol and his team focused on three legal topics: abuse of position, invalidity of agreements due to lack of shareholder approval, and unlawful distributions on the part of Hessel and Haico Halbesma. They identified several agreements, transactions, and matters that in their view constitute likely unlawful distributions. Attempts to charge for services not delivered, as well as any other invoices for services not delivered or use of company funds to pay private expenses, can potentially constitute violations of provisions in the penal code.

In the executive summary of the factual report, Sands (2019a) lists Catharina Petronella Pos, James Wingett Hill, Bote De Vries, and Diederik Legger as board members who benefited from related party transactions. While Hessel and Haico Halbesma received total remuneration of €4.5 million and €2.8 million, respectively, from 2013 to 2017, Chatrina Int Petronella Pos and James Wingett Hill received €0.5 million each. Hessel Halbesma and his firm Feastwood stood out with the largest transaction amounts over the period from 2013 to 2017. For 2013 and 2014, examiners found examples where timesheets from Hessel Halbesma showed the number of working hours exceeding the limit of 8 hours and €2,400 per day. In 2014, the total invoiced amount exceeded the maximum possible figure for a whole year. In 2015, Hessel Halbesma through Feastwood invoiced 3,600 additional hours. In 2016, as the hourly fee increased from €300 to €500, Feastwood charged for Hessel Halbesma an additional €608,400 for already invoiced hours concerning 2015.

In the executive summary of the legal review, Sands (2019b) conclude that they have uncovered several agreements and transactions that have or may have comprised elements of unlawful distributions of funds to individual associated with Oceanteam. Fraud examiners suggest that recipients of such potentially unlawful distribution of funds have an obligation to return the money. They also suggest that persons who assisted in adopting or carrying out the deviant acts might be liable as well. Fraud examiners base their suggestions on reviews of documents and interviews that leave an impression of an organization that operated under very distinct control by Hessel and Haico Halbesma.

Private policing evaluation

It seems that Sands' fraud examiners have done a thorough investigation by reconstructing past events and sequences of events related to privileged individuals' abuse of positions at Oceanteam for personal gain. The private policing by Sands (2019a, 2019b) thus deserves an allocation at least at level 4 in the maturity model. Since there was continued dispute after release of the report, the investment level is not obvious. In fact, after release of the report to Bergen District Court, Halbesma and others attempted to prevent shareholders to access the report. They had previously attempted to terminate the investigation (Strandli, 2019). While the report was completed and submitted to the court on November 4, 2019, the secrecy went on until April 2020, when a shareholders meeting needed the report. Oceanteam then decided to make the report public on their website, commenting that they were not responsible for the contents (Figure 7.2).

A letter sent to all shareholders of Oceanteam on March 30, 2020, illustrates the dispute, dissatisfaction, and reluctance to distribute the private policing report, as the letter emphasizes the lack of trust that major shareholders and the company places in the report by Skridshol's team:

> Following a joint petition from the company and the investigation requester, on 4 October 2019, the Bergen district court decided to cease the ongoing investigation. In the decision it was further resolved that the investigation report, as far as the report had been written at the time the decision was legally binding, was to be submitted to the Bergen district court.
>
> In accordance with the Public Limited Companies Act section 5-28 second paragraph the Bergen district court convenes the EGM (extraordinary general meeting) to deal with the investigation report. …
>
> The investigation report has been prepared solely by the investigator, Mr. Nicolai Skridshol, and his investigation team, and the company is not liable for the content of the report. The report was not presented to Oceanteam for review and clarification before being submitted to the court, and the company has not taken any position with respect to the correctness of the factual

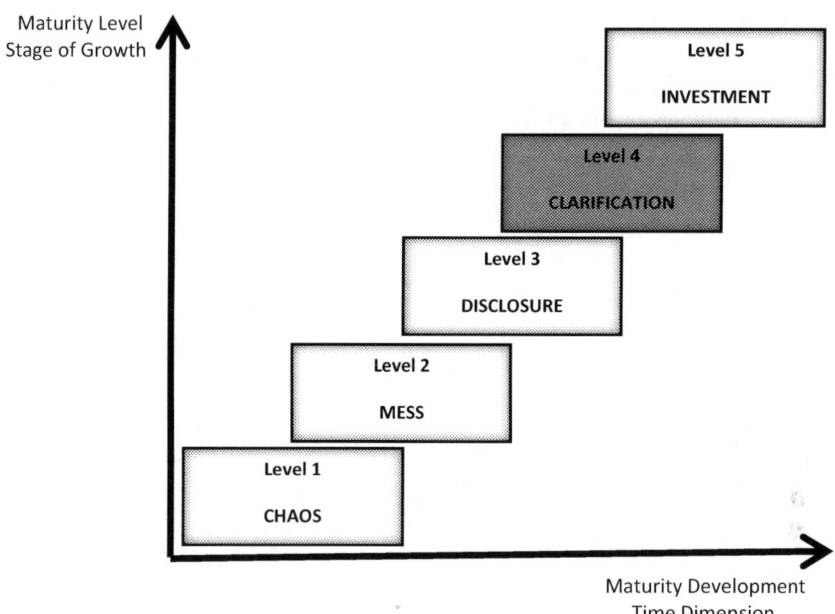

Figure 7.2 Maturity model for internal private investigations applied to Sands

> or legal circumstances described in the report. Oceanteam is in the process of evaluating the report and the company's legal position.

To evaluate Sand's (2019a, 2019b) investigation as an investment, benefits and costs need assessment. In terms of costs, Riisnæs (2018) reported in the media that Skridshol and his team had received an additional 3 million Norwegian kroner to complete their review at Oceanteam. Without knowing the initial budget, we assumed that it might be a more substantial number such as 6 million kroner initially. The total estimate for costs is thus 9 million kroner, which is the equivalent of 1 million USD. The benefits include clarification and removal of rumors, which might influence both management efficiency and market opportunities for Oceanteam. Another benefit might be that elite members in the company in the future will avoid abusing their positions for personal financial gain.

The report gives a clear picture that examiners did not have a functioning working relationship with people at Oceanteam. They had to ask for information repeatedly, and some documents were very hard to retrieve. The lack of communication caused a need to expand the budget for the investigation. When the mandate was ready in its formulation, 3 million Norwegian kroner should cover the investigative work. The budget increased twice. First on September 24, 2018, by another 3 million kroner. Then yet another 3 million kroner on January 23, 2019. The fact that the budget increased by 300% is an indication of many tasks that went wrong during the investigation.

One consequence of the private policing was that Haico and Hessel Halbesma had to leave their positions at Oceanteam. Another consequence was the restructuring of compliance functions. However, the new management did not appreciate the investigation report by Sands (2019a,b). They distanced themselves from the whole investigation affair, and they expressed dissatisfaction with the costs that the company had to carry for the investigation.

Bibliography

Benson, M.L. and Simpson, S.S. (2018). *White-Collar Crime: An Opportunity Perspective*, 3rd Edition, New York: Routledge.

Cohen, L.E. and Felson, M. (1979). Social change and crime rate trends: A routine activity approach, *American Sociological Review*, 44, 588–608.

Galvin, B.M., Lange, D. and Ashforth, B.E. (2015). Narcissistic organizational identification: Seeing oneself as central to the organization's identity, *Academy of Management Review*, 40 (2), 163–181.

Goldstraw-White, J. (2012). *White-Collar Crime: Accounts of Offending Behavior*, London: Palgrave Macmillan.

Nichol, J.E. (2019). The effects of contract framing on misconduct and entitlement, *The Accounting Review*, 94 (3), 329–344.

Riisnæs, M.G. (2018). Advokat gransker Oceanteam videre (Attorney continues Oceanteam investigation), *Daily Norwegian Business Newspaper Dagens Næringsliv*, www.dn.no, published September 26.

Sands (2019a). *Factual Report: Oceanteam ASA Investigation of Related Party Transactions*, November 4, Oslo: Law Firm Sands.

Sands (2019b). *Report – Legal Review: Oceanteam ASA Investigation of Related Party Transactions*, November 4, Oslo: Law Firm Sands.

Strandli, A. (2019). Oceanteam vil stanse granskningen av selskapet (Oceanteam wants to stop the investigation of the company), *Daily Norwegian Financial Newspaper Finansavisen*, www.finansavisen.no, published May 5.

Zvi, L. and Elaad, E. (2018). Correlates of narcissism, self-reported lies, and self-assessed abilities to tell and detect lies, tell truths, and believe others, *Journal of Investigative Psychology and Offender Profiling*, 15, 271–286.

8 Oslo housing by Deloitte

The capital of Norway, the city of Oslo, owns several housing facilities that less fortunate inhabitants occupy often on a permanent basis. The municipality has an agency that purchases apartments and other housing facilities for this purpose. Rumors in the housing market suggested that an in-house consultant in the municipal agency made purchases far above market value. In return, the consultant faced accusations regarding receipt of bribes from sellers of apartments. Previous investigations had indeed confirmed overpriced procurements, and the police initiated an investigation in 2018. Then a new case emerged, and Deloitte (2019) had the task of investigating whether the new case involved another example of overpriced procurement. The media did already speculate in a new corruption scandal in the municipality of Oslo (Linstad, 2019):

> The politicians believed the Housing scandal in Oslo was completely examined. But then a new, unexplainable million purchase emerges. The scandals in Oslo municipal agency Boligbygg does not seem to end. Wednesday evening, the municipal council was to make a final mark for the investigation. However, it is now postponed again because a new, unknown procurement episode of 24 million kroner suddenly came to light.
>
> Boligbygg recently became aware that in the fall 2017, a contract was signed for the purchase of six separate housing units in Lilleaker housing apartments, with address Lilleaker road 39A. The total purchase price is NOK 24 million.

The auditing firm BDO and the municipal audit function had conducted previous investigations. In addition, auditing firm Deloitte, who got the task of this additional investigation, had already conducted investigations into procurements of housing facilities for the city of Oslo.

White-collar convenience

Both the briber and the bribed in a corruption relationship have their financial motives, organizational opportunities, and willingness for deviant behaviors. In

Figure 8.1, illustrations for the briber are with texture, while illustrations for the bribed are in dark gray.

The briber has a motive of selling overpriced housing facilities to the municipality of Oslo (Huang and Knight, 2017), while the bribed can make an extraordinary profit (Goldstraw-White, 2012), which is possible because of the individual's procurement position in the municipality (Patel and Cooper, 2014). The internal consultant had substantial experience from the real estate market and enjoyed status in the agency, as suggested by the axis opportunity-commit-status in Figure 8.1. The bribed consultant had the opportunity to divide procurements into parts so that each part seemed small and thus did not require approval from any political body in the city. The property owner had access to resources in terms of corruption payments (Ramoglou and Tsang, 2016), as suggested by the axis opportunity-commit-access. It is a rational choice for the briber to get involved in corruption to improve corporate profitability in his real estate empire (Pratt and Cullen, 2005). The bribed can neutralize potential feelings of guilt by arguing that he would have triggered the same purchases anyway (Sykes and Matza,

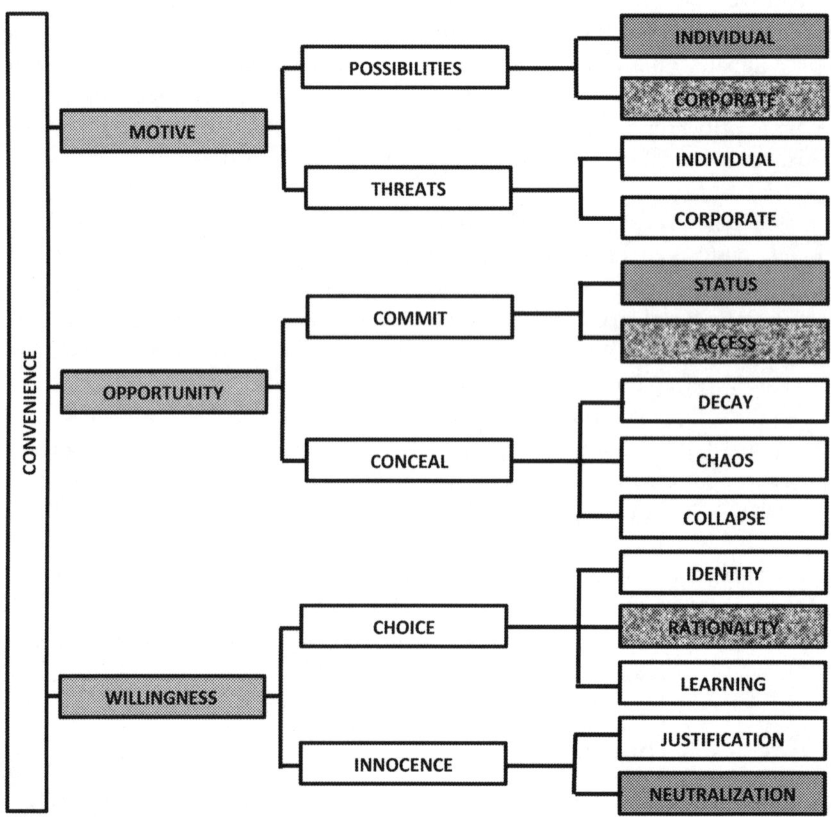

Figure 8.1 Convenience themes in the case of Oslo housing

1957), possibly sliding on a slippery slope from the right side to the wrong side of the law (Welsh et al., 2014).

Fraud examination outcome

Fraud examiners from Deloitte (2019: 5) draw the following conclusion:

> Deloitte's valuation shows that the agreement for the purchase of the housing shares in Lilleaker road 39A for a total of NOK 23 million is three to five million above estimated market value at the time the purchase agreements were entered. In addition, Deloitte finds that the agreement to purchase three parking spaces at NOK 300.000 per place was significantly above market value.

Fraud examiners approached the valuation systematically by reviewing variables that influence apartment prices in Oslo. Examples include the floor level, where ground floor apartments are less attractive and top floor apartments are more attractive. They included the size of apartments, where the value of additional square meters declines. Furthermore, Lilleaker road has much traffic to a nearby shopping mall, harming some of the apartments more than others. Finally, fraud examiners obtained actual sale prices for other apartments in the neighborhood.

The fraud examiners were quite confrontational in their interviews with the allegedly bribing seller, as indicated by email exchanges between the examiner and the seller referenced in the investigation report. After several email exchanges, fraud examiners wrote in their next email (Deloitte, 2019: 71):

> Thank you for your answers and the documents from you. We do understand that it is not an optimal point in time for you to provide answers to our queries regarding the contract for procurement of housing units in Lilleaker road 39A, but do appreciate that you found some time for it anyway. It is useful for the report we are to deliver that our description becomes as complete as possible. Based on the answers you have sent us, there are some places where you provide answers to issues slightly different from those where we really want answers. To make matters simple, we have included our follow-up questions in your answers in the attached document and are grateful for your expected responses to these questions, and then preferably as concrete as possible.

The suspected briber did not respond anymore. This is obvious from the following email, which the examiners sent one week later (Deloitte, 2019: 75):

> We have noticed that we have received no answers to our follow-up question. We are now about to deliver our report this Friday and would really appreciate answers to those questions. We want to offer you the opportunity of contradiction to the draft report and assume that this might most conveniently

take place in our offices. This implies that you will get a separate PC and a separate room at your disposal, where you will have the chance to review all parts of the report that deal with you. You will thus have the opportunity to contradict information relating to you to ensure that the information is correct. You will receive further information about the process when you do the contradiction.

Private policing evaluation

The private investigation was very limited in scope, as the examination focused solely on the issue of whether there was yet another case of overpriced procurement by the municipality of Oslo. Deloitte's (2019) fraud examiners were successful in establishing the facts in a convincing manner in their report. Therefore, this case of private policing could result in a maturity assessment at level 5 in Figure 8.2.

Of course, compared to other private policing cases in this book, the current case was not very difficult for the fraud examiners. Nevertheless, given the examination task handled by investigators Thorvald Nyquist and Stein Ove Songstad, Deloitte (2019) successfully completed their assignment.

One reason for the allocation of the private policing effort in Figure 8.2 at level 4 rather than 5 is the question whether this large-scale investigation was indeed necessary. There is an 83-page report filled with documentation about various

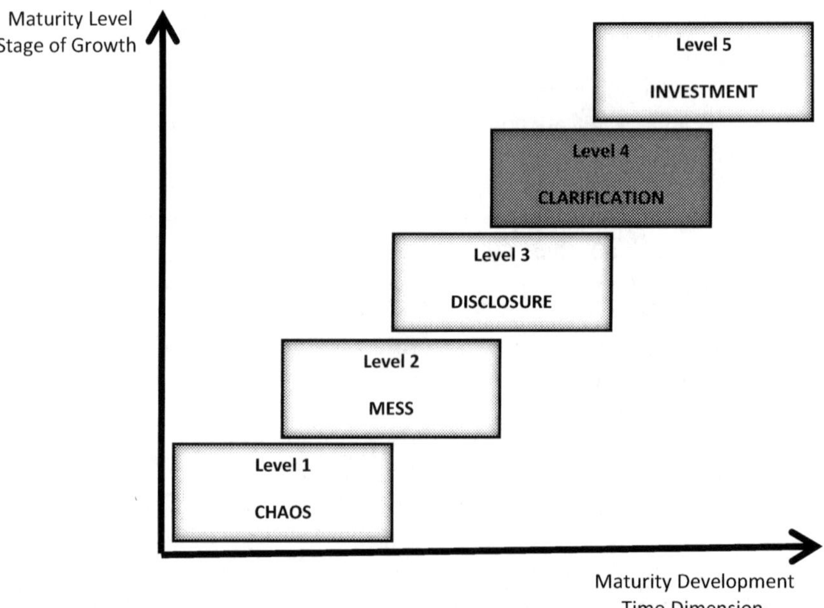

Figure 8.2 Maturity model for internal private investigations applied to Deloitte

housing prices, market values, and market parameters. It is not at all obvious that the benefits are exceeding the costs for this examination. Thus, while Deloitte (2019) has done a professional job, there is a question whether this examination – at least at the substantial scale performed – can be justified by the city of Oslo.

Oslo Boligbygg paid Deloitte 1 million Norwegian kroner for the report. Compared to the previous Deloitte report, where the investigators examined several purchases and Oslo Boligbygg paid 13 million, this examination was inexpensive.

The recommendations and measures that Deloitte concludes are in accordance with the mandate they have worked according to, and they provide relevant recommendations to Boligbygg. They also note that one suspect has tried to remain reluctant to follow the guidelines relevant for his position and has exceeded the amount limit he had permit to spend. This has probably been in the gray zoned for Boligbygg, and Boligbygg now must rewrite these guidelines so that they no more can be ignored.

Almost all the old board members at Boligbygg had to resign after yet another scandal emerged. Because of the poor follow-up, the retired board enabled deviant behavior to continue. While Boligbygg has restarted procurements of housing, it is not obvious whether waterproof routines are in place. However, this is not the responsibility of the fraud examiners but rather of the board and management at Boligbygg.

The price for the investigation of Lilleaker road 29 A was 1,145,900 Norwegian kroner. Stein Ove Songstad was the responsible partner at Deloitte for both the previous and the current investigations. The examiners interviewed only three persons for the current report, while they interviewed 70–80 persons for the previous report.

Bibliography

Deloitte (2019). *Lilleakerveien 39 A – Boligbygg Oslo KF Gransking (Lilleaker road 39 A – Housing Oslo Investigation)*, May, Oslo: Auditing Firm Deloitte.

Goldstraw-White, J. (2012). *White-Collar Crime: Accounts of Offending Behavior*, London: Palgrave Macmillan.

Huang, L. and Knight, A.P. (2017). Resources and relationships in entrepreneurship: An exchange theory of the development and effects of the entrepreneur-investor relationship, *Academy of Management Review*, 42 (1), 80–102.

Linstad, A. (2019). Politikerne trodde Boligbygg-skandalen i Oslo var ferdig gransket. Men så dukket et nytt, uforklarlig millionkjøp opp (The politicians believed that the Boligbygg scandal in Oslo was completely examined. Butt hen a new, inexplainable million purchase popped up), *Web-Based Norwegian Newspaper Vårt Oslo*, www.vartoslo.no, published March 28.

Patel, P.C. and Cooper, D. (2014). Structural power equality between family and nonfamily TMT members and theperformance of family firms, *Academy of Management Journal*, 57 (6), 1624–1649.

Pratt, T.C. and Cullen, F.T. (2005). Assessing macro-level predictors and theories of crime: A meta-analysis, *Crime and Justice*, 32, 373–450.

Ramoglou, S. and Tsang, E.W.K. (2016). A realist perspective of entrepreneurship: Opportunities as propensities, *Academy of Management Review*, 41, 410–434.

Sykes, G.M. and Matza, D. (1957). Techniques of neutralization: A theory of delinquency, *American Sociological Review*, 22 (6), 664–670.

Welsh, D.T., Ordonez, L.D., Snyder, D.G. and Christian, M.S. (2014). The slippery slope: How small ethical transgressions pave the way for larger future transgressions, *Journal of Applied Psychology*, 100 (1), 114–127.

9 Oslo energy recovery by PwC

This case is not directly concerned with private policing of economic crime. The internal investigation by examiners from PwC (2019a) investigated violation of the Working Environment Act in Norway, where law violations can have financial motives. The reason for the investigation assignment was that the notification system had received warnings regarding allegations of breach of the procurement regulations, extensive and deviant use of external consultants, and hiring people without internal or external announcements of vacant positions. The audit firm was engaged in investigating the agency for incidents back in time based on notifications and reports of breaches of working time regulations.

Daily Norwegian newspaper *Aftenposten* reported from the presentation of the private policing report by fraud examiner Gunnar Holm Ringen from PricewaterhouseCoopers (Sørgjeld, 2019):

> They have examined the municipality of Oslo where they found violations of procurement rules, illegal overtime, and unruly employments. In 28 out of 47 external procurements that have been examined in the energy recovery agency, there are errors and omissions. Only one in sixteen management positions were announced publicly. The review report on the Energy Recovery Agency in Oslo Municipality was presented by the audit firm PwC on Friday. The reason why the City Council in March ordered a review was anonymous whistleblowing.
>
> A review of 47 supplier relationships shows major flaws and shortcomings, says Gunnar Ringen of PwC.

The chief executive at the energy recovery agency resigned when the internal investigation started, and the newly appointed chief executive had as priority to stop occurrences of rule violations in the agency.

White-collar convenience

Assuming the allegations are correct, we briefly study the alleged white-collar crime by application of convenience theory. The suspected offenders are executives at the energy recovery agency in the municipality of Oslo. They had their focus on operations, so the motive seems to be removal of strain and pain

(Langton and Piquero, 2007) and avoidance of organizational collapse (Blickle et al., 2006). The energy recovery agency was committed to keeping operations running around the clock, no matter what. This had financial implications. In addition, the goal of the agency is to be a leader in sustainable waste utilization, which put pressure on them to reach the goal at the expense of means (Jonnergård et al., 2010). They lost focus from anything else but achievement of their goal. The main task for the unit was to sort and recycle energy from residual waste through the production of district heating, biogas, and bio-fertilizers. This task appears, according to the review report (PwC, 2019a), as so overriding that it has caused reluctance to keep spending down. They have spent more money than allowed. Finance was obviously less important than keeping operations going and being a leader in sustainable waste utilization.

In the opportunity dimension, abuses of working regulations and procurement guidelines were possible because of decay by institutional deterioration (Rodriguez et al., 2005) and inability to control because of social disorganization (Hoffmann, 2002). Municipal politicians were unable to review performance because of the chaotic situation leading to lack of control in the principal-agent relationship (Bosse and Phillips, 2016). In the recycling agency, a lack of routines and systems in operations and among the units meant that there was poor communication among employees. There were many issues reported incorrectly, issues that were not reported, misunderstandings of reporting, and little staff responsible for overseeing that reporting was according to regulations. In several interviews with staff, examiners found that some knew about violations of laws and regulations, and about the illegalities that occurred. However, most concluded that was simply the way it was and should be. Therefore, everyone just worked like before. Performing illegalities and doing things that were a bit beyond the borderline was almost a routine. Illegality became a norm in operations. Some people quit because they did not want to do anything illegal, and they considered it difficult if not impossible to change behaviors internally.

In the behavioral dimension, executives seem to argue that the misconduct as acts of wrongdoing was morally justifiable (Schnatterly et al., 2018). They could neutralize potential guilt feelings by loyalty to higher authority or by loyalty to keeping operations working daily (Sykes and Matza, 1957). Willingness might be a result of differential association (Sutherland, 1983), where people learn from each other that misconduct becomes a norm. It is easy to follow along when everyone does the same. Agency staff may have been sliding on a slippery slope to the wrong side of the law. Sliding on a slippery slope can make the offender feel innocent, as the offender did not notice ending up on the wrong side of the law (Welsh et al., 2014). Arjoon (2008: 78) explains the slippery slope in the following way: "As commonsense experience tells us; it is the small infractions that can lead to the larger ones". A series of small infractions gradually increase over time. Committing small indiscretions over time gradually leads people to complete larger unethical acts that they otherwise would have judged impermissible (Murphy and Dacin, 2011; Pettigrew, 2018). Figure 9.1 illustrates these suggested convenience themes.

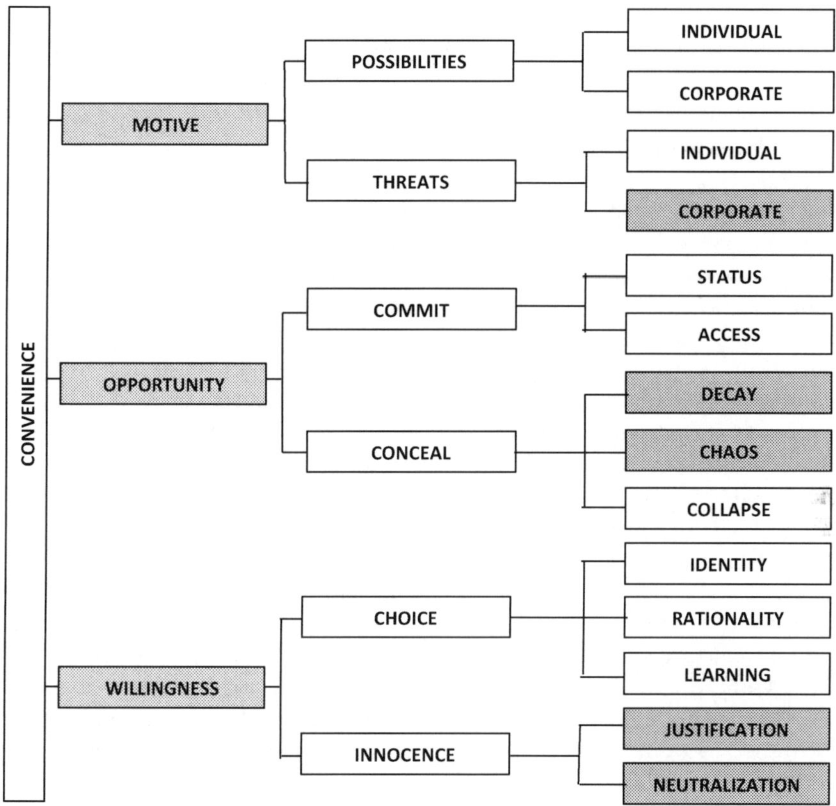

Figure 9.1 Convenience themes in the case of Oslo energy recovery

Fraud examination outcome

On behalf of the city council department for environment and transport, PwC (2019a) conducted a study of working hours, procurement, and employment in the energy recovery agency. The examination report documents violations of procurement rules and working time regulations, and that there is a lack of evidence for recruitment to many positions. The report states that the city agency had all its focus on operations, and that this happened at the expense of complying with rules and regulations.

For example, fraud examiners question whether the most qualified person always was the first choice and became recruited to a position (PwC, 2019a: 152):

> In light of the qualification principle that applies to the public sector, and the assumption that vacancies are to be announced, the practice represents, both isolated to individual cases and overall, a risk that the qualification principle

> is not followed. This applies to the large scope of commanding employees to new positions as well as frequent reorganization. Only one executive position was ever advertised. Regardless of whether each of the changes is objectively justified, the disclosed practice contributes to weakening public confidence, by asking whether the hiring has been made on a factual basis, and whether irrelevant circumstances have been taken into account.

The mandate for the private policing at the energy recovery agency was to confirm or reject allegations and accusations from whistleblowers concerning violations of laws and rules, extensive use of external consultants, employment without announcement of vacant positions, and working environment deviations. The information strategy applied by examiners was first to ask for a large number of documents related to the topics in the mandate. They looked at financial transactions, contract, procurements, employments, systems, and routines.

Next in the information strategy, examiners conducted interviews with former chief executives, department heads, employees in the procurement department, and human resource staff.

PwC (2019a: 152) comments on the recruitments of employees:

> In PwC's assessment, there is not sufficient documentation in the agency that the regulations for ordering, hiring outside the qualification principle and lack of information have been followed. It can then be questioned whether the underlying processes are satisfactory and legitimate since this cannot be confirmed. In PwC's view, there is a risk that the employment processes in the agency may in certain cases have occurred in contravention of current regulations.

The outcome of the fraud examination was sufficiently specific for the responsible politician Lan Marie Berg in the city council to act and correct deviance. The report became public in October 2019, and the Norwegian labor inspectorate was satisfied with Berg's cleanup in March 2020. The labor inspectorate had completed its audit of the energy recovery agency. They waived all orders related to breaches of the Working Environment Act (NTB, 2020).

Private policing evaluation

The private policing by PwC (2019a) deserves level 4 in the maturity model as illustrated in Figure 9.2. Fraud examiners contributed to clarification that enabled Lan Marie Berg to correct the situation (NTB, 2020).

The examination by PwC (2019a) resulted in a quantitative measure of violations of various rules and regulations. The numbers were surprisingly high according to most stakeholders, which meant that the quantification was useful. They found 431 violations of the Working Environment Act in 2017, and 300 violations in 2018. Seventy-nine persons were harmed by such violations in 2017, and 61 persons were harmed in 2018.

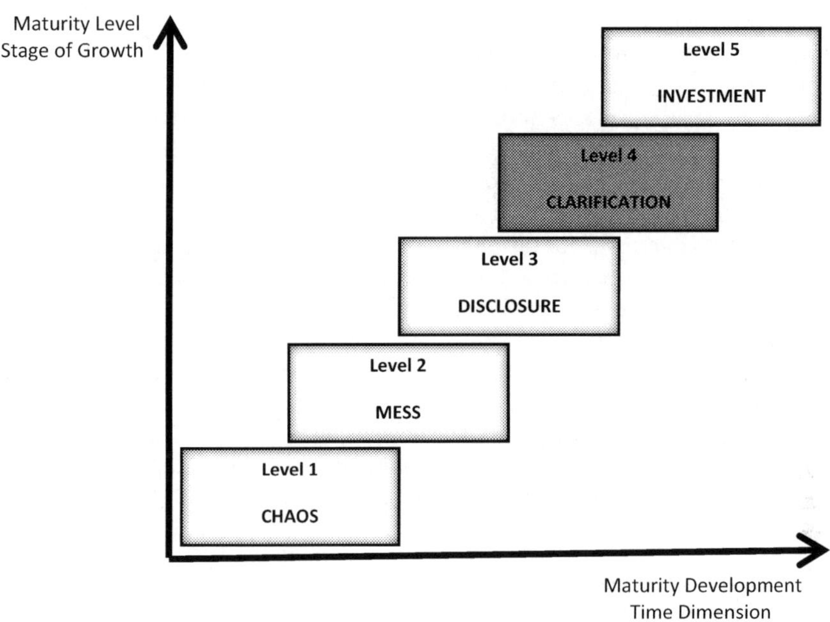

Figure 9.2 Maturity model for internal private investigations applied to PwC

However, the examination lacks an analysis of causes and effects, thereby not justifying a level 5 of maturity. There are indications of causality that the report vaguely formulates, such as the following example (PwC, 2019a: 76):

> According to what PwC has been told, the lack of cooperation between procurement functions and operational units is a contributing factor to the uncovered findings.

Fraud examiners explicitly blame executives for lack of involvement in the problems. As the investigation report was moving close to completion and publication, the chief executive resigned from his position.

There is little criticism to come to the report presented by PwC (2019a). The report is neat, well structured and responds to the mandate assigned. PwC has an important responsibility to ensure that findings surface, and in this case, they produce a good number of findings that prove to be serious. However, it can sometimes be a little difficult to know where to find potential content for specific issues. Examiners could easily summarize findings toward the end of some issues covered in the report.

PwC has conducted an investigation that has a comprehensive mandate – focusing on the systemic side of deviance. There is avoidance of the individual side of deviance. Although the mandate finds answers to an acceptable extent, deeper inquiries into individuals in the agency are missing, especially with regard to management. At the same time, it seems that PwC had a team with high competence, both from a legal and financial background, but the sector-specific competence was lacking. As the influence on the mandate from PwC seems to have been great, it can therefore be questioned why no changes were made that would have benefited the result in terms of responsibility for deviance among key personnel in the agency.

The investigators have obtained large amounts of documentation, some documents they requested were difficult to obtain, because they apparently did not exist, which, of course, has led to something they should have seen that they have not had the opportunity to examine. They have interviewed over 20 people, and some several times. One former section manager did not want to answer questions from PwC or contradict relevant parts of the report beyond an initial interview. This means that PwC has not obtained key information related to the management dialogue, and that allegations related to the relevant role are not contradicted. Nevertheless, the examination deserves level 4, as it seems that the investigators have been active in the inquiry process and have interviewed people with different roles.

Bibliography

Arjoon, S. (2008). Slippery when wet: The real risk in business, *Journal of Markets & Morality, Spring*, 11 (1), 77–91.

Blickle, G., Schlegel, A., Fassbender, P. and Klein, U. (2006). Some personality correlates of business white-collar crime, *Applied Psychology: An International Review*, 55 (2), 220–233.

Bosse, D.A. and Phillips, R.A. (2016). Agency theory and bounded self-interest, *Academy of Management Review*, 41 (2), 276–297.

Hoffmann, J.P. (2002). A contextual analysis of differential association, social control, and strain theories of delinquency, *Social Forces*, 81 (3), 753–785.

Jonnergård, K., Stafsudd, A. and Elg, U. (2010). Performance evaluations as gender barriers in professional organizations: A study of auditing firms, *Gender, Work and Organization*, 17 (6), 721–747.

Langton, L. and Piquero, N.L. (2007). Can general strain theory explain white-collar crime? A preliminary investigation of the relationship between strain and select white-collar offenses, *Journal of Criminal Justice*, 35 (1), 1–15.

Murphy, P.R. and Dacin, M.T (2011). Psychological pathways to fraud: Understanding and preventing fraud in organizations, *Journal of Business Ethics*, 101, 601–618.

NTB (2020). Arbeidstilsynet fornøyd med Lan Marie Bergs opprydding (The Labor Inspection Authority satisfied with Lan Marie Berg's clean-up), *Daily Norwegian Newspaper VG*, www.vg.no, published March 18.

Pettigrew, W.A. (2018). The changing place of fraud in seventeenth-century public debates about international trading corporations, *Business History*, 60 (3), 305–320.

PwC (2019a). *Undersøkelse av Energigjenvinningsetaten i Oslo Kommune (Inquiry into the Energy Recycling Authority at Oslo Municipality)*, October 22, Oslo: Auditing Firm PwC.

Rodriguez, P., Uhlenbruck, K. and Eden, L. (2005). Government corruption and the entry strategies of multinationals, *Academy of Management Review*, 30 (2), 383–396.

Schnatterly, K., Gangloff, K.A. and Tuschke, A. (2018). CEO wrongdoing: A review of pressure, opportunity, and rationalization, *Journal of Management*, 44 (6), 2405–2432.

Sutherland, E.H. (1983). *White Collar Crime – The Uncut Version*, New Haven, CT: Yale University Press.

Sykes, G.M. and Matza, D. (1957). Techniques of neutralization: A theory of delinquency, *American Sociological Review*, 22 (6), 664–670.

Sørgjeld, C. (2019). Har gransket Oslo kommune: Brudd på anskaffelsesregler, ulovlig overtid og uryddige ansettelser (Have examined Oslo municipality: Violations of procurement rules, illegal overtime and messige employments), *Daily Norwegian Newspaper Aftenposten*, www.aftenposten.no, published October 25.

Welsh, D.T., Ordonez, L.D., Snyder, D.G. and Christian, M.S. (2014). The slippery slope: How small ethical transgressions pave the way for larger future transgressions, *Journal of Applied Psychology*, 100 (1), 114–127.

10 Samherji fishing by Al Jazeera

Johannes Stefansson came to Namibia in Africa in 2011, where he was assigned the task by the Icelandic seafood company Samherji of looking for business opportunities. To complete the mission, he involved himself in questionable payments to politicians and business people in Namibia and Angola. After a while, he developed a bad conscience and felt guilty of wrongdoing. He decided to give notice of the situation. The police arrested the former minister of fisheries in Namibia, Bernhard Esau, and indicted him for corruption and money laundering in November 2019. Stefansson provided information to WikiLeaks and Al Jazeera, where investigative journalist James Kleinfeld interviewed local sources in Namibia. Kleinfeld (2019) then wrote a report on the "Anatomy of a bribe: A deep dive into an underworld of corruption".

White-collar convenience

Both the briber and the bribed in a corruption relationship have their financial motives, organizational opportunities, and willingness for deviant behaviors. They enter into a relationship with mutual illegal benefits (Huang and Knight, 2017). In Figure 10.1, themes for the briber are with texture, while themes for the bribed are in dark gray. The briber has a motive of obtaining fishing rights in the Namibian ocean zone, which is corporate crime (Bittle and Hébert, 2020), while the bribed can make an extraordinary profit, which is possible because of the individual's decision rights as the minister of fishery. This is occupational crime (Goldstraw-White, 2012; Shepherd and Button, 2019). Johannes Stefansson had access to resources (Berghoff and Spiekermann, 2018) in terms of corruption payments from Samherji via the Norwegian bank DNB to Esau in Namibia, as suggested by the axis opportunity-commit-access in the figure. It is a rational choice for the briber (Kamerdze et al., 2014) to get involved in corruption to improve corporate profitability in the Icelandic fishing empire of Samherji. The bribed can neutralize potential feelings of guilt by arguing that he would have triggered the same agreements anyway (Benson, 1985).

The briber, Samherji, can neutralize guilt feeling by claiming that they do so much good in Namibia by creating jobs in fisheries and paying taxes to the local government. Samherji can claim that it was necessary to carry out the offense

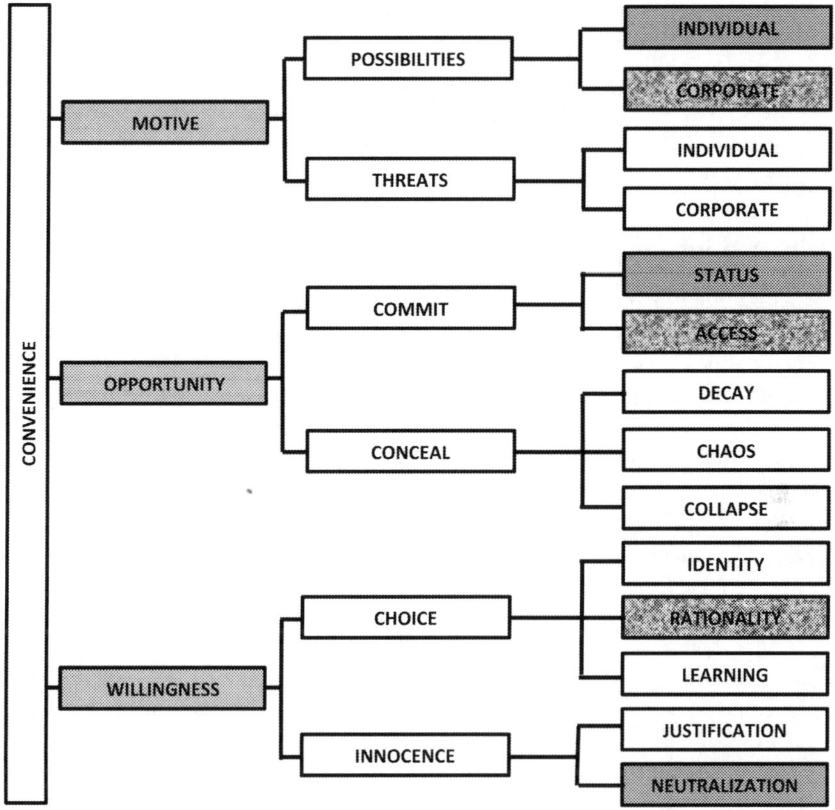

Figure 10.1 Convenience themes in the case of Samherji

since Namibia is a corrupt country. The offender then claims that the offense belongs in a larger context, where the crime is an illegal element among many legal elements to ensure an important result. The offense was a required and necessary means to achieve an important goal. A bribe represents nothing in dollar value compared to the potential income from a large contract abroad, and compared to the local benefit of jobs and business abroad.

Fraud examination outcome

Iceland public broadcasting, similar to BBC in the United Kingdom, interviewed the whistleblower and cooperated with Al Jazeera. Al Jazeera's investigative unit secretly filmed officials in Namibia demanding cash in exchange for political favors. It was a story of how foreign companies plunder Africa's natural resources. Using confidential documents provided to Al Jazeera by WikiLeaks, "Anatomy of a Bribe" exposes the government ministers and public officials willing to sell off

Namibia's assets in return for millions of dollars in bribes. Al Jazeera journalists spent three months undercover posing as foreign investors looking to exploit the lucrative Namibian fishing industry. The country's minister of fisheries demonstrated a willingness to use a front company to accept a $200,000 "donation". Exclusive testimony from a whistleblower, who worked for Iceland's biggest fishing company, reveals that his employer instructed him to bribe ministers and even the president in return for fishing rights worth hundreds of millions of dollars.

Private policing evaluation

The investigation report by Kleinfeld is a documentary television program of 51 minutes accessible at Al Jazeera, YouTube, and other platforms. The documentary was a tremendous success and caused police involvement in Iceland, Norway, and Namibia. It was mature work by investigative journalists at level 4, as indicated in Figure 10.2. The media coverage represented disclosure and clarification of misconduct and crime.

Al Jazeera exposed public figures close to Namibian President Hage Geingob discussing laundering of political contributions. Posing as Chinese investors, Al Jazeera journalists attempted to enter the Namibian fishing industry to acquire highly lucrative fishing quotas for a proposed joint venture with Namibian fishing

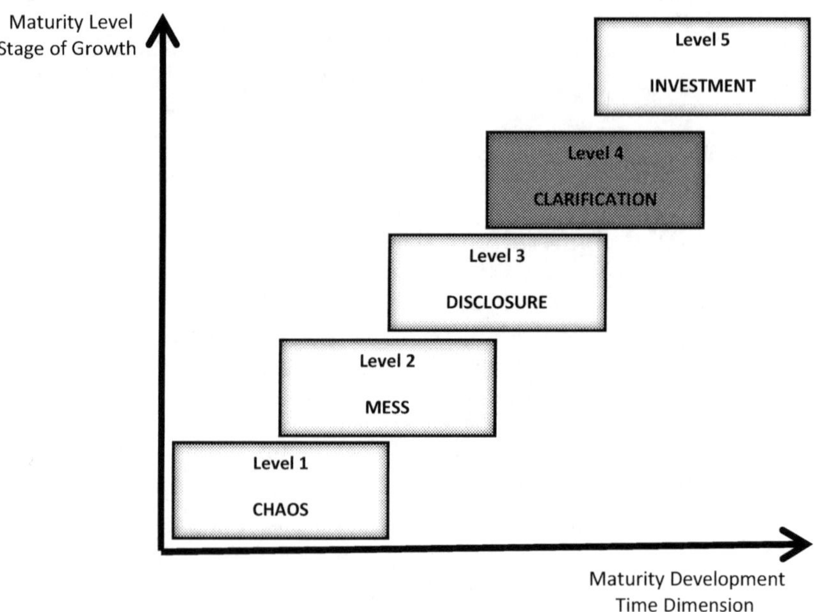

Figure 10.2 Maturity model for investigative journalism applied to Kleinfeld at Al Jazeera

company Omualu. During the Al Jazeera investigation, Esau requested a donation of $200,000 from the Chinese "investors" to the ruling Swapo party, preferably ahead of the nation's general election that was scheduled at that time. Filmed with hidden cameras, Esau is visible when accepting an iPhone from Al Jazeera's reporter.

Under the instructions of Omualu's managing director Sacky Kadhila-Amoomo, the assumed donation should secretly move into the Swapo party, under the disguise of a foreign investment in real estate. Furthermore, the assumed donation should channel through the trust account of Sisa Namandje, who had been the personal lawyer for all Namibian presidents since the nation's independence in 1990.

Norwegian bank investigation

The alleged corruption payments from Samherji traveled via the Norwegian bank DNB to Esau in Namibia. DNB is Norway's largest lender that faced allegations concerning the Icelandic company had transferred money via the bank to bribe Namibian officials. DNB had to investigate the claims. When DNB made the announcement of an internal investigation, Iceland's biggest fishing company, Samherji, said in a statement that it had also hired a law firm to investigate the allegations (Schultz, 2019).

However, at first, Samherji denied any wrongdoing (Samherji, 2019a):

> It has recently been brought to our attention that a former executive of a subsidiary of the company in Namibia, Johannes Stefansson, has spoken to the media and made serious allegations against Samherji's executives, both current and former. We take this very seriously and have engaged the international law firm Wikborg Rein based in Norway to assist us in thorough investigation of our operations in Africa. Until the investigation has been concluded we will not comment on specific allegations. …
>
> "All the activities of Samherji and its affiliates were under investigation by authorities for years and no wrongdoings were ever found. All our accounting, e-mails and all other data were thoroughly examined, including that of the companies that have been operating in African waters since 2007. We will not now, like in the past, accept false and misleading allegations of a former employee who once again are prepared by the same parties and media as in the Central Bank-case a few years back", says Thorsteinn Mar Baldvinsson, CEO of Samherji.
>
> At this point in time we believe it is important to disclose that in the beginning of 2016 we came to suspect that something was wrong without operations in Namibia. In order to get better information, we hired a former police officer from the special prosecutor's office to go to Namibia and look into the matter. His investigation led to the dismissal of the aforementioned employee in mid-2016 for unacceptable behavior and conduct. Since then our staff has been trying to take control of our operations in Namibia.

> During this process the former employee has demanded large sums of money from Samherji.

This statement in a press release from Samherji (2019a) carries the date November 11. It denies any knowledge of wrongdoing and blames the whistleblower Stefansson, who received the blame for misconduct in Namibia. This kind of initial statement is common and similar to initial accounts from companies when they face allegations of misconduct and crime (Gottschalk and Benson, 2020: 1):

> Our analysis shows that denial of wrongdoing in several cases is replaced by admission of wrongdoing and scapegoating, while obfuscation of wrongdoing is replaced denial or acceptance of responsibility and scapegoating.

A scapegoat is a person burdened with the wrongdoing of others (Eren, 2020). While CEO Baldvinsson spoke in the above statement on November 11, he had to step aside three days later, on November 14, when Samherji issued a new press statement (Samherji, 2019b):

> The CEO and board of directors of Samherji have agreed that the CEO Thorsteinn Mar Baldvinsson will step aside for the time being until the pending internal investigation into the company's subsidiaries' alleged wrongdoing in Namibia has revealed the key material facts of the matter.

This executive destiny for Baldvinsson is typical as illustrated in the research by Gottschalk and Benson (2020). They found that corporations tend to distance themselves from individuals so that the corporations can survive. Corporations reassign, force to resign, or fire senior leaders. At Samherji, the board hired a new CEO, Bjorgolfur Johannsson, when Baldvinsson had to step down in November 2019. Four months later, Baldvinsson returned to Samherji, now in a position as co-CEO with Johannsson without any real executive power. The company then stated that the fraud examination by Wikborg Rein was to continue (Samherji, 2020):

> Wikborg Rein's reporting lines will remain to the board of directors, and Mr. Johannsson will remain dedicated to providing any assistance needed for Wikborg Rein.

According to Reuters (2019), Samherji transferred more than $70 million through a shell company in the tax haven Marshall Islands from 2011 to 2018. Samherji transferred the money through bank accounts in DNB Norway. The bank's largest shareholder is the Norwegian state, which holds a 34% stake in the bank (Reuters, 2019):

> The money consisted partly of proceeds from Samherji's questionable and possibly unlawful operations in Namibia where the company bribes officials

> to get secure access to fishing quotas. The company in the Marshall Islands was used to pay salaries to the crews of Samherjis factory trawlers. These trawlers fished horse mackerel in Mauritania, Morocco, and Namibia.

The Norwegian bank DNB was heavily involved in the Panama Papers scandal, where the bank had helped rich people in their wealth management program to hide large sums of money in tax havens (Brustad and Hustadnes, 2016; Langset et al., 2016; Tanum, 2016). Fraud examiners from law firm Hjort (2016) investigated the case. The bank ignored to monitor its client transactions through the bank and thus risked being a vehicle for money laundering and tax evasion.

The Samherji scandal forced the bank to conduct yet another internal investigation (Reuters, 2019):

> "Like every other bank, we are guided to take action if the clients do not give us the necessary information that we need to have so that the bank can have good control over how the client uses the bank", said DNB's spokesman, Even Westerveld. "This can sometimes mean that the bank freezes the accounts of clients or off boards him. Unfortunately, we do not officially hold count how often this happens within the bank".

On April 20, 2020, Margret Olafsdottir, chief communications officer at Samherji on Iceland, responded to my request for the Wikborg Rein report:

> Wikborg Rein has informed the Samherji board of directors that the investigation is likely to conclude during the course of this 2nd quarter of 2020. When their work is finished they will first meet with the Samherji board and present the results. They will next meet with relevant authorities and present their findings and conclusions to them. There will then be a number of considerations to be taken into account in terms of what can be published and how, including whether publishing information will jeopardize ongoing investigations by public authorities in any country, whether publishing certain information will infringe upon laws and regulations concerning protection of individuals mentioned in any findings, etc. All such questions will be discussed thoroughly with relevant authorities at such time.

Norwegian police investigation

Økokrim is the Norwegian national authority for investigation and prosecution of economic and environmental crime, similar to the serious fraud office in the United Kingdom or the fraud units at the FBI in the United States. They started investigating Samherji and DNB in November 2019 (Ekroll et al., 2019):

> Økokrim is launching an investigation into DNB related to the Icelandic fisheries case. Økokrim has started an investigation at DNB after disclosure

> of possible corruption and money laundering in an Icelandic fishing company where DNB has been their bank. The Icelandic fishing group Samherji faced accusation of corruption and illegal cooperation with Namibian state officials. Several of them are now in prison, and others are on the run in the country. Samherji faces allegations of having used DNB to transfer money via tax havens, and to an African official who owns a company in Dubai. In total, Samherji allegedly used DNB to transfer NOK 640 million to a tax haven, according to Icelandic media. Økokrim is now investigating Norway's largest financial group.
>
> "The purpose of the investigation is to find out what has happened and whether criminal offenses have been committed. It is natural that we cooperate with the authorities of other countries working on the case complex. We are at an early stage, and will not be providing more information about the investigation now", acting Økokrim chief, Hedvig Moe, writes in a press release.

On April 20, 2020, Even Westerveld, chief communications officer at DNB in Norway, responded to my request for their report:

> No investigation has been conducted in this case, and consequently no investigation report has been made. The board of directors has discussed the matter thoroughly several times, and the matter is – as you know – subject to investigation at Økokrim. We do not know where the investigation is right now.

Bibliography

Benson, M.L. (1985). Denying the guilty mind: Accounting for involvement in a white-collar crime, *Criminology*, 23 (4), 583–607.

Berghoff, H. and Spiekermann, U. (2018). Shady business: On the history of white-collar crime, *Business History*, 60 (3), 289–304.

Bittle, S. and Hébert, J. (2020). Controlling corporate crimes in times of de-regulation and re-regulation, in: Rorie, M.L. (editor), *The Handbook of White-Collar Crime*, Hoboken, NJ: Wiley & Sons, chapter 30, pages 484–501.

Brustad, L. and Hustadnes, H. (2016). –Bjerke har forsømt lederansvaret uansett (-Bjerke has neglected the management responsibility regardless), *Daily Norwegian Newspaper Dagbladet*, www.dagbladet.no, published April 11.

Ekroll, H.C., Breian, Å. and NTB (2019). Økokrim starter etterforskning av DNB i forbindelse med islandsk fiskerisak (Økokrim is launching an investigation into DNB related to the Icelandic fisheries case), *Daily Norwegian Newspaper Aftenposten*, www.aftenposten, published November 29.

Eren, C.P. (2020). Cops, firefighters, and scapegoats: Anti-money laundering (AML) professionals in an era of regulatory bulimia, *Journal of White Collar and Corporate Crime*, 1–12, published online https://doi.org/10.1177/2631309X20922153.

Goldstraw-White, J. (2012). *White-Collar Crime: Accounts of Offending Behavior*, London: Palgrave Macmillan.

Gottschalk, P. and Benson, M.L. (2020). The evolution of corporate accounts of scandals from exposure to investigation, *British Journal of Criminology*, published online https://doi.org/10.1093/bjc/azaa001.

Hjort (2016). *Rapport til styret i DNB ASA (Report to the Board at DNB)*, September 11, Oslo: Law Firm Hjort.

Huang, L. and Knight, A.P. (2017). Resources and relationships in entrepreneurship: An exchange theory of the development and effects of the entrepreneur-investor relationship, *Academy of Management Review*, 42 (1), 80–102.

Kamerdze, S., Loughran, T., Paternoster, R. and Sohoni, T. (2014). The role of affect in intended rule breaking: Extending the rational choice perspective, *Journal of Research in Crime and Delinquency*, 51 (5), 620–654.

Kleinfeld, J. (2019). Anatomy of a bribe: A deep dive into an underworld of corruption, *Al Jazeera*, www.aljazeera.com, published December 1.

Langset, M., Ertesvåg, F. and Ensrud, S. (2016). BI-professor: -Det vil bli rettssaker (BI professor: -There will be court cases), *Daily Norwegian Newspaper VG*, Wednesday, April 6, page 7.

Reuters (2019). Norway's DNB investigates allegedly improper Samherji payments to Namibia, *Under Current News*, www.undercurrentnews.com, published November 15.

Samherji (2019a). *Statement from Samherji*, Press Release, www.samherji.is, published November 11.

Samherji (2019b). *Samherji CEO Steps Aside While Investigations Are Ongoing*, www.samherji.is, published November 14.

Samherji (2020). *Thorsteinn Mar Baldvinsson Returns as co-CEO of Samherji*, www.samherji.is, published March 27.

Schultz, J. (2019). Wikborg Rein-gransker om Samherji: -Planen er å være ute av Namibia innen få måneder (Wikborg Rein investigator about Samherji: -The plan is to be out of Namibia within a few months), *Daily Norwegian Business Newspaper Dagens Næringsliv*, www.dn.no, published December 1.

Shepherd, D. and Button, M. (2019). Organizational inhibitions to addressing occupational fraud: A theory of differential rationalization, *Deviant Behavior*, 40 (8), 971–991.

Tanum, A.C. (2016). *DNB Luxembourg – Redegjørelse fra styret (DNB Luxembourg – Statement from the Board), brev til Nærings- og fiskeridepartementet ved statsråd Monica Mæland* (letter to the department of industry and fishery attention minister Monica Mæland), April 11, Oslo.

11 Social security by PwC

The National Board of Social Services in Denmark hired corporate investigators from global auditing firm PricewaterhouseCoopers (PwC) (2019). The social services board (Socialstyrelsen) is a government agency under the Ministry of Social Affairs and Interior. Socialstyrelsen aims at actively contributing to social initiatives for the benefit of citizens. Socialstyrelsen is responsible for a variety of tasks and projects in the social area, including children, young people and families, disabilities, aids and psycho-social initiatives, and adults with social problems. Socialstyrelsen does not only support vulnerable groups such as unemployed and homeless people; it also provides social benefits to a large fraction of the Danish population.

The initial account from Socialstyrelsen was a denial of any misconduct internally in the organization. Denial is a false response about occurrence of misconduct, wrongdoing, and crime (Gago-Rodriguez et al., 2020). Denial of knowledge, denial of deviance, denial of responsibility as well as scapegoating represent typical initial responses to accusations and allegations (Schoultz and Flyghed, 2020). A scapegoat is a person burdened with the wrongdoing of others (Eren, 2020).

Allegations of fraud at Socialstyrelsen were not consistent with the self-image of the Danish state that Transparency International and other global organizations have regarded as having the lowest rate of corruption in the world according to Transparency International. Allegations that employee Britta Nielsen had embezzled funds amounting to more than 100 million Danish kroner over the course of 25 years became evident in August 2018 and then taken seriously. The agency terminated her employment, and she fled to South Africa. In November 2018, South African police arrested her and extradited her to Denmark. In February 2020, a Danish court sentenced her to prison (Ottermann, 2020).

White-collar convenience

"Britta Nielsen is a committed employee, who takes on significant tasks in grant administration and is always willing when extra work is required". This is what Danish Britta Nielsen's (64) employer wrote in a recommendation for the

Queen's Merit Medal in 2016. Nielsen received the medal in silver. The occasion was 40 years of service as an employee at Socialstyrelsen. It is from that point in time that Nielsen faces an accusation of having embezzled 117 million Danish kroner, about US$20 million. In 2018, the police arrested her in South Africa, having been on the run for more than a month (Newth, 2018).

The following year, Britta Nielsen was the defendant in court facing the charge of embezzlement (NTB, 2019):

> The 65-year old woman faced the accusation of stealing DKK 117 million from Socialstyrelsen. When she appeared in court on Thursday, she admitted the charges, but not the amount for which the prosecution charged her.

BBC (2020) reported the following year:

> A Danish court is due to deliver its verdict in the case of a woman accused of stealing 117 million Danish kroner (£13m; $17m) of government funding. Britta Nielsen worked at Denmark's social services board for 40 years, distributing funding to people in need.

In their report, PwC (2019b: 3) label Britta Nielsen as BN and mention that acronym 141 times in the 80-page report, for example:

> In the period from1993 to 2018, a total of 66 bank accounts have been identified, which belong to BN, spread to nine Danish financial institutions or credit card institutions.

By exploitation of fundamental insights into the social security processes and because of her central employment in benefits administration, Britta Nielsen was able to conceal her fraud for a very long period. From 2000 to 2007, she abused the PAS system, while she later abused the TAS system for benefits payments. TAS (tilskuddsadministrationssystem/benefits administration system) did not separate between users of the system who registered information about potential receivers of benefits and users of the system who initiated actual benefit payments. Nobody controlled Nielsen when she created fake receivers with her bank accounts attached, and when she initiated payments to the same fake benefit receivers (Benson and Simpson, 2018; Cohen and Felson, 1979). There was obviously a lack of control in principal-agent relationships (Bosse and Phillips, 2016). She was supposed to distribute funding to people in need. Instead, she took some of the money herself. Maybe she had traces of sensation seeking to experience adventure (Craig and Piquero, 2017).

Britta Nielsen embezzled funds intended for vulnerable and disabled people by creating fake receivers of social benefits. She received a sentence of 6.5 years in prison for embezzling 117 million Danish kroner of government funding intended for social security needs (Ottermann, 2020).

Nielsen did not only create fictitious receivers of benefits. She also created fictitious projects – one of them she called "help for self-help" – that were eligible for funding. However, most of the money ended up in her personal bank accounts. Her defense lawyer argued in court that barriers against fraud were nonexistent, and that all colleagues knew how easy it was to embezzle money (Ottermann, 2020):

> Nielsen reportedly told the court: "It was a standing joke that you could easily add your own account number and then be off to the Bahamas".

Nielsen's motive was greed (Goldstraw-White, 2012; Schoepfer and Piquero, 2006), as she over the years had acquired luxury properties in Denmark and South Africa. She gave some of the embezzled money to her three adult children, who have all pleaded guilty of gross robbery for each receiving funds. One of the daughters had allegedly spent the money on a competition horse. The Danish treasury had thus a hard time retrieving money from Nielsen's swindle (Ottermann, 2020).

"She has betrayed the trust she was given when she became employed by the National Board of Social Services", prosecutor Lisbeth Jorgensen told the court during the trial (Ottermann, 2020), maybe because of a professional deviant identity (Obodaru, 2017) and a rational choice (Pratt and Cullen, 2005). During the trial, Nielsen explained that she had moved involuntarily into a vicious circle where she wanted to improve the lifestyle of her children (Agnew, 2014). Her lawyer, Nima Nabipour, pleaded mitigating circumstances, including Nielsen's age and health. On several occasions, the trial interrupted where Nielsen felt bad and needed transportation by ambulance for medical checks.

Figure 11.1 illustrates convenience themes suggested above. Her perceived innocence – lack of a guilty mind – might be explained by a disappointing work context that caused entitlement (Nichol, 2019), sliding on a slippery slope to the wrong side of the law (Welsh et al., 2014), as well as lack of self-control (Gottfredson and Hirschi, 1990).

Fraud examination outcome

Fraud examiners from PwC (2019b: 6) concluded that the main convenience theme in the organizational opportunity dimension was lack of division of functions:

> We can ascertain that the main reason why it has been possible for BN to carry out the presumptive fraud against the grant administration has been the lack of functional separation between persons with access to change recipients' master data, including account numbers, and persons who can make payments to the beneficiaries.

The investigative approach chosen by fraud examiners from PwC (2019) was mainly to review accounts and accounting. They followed financial transactions

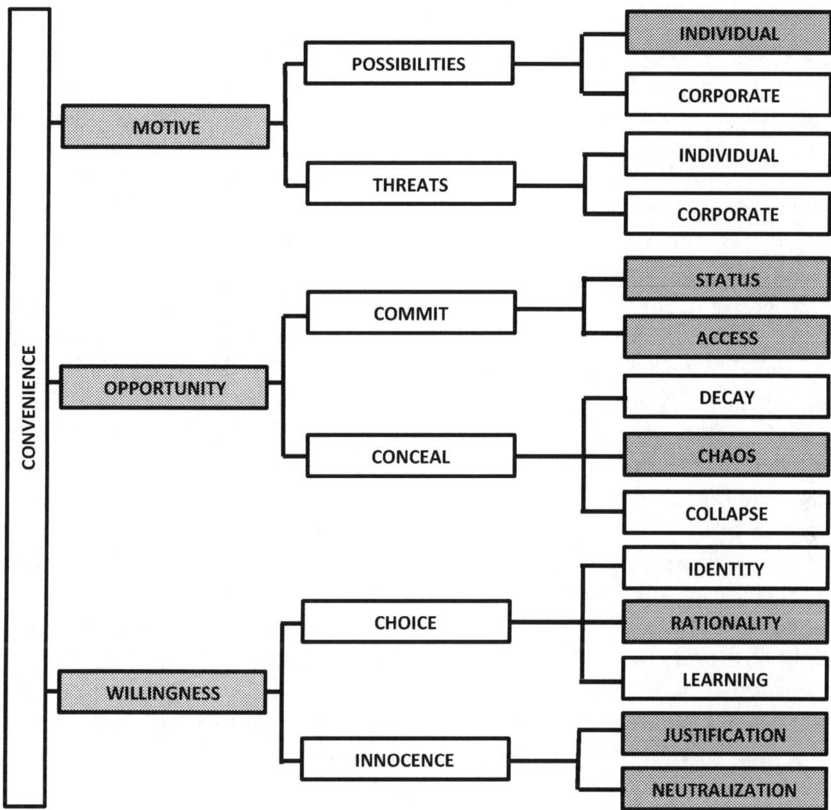

Figure 11.1 Convenience themes in the case of Britta Nielsen at Socialstyrelsen

from TAS payments to Navision Stat, a system for business accounting. They reviewed accounting statements from 1993 to 2018 and identified 37 bank accounts belonging to Nielsen. However, the individual banks were not able to retrieve all relevant transactions that Nielsen conducted.

The fraud examiners found that the grant administration since 2016 automatically issued notifications to grant recipients' email addresses when allocation of grants occurred. As email addresses are part of the basic data, administrative case handlers had the opportunity to change email addresses without any barriers. By changing email addresses, the entitled receivers of funds had no way of knowing that the grant administration had approved their applications.

The Auditor General in Denmark had conducted performance audits at Socialstyrelsen, but fraud examiners from PwC failed in obtaining their results. Therefore, they ignored other sources of information related to the Auditor General's work. Instead, fraud examiners simply state that if they had looked into the matter in documents from the Auditor General, then investigation conclusions might have been different. However, fraud examiners emphasize that the Auditor General had made recommendations in the past that might have prevented the extent of convenience experienced by Nielsen.

To the extent that fraud examiners were able to retrieve the contents in Nielsen's email accounts, they claim to have made some interesting findings. They applied simple search words and search combinations based on their knowledge of the case so far. Unfortunately, these pages in the report are blank in the publicly available version.

The PwC (2019) report describes 13 control weaknesses in the Danish social security agency. The main flaw was the ability for an employee to both create projects and pay grants (Nielsen, 2019). Management was not required to approve transfers or to control who had access to financial systems. The investigation confirmed that a number of control functions had failed that might explain the convenience of Nielsen's fraud.

PwC (2019) conducted no interviews, at least they do not write about interviews in their report of investigation. This is surprising, as informants and witnesses typically have observed behaviors that can lead to new disclosures and more evidence related to disclosures that have already occurred. While the embezzled amount confirmed is already significant, there is in similar cases often more money out there that professional examiners might detect. Typically, offenders admit to amounts that already are subject to hard evidence, while being reluctant to tell about further instances of fraud that investigators have not detected. In such situations, other people can lead investigators into new avenues for their inquiries. Very often, colleagues and others are willing to tell what they have observed, as long as interviewers treat interviewees fairly and honestly.

The mandate for PwC's (2019) investigation was to reconstruct sequences of events for abuse of social benefit payments and to explain how such financial abuse could take place. Furthermore, the mandate asked investigators to determine the magnitude of the fraud for the period from 1977 to 2018. Finally, the mandate asked investigators to evaluate the control systems and control culture at Socialstyrelsen. It seems that investigators failed in completing their examinations in accordance with the mandate.

PwC label their fraud examinations as forensic investigations, where they establish facts and analyze issues. They employ forensic accountants, lawyers, regulators who have retired, law enforcement agents such as police detectives, information technology experts, and corporate intelligence experts. They suggest that fraud hides in the shadows, and fraudsters willingly exploit the lack of awareness that creates one of fraudsters' most convenient opportunities.

The examination team at PwC consisted of Brian Christiansen, partner and head of risk assurance, Mads Johansson, certified auditor, and Thomas Riis, certified auditor.

Private policing evaluation

The 80-page report from PwC (2019) is a document full of repetition of facts that the police and the public knew already before the fraud examination took

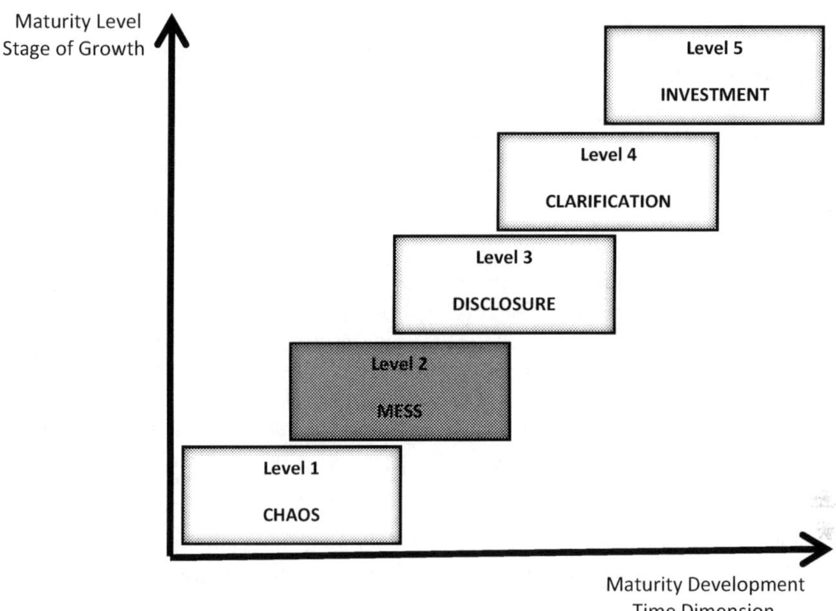

Figure 11.2 Maturity model for internal private investigations applied to PwC

place. Consequently, the report is at level 2 in Figure 11.2 since the presentation is a mess without any new insights.

Fraud examiners were unable to find more embezzled money than was already known (PwC, 2019b: 31):

> Thus, there is still a risk that there will be disbursements to accounts where we do not know the real owners for all or part of the period 2002 to 2018. To address this, we have attempted to obtain account information from banks, curators, and tax authorities to identify as many of BN's accounts as possible.

It is an obvious shortcoming in the investigation that fraud examiners did not approach witnesses, informants, and others for interviews, but they only relied on digital searches and public authorities.

Bibliography

Agnew, R. (2014). Social concern and crime: Moving beyond the assumption of simple self-interest, *Criminology*, 52 (1), 1–32.

BBC (2020). Britta Nielsen: Danish social worker accused of stealing millions, *British Broadcasting Corporation*, www.bbc.com, published February 18.

Benson, M.L. and Simpson, S,S. (2018). *White-Collar Crime: An Opportunity Perspective*, 3rd Edition, New York: Routledge.

Bosse, D.A. and Phillips, R.A. (2016). Agency theory and bounded self-interest, *Academy of Management Review*, 41 (2), 276–297.

Cohen, L.E. and Felson, M. (1979). Social change and crime rate trends: A routine activity approach. *American Sociological Review*, 44, 588–608.

Craig, J.M. and Piquero, N.L. (2017). Sensational offending: An application of sensation seeking to white-collar and conventional crimes, *Crime & Delinquency*, 63 (11), 1363–1382.

Eren, C.P. (2020). Cops, firefighters, and scapegoats: Anti-money laundering (AML) professionals in an era of regulatory bulimia, *Journal of White Collar and Corporate Crime*, 1–12, published online https://doi.org/10.1177/2631309X20922153.

Gago-Rodriguez, S., Marquez-Illescas, G. and Nunez-Nickel, M. (2020). Denial of corruption: Voluntary disclosure of bribery information, *Journal of Business Ethics*, 162, 609–626.

Goldstraw-White, J. (2012). *White-Collar Crime: Accounts of Offending Behavior*, London: Palgrave Macmillan.

Gottfredson, M.R. and Hirschi, T. (1990). *A General Theory of Crime*, Stanford, CA: Stanford University Press.

Newth, M. (2018). Britta Nielsen (64) mistenkt for å ha stjålet 140 millioner (Britta Nielsen (64) suspected of having stolen 140 million), daily Norwegian newspaper *VG*, www.vg.no, published November 5.

Nichol, J.E. (2019). The effects of contract framing on misconduct and entitlement, *The Accounting Review*, 94 (3), 329–344.

Nielsen, M.K. (2019). New report concludes: How Britta Nielsen could swindle for DKK 120 million for 25 years, *Danish Public Broadcasting Danmarks Radio*, www.dr.no, published March 1.

NTB (2019). Dansk kvinne for retten i storstilt svindelsak (Danish women prosecuted in court in a big fraud case), *ABC Nyheter*, www.abcnyheter.no, published October 24.

Obodaru, O. (2017). Forgone, but not forgotten: Toward a theory of forgone professional identities, *Academy of Management Journal*, 60 (2), 523–553.

Ottermann, P. (2020). Danish social worker jailed for stealing £13m of government funds, *The Guardian*, www.theguardian.com, published February 18.

Pratt, T.C. and Cullen, F.T. (2005). Assessing macro-level predictors and theories of crime: A meta-analysis, *Crime and Justice*, 32, 373–450.

PwC (2019). *Ekstern Undersøgelse af Tilskudsadministrationen 1977-2018 (External Examination of the Benefits Administration 1977–2018)*, February, Oslo: Auditing Firm PwC.

Schoepfer, A. and Piquero, N.L. (2006). Exploring white-collar crime and the American dream: A partial test of institutional anomie theory, *Journal of Criminal Justice*, 34 (3), 227–235.

Schoultz, I. and Flyghed, J. (2020). "We have been thrown under the bus": Corporate versus individual defense mechanisms against transnational corporate bribery charges, *Journal of White Collar and Corporate Crime*, published online https://doi.org/10.1177/2631309x20911883.

Welsh, D.T., Ordonez, L.D., Snyder, D.G. and Christian, M.S. (2014). The slippery slope: How small ethical transgressions pave the way for larger future transgressions, *Journal of Applied Psychology*, 100 (1), 114–127.

12 Social security by Kammeradvokaten

The Danish government hired the law firm Paul Schmith (Kammeradvokaten, 2019) in parallel with PwC (2019) hired by Socialstyrelsen to determine whether executives had failed in the management of controls, which made it convenient for Britta Nielsen to commit fraud over such a long period (BBC, 2020; Newth, 2018; Nielsen, 2019; NTB, 2019; Ottermann, 2020). The mandate asked investigators to examine whether any official responsibility could transfer into blame at individuals. Relevant individuals worked as executives in the social security service in Denmark, in the ministry, or elsewhere.

This is an interesting mandate, as attribution of guilt is a frequent issue in private policing of economic crime. Attribution theory (Keaveney, 2008) and the blame game hypothesis (Lee and Robinson, 2000) suggest that establishing causality for a negative event is concerned with efforts by suspects to assign misleading attribution to others (Eberly et al., 2011). Self-blame is rare and often nonexistent. Nobody will blame oneself for a negative event. Self-blame is attributing a negative event to one's behavior or disposition. Some are too powerful to blame. Pontell et al. (2014) found that the financial crisis obviously had its cause in mismanagement in the financial sector, but all in the financial sector avoided serious blame. The investigation of the collapse at Lehmann Brothers is a typical example. Status-related factors such as influential positions often preclude perceptions of blameworthiness (Slyke and Bales, 2012).

Compared to the PwC (2019) examination, Kammeradvokaten (2019) included a responsibility analysis and personal contact reflection with the social security agency. However, Kammeradvokaten builds to a substantial extent on the work by PwC. The whistleblower was Søren Madsen.

White-collar convenience

Executives are supposed to control their own organization. If they fail in implementing guardianship against financial crime such as embezzlement, they become responsible for misconduct and wrongdoing. Figure 12.1 illustrates convenience themes that seem applicable to the management at Socialstyrelsen.

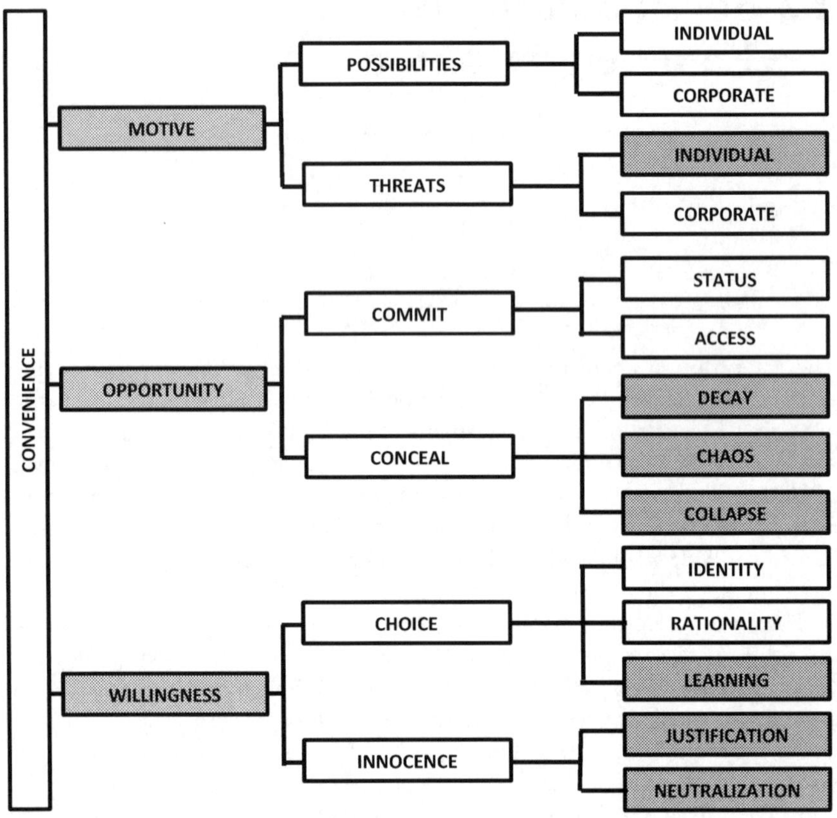

Figure 12.1 Convenience themes in the case of executives at Socialstyrelsen

The motive might be avoidance of strain and pain in a stressful executive everyday working life (Agnew, 2005, 2012; Thaxton and Agnew, 2018). Executives were responsible for decay in terms of institutional deterioration (Rodriguez et al., 2005), causing inability to control because of social disorganization (Hoffmann, 2002). In addition, a third theme might be collapse in terms of rule complexity preventing compliance (Lehman et al., 2019).

Executive ignorance can result from differential association (Sutherland, 1983), where executives among themselves reinforce the belief that they are in control since upper echelon information selection often occurs (Gamache and McNamara, 2019). They can deny knowledge of crime (Cohen, 2001) and claim that not knowing implies innocence. They may suffer from narcissism (Zhu and Chen, 2015; Zvi and Elaad, 2018), where they had grandiose trust in their own abilities to run the social security agency. Executives might claim that crime went under the corporate radar (Williams et al., 2019). They may neutralize any guilt feeling of ignorance and reluctance by claiming that they are victims of the offense committed by Britta Nielsen.

Fraud examination outcome

Law firm Kammeradvokaten (2019) reached the conclusion that no former or current executives at Socialstyrelsen deserved blame for such failures. This was in contrast to Nielsen's defense attorney, who argued in court that the safeguards around welfare were too lax, and that both management and her colleagues knew how convenient it was to commit embezzlement at work (Ottermann, 2020).

The investigators found that there were no indications or suspicion of fraud or similar irregularities in the ministry and other authorities responsible for social security services. Based on this finding, they conclude that boards and others had no reason to react to something they did not know was taking place (Kammeradvokaten, 2019: 123):

> Based on the available material, we first assess that the management's handling of the government audit's comments on accounts and reports was immediately deficient, given that the situation was not completely rectified over a period of at least three years. However, this criticism for not following up the national audit office's comments regarding accounts and reports cannot be directly linked to the alleged audit weakness number 6 identified by PwC regarding accounts and reports. The alleged control weakness number 6 concerns Britta Nielsen's ability to override the reminder function for these, and thus not, as pointed out by the auditor general, that the accounting review has been slow. Regardless of the fact that it must be considered obvious that the large case-file of accounts and reports has been instrumental in creating a control environment where it has been easier for Britta Nielsen to hide her fraud, the criticism here must be compared with the fact that there is not necessarily correlation Britta Nielsen's fraud and the lack of review of accounts and reports.

In this quote, lawyers from Kammeradvokaten (2019) express disagreement with auditors from PwC (2019) and thereby create confusion. One reason for the gap in their understanding of weaknesses might be the different levels of probability for evidence. If auditors apply the rule of more likely than not, while lawyers apply the rule of beyond any doubt, then they may certainly conclude differently about various pieces of evidence.

However, Kammeradvokaten (2019) continue in their report to downplay the lack of management attention as identified by PwC (2019):

> In addition, it could immediately appear questionable that the management did not seem to adequately respond to the government audit's comments regarding control of disbursements and user access. However, we cannot rule out, on the present basis, that there was a follow-up to this in the period.

While attorneys at Kammeradvokaten (2019) according to the mandate should identify potentially responsible individuals and institutions for lack of controls, they do instead contribute to diffusion of responsibility in their report.

Niels Banke and Lene Damkjær Christensen, who are both lawyers and partners at Kammeradvokaten, conducted the investigation. The examiners conclude that no responsibility or blame belongs in the grant administration or the national board of health and welfare either personally or functionally, and therefore suggest no actions, except what PwC already had emphasized. The only thing examiners suggest is that the national board of health and welfare if they desire may improve their own control mechanisms to compensate for weaknesses.

Private policing evaluation

The lawyers at Kammeradvokaten (2019) discuss back and forth in their lengthy report of 163 pages. They assess responsibilities for time intervals 2000–2007 and 2018–2019. They evaluate responsibility of management, board, and ministry. The report is an example of a blame game with no conclusion (DeScioli and Bokemper, 2014; Keaveney, 2008; Lee and Robinson, 2000; Resodihardjo et al., 2015; Xie and Keh, 2016). Therefore, the investigation belongs at level 1 in the maturity model in Figure 12.2.

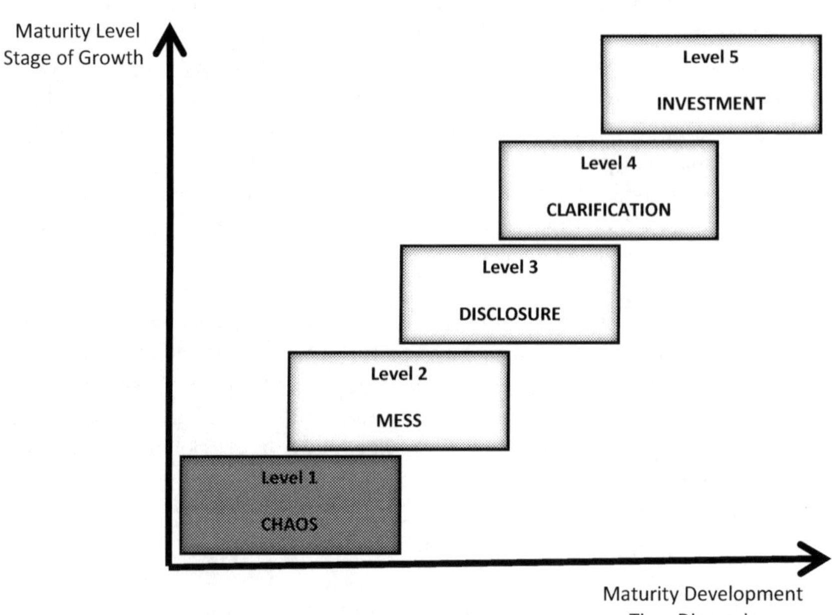

Figure 12.2 Maturity model for internal private investigations applied to Kammeradvokaten

Responsibility is not only a matter of what you know, as the examiners suggest. They implicitly argue that if responsible persons do not know of misconduct and crime, then they are not responsible for criminal incidents. This is indeed a chaotic perspective, first because responsible persons have a duty of keeping themselves informed of what is going on. In addition, whether you know or not is less important, as you are responsible for whatever goes on in an agency for which you are politically or managerially responsible. Very different from several internal investigations presented in this book, where executives had to leave their positions even when they did not have personal knowledge of wrongdoing, such as at Swedbank and Oslo Energy Recovery, Danish fraud examiners in this case try to place the blame elsewhere. This is in fact an interesting theme in many private policing efforts, where some investigators suggest innocence and lack of blameworthiness if someone does not know, while other investigators suggest that personal knowledge is irrelevant for assessing personal responsibility.

Both reports by PwC (2019) and Kammeradvokaten (2019) focus exclusively on the fraudster and her organizational opportunities. It is surprising that investigators examined nobody else, given that system's weaknesses and cultural disorganization had existed long before the fraudster started her embezzlements.

Bibliography

Agnew, R. (2005). *Pressured into Crime: An Overview of General Strain Theory*, Oxford: Oxford University Press.

Agnew, R. (2012). Reflection on "A Revised Strain Theory of Delinquency", *Social Forces*, 91 (1), 33–38.

BBC (2020). Britta Nielsen: Danish social worker accused of stealing millions, *British Broadcasting Corporation*, www.bbc.com, published February 18.

Cohen, S. (2001). *States of Denial: Knowing about Atrocities and Suffering*, Cambridge: Polity Press.

DeScioli, P. and Bokemper, S. (2014). Voting as a counter-strategy in the blame game, *Psychological Inquiry*, 25, 206–214.

Eberly, M.B., Holley, E.C., Johnson, M.D. and Mitchell, T.R. (2011). Beyond internal and external: A dyadic theory of relational attributions, *Academy of Management Review*, 36 (4), 731–753.

Gamache, D.L. and McNamara, G. (2019). Responding to bad press: How CEO temporal focus influences the sensitivity to negative media coverage of acquisitions, *Academy of Management Journal*, 62 (3), 918–943.

Hoffmann, J.P. (2002). A contextual analysis of differential association, social control, and strain theories of delinquency, *Social Forces*, 81 (3), 753–785.

Kammeradvokaten (2019). *Ansvarsvurdering Vedrørende Sagen om Svindel med Tilskuddsmidler – Offentlig Rapport (Responsibility Assessment Regarding the Case of Fraud with Benefits Funds – Public Report)*, February 22, Copenhagen: Law Firm Poul Schmith.

Keaveney, S.M. (2008). The blame game: An attribution theory approach to marketer-engineer conflict in high-technology companies, *Industrial Marketing Management*, 37, 653–663.

Lee, F. and Robinson, R.J. (2000). An attributional analysis of social accounts: Implications of playing the blame game, *Journal of Applied Social Psychology*, 30 (9), 1853–1879.

Lehman, D.W., Cooil, B. and Ramanujam, R. (2019). The effects of rule complexity on organizational noncompliance and remediation: Evidence from restaurant health inspections, *Journal of Management*, 1-33, published online https://doi.org/10.1177/0149206319842262.

Newth, M. (2018). Britta Nielsen (64) mistenkt for å ha stjålet 140 millioner (Britta Nielsen (64) suspected of having stolen 140 million), *Daily Norwegian Newspaper VG*, www.vg.no, published November 5.

Nielsen, M.K. (2019). New report concludes: How Britta Nielsen could swindle for DKK 120 million for 25 years, *Danish Public Broadcasting Danmarks Radio*, www.dr.no, published March 1.

NTB (2019). Dansk kvinne for retten i storstilt svindelsak (Danish women prosecuted in court in a big fraud case), *ABC Nyheter*, www.abcnyheter.no, published October 24.

Ottermann, P. (2020). Danish social worker jailed for stealing £13m of government funds, *The Guardian*, www.theguardian.com, published February 18.

Pontell, H.N., Black, W.K. and Geis, G. (2014). Too big to fail, too powerful to jail? On the absence of criminal prosecutions after the 2008 financial meltdown, *Crime, Law and Social Change*, 61 (1), 1–13.

PwC (2019). *Ekstern Undersøgelse af Tilskudsadministrationen 1977-2018 (External Examination of the Benefits Administration 1977–2018)*, February, Oslo: Auditing Firm PwC.

Resodihardjo, S.L., Carroll, B.J., Eijk, C.J.A. and Maris, S. (2015). Why traditional responses to blame games fail: The importance of context, rituals, and sub-blame games in the face of raves gone wrong, *Public Administration*, 94 (2), 350–363.

Rodriguez, P., Uhlenbruck, K. and Eden, L. (2005). Government corruption and the entry strategies of multinationals, *Academy of Management Review*, 30 (2), 383–396.

Slyke, S.V. and Bales, W.D. (2012). A contemporary study of the decision to incarcerate white-collar and street property offenders, *Punishment & Society*, 14 (2), 217–246.

Sutherland, E.H. (1983). *White Collar Crime – The Uncut Version*, New Haven, CT: Yale University Press.

Thaxton, S. and Agnew, R. (2018). When criminal coping is likely: An examination of conditioning effects in general strain theory, *Journal of Quantitative Criminology*, 34, 887–920.

Williams, M.L., Levi, M., Burnap, P. and Gundur, R.V. (2019). Under the corporate radar: Examining insider business cybercrime victimization through an application of routine activities theory, *Deviant Behavior*, 40 (9), 1119–1131.

Xie, Y. and Keh, H.T. (2016). Taming the blame game: Using promotion programs to counter product-Hhrm crises, *Journal of Advertising*, 45 (2), 211–226.

Zhu, D.H. and Chen, G. (2015). CEO narcissism and the impact of prior board experience on corporate strategy, *Administrative Science Quarterly*, 60 (1), 31–65.

Zvi, L. and Elaad, E. (2018). Correlates of narcissism, self-reported lies, and self-assessed abilities to tell and detect lies, tell truths, and believe others, *Journal of Investigative Psychology and Offender Profiling*, 15, 271–286.

13 Swedbank by Clifford Chance

Swedbank carried out bank transactions of more than €37 billion (about US$40 billion) with a high risk for money laundering over a five-year period according to private policing in terms of an internal investigation by fraud examiners from law firm Clifford Chance (2020). The investigation report suggests that the Swedish bank actively targeted high-risk individuals in the Baltic region and points to failings from both top management and the board (Milne, 2020).

Birgitte Bonnessen was the chief executive officer (CEO) at Swedbank. She had to leave the position in 2019 (Makortoff, 2019). When Clifford Chance (2020) presented their report of investigation, the new Swedbank board decided to withdraw her final compensation of 26 million Swedish kroner (US$2.7 million). At the same time, Swedbank accepted a fine of 4 billion Swedish kroner (US$408 million) from the Swedish finance inspection (Johannessen and Christensen, 2020).

White-collar convenience

The bank benefited from having oligarchs and other Russians as customers without implementing anti-laundering procedures. The motive for violating anti-money laundering (AML) laws was for Swedbank to make extraordinary profits by corporate crime (Naylor, 2003), as illustrated by the convenience theme motive-possibilities-corporate in Figure 13.1. Swedbank executives had a high status (Agnew, 2014), which allowed them to implement special arrangements for non-resident clients. They could claim that the act of wrongdoing is morally justifiable (Schnatterly et al., 2018), probably based on upper echelon information selection (Gamache and McNamara, 2019). A CEO such as Birgitte Bonnessen might suffer from narcissistic traits (Zhu and Chen, 2015), where she constructed her own professional world (Chatterjee and Pollock, 2017). Many CEOs tend to have a temporal focus (Gamache and McNamara, 2019). Schnatterly et al. (2018) found that pressure, opportunity, and rationalization cause CEO wrongdoing.

Bonnessen and her colleagues may have been sliding on a slippery slope to the wrong side of the law. Sliding on a slippery slope can make the offender feel innocent, as the offender did not notice ending up on the wrong side of the law (Welsh et al., 2014). Arjoon (2008: 78) explains the slippery slope in the

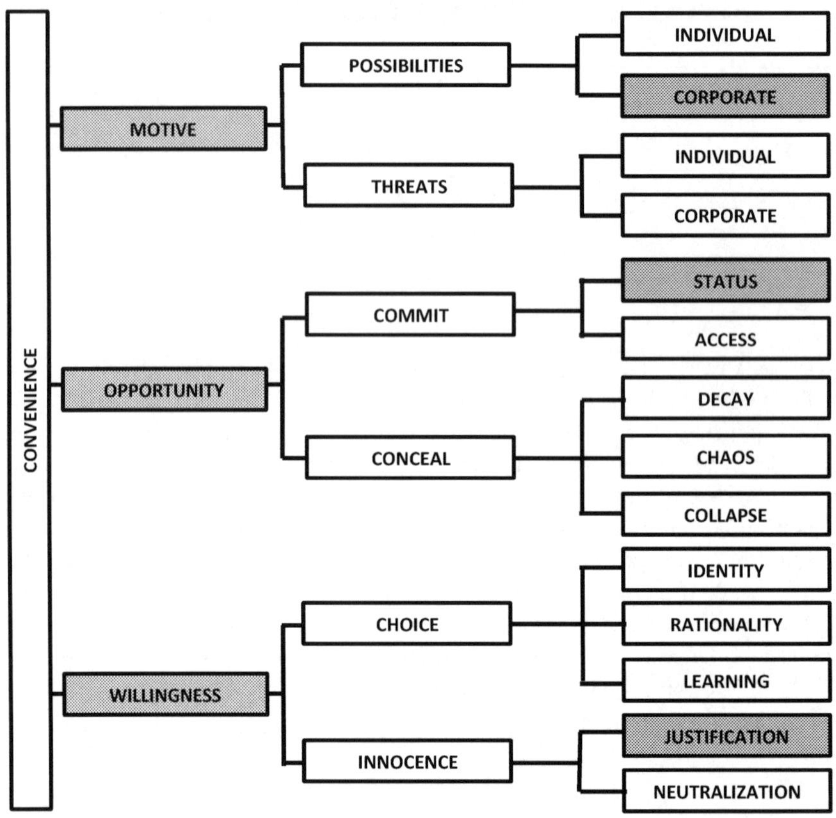

Figure 13.1 Convenience themes in the case of Swedbank

following way: "As commonsense experience tells us, it is the small infractions that can lead to the larger ones". A series of small infractions gradually increase over time. Committing small indiscretions over time gradually leads people to complete larger unethical acts that they otherwise would have judged impermissible (Murphy and Dacin, 2011; Pettigrew, 2018).

Birgitte Bonnessen resigned from the position of chief executive officer at Swedbank while Clifford Chance were still conducting their investigation. Viveka Stangert resigned from the position of chief compliance officer when the bank publicized the report of investigation.

Fraud examination outcome

The ideal background for an investigation is the leadership's desire to reconstruct past events and sequence of events caused by internal forces. People internally have raised issues, and the board has responded by initiating an internal investigation by fraud examiners. People in the organization unite in their ambition to find the underlying causes of whatever rumors, accusations, tips, reports, or other statements that have emerged internally. The investigation becomes an internally driven process characterized by joint ambitions and trust that the organization will handle examination outcomes professionally and fairly, and that accountability will reflect relevant attribution of responsibility.

The far less than ideal motive for an investigation is an externally driven process characterized by media accusations against the organization, where people internally feel the need to defend themselves. The initial account from the leadership will typically be denials, excuses, or justifications. An account is a statement made by an actor to explain unanticipated or untoward behavior that is subject to some sort of evaluative inquiry by other actors (Gottschalk and Benson, 2020).

In late 2018, media reports raised questions regarding Swedbank's exposure to money laundering scandals involving the Baltic region and Estonia in particular. At the time, Swedbank publicly maintained in its initial account that the bank had limited exposure to money laundering risks because Swedbank had anti-money laundering procedures in place to ensure that it acted forcefully in response to suspicious activity. Swedbank thus denied any wrongdoing, and claimed they protected themselves against money laundering. This initial account from executive management was far from the truth. In fact, Swedbank had taken on customers who other Baltic banks had denied access.

On February 20, 2019, the Swedish public television network program "Uppdrag gransking" (Assignment investigation) – broadcast on Sveriges Television (SVT) – began a series of programs alleging that customers of Swedbank's Baltic subsidiaries in Estonia, Latvia, and Lithuania had engaged in suspicious transactions indicative of money laundering. Following the first SVT program, Swedbank engaged law firm Clifford Chance (2020) to conduct an investigation into the allegations that investigative journalists had presented and more broadly into Swedbank's Baltic banking business from January 2007 through March 2019.

Fraud examiners interviewed 37 current and former employees of Swedbank, and 30 current and former employees of Baltic subsidiaries. Investigators interviewed certain individuals multiple times, resulting in nearly 100 interviews (Clifford Chance, 2020: 32):

> Such interviews, along with a significant number of scoping and background discussions with numerous bank employees across a variety of positions, assisted Clifford Chance in focusing on key document locations and document types.

Interviews of board members at Swedbank indicated that the board believed that bank management had anti-money laundering matters under control. Interviews of AML employees indicated that business units tended to have greater influence over the final decision whether to on-board a customer than the compliance function had at that time. During an interview conducted in Estonia, an employee recalled that the practice of storing customer documentation relating to beneficial ownership in a safe was a common practice. When another Estonian employee answered questions regarding email exchanges, the employee recalled that there were enhanced concerns regarding the confidentiality of Russian oligarchs, and that documents relating to these customers were stored separately.

During an interview with the former Swedbank Estonia CEO, the CEO explained that they had operated under relevant standards. The CEO argued that their operational procedures were consistent with what the CEO characterized as then-prevailing standards. Swedbank Estonia operated under the assumption that, so long as the bank knew or believed it knew the true beneficial owner of a customer, there was no need to ensure that there was supporting documentation in the relevant bank systems.

A senior manager at Swedbank Lithuania recalled deciding to expand the non-resident market segment, although AML was difficult or even impossible, since the segment was so profitable. Another senior manager at Swedbank Lithuania claimed the opposite (Clifford Chance, 2020: 79):

> A senior manager in Baltic Banking's Risk and Compliance function also told Clifford Chance during an interview that the senior manager and others objected to developing a non-resident business in Lithuania due to AML concerns and that, by June 2013, the proposal was abandoned.

Yet another interviewed manager in the Baltic region acknowledged that, in retrospect, AML compliance in the Baltic subsidiaries should have been more of a priority at the time, and it had simply not been a focal point until the latter half of 2015. Several interviewees said that they perceived skeptical reviews and audits as implicit criticism of their customer knowledge. An employee recalled that they used Excel spreadsheet for sanctions screening, which the employee characterized as primitive, because it predominantly relied on manual input into the spreadsheet and would not automatically download from or update relevant data segments in bank systems. A senior executive recalled that setting risk tolerance limits was a result of risk appetite.

In addition to interviews, fraud examiners from Clifford Chance (2020) analyzed external payment transactional activities of high-risk nonresident (HRNR) customers of the Baltic subsidiaries. HRNR customers were nonresident legal entities registered outside of the European Union and Norway, but also including customers registered in Malta, Cyprus, the United Kingdom, and Luxembourg. All entities considered to have high AML risk were part of the investigation.

Before any interviews, document reviews, and digital searches, fraud examiners from the law firm conducted a scoping study. The purpose of the scoping exercise was to understand Swedbank's information systems architecture and to identify repositories of structured and unstructured electronic data. The purpose was also to identify knowledgeable people and sources of hardcopy documents potentially relevant to the investigation, including archives and backup repositories (Clifford Chance, 2020: 15):

> Critical to the exercise was a thorough understanding of the organizational structure of Swedbank and its branches, subsidiaries and affiliates in order to: (a) understand Swedbank's senior management and reporting architecture, and (b) identify the functional areas within Swedbank where potentially relevant employees might work, including employees in compliance or customer relationship management.

Clifford Chance (2020) mapped the locations of information sources related to organizational structure, customers, customer identification information, transactions, current and former employees, policies and procedures, meeting minutes and materials, and prior reports. Erling Grimstad, a fraud examiner from Norway, was one out of several investigators who had submitted prior reports.

Fraud examiners from law firm Clifford Chance failed in determining whether money laundering had actually occurred in Swedbank's subsidiaries in Estonia, Latvia, or Lithuania. In fact, they did not even try to collect evidence of money laundering activities (Clifford Chance, 2020: 8):

> Inclusion in the group of AML risk identified customers is not necessarily indicative of suspicious behavior or improper conduct. Rather, these parameters were designed to capture the portion of the Baltic subsidiaries' customer population that warranted further review. In addition, the fact that an external payment to or from one of these customers hit against one or more of the detection algorithms does not mean that the payment should have been considered suspicious at the time, let alone is it evidence that a customer engaged in money laundering or other financial crime. Rather the detection algorithms are designed to identify transactions with risk indicators similar to those that a transaction monitoring system would flag for further review.

Rather than collecting evidence on money laundering activities, such as circular transfers by suspected nonresident companies, fraud examiners collected only evidence on misconduct in terms of failing anti-money laundering work in the Baltic subsidiaries. The word "evidence" is subject to repetition several times in the investigation report, however, mainly in terms of not identifying evidence rather than identifying evidence. For example, "the investigation did not identify evidence that these issues were presented to the Board" (Clifford Chance, 2020: 83), which simply means that to the extent board members learned about misconduct, this was of course not documented in formal ways. Clifford Chance (2020: 84) continues to emphasize that reports were not "provided to the Board or its committees".

Investigators found evidence of two Russian oligarchs who moved "funds among related accounts in Swedbank Estonia" (Clifford Chance, 2020: 87). Again, investigators failed in identifying potential evidence of money laundering activities among Russian oligarchs and other nonresident bank clients in Estonia, Latvia, or Lithuania.

Nick Hourigan at FTI Consulting provided forensic support to Clifford Chance. They collected and analyzed transactions processed by Swedbank Estonia, Latvia, and Lithuania. In Estonia, FTI identified 338,000 messages that reflected search terms. FTI then determined that 7,100 of these messages contained true hits against search terms defined by the United States Treasury Department's Office of Foreign Assets Control. From further study of those messages, FTI assembled 3,037 transactions for legal review, supplemented by customers from Internet addresses in embargoed countries. The fraud examiners ended up identifying 19 sanctioned corporate customers. The fraud examiners obtained similar results for Latvia and Lithuania.

The fraud examination outcome included evidence that bank clerks had received gifts from bank clients, extreme difference in risk assessments among banks regarding customer segments, bank clerks who purposely withheld information, deviance in the storage of documents according to bank guidelines, and approval of customers and transactions despite obvious red flags.

Clifford Chance have described sequences of events in quite many details: they find violations in not following rules, they emphasize mistakes that people have done, shortcomings and weaknesses in anti-money laundering routines, and processes and controls. They have identified transactions that obviously transgressed the rules at that time.

However, it says in the mandate that the investigation should examine exposures to money laundering. Clifford Chance has not addressed this issue in the mandate. Although they indicate obvious incidents of money laundering, they seem reluctant to conclude that money laundering has occurred, and who might be the money launderers. They argue that they need evidence of the origins of funds before they can make a conclusion regarding anti-money laundering incidents. It seems that examiners wanted to avoid the theme of actual incidents and thus were reluctant to identify evidence.

Private policing evaluation

Chapter VII in the report is presenting the investigation's findings and conclusions. The chapter is 125 pages out of the 216-page report. The chapter tells a story of developments, but it does not reconstruct past events or sequences of events as required from a fraud examination. Even worse, there are no real conclusions, although the title of Chapter VII claims there will be a conclusion. As a result, and because of the lack of evidence of money laundering, Figure 13.2 illustrates that the Clifford Chance (2020) investigation report only reaches level 2 in terms of fraud examination maturity.

Rather than trying to find the underlying cause of rumors and accusations concerning misconduct and crime in the form of money laundering, examiners spend time telling how Swedbank's current board and management intend to implement new approaches to compliance and anti-money laundering (Clifford Chance, 2020: 178):

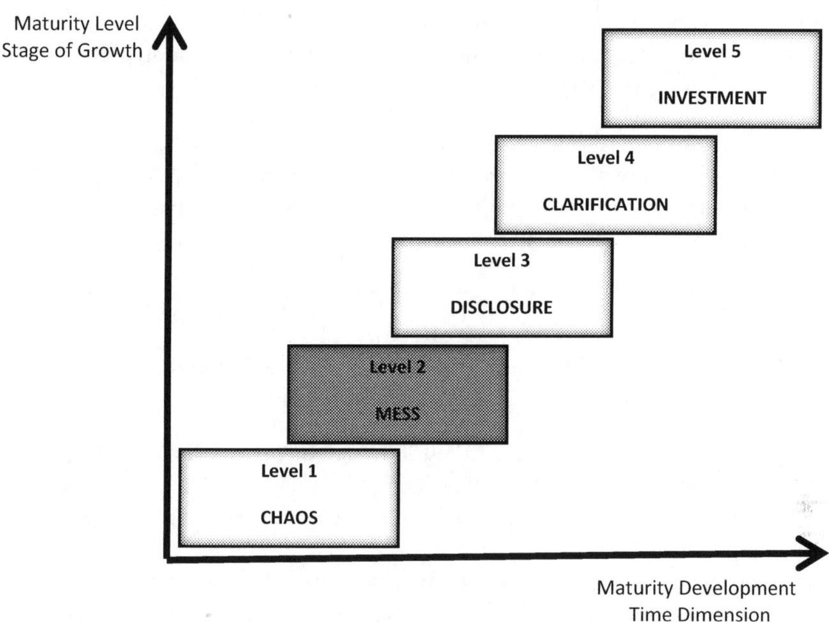

Figure 13.2 Maturity model for internal private investigations applied to Clifford Chance

> Swedbank has focused over the past year on transforming its approach to AML/CTF and sanctions compliance, creating new roles, appointing new personnel, increasing resources, revising and strengthening policies and procedures, and taking steps to de-risk its customer portfolio including in the Baltic subsidiaries.

It is naïve to believe that things will change simply because there are changes in top management and because those new executives in charge express ethical intentions. Fraud examiner David DiBari chose to include a whole chapter on remediation and nice words about the current bank management. Maybe he did so to please the new top executives, who are to pay for the investigation by Clifford Chance (2020).

Jens Henriksson became the chief executive officer at Swedbank in October 2019. Henriksson told that the costs of the Clifford Chance investigation were 1.9 billion Swedish kroner (approximately US$190 million). This figure includes work by subcontractors FTI Consulting, Forensic Risk Alliance (FRA), and other consultants. FRA had the task of examining 50 bank clients who the Swedish public television program "Uppdrag gransking" had identified. According to the program, those 50 clients had suspicious transactions amounting to 40 billion Swedish kroner (approximately US$4 billion). Out of the 1.9 billion kroner, 1.5

billion kroner went to Clifford Chance, while the remaining 0.4 billion kroner went to the other investigation partners.

On their website, Clifford Chance lists the following four strategies for their "responsible business strategy":

- Doing business responsibly through market-shaping practice in relation to ethics, professional standards, and risk management is a top priority.
- People are central to everything we do. We realize our potential by creating a safe, healthy, and inclusive workplace, and by broadening our skills and experience.
- Community sits at the heart of our firm. We partner to support our community by widening access to justice, finance, and education.
- Environment and contributing to a more sustainable world is important to how we advise our clients and manage our business.

There seems to be a gap between these fine statements by Clifford Chance and the lack of problem-solving at Swedbank combined with a bill of a magnitude that is exceptionally expensive compared to all other private policing cases presented in this book. Swedbank paid for David DiBari, Daniel Silver, Michelle Williams, Celeste Koeleveld, Glen Donath, Steven Gatti, Robert Houck, Steve Nicklesburg, George Kleinfield, Megan Gordon, and Michael Lyons at Clifford Chance.

Clifford Chance has written a comprehensive and probably useful review report, although parts of what have emerged in the review report were already known. Examiners wrote the report text in such a way that it gives Swedbank a feasible starting point for required control mechanisms at the executive level. The structure and quality of the report appears professional. However, the report is very comprehensive and relatively heavy to read. Among other things, there are many abbreviations to get into, and not least remember, actually to understand the context of what you read.

Bibliography

Agnew, R. (2014). Social concern and crime: Moving beyond the assumption of simple self-interest, *Criminology*, 52 (1), 1–32.

Arjoon, S. (2008). Slippery when wet: The real risk in business, *Journal of Markets & Morality, Spring*, 11 (1), 77–91.

Chatterjee, A. and Pollock, T.G. (2017). Master of puppets: How narcissistic CEOs construct their professional worlds, *Academy of Management Review*, 42 (4), 703–725.

Clifford Chance (2020). *Report of Investigation on Swedbank*, March 23, Washington, DC: Law Firm Clifford Chance.

Gamache, D.L. and McNamara, G. (2019). Responding to bad press: How CEO temporal focus influences the sensitivity to negative media coverage of acquisitions, *Academy of Management Journal*, 62 (3), 918–943.

Gottschalk, P. and Benson, M.L. (2020). The evolution of corporate accounts of scandals from exposure to investigation, *British Journal of Criminology*, published online https://doi.org/10.1093/bjc/azaa001.

Johannessen, S.Ø. and Christensen, J. (2020). Swedbank vil ikke betale sluttpakke til toppsjef som måtte gå av etter hvitvaskingsskandale (Swedbank will not pay final package to top executive who had to leave after money laundering scandal), *Daily Norwegian Business Newspaper Dagens Næringsliv*, www.dn.no, published March 23.

Makortoff, K. (2019). Swedbank chief sacked amid money laundering scandal, *The Guardian*, www.theguardian.com, published March 28.

Milne, R. (2020). Swedbank failings on E37bn of transactions revealed in report, *Financial Times*, www.ft.com, published March 23.

Murphy, P.R. and Dacin, M.T (2011). Psychological pathways to fraud: Understanding and preventing fraud in organizations, *Journal of Business Ethics*, 101, 601–618.

Naylor, R.T. (2003). Towards a general theory of profit-driven crimes, *British Journal of Criminology*, 43, 81–101.

Pettigrew, W.A. (2018). The changing place of fraud in seventeenth-century public debates about international trading corporations, *Business History*, 60 (3), 305–320.

Schnatterly, K., Gangloff, K.A. and Tuschke, A. (2018). CEO wrongdoing: A review of pressure, opportunity, and rationalization, *Journal of Management*, 44 (6), 2405–2432.

Welsh, D.T., Ordonez, L.D., Snyder, D.G. and Christian, M.S. (2014). The slippery slope: How small ethical transgressions pave the way for larger future transgressions, *Journal of Applied Psychology*, 100 (1), 114–127.

Zhu, D.H. and Chen, G. (2015). CEO narcissism and the impact of prior board experience on corporate strategy, *Administrative Science Quarterly*, 60 (1), 31–65.

14 XXL Sports by DLA Piper

Fraud examiners from law firm DLA Piper (2020) in Oslo conducted the private policing of suspected economic crime at store chain XXL Sports in Norway. Management faced suspicion of having manipulated sale prices for sporting goods in their stores. They claimed in many sales campaigns that they had cut original prices quite drastically, sometimes down to half of the prices that they had before. XXL management argued in their campaign that they could document that people previously had bought the same goods at twice the prices. However, the overpricing occurred when employees at XXL followed instructions to buy goods, and then return the goods and get the money back (Jordheim and Wig, 2019):

> Former XXL managers say: That's how they cheated on prices. Four former sales managers tell E24 that XXL stores fabricated sales figures so as not to be caught for misleading marketing. The chief executive at XXL now initiates internal investigations.
>
> It was often cheated with larger, expensive goods that it might be difficult to sell, says Christian Sandmo Olsen (24). He is one of four former sales leaders at three different XXL department stores who have told E24 about long-term and systematic fabrication of sales figures in order to be able to advertise with pre-prices in new offer announcements. A sales manager has overall responsibility for a department and is part of the store's management group. The fraud is carried out by employees who themselves buy an item and then return it immediately afterwards. So, if you look up the product in XXL's computer system, the store seems to have sold more goods than it actually has, explains the sales manager.

The treatment of employees was bad by Norwegian standards, as there was almost a military practice forcing employees to participate in price manipulation. The purpose of this wrongdoing carried out by employees at the sports department stores was to avoid detection by public agencies that they were violating Norwegian marketing regulations.

White-collar convenience

Again, we assume that the allegations are correct, and we study the deviant behavior at XXL by convenience themes as suggested in Figure 14.1.

The financial situation for sport chains in Norway was at that time weak, and one of XXL's competitors, G Sport, went bankrupt. XXL also faced the threat of bankruptcy. As indicated in the figure, motive-threats-corporate is the relevant theme for price manipulation to strengthen sales. The threat of corporate collapse and bankruptcy might cause exploration and exploitation of illegal avenues to survive, where moral panic can occur (Chattopadhyay et al., 2001; Kang and Thosuwanchot, 2017). The survival of the corporation can become so important that no means come across as unacceptable in the current situation (Blickle et al., 2006). Sometimes, fraud and corruption are considered temporary measures to

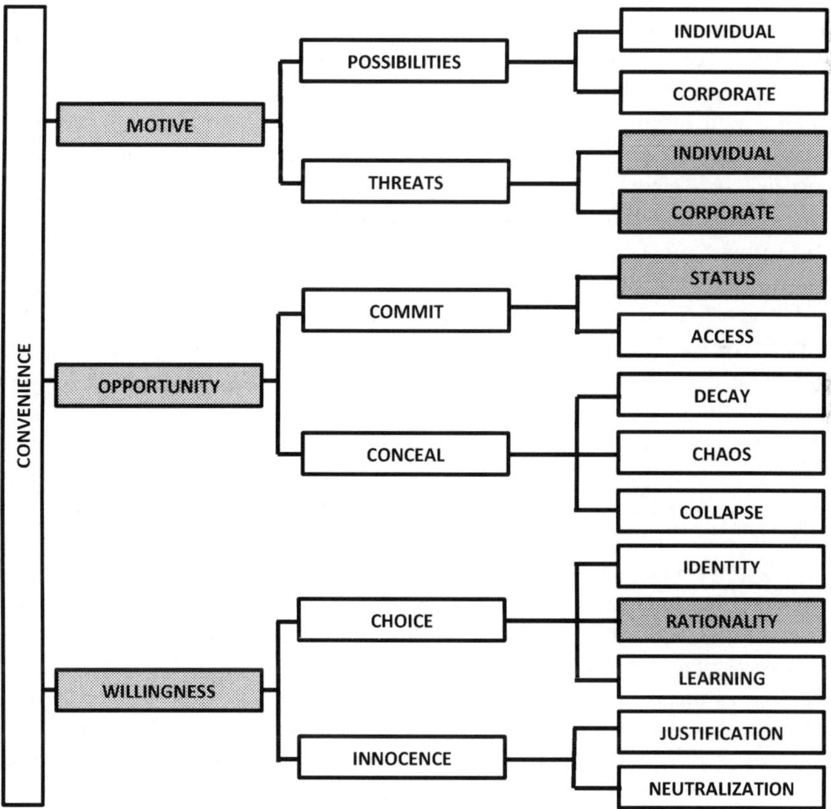

Figure 14.1 Convenience themes in the case of XXL

recover from a crisis (Geest et al., 2017), where the measures will be terminated when the crisis is over. As indicated in Figure 14.1, there was a corporate threat of bankruptcy as potential motive since the company was struggling with heavy losses (Hopland, 2020):

> XXL has never had a weaker result in the first quarter. Norway's largest sports chain has never had a tougher start to the year than in 2020.

A potential threat to the planned sales campaign was the failure to succeed if previous prices were not substantially different from bargain prices. Potential customers do not run to the store if there is a discount of only 10%. The discount has to be much larger to make sure the sales campaign is a success.

Another threat from weak corporate performance was that employees had to work free, without pay, to compensate for missing sales targets. Many were young and had temporal employment that they could lose quickly. They feared harassment and various forms of punishment if they did not perform, if their store did not perform, and if XXL as a whole did not perform.

There was a strong goal orientation, where goals justify means. Profit orientation dominates in both good times and bad times in goal-oriented organizations, where the financial bottom line is the only concern in the business (Jonnergård et al., 2010). There is a greater extent of criminogenity (that is propensity to financial crime) in organizations where executives primarily or exclusively control and manage by ambitious financial goals. This is because failing achievement will lead to negative consequences, while achievement of goals will lead to positive consequences for the organization.

In the organizational opportunity dimension of convenience theory, the status of executives at XXL was strong, since most of the sales personnel were temporarily hired while otherwise being unemployed or being young as high school or college students. Some offenders know that they are too big to fail and too powerful to jail (Pontell et al., 2014; Schnatterly et al., 2018). They are too important to blame (Eberly et al., 2011; Slyke and Bales, 2012). They enjoy high social status in privileged positions. White-collar offenders "are now regarded as the untouchables, too well-heeled and powerful to lock up" (Hausman, 2018: 381). Katz (1979) found that financial crime higher up in the organization will be ignored to a larger extent than lower down in the organization, or blame is allocated elsewhere (Keaveney, 2008; Lee and Robinson, 2000; Sonnier et al., 2015).

It was organizationally convenient for employees at XXL to buy goods and then return the goods later. It looked like completed sales. These fake sales did not look different from real sales in the system, as they looked the same. To find a fake sale would be like looking for a needle in a haystack, and it would be hard to find evidence. It was easy to commit the action of fake sales, while the action was difficult to detect. The organizational opportunity thus means that everyone employed at XXL could make a fictitious purchase, where there was a minimal risk of detection. There were simply too many transactions to find a few deviant ones.

As indicated in Figure 14.1, it was probably a rational choice to manipulate prices at XXL, where advantages should exceed disadvantages (Barry and Stephens, 1998; Hefendehl, 2010; Lyman and Potter, 2007). Some employees perceived XXL as a family, since many of them had been in the company from the beginning, ever since Øyvind Tidemandsen founded the business (Solgård, 2020). They were loyal without any skepticism or critical attitude. They did what XXL expected of them without posing any questions. Some employees remained in the dark whether fake purchases represented a violation of the law. They simply did what executives expected of them and did not feel bad about it. Some thought that customers did a bargain anyway, despite the fake discount.

Executives made jokes about price manipulation, which distracted from deviant behavior and made it acceptable (Yam et al., 2018). In addition to military discipline, executives drilled employees in competitive thinking. It was important to beat the competition in the sports department business, whatever it takes. The personal willingness for deviant behavior thus derives from naïve loyalty to leaders and the company, a culture of winning at any costs, lack of communication about what is illegal and illegal, and competition among employees, departments, and stores. In addition, a management style of authority, cynicism, and punishment left little choice rather than to follow their leaders. While some found armpits quite amusing as punishment in a department store for sporting goods, others disliked it very much.

Executives at XXL could neutralize potential guilt feelings by not remembering that they had encouraged deviant behavior. They had not specifically encouraged crime, they simply said: "we have to make it", "this is extremely important", and "you just have to find a way of doing it".

Executives and others in the elite may use language that followers do not necessarily understand. Followers nevertheless trust executive messages. Language shapes what people notice and ignore (Ferraro et al., 2005), and language is a window into organizational culture (Holt and Cornelissen, 2014; Srivastava and Goldberg, 2017; Weick, 1995). Offender language can cause obedience among followers (Mawritz et al., 2017).

Employees who completed purchases and then returned the goods may have felt stress from executives' expectations. They wanted to remove strain, pain, and uncertainty (Langton and Piquero, 2007).

Fraud examination outcome

The fraud examination by DLA Piper (2020: 7) draws the following conclusion:

> A practice of establishing incorrect pre-prices in XXL has been revealed. During the mandate period from 2017 to the present, six cases have been revealed that are considered confirmed on the basis of interviews and other evidence. In addition, we got confirmed two cases relation to the time before 2014. One case concerns 2008–2010 and one case concerns 2013. However, the investigation has shown that a significant number of informants have

"heard of" fictitious purchases without being able to identify individual events so that they are verifiable. In our assessment, it must be assumed that the practice is somewhat more widespread than the eight identifiable cases, but that the scope has not been significant. We find that this practice has been used as an exception over a long period of time. We conclude that the practice has not been widespread and systematic.

XXL sent the DLA Piper (2020) to the relevant government agency, which is the Consumer Authority that is an independent administrative body. The Norwegian Consumer Authority has the responsibility of supervising measures in the market and seeks to exert influence on traders to observe the regulatory framework.

Fraud examiners created a special whistleblowing channel for persons at XXL who wanted to contribute information to the investigation. Examiners promised people anonymity. Only two notices arrived at the examiners, which indicate that people at XXL did not trust the investigation.

Private policing evaluation

A response letter from the Consumer Authority to XXL indicates that the authority is not at all happy with the report (Forbrukertilsynet, 2020a). They emphasize that the marketing law prohibits deviant and misleading trade practices. The authority decided to report the case to the police, where they accuse XXL of violating statute 160 of the penal code (Forbrukertilsynet, 2020b). While it is not obvious the authority is right in considering the misconduct at XXL to be far more serious than the fraud examiners, the gap and discrepancy between the two assessments is indeed striking. It would thus be wrong to conclude that DLA Piper (2020) have contributed to clarification at level 3 in the maturity model. Rather, the private policing seems more appropriately allocated at level 2 in Figure 14.2.

It was a superficial investigation. The report is short and imprecise. The investigation highlights the problem but not more than that. Although it responds to the mandate, the investigation does not take any deep dive into the problem. Brief and nonreflected conclusions characterize level 2. The report highlights problems but fails in reconstructing events and causes of events.

One of the obvious shortcomings in the work by investigators was their failing information strategy in terms of interviews. They failed in accessing potential informants, probably because they applied an approach that caused informants to deny participation. Those informants they succeeded in interviewing seem to have had concerns about telling all they knew about the price fixing. Again, the examiners deserve criticism for not providing a trustworthy climate for employees to tell freely what they have observed.

Rather than focusing on individuals responsible for the wrongdoing, the examiners seem to protect executives by blaming a mixture of corporate culture, organizational systems, business routines, and individuals completing fake

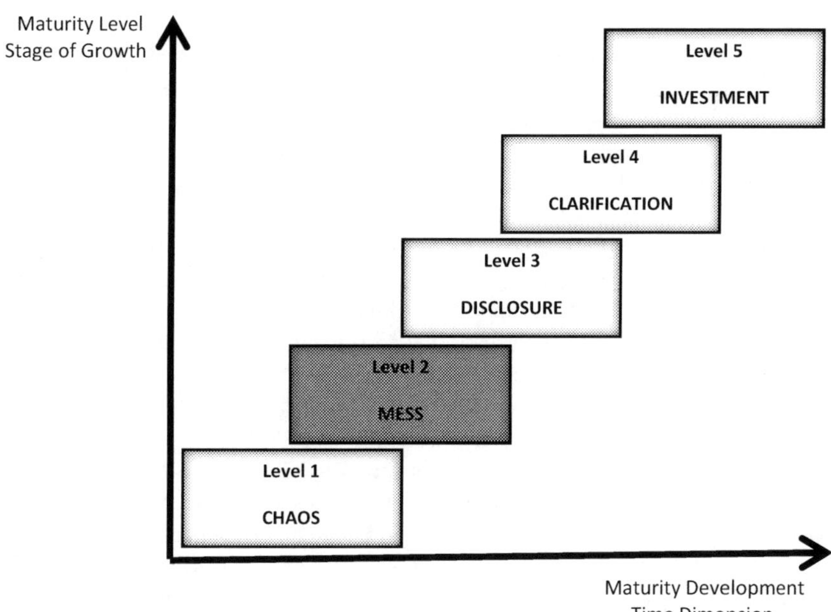

Figure 14.2 Maturity model for internal private investigations applied to DLA Piper

purchases. This creates a messy picture. Obviously, management is responsible for both culture and systems, and even what individuals do in the organization. However, examiners avoided that perspective. Responsible executives, including Anders Kjellen, Tom Erik Kjønø, and Jakob Olsbø, avoided attention.

The 41-page report from DLA Paper (2020) starts with a picture of attorney Berit Reiss-Andersen, who was in charge of this investigation. Both her email address and telephone number are listed, together with the text "Berit is head of DLA Pipers department for civil solutions, legal procedures, and economic crime". While it is certainly uncommon to have a photo of an examiner in a report of investigation, it is not surprising that Reiss-Andersen becomes an exception. In addition to be a famous white-collar defense lawyer, she also heads the Norwegian Nobel Committee that awards the Nobel Peace Prize. This position combined with her legal merits gives her an impressive status in Norwegian society. However, the discrepancy between her photo and the contents of her report makes the investigation even less reliable. A potential explanation is that she mainly posed as a figurehead, while other less skilled and less experienced did the actual investigative work, such as Ellen Haug-Svendsen, Ivar Valter Kristiansen, Kjetil Hare Johansen, Egil Hatling, Silje Gjølberg Finnanger, and Victoria Palm at DLA Piper.

The report appears as a commissioning work where the client gets the desired result. DLA Piper wanted to help management clean themselves of any suspicions of wrongdoing. Examiners quickly draw conclusions that there are no systematics in the deviant actions and thus no blame to assign to XXL as such.

Maybe the board was satisfied with the investigation outcome. Board members included Hugo Lund Maurstad (chair and representative of an investment fund that had invested heavily in XXL shares), Øivind Tidemandsen (founder of XXL), Ronny Blomseth, Kjersti Helen Krokeide Hobøl, and Maria Anna Kristina Aas-Eng.

Pål Wibe replaced Tolle Grøterud as chief executive officer at XXL when business performance deteriorated shortly before the investigation was initiated by the XXL board (Solgård, 2020). Grøterud's predecessor, Fredrik Steenbuch, found that competitors tried to sabotage XXL by denying vendors to trade with XXL, and thus XXL had to respond accordingly.

Whistleblower Olsen blew the whistle on XXL in the media. Shortly after, examiners invited him to DLA Piper's offices, where he met Reiss-Andersen and five other attorneys. The interview started politely and nicely, but after a while, he felt that it was more like an interrogation. He considered leaving the place. However, he did understand that they had to present some critical questions to him regarding his allegations in the media. Without access to any digital information, he was unable to answer some of the examination questions. After the interview, he received a transcript of the interview from the examiners, but he decided not to sign it. He was convinced that top management was involved and maybe had initiated the fraud, but examiners did not include that issue as a topic in the interview.

Norwegian consumer authority

The Norwegian consumer authority decided to report the case to the police, where they accused XXL of violating statue 160 of the penal code (Forbrukertilsynet, 2020b: 2):

> The XXL report states (on page 19) that out of 84 persons interviewed at XXL, 22 persons have direct knowledge of fictitious transactions. Eight of these persons confirmed that they had completed fictitious transactions themselves. Furthermore, four persons have explained that their executives told them to make fictitious purchases, but in the last minute managed to make real sales to customers, so that the need for fictitious purchases disappeared. The remaining 10 persons in this group have reported having first-hand knowledge of fictitious pre-prices, because they have either observed the incident or someone told them about it as it occurred. …
>
> The consumer authority can see no other purpose for XXL's practice of manipulating sales figures than that XXL has deliberately tried to put consumers and the consumer authority behind the light. The intention of carrying out the fictitious transactions in our opinion must have been to hide violations of the marketing act vis-à-vis the consumer authority, which is the public regulatory body that is set to enforce marketing law violations.

Bibliography

Barry, B. and Stephens, C.U. (1998). Objections to an objectivist approach to integrity, *Academy of Management Review*, 23 (1), 162–169.

Blickle, G., Schlegel, A., Fassbender, P. and Klein, U. (2006). Some personality correlates of business white-collar crime, *Applied Psychology: An International Review*, 55 (2), 220–233.

Chattopadhyay, P., Glick, W.H. and Huber, G.P. (2001). Organizational actions in response to threats and opportunities, *Academy of Management Journal*, 44 (5), 937–955.

DLA Piper (2020). *Granskingsrapport XXL ASA (Examination Report XXL Ltd.)*, January, Oslo: Law Firm DLA Piper.

Eberly, M.B., Holley, E.C., Johnson, M.D. and Mitchell, T.R. (2011). Beyond internal and external: a dyadic theory of relational attributions, *Academy of Management Review*, 36 (4), 731–753.

Ferraro, F., Pfeffer, J. and Sutton, R.I. (2005). Economics language and assumptions: How theories can become self-fulfilling, *Academy of Management Review*, 30 (1), 8–24.

Forbrukertilsynet (2020a). *XXL – fiktive priser og manipulering av dokumentasjonsgrunnlag (XXL – Fictive Prices and Manipulation of Documentation Foundation)*, Norwegian Consumer Authority, case 19/1721-21, Oslo.

Forbrukertilsynet (2020b). *Anmeldelse for mulig brudd på straffeloven § 160 om bevispåvirkning (Report for Possible Violation of the Penal Code § 160 Regarding Evidence Influence)*, Norwegian Consumer Authority, case 19/1721-20, Oslo.

Geest, V.R., Weisburd, D. and Blokland, A.A.J. (2017). Developmental trajectories of offenders convicted of fraud: A follow-up to age 50 in a Dutch conviction cohort, *European Journal of Criminology*, 14 (5), 543–565.

Hausman, W.J. (2018). Howard Hopson's billion dollar fraud: The rise and fall of associated gas & electric company, *Business History*, 60 (3), 381–398.

Hefendehl, R. (2010). Addressing white collar crime on a domestic level, *Journal of International Criminal Justice*, 8, 769–782.

Holt, R. and Cornelissen, J. (2014). Sensemaking revisited, *Management Learning*, 45 (5), 525–539.

Hopland, S. (2020). XXL har aldri hatt et svakere resultat i første kvartal. Norges største sportskjede har aldri hat ten tøffere start på året enn i 2020 (XXL has never had a weaker result in the first quarter. Norway's largest sports chain has never had a tougher start to the year than in 2020), *Web-Based Norwegian Newspaper E24*, www.e24.no, published April 29.

Jonnergård, K., Stafsudd, A. and Elg, U. (2010). Performance evaluations as gender barriers in professional organizations: A study of auditing firms, *Gender, Work and Organization*, 17 (6), 721–747.

Jordheim, H. and Wig, K. (2019). Tidligere XXL-ledere forteller: Slik jukset de med prisene (Former XXL leaders tell: So did they cheat with the prices), *Web-Based Norwegian Newspaper E24*, published August 17.

Kang, E. and Thosuwanchot, N. (2017). An application of Durkheim's four categories of suicide to organizational crimes, *Deviant Behavior*, 38 (5), 493–513.

Katz, J. (1979). Concerted ignorance: The social construction of cover-up, *Urban Life*, 8 (3), 295–316.

Keaveney, S.M. (2008). The blame game: An attribution theory approach to marketer-engineer conflict in high-technology companies, *Industrial Marketing Management*, 37, 653–663.

Langton, L. and Piquero, N.L. (2007). Can general strain theory explain white-collar crime? A preliminary investigation of the relationship between strain and select white-collar offenses, *Journal of Criminal Justice*, 35 (1), 1–15.

Lee, F. and Robinson, R.J. (2000). An attributional analysis of social accounts: Implications of playing the blame game, *Journal of Applied Social Psychology*, 30 (9), 1853–1879.

Lyman, M.D. and Potter, G.W. (2007). *Organized Crime*, 4th Edition, Upper Saddle River, NJ: Pearson Prentice Hall.

Mawritz, M.B., Greenbaum, R.L., Butts, M.M. and Graham, K.A. (2017). I just can't control myself: A self-regulation perspective on the abuse of deviant employees, *Academy of Management Journal*, 60 (4), 1482–1503.

Pontell, H.N., Black, W.K. and Geis, G. (2014). Too big to fail, too powerful to jail? On the absence of criminal prosecutions after the 2008 financial meltdown, *Crime, Law and Social Change*, 61 (1), 1–13.

Schnatterly, K., Gangloff, K.A. and Tuschke, A. (2018). CEO wrongdoing: A review of pressure, opportunity, and rationalization, *Journal of Management*, 44 (6), 2405–2432.

Slyke, S.V. and Bales, W.D. (2012). A contemporary study of the decision to incarcerate white-collar and street property offenders, *Punishment & Society*, 14 (2), 217–246.

Solgård, J. (2020). XXL-gründer Øivind Tidemandsen har solgt aksjer for 117 millioner kroner i XXL (XXL founder Øivind Tidemandsen has sold shares for 117 million kroner in XXL), *Daily Norwegian Business Newspaper Dagens Næringsliv*, www.dn.no, published April 30.

Sonnier, B.M., Lassar, W.M. and Lassar, S.S. (2015). The influence of source credibility and attribution of blame on juror evaluation of liability of industry specialist auditors, *Journal of Forensic & Investigative Accounting*, 7 (1), 1–37.

Srivastava, S.B. and Goldberg, A. (2017). Language as a window into culture, *California Management Review*, 60 (1), 56–69.

Weick, K.E. (1995). What theory is not, theorizing is. *Administrative Science Quarterly*, *40*, 385–390.

Yam, K.C., Christian, M.S., Wei, W., Liao, Z. and Nai, J. (2018). The mixed blessing of leader sense of humor: Examining costs and benefits, *Academy of Management Journal*, 61 (1), 348–369.

15 Navy logistics by PwC

Seven decommissioned Norwegian naval vessels ended up in the hands of a warlord in Nigeria. The 2012 sale took a surprising turn when an investigative journalist in a Norwegian daily newspaper (Egeberg, 2014, 2015) revealed that the vessels were serving, two years later, in the private flotilla of a former Nigerian rebel (Evans, 2017; Tufts, 2018). Nigeria is rich in oil resources where the rebels fight for control (Ezeonu, 2020; Reporter, 2013). The news about the six demilitarized missile torpedo boats and one naval support vessel triggered both an internal fraud examination by PwC (2014, 2015) for the Ministry of Defense in Norway and a police investigation by Økokrim (Norwegian national authority for investigation and prosecution of economic and environmental crime).

The police investigation led to the conviction in May 2017 of a Norwegian official on bribery charges and the revelation of the role played by a UK intermediary, CAS-Global Ltd. The firm applied for export licenses in Norway and for a re-export license for the naval support vessel from the UK, telling the Norwegians that the ships would support an official West African mission, and the British that the ships should serve the Nigerian government (Tufts, 2018).

The Norwegian official appealed the conviction in a district court in Norway in May 2017 via a court of appeals and further to the Supreme Court (Oslo tingrett, 2017; NTB, 2019a). The Supreme Court confirmed in May 2019 the sentence in Borgarting court of appeals from October 2018 of 4 years and 3 months in prison for the former commander Bjørn Stavrum in the Norwegian navy (Borgarting, 2018; Eriksen, 2019; Høyesterett, 2019).

White-collar convenience

Motive, opportunity, and willingness determine the extent of white-collar crime convenience in the naval logistics case, as illustrated in the structural model in Figure 15.1. A video on YouTube posted by personal coach May Britt Lian can shed some light upon Bjørn Stavrum's motive for illegal financial gain. The video seems to be a marketing stunt for the coaching firm, where the coach interviews Stavrum by letting him tell his own story (Lian, 2017):

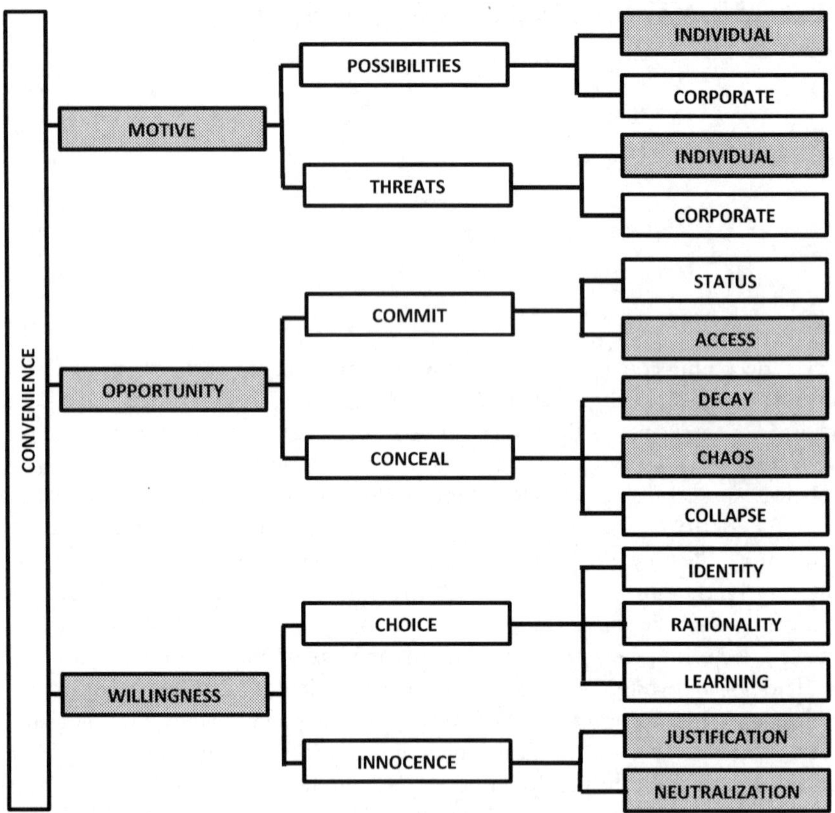

Figure 15.1 Convenience themes in the case of the naval commander

> Yes, Bjørn, now you can tell a little about who you are: The name is Bjørn Stavrum, 60 years. I was an employee in the armed forces for 37 years until I retired in 2014. It was a sad departure since Økokrim is currently investigating me for selling vessels to Nigeria. The fact that I am sitting here today has its cause in my search for help after I came in the spotlight of the police in relation to my job. I am glad for the help I have received. It has provided me with incredible results in that I have managed to calm myself and look ahead. Do not dwell on things that have taken all my energy. I urge everyone to dare to challenge themselves in relation to not sitting with problems, but rather seeking help from other people.

A motive emerges in the middle of the video, where Stavrum tells his story as a single parent (Lian, 2017):

> I have been a single dad since 1989 for three children that I took over after my wife left me to Canada. The children were two, three, and six years of

> age respectively. One child was born with water retention and has had major problems. This went on up through childhood and today as well. It has been a challenge, and I chose to stay in the armed forces to take care of the kids. The army as employer was incredibly good at supporting my everyday life as a single dad. After all, I found myself left alone with three children in 1989, and that was not normal for a father to end up left alone with three children. There have been numerous obstacles on the way forward over the years as the kids grew up. I have had my rounds with public child welfare protection in the city of Tromsø, among other things, with the risk of losing the children.

The single parent story is in line with the perspective of negative life events in convenience theory (Engdahl, 2015). The perspective of negative life events suggests that events such as divorce, accident, lack of promotion, and cash problems can cause potential offenders to consider white-collar crime a convenient solution. Other relevant perspectives on Stavrum's crime motive include avoiding loss of self-esteem (Crosina and Pratt, 2019), removal of strain, pain, and uncertainty (Langton and Piquero, 2007), restoring the perception of equity and equality (Leigh et al., 2010), and satisfying the desire to help others as social concern (Agnew, 2014). The latter perspective of helping others based on social concern moves white-collar crime beyond the assumption of simple self-interest. However, as argued by Paternoster et al. (2018), helping others can be a self-interested, rational action. The self-interest or self-regarding preference and the implicit rationality can imply interest in other's materialism.

In the organizational opportunity dimension of convenience theory, investigative journalist Egeberg (2015: 44) found that lack of controls caused the Norwegian government's embarrassment to tighten quickly the legislation:

> The disclosures have led the government to tighten immediately export legislation by amending regulations on exports of defense equipment, multipurpose goods, technology and services on Friday, September 12, 2014.

Stavrum had legitimate access to premises and systems (Benson and Simpson, 2018), and he had legitimate access to resources (Adler and Kwon, 2002). More importantly, however, there was an inability to control Stavrum because of institutional deterioration (Rodriguez et al., 2005), social disorganization (Forti and Visconti, 2020; Hoffmann, 2002), inference and noise in crime signals (Karim and Siegel, 1998), and lack of principal-agent relationships (Bosse and Phillips, 2016).

The control and constitution committee in the Norwegian parliament had an open hearing in October 2016 concerning the sale of army material, and they invited Stavrum to present himself (Dagbladet, 2015):

> This is not an attempt to cleanse myself. I know I have a serious charge against me. I have made some assessments that were not very successfully,

> and I strongly apologize for this. However, in my 37 years in the armed forces, I have never done anything that has been devastating or negative for my employer in any way. I hope this will become evident when Økokrim has completed the police investigation.

The above quote is interesting to analyze with the perspectives of choice and innocence in the theory of convenience dimension of willingness for deviant behavior. There is little evidence of deviant identity (e.g., Obodaru, 2017), rationality (Pratt and Cullen, 2005), and learning (Sutherland, 1983) that characterize the choice perspective. Similarly, there is little evidence of justification (e.g., Schnatterly et al., 2018) in the innocence perspective. Stavrum may have been sliding on a slippery slope over on the wrong side of the law (Welsh et al., 2014) when he lacked self-control (Gottfredson and Hirschi, 1990).

The quote mainly supports the perspective of neutralization techniques (Sykes and Matza, 1957). First, Stavrum applies the neutralization technique of no damage. He refuses damage from crime, as there is no visible harm from his action to his employer. The offender seeks to minimize or deny the harm done. Denial of injury involves justifying an action by minimizing the perception of the harm it causes. The misbehavior is not very serious because no relevant party suffered directly or visibly because of it. Statements of denial are "assertions that something did not happen, does not exist, is not true or is not known about" (Cohen, 2001: 3).

Next, Stavrum applies the neutralization technique of no victim. He refuses the existence of any victim from his crime, as he claims there is nobody suffering from his action. The offender could here acknowledge an injury, which he does not, but deny any existence of victims or claim that the victims are unworthy of concern. Any potential blame for illegal actions is unjustified because the violated party deserves whatever injury they receive.

A third neutralization technique is concerned with blunder quota. After 37 years in the armed forces, Stavrum suggests that he has made some mistakes during those years. The offender can feel that after having done so much good for so many for so long time, others should excuse him for some unfortunate misconduct. Others should understand that the alleged crime was an acceptable mistake. This is in line with the metaphor of the ledger, which uses the idea of compensating bad acts for good acts. That is, the offender believes that he has previously performed a number of good acts and has accrued a surplus of good will, and, because of this, can afford to commit some bad actions.

Fraud examination outcome

The fraud examination report by PwC (2014: 9) describes a number of phenomena known from the organizational opportunity dimension of convenience theory:

> PwC has assessed the extent to which the case handling and process related to the disposal of end-of-life vessels had a sound organizing and structure

> in line with the requirements for professional management practice. Our main conclusion is that there is a clear need for improvement regarding the structuring of and management involvement in the process throughout the course of case handling at all levels.
>
> There are no routines for FLO, after receiving a disposal order, to prepare a plan or risk assessment for the implementation of the impending divestment process. At the same time, there is also no governance structure with associated decision-making authority on disposal actions within FLO, as it does at procurements and acquisitions. Thus, no amount limits exist for what the individual caseworker can dispose of.

The following year, PwC (2015: 5) continued its criticism of ignorance and lack of control:

> PwC believes there is reason to question that for five of the sales where the settlements have gone through the NMA there is no signed contract. PwC finds it unreasonable for the armed forces not to ensure that at every sale there is a contract signed by the buyer and the armed forces where the sales price is clearly stated.

Private policing evaluation

The first investigation by PwC (2014) had a mandate where fraud examiners should detect whether employees in Norwegian defense and vendors involved in sales had made mistakes and were responsible for misconduct, which would represent new insights into the sale of decommissioned naval vessels. The private police force failed to reveal new insights in their examination. It seems thus useless at level 1 in the maturity model in Figure 15.2.

The second investigation by PwC (2015) had a mandate where fraud examiners should analyze patterns and procedures in decommissioning processes. As suggested in Figure 15.3, the report by the investigators contributes to clarification concerning actors and their roles in the sales processes. Public and private actors, both domestic and foreign, are included in the analysis.

Court sentencing evaluation

First, the district court Oslo tingrett (2017), then the court of appeals Borgarting (2018), and finally the Supreme Court Høyesterett (2019) sentenced white-collar offender Bjørn Stavrum to prison for 4 years and 3 months. The district court verdict is 56-pages long; the court of appeal verdict is 29-pages long, while the Supreme Court verdict is 6-pages long. To sentence someone to prison requires that judges identify evidence of crime that is beyond any reasonable and sensible doubt. It is an interesting exercise to evaluate court judges' work similar to fraud examiners' work. However, evaluation criteria have to be different, as judges receive information in a courtroom, normally over a period of a few weeks,

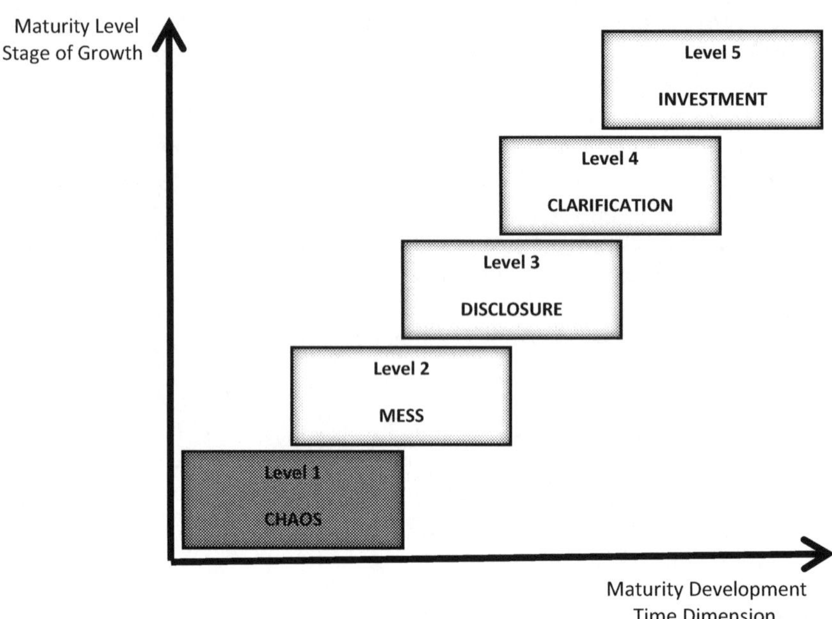

Figure 15.2 Maturity model for internal private investigations applied to PwC (2014)

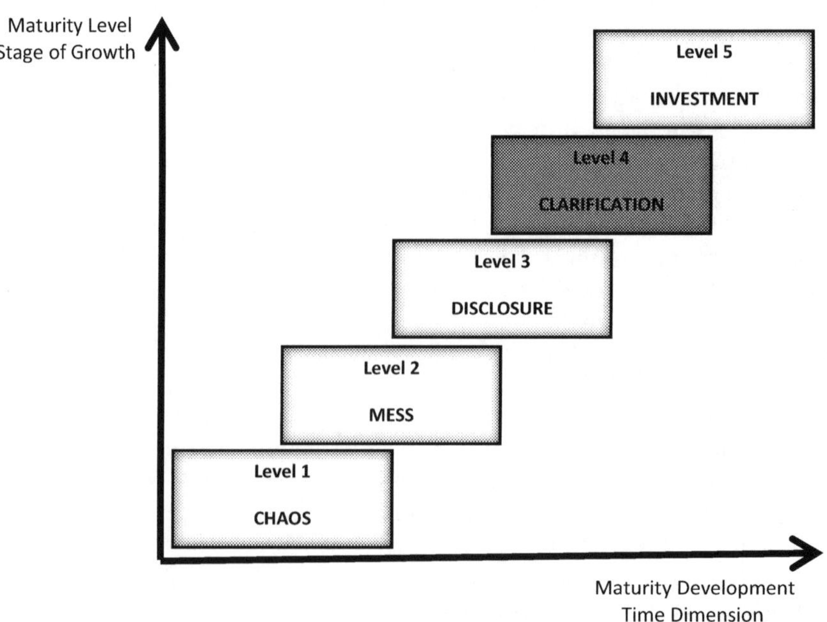

Figure 15.3 Maturity model for internal private investigations applied to PwC (2015)

while examiners investigate matters by collecting information from various relevant sources.

Oslo tingrett (2017: 7) states that "it is not required, that each element of evidence in a case needs to be proven beyond any reasonable doubt, as long as a combined assessment of all facts leave no doubt about the conclusion in the case". Borgarting (2018: 10) states:

> The court of appeal finds it beyond any reasonable and sensible doubt that the payments from CAS were a gift in the form of bribes or monetary lubrication – and not a loan. Bribe is a form of corruption. The deciding factor for the court's assessment is the following. On January 24, 2013, Stavrum sent an email to Stuart MacGregor, where the subject was "financial support". We repeat from the email:
>
> "Dear Stuart. With reference to earlier conversation and e-mail regarding financial support. Enclosed you will find a signed draft contract that I have made, for loaning money of you. This is for tax authority. I must either loan or get this money as a gift. This is how I prefer to do it. I hope it is suitable for you. I do rely hope that you can manage to help me as you said".

While Stavrum claimed the payments were a loan, the court was convinced they were bribes. This is an example where evaluation is relevant, as the interpretation of the above email is not obvious to every reader of it.

Generally, a court sentence is a document that needs evaluation on a number of criteria, in addition to the extent of evidence for the statement of proof beyond any reasonable and sensible doubt. First, the structure of a verdict needs to satisfy certain requirements, where one finds the issue explained, the relevant statutes included, the story told, and a discussion of what is proven and not proven. Next, the quality of the subsumption is important, where the judge attempts to apply a law text to facts in the case. Third, the presentation is important, where explanations by witnesses in court become relevant in the verdict only to the extent that witness statements find application in the sentencing. Finally, the core of the case needs emphasized text and should not be lost in a lot of more or less irrelevant information.

Therefore, a low-quality court sentence has a number of characteristics. First, the structure of the document is messy without any clear direction. The issue is not clearly stated, and the relevant statutes not applied. The subsumption is not convincing, and thus the sentence lacks convincing evidence application. Next, the verdict document tells a lengthy story without any focus on relevant facts. Third, the document jumps to conclusion without any backing evidence. Finally, the judge left out or forgot important pieces of evidence to build the case.

The fundamental question one has to ask oneself when evaluating a court verdict: Is this a case of injustice? Norwegian courts are normally so afraid of injustice – having incarcerated innocent people – that they prefer to release guilty defendants if there is any doubt at all. Is Stavrum a case of the opposite? An evaluation should search to clarify whether the evidence against Stavrum was sufficient to exclude the possibility of sentencing him to prison if he is not guilty.

The case of a convicted white-collar offender in the Norwegian defense logistics in this chapter is an alternative for students to the 14 cases presented in the 14 previous chapters of this book. If business school students chose the case of Bjørn Stavrum in the spring term 2020, then they evaluated the court sentences in their term papers.

To evaluate court sentencing, there is a need for evaluation criteria. These are potential criteria:

1. The rationale must be professional: This first criterion implies that the court sentencing should be legally and procedurally professional. There is a requirement for good legal quality. Once the judge or judges have decided in terms of a verdict, it is reasonable to state who has made the decision, what legal statute is relevant, and that the court has followed all adopted procedures. This criterion is met at all three court levels.
2. The rationale must be functional: This means that the court should structure the sentence document in a logical way, and make it efficiently organized and clearly designed. The conclusion reached by the judges must appear as logical consequence of the discussion. The rationale must explain assessments, premises, and facts so that it sufficiently and fully communicates to all stakeholders. This must be done in an understandable language and be adapted to those affected by the decision. The documents from the district court and court of appeal have a clear set of points for the offender's violations of law statutes. In the Supreme Court judgment, only the appeal over the application of the law went through to the court. The Supreme Court judge reasoned his view on the facts and previously given conclusions in a functional manner.
3. The rationale must be open and complete: This criterion emphasizes that the motivation and the basis for the decision are clearly stated. Here, the courts must clearly explain the discretionary assessments and the bases for them. What assumptions the courts use and can lead to the discussion and the direction of potential trade-offs. One must also look at the considerations that the courts have taken into account and the connection to any predatory legal work, legal purposes, previous verdicts, legal purposes, regulations, and real assessments. Most arguments refer to the facts that form the evidence picture and that justify the courts' conclusions. The sentence from the court of appeals refers to the general preventive considerations. The court states that the general preventive considerations usually apply strongly in the sentencing for both active and passive corruption.
4. The rationale must have a design from the perspective of the normative effect of the judgment: The aim here is that the sentence should be guiding and contributing to a clarification of the law and possible legal development in facts of this kind. For a sentence to have normative effects, it is essential that, by conclusions, there is no room for alternative interpretations. In the Supreme Court's assessment, the court stated that the content of the penal code needs clarification on a case-by-case basis. Clarification on a case-by-case

> basis is a natural part of legal methodology. At the same time, the court has to safeguard predictability in a perspective of generalizing penalties for categories of offenses.

A court document includes the reasoning and sentencing of an offender. The court process needs to be effective, where the hearings should take place without unreasonable delay and in a time frame that is limited. Surprisingly many white-collar crime cases in Norway last for weeks and months, while traditional street crime cases last for days or weeks in the courts. Poverty and powerlessness tend to be the cause of street crime, while excessive power and greed is frequently the cause of white-collar crime. In both cases, the verdict should be fair and unbiased, and it should derive from knowledge rather than opinions.

The criterion of beyond any reasonable and sensible doubt is concerned with human rights and the rule of law. For example, anyone who faces charges of a criminal offense shall have the status of innocence until proved guilty by law. The formulation of reasonable and sensible implies that the threshold for sentencing in criminal cases should be very high. Any reasonable doubt should benefit the accused. Distinguishing between the doubt that can lead to acquittal and the doubt the evidence assessment can disregard is a challenging task for judges. In light of the sentences in the Stavrum case, there is no reasonable doubt regarding facts that transgress laws. The circumstances of the indictment had proofs beyond any reasonable and sensible doubt.

Preventive and detective measures

Business school students who chose the case of Bjørn Stavrum were also supposed to suggest preventive and detective measures related to white-collar crime. Preventive measures in the research literature include:

- Corporate governance: Promoting fairness, honesty, integrity, and accountability
- Corporate culture: Promoting transparency rather than secrecy, direct talk rather than indirect talk, relational orientation rather than task orientation, speaking rather than silence, cooperation rather than competition, and mastery rather than fumbling
- Compliance risk assessment: Introducing a systematic approach to the entity's identification of relevant risks to achievement of its objectives
- New tone from the top: Correcting deficiencies in the previous tone that might have triggered misconduct and crime
- Recruitment processes: Selecting individuals who share the new core values and ethical understanding
- Policies and procedures: Introducing core value statements, mission statements, code of conduct, and segregation of duties
- Communication and training: Advancing beyond ethics an awareness of proper conduct within the organization

- Individual sanctioning: Implementing tough procedures so that potential offenders can notice and learn about the consequences of deviant behavior that will work as a deterrent against misconduct and crime
- Bureaucratic routines: All incoming invoices need the four-eyes principles, independent of the amount
- Sales reporting: Information should include how payments occurred, from someone to someone, items, contact information, and signatures.

Detective measures in the research literature include:

- Whistleblowing routines: Enabling individuals who believe they observe wrongdoing to report their observations in a safe way to trusted individuals, where there is no danger of reprisals
- Monitoring systems: Assessing and ensuring the quality of internal performance over time
- Audit functions: Identifying misstatements by looking from deviance rather than confirmation
- Fraud examination: Developing internal capability to reconstruct past events and sequences of events

Bibliography

Adler, P.S. and Kwon, S.W. (2002). Social capital: Prospects for a new concept, *Academy of Management Review*, 27 (1), 17–40.

Agnew, R. (2014). Social concern and crime: Moving beyond the assumption of simple self-interest, *Criminology*, 52 (1), 1–32.

Benson, M.L. and Simpson, S.S. (2018). *White-Collar Crime: An Opportunity Perspective*, 3rd Edition, New York: Routledge.

Borgarting (2018). *Case Number 17-108216AST-BORG/02, Borgarting Lagmannsrett (Borgarting Court of Appeals)*, October 10, Oslo.

Bosse, D.A. and Phillips, R.A. (2016). Agency theory and bounded self-interest, *Academy of Management Review*, 41 (2), 276–297.

Cohen, S. (2001). *States of Denial: Knowing about Atrocities and Suffering*, Cambridge: Polity Press.

Crosina, E. and Pratt, M.G. (2019). Toward a model of organizational mourning: The case of former Lehman Brothers bankers, *Academy of Management Journal*, 62 (1), 66–98.

Dagbladet (2015). –Jeg er ikke ute etter hevn (I am not out for revenge), *Daily Norwegian Newspaper Dagbladet*, www.dagbladet.no/dbtv.no, November 26. published online https://www.youtube.com/watch?v=1x0I1FKhA5Q.

Egeberg, K. (2014). Norske krigsskip havnet i Nigeria – Langt i fra hva som var avtalen, sier Forsvaret (Norwegian warships ended up in Nigeria – Far from what was the agreement, the Military Defense says), *Daily Norwegian Newspaper Dagbladet*, www.dagbladet.no, published June 14.

Egeberg, K. (2015). *Nigeria-båtene: Metoderapport til Skup-prisen 2014 (The Nigeria Boats: Methods Report to the Skup Prize 2014)*, Oslo: Dagbladet.

Engdahl, O. (2015). White-collar crime and first-time adult-onset offending: Explorations in the concept of negative life events as turning points, *International Journal of Law, Crime and Justice*, 43 (1), 1–16.

Eriksen, N. (2019). Rettskraftig korrupsjonsdom i Nigeriabåt-saken (Enforceable corruption verdict in Nigeria boat case), *Daily Norwegian Newspaper Dagbladet*, www.dagbladet.no, published May 15.

Evans, R. (2017). Anti-corruption police investigate UK firm over ex-Nigerian warlord deal, *The Guardian*, www.theguardian.com, published May 14.

Ezeonu, I. (2020). Market criminology: A critical engagement with primitive accumulation in the petroleum extraction industry in Africa, in: Rorie, M.L. (editor), *The Handbook of White-Collar Crime*, Hoboken, NJ: Wiley & Sons, chapter 25, pages 398–417.

Forti, G. and Visconti, A. (2020). From economic crime to corporate violence: The multifaceted harms of corporate crime, in: Rorie, M.L. (editor), *The Handbook of White-Collar Crime*, Hoboken, NJ: John Wiley & Sons, chapter 5, pages 64–80.

Gottfredson, M.R. and Hirschi, T. (1990). *A General Theory of Crime*, Stanford, CA: Stanford University Press.

Hoffmann, J.P. (2002). A contextual analysis of differential association, social control, and strain theories of delinquency, *Social Forces*, 81 (3), 753–785.

Høyesterett (2019). Dom avsagt 13. mai 2019i anke over Borgarting lagmannsretts dom 23. oktober 2018 (Verdict announced May 13, 2019 regarding appeal for Borgarting court's verdict October 23, 2018), *Høyesterett* (Norwegian Supreme Court), Oslo.

Karim, K.E. and Siegel, P.H. (1998). A signal detection theory approach to analyzing the efficiency and effectiveness of auditing to detect management fraud, *Managerial Auditing Journal*, 13 (6), 367–375.

Langton, L. and Piquero, N.L. (2007). Can general strain theory explain white-collar crime? A preliminary investigation of the relationship between strain and select white-collar offenses, *Journal of Criminal Justice*, 35 (1), 1–15.

Leigh, A.C., Foote, D.A., Clark, W.R. and Lewis, J.L. (2010). Equity sensitivity: A triadic measure and outcome/input perspectives, *Journal of Managerial Issues*, 22 (3), 286–305.

Lian, M.B. (2017). *Bjørn Stavrum – Velger å se Fremover (Bjørn Stavrum – Chooses to Look Ahead*, August 29, published online https://www.youtube.com/watch?v=fQwBgiuu4I4.

NTB (2019a). En del av Nigeriabåt-saken opp i Høyesterett (Part of the Nigerian boat case in the Supreme Court), *Daily Norwegian Newspaper Dagbladet*, www.dagbladet.no, published May 1.

Obodaru, O. (2017). Forgone, but not forgotten: Toward a theory of forgone professional identities, *Academy of Management Journal*, 60 (2), 523–553.

Oslo tingrett (2017). Verdict 16–110357MED-OTIR/04, judge Lise Bogen Behrens, *Oslo Tingrett* (Oslo district court), May 16.

Paternoster, R., Jaynes, C.M. and Wilson, T. (2018). Rational choice theory and interest in the "fortune of others", *Journal of Research in Crime and Delinquency*, 54 (6), 847–868.

Pratt, T.C. and Cullen, F.T. (2005). Assessing macro-level predictors and theories of crime: A meta-analysis, *Crime and Justice*, 32, 373–450.

PwC (2014). *Forsvarets logistikkorganisasjon: Rapport etter gjennomgang av salg av fartøy (Military Logistic Organization: Report after Review of Sales of Vessels)*, October 31, Oslo: Auditing Firm PricewaterhouseCoopers.

PwC (2015). *Forsvarsdepartementet: Undersøkelse av forhold knyttet til Forsvarets Avhending av fartøyer (Ministry of Defense: Examination of Circumstances Relatet to the Military's Sale of Vessels)*, March 20, Oslo: Auditing Firm PricewaterhouseCoopers.

Reporter (2013). Nigerians yawn over missing billions, *The Sun*, December 31, published online https://infoweb.newsbank.com/apps/news/document-view?p=AWNB&t=&sort=YMD_date%3AD&maxresults=20&f=advanced&val-base-0=NNPC&fld-base-0=alltext&bln-base-1=and&val-base-1=oil%20revenues&fld-base-1=alltext&bln-base-2=and&val-base-2=2013&fld-base-2=YMD_date&docref=news/14C0EF3456A37C88, retrieved November 3, 2018.

Rodriguez, P., Uhlenbruck, K. and Eden, L. (2005). Government corruption and the entry strategies of multinationals, *Academy of Management Review*, 30 (2), 383–396.

Schnatterly, K., Gangloff, K.A. and Tuschke, A. (2018). CEO wrongdoing: A review of pressure, opportunity, and rationalization, *Journal of Management*, 44 (6), 2405–2432.

Sutherland, E.H. (1983). *White Collar Crime – The Uncut Version*, New Haven, CT: Yale University Press.

Sykes, G.M. and Matza, D. (1957). Techniques of neutralization: A theory of delinquency, *American Sociological Review*, 22 (6), 664–670.

Tufts (2018). *CAS-Global Ltd. and the Private Nigerian Coast Guard Fleet*, Compendium of Arms Trade Corruption, World Peace Foundation, The Fletcher School, Tufts University, published online www.sites.tufts.edu/corruptarmsdeals/.

Welsh, D.T., Ordonez, L.D., Snyder, D.G. and Christian, M.S. (2014). The slippery slope: How small ethical transgressions pave the way for larger future transgressions, *Journal of Applied Psychology*, 100 (1), 114–127.

16 Kraft & Kultur by Ernst & Young

Boris Benulic was the chief executive officer (CEO) at energy company Kraft & Kultur in Sweden, which was a subsidiary of the Norwegian energy corporation Troms Kraft (Nergaard, 2013a, 2013b). It seems that Benulic made the choice of crime based on a perception of benefits exceeding costs as rational, and it seems that behavioral reinforcement of deviance took place over time. His salary increased substantially, as board members believed they observed growth in sales and profits, especially growth in financial contributions to the group and parent company, and the board paid him bonuses for seemingly successful entrepreneurship (Benulic, 2018).

However, in 2012, Troms Kraft hired corporate examiners from global auditing firm Ernst & Young (2012) to conduct an internal investigation at Kraft & Kultur. The examiners were surprised to find a series of emails from Benulic instructing accountants to manipulate figures in such ways that the bottom lines in terms of profits would result in predetermined numbers. For example, in an email dated June 5, 2008, Benulic wrote that the electricity income had to be set in such a way that the income from electricity would result in a sum that made the firm complete at 16.1 million Swedish kroner (about US$1.61 million) in profits after tax (Ernst & Young, 2012: 10):

> Elintäkterna – ta en summa där som gör at vi landar på 16,1 MSEK i resultat etter skatt (Electricity income – take a sum that makes us end up at 16,1 million Swedish kroner in result after tax).

In 2018, the Supreme Court in Sweden upheld the final verdict of 3.5 years in prison for Boris Benulic for accounting fraud (Mo, 2018), which had previously been determined by the district court of Södertörn (2015) and the appellate court of Svea (2017).

White-collar convenience

Boris Benulic argued in court that the prosecution had made allegations based on incorrect and defective investigations. Among other things, the prosecutor did not take into consideration that Kraft & Kultur had different types of electricity agreements, nor did the prosecutor consider the in-depth balance on the issue of accrued income. He further pointed out that he, as the defendant, suffered an unfair trial. He referred to guidelines that a trial must be impartial and independent. Investigator Annicka Holmgren, who the court appointed as an expert, was not objective according to Benulic, because she had worked for Troms Kraft. The company had paid for her investigation and the expertise she stands for.

Benulic blamed start-up problems that Kraft & Kultur had with regard to difficulties in linking electricity consumption to the correct period during billing, and that there had therefore been substantial billing delays, in some cases for several years. He also pointed out that customers had not reported power consumption on time, which contributed to shifts in power costs. Nor with the help of Enita AS, the company that was supposed to help with structuring and consulting, did Kraft & Kultur obtain a complete and correct annual report on accrued revenues. Benulic thus claimed that he had tried as far as he could to make the accounting items for earned annual income as accurate as possible. He blamed low effectiveness and quality of internal controls for potential errors.

In an interview, Benulic envisioned himself as the CEO of Kraft & Kultur to be a major enterprise with headquarters in New York. This illustrates his desire to grow the company and run a large organization (Nødset, 2012: 58):

> The motivation to grow is what usually makes a good CEO. Due to the high competitive pressure, the company had to offer extremely low prices in order to grow and outbid competitors. K&K's competitors could not understand how the company was able to offer such low prices.

In addition to growth and fame, Benulic was also interested in personal financial benefits. When the company seemingly doubled its sales from 2008 and 2010, Benulic's salary almost doubled from 900,000 Swedish kroner (US$ 90,000) to 1600,000 Swedish kroner (US$160,000). While Figure 16.1 illustrates growth by the motive-possibilities-corporate theme, the figure illustrates greed by the motive-possibilities-individual theme.

At the same time, there is also the motive-threats-corporate theme, where the chief executive registered "fake future income that was used to hide losses at K&K" (Nergaard, 2013b: 277).

While Benulic justified his actions as illustrated in Figure 16.1, he also took on the sole responsibility for any mistakes in an email to the board on November 12, 2011, two weeks before the board fired him (Ernst & Young, 2012: 10):

> The chief executive writes in the email that nobody else in the company was involved, and that the mistake is his responsibility alone.

Benulic was a well-known person in Sweden because of his career background as a media reporter, investigative journalist, newspaper editor, participant in public debates, and left-wing politician. People perceived him as charismatic and influential with personal skills to be successful. However, he implemented an

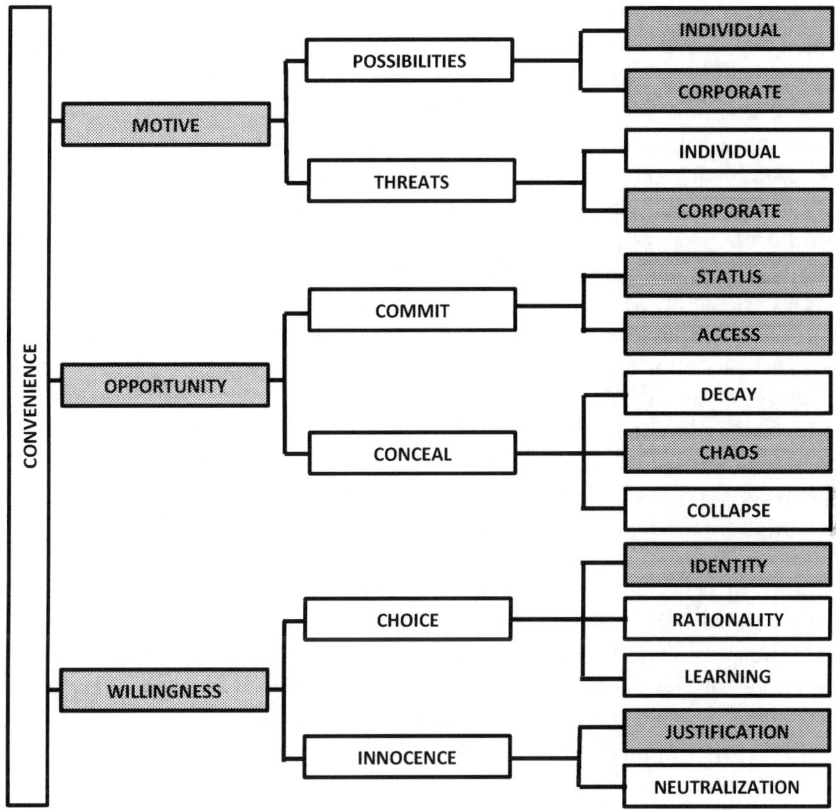

Figure 16.1 Convenience themes in the case of Kraft & Kultur

authoritarian management style when he took on the leadership at Kraft & Kultur (Nødset, 2012).

As illustrated in Figure 16.1, Benulic had high status and convenient access to resources by telling people what to do. He had control over the external auditor Elisabeth Simonssons from auditing firm Grant Thornton (Deloitte, 2013).

Benulic had a strong identification with the business and justified his wrongdoings. Nergaard (2013a) suggests that the opportunity structure also consisted of weak management competence in the parent company Troms Kraft, incompetent and marginal financial management function, minimal and absent control systems, and board members knowing energy but not business.

In the willingness dimension of convenience theory in Figure 16.1, Benulic came to Kraft & Kultur with a tendency to act on both the wrong side and the right side of the law in his previous positions. For example, as a publisher at Ordfront ('Word front') in Sweden, he regularly exceeded his authorization, was reluctant to inform the board about new contracts, and let the company cover his private expenses. When the Ordfront board discovered his wrongdoing, Benulic got the choice of leaving voluntarily, or they would terminate him. The board considered reporting him to the police. However, since that would imply bad publicity, the board instead entered into an agreement with Benulic that he should repay his unjust gain (DN, 2014).

Benulic (2018), on the other hand, has a slightly different version of what happened in his autobiography. He says he had to choose between leaving Ordfront and dismissal after dissatisfying top management, and that he was neither the first nor the last to have conflicts with them. Benulic felt that one of the reasons for the resignation was that the CEO of Ordfront got news of some rumors that employees at the company whispered at times that Benulic had been a better executive than he was. Benulic himself claims in his autobiography that he was not interested in the position, and that he was already mentally elsewhere.

After his time at Ordfront, he started what was to become the precursor and predecessor to Kraft & Kultur, Hellefors Kulturdistribution. However, this company went bankrupt already in 2001. The bankruptcy report shows that in the summer of 2000, the company bought book clubs with associated customer information databases from Ordfront for the equivalent of $200,000. The bankruptcy report emphasizes that this obligation was initially Benulic's personal liability, but that he transferred it to the newly started company. Following the acquisition of clubs and databases, the company's financial situation deteriorated quickly, and the company tried to raise new capital without succeeding. Benulic (2018) tells in his book that Hellefors started running out of money as they had spent a lot on redeeming member registers and customer orders from Ordfront. He does not mention that this was his personal debt. What he does, on the other hand, is to spend many pages reflecting on the desperation he felt when they started running out of money and bankruptcy could become a fact. He says that he spent a lot of time thinking about how to solve the situation. He says that at some point a Hells Angels member who offered to borrow him money contacted him. The next day another person invited him to a deserted cottage where the person offered him a loan. On the third day, the bank called him, telling him that they wanted to lend him four times the amount offered by the previous two. Benulic says he was doubtful about the first two and ended up refusing. The offer from the bank, however, was what made him most frightened. He would rather see the company go bankrupt than accept this loan. So says Benulic (2018) in his autobiography. However, the whole scene seems written in a way that makes it unclear if it actually happened or if this is something he simply made up. He appears distant and strange, especially considering that he writes that borrowing from a bank is the scariest option, without presenting any reasons for it.

Benulic seems to have suffered from narcissistic identification with Kraft & Kultur since he created the business. Narcissistic identification is a special type of narcissism where the offender sees little or no difference between the self and the corporation. The company money is personal money that can be spent whatever way the narcissist prefers (Galvin et al., 2015). While narcissistic grandiosity and admiration belong to the motivational dimension of convenience theory, narcissistic empathy deficit belongs to the willingness dimension of convenience theory where the offender possesses a sense of entitlement (Nichol, 2019). The narcissistic offender shows unreasonable expectations to receive and obtain preferential treatments (Zvi and Elaad, 2018).

Kraft & Kultur was a dormant company from 1998 to 2001. The year 2002 was the first with real business. In 2001, however, several transactions took place with Hellefórs Kulturdistribution in advance of their bankruptcy. Some transactions had no accounting documents at all. These transactions totaled the equivalent of $100,000. The board requested a statement from Benulic on these transactions for the next board meeting. Benulic never made a statement, and the case ended with it.

In the willingness dimension of convenience theory, Benulic was always ambivalent in accepting responsibility. On November 12, 2011, Benulic wrote in an email to the CEO at Troms Kraft that Kraft & Kultur had misleading number in accounts receivable. In the same email, he took on all the blame and wrote that nobody else had been involved. A few days later, he wrote a new email in which he resigned as general manager because of his health condition, but at the same time he wanted to continue in the company in another function. Another couple of days after that he wrote a third email suggesting this time that he can take over the culture part of the company and the employees there as a management buyout (Ernst & Young, 2012).

Benulic later changed his explanation. During the trial in Södertörn (2015) district court, he denied that he had done anything wrong or punishable. Benulic claimed that he always tried to provide a true picture of Kraft & Kultur's finances. He blamed start-up problems. Benulic claimed that he had tried to make the accounting records for billable revenues as accurate as possible. Because he found that the accounting system provided misleading financial results, he manually changed the accounts to show the company's real economic volume. According to himself, he has thus done nothing wrong, since he only manually has entered existing contracts and agreements in the accounts, and thus entered real expected income.

During interviews with fraud examiners from Ernst & Young (2012), Benulic said that he felt that he was not to blame for something going wrong. He named others to blame. Elite members can apply the blame game by misleading attribution to others (Eberly et al., 2011), or they can apply offender humor to distract attention from deviant behavior (Yam et al., 2018). Benulic blamed other executives at Kraft & Kultur for pricing electricity too low. He said during interviews that he relied on other executives' explanations and reports, and that if electricity deliveries subsequently proved to suffer from incorrect pricing, then Troms Kraft should hold other executives accountable.

Another example of misleading attribution in the interviews with Ernst & Young (2012) was when asked if there was any possibility that he had miscalculated. Benulic replied that he could not have been wrong. However, he pointed out that the supporting material, the Excel files, that he got from others might have had errors from manipulation. Benulic's answer might be interpreted as meaning that he admits that something might have been wrong, but that he at the same time slides the responsibility for potential wrongdoing away from himself and over to other executives.

In his autobiography, Benulic (2018) stands completely unaware of the charges against him. He claims that even his lawyers do not understand at all why the prosecutor has indicted him. Benulic points out that he had no personal financial gain from the alleged wrongdoing. He spent much time delegating tasks to other people in the organization. He argues that it would not have been rational for him to manipulate accounts. He had also made it clear to the board of Kraft & Kultur and corporate management that he did not want to be part of the audit work. Benulic uses the last part of his autobiography to explain why it was not he who performed the manipulation. It is thus obvious from reading his autobiography that Benulic does not take on any responsibility, admits no guilt, and argues that nobody should hold him accountable for any wrongdoing.

Benulic seems smart in a strange way. In some of the email examples cited by Ernst & Young (2012), it should normally be difficult for him to explain some formulations away. Phrases like "I can't conjure up the cheat every six months", "the auditors seem to buy all my explanations", and "triumph with them too, soon we can perform in Las Vegas with this act" are all pointing in the direction that he knew he did something that was at best in the gray zone of the law.

During the interviews with examiners, it appears that Benulic on several occasions has been sitting on information about Kraft & Kultur, which he has chosen not to share with the board. For example, Benulic was aware that Troms Kraft had prepared an electricity trading policy, and he was familiar with it. Nevertheless, he decided that Kraft & Kultur should not follow this and not price-hedge the fixed-price contracts. While this convenience theme of Benulic deviating from official policy without reactions from anyone belongs in the opportunity dimension of convenience theory, his ability to convince himself of being right belongs in the willingness dimension. He gave clear instructions to employees at Kraft & Kultur that they could not talk to anyone in other parts of the group about this. Since they were obedient, this phenomenon belongs in the opportunity dimension. Obedience in human behavior is a form of social influence receipt in which a person learns how to adhere to instructions or orders from a person of authority (Baird and Zelin, 2009; Hollow, 2014).

It is thus clear that Benulic deliberately chose to hide information about corporate deviance from the board of directors as well as the group as a whole. Another example is that Benulic, during an interview with examiners, acknowledged that he was aware of weaknesses in the basic documentation of the financial statements, and that he chose not to inform the board about this. In this instance, too, he chose to hide information from the board and the rest of the group.

Benulic admits in his autobiography that during the first years of Kraft & Kultur they engaged in misleading marketing. They marketed themselves as a company that operated within culture and environmental protection, while until 2006 the company offered only green energy in the alleged form of electricity from hydropower. This changed when they in 2006 decided to offer more environmental-friendly products, books, and films. Kraft & Kultur bought power from Nord Pool. That is, they bought energy from a common source, and they thus had no way of telling what proportion of the power they resold would come from renewable sources such as waterfalls. The green energy they marketed might not have been as green as he claimed it to be (Benulic, 2018).

For a while, financial performance at Kraft & Kultur looked good. Margins in 2003 were high due to a currency gain. This foreign exchange gain was not clearly reflected in the accounts and was not reported to the board, as can been seen in the board minutes (Ernst & Young, 2012). It was probably a deliberate act by Benulic to make the revenues for that year look better than what reality could tell.

Deviant personality traits

Elements of pride, patronizing attitude, and lack of sense of or need for belonging are some of the personal attributes of Benulic as an offender. In his autobiography, he says that in the first period at Helleförs Kulturdistribusjon, he worked with two others at their home before renting a small office space in what he calls a bad area in Stockholm. For a while, the three persons worked without pay. Benulic's (2018) formulations seem to indicate that he experienced a great deal of pride and high work ethics among the three because they worked hard despite poor working conditions. Furthermore, he says that at the beginning of the 21st century, it was new and unfamiliar to Swedish customers that they could freely choose electricity providers. He proudly states that Kraft & Kultur carried customers out of prisons where they seemed trapped, and then offered them a better deal. He believes that their initial marketing strategy is the reason why the company became one of Sweden's largest electricity providers a few years later.

In Benulic's testimony as explanation in court, Benulic revealed that he, according to himself, was the only one who could give a correct calculation of accrued income, and thus the correct presentation of the economy and business performance in Kraft & Kultur. According to Benulic, neither systems for accounting nor consultants for auditing were capable of generating correct numbers for expenses and revenues (Södertörn, 2015).

Benulic gives the impression that he has hight thoughts about himself, also relative to other people, in his autobiography. He considers himself an important person, even after conviction and incarceration. He also gives the impression that he has little confidence in professionals such as engineers and lawyers, and the systems in society in general. He thinks he has better knowledge and understanding than others have. This is evident, for example, when he tells about an incident at the bank. He says he noticed that he was an important customer at the bank, which he does not think is strange considering the amounts they borrowed from the bank. Evidence of his importance is the serving of coffee in a porcelain cup rather than a cardboard mug in the bank. In addition, he had the opportunity to review his personal finances during the meeting. However, he is not interested. He describes the bank adviser as a young woman wearing tailor-made clothing and pearl jewelry. He believes that she has not read more than a few lines about the funds she presents. He has devised many questions that he does not ask, because he does not want to offend or embarrass her. He says instead that he would rather put all his money under his mattress than buy funds, as he considers it a better choice considering the world economy. He says this in all seriousness.

Benulic (2018) also writes about several meetings with the chief financial officer at Troms Kraft concerning whether to fix interest rates or not, and he considers these meetings to be completely absurd. He ponders complex financial issues every day and fails to make decisions. Maybe his lack of financial training makes it difficult for him to understand the meaning of meetings. He wonders why they are important, and what is most appropriate to do. He does not trust that the bank adviser in tailor-made clothes can provide relevant information. He is even more puzzled about the woman who recommends a product she does not understand. He notices lack of knowledge among people who make recommendations, which they do not understand themselves.

Benulic is concerned with high work ethics and believes that many people lack it. For example, he feels relief when Hellefórs Kulturdistribution goes bankrupt because he no longer had to deal with others' reluctance on a daily basis toward all demands to make an effort. He also complains that employees will not work overtime without pay (Benulic, 2018).

Benulic (2018) is concerned about what he perceives as people's care to fit in. Sweden is a country with a consensus culture. Already in his time as a journalist, he reacted to other journalists who were more concerned with fitting in than doing a good job and telling the important stories. He describes in his autobiography several situations where he was not at all in agreement with other people. An example is when some representatives from Troms Kraft showed up in Stockholm, and Benulic joined them for dinner. He describes the representatives as seven little drunk dwarves.

An example of him not interested in fitting in is from the first period at Kraft & Kultur, when it was important for the company to sign new customers. He did not want to go. Instead, a young woman went, who he claims was interested in meeting new people, and who was interested in what the customers had to say.

He says he arrived at the office every day and was surprised to see all the strange people. He pauses by the women only discussing silicone, while the men played video games in the lunchroom. He believes that too few read the books and magazines that the company published. He thinks that their hiring is a result of managers who do not want to hire anyone who can challenge their positions in the company. Other executives were only interested in talking about company cars for themselves, about summer resorts, and about where to go on the next holiday. He was thus not encouraged to talk to them either (Benulic, 2018).

It is time to summarize the three dimensions of convenience theory in the case of Boris Benulic. His motives were at several levels. At the global level, he wanted to create a better world by combining energy and culture. At the business level, he wanted to expand so quickly that the company could become a global leader.

At the individual level, illegitimate gain was needed so that he could spend money developing networks nationally and internationally.

In the opportunity dimension of convenience theory, Benulic was powerful, influential, and charismatic. The employees were loyal and obedient. Control mechanisms did not work, neither those locally in Sweden nor those imposed on the company from Troms Kraft in Norway. The corporate structure at Troms Kraft with subsidiaries, one of them being Kraft & Kultur, lacked transparency. There was no organization chart for Kraft & Kultur, and nobody knew who was responsible for what. The board members in the subsidiary Kraft & Kultur were appointed by the parent company Troms Kraft with an emphasis on energy competence rather than business or management competence.

In the willingness dimension of convenience theory, Benulic was used to slide on the slippery slope being sometimes in gray zones. He felt entitled to whatever he did. He used the neutralization technique of denying responsibility.

Fraud examination outcome

Accounting manipulation is the misrepresentation of financial figures for income, costs, and assets. Financial statement fraud in terms of financial information manipulation is a distorted presentation, a misstatement of the financial performance and position of an enterprise. The purpose is to create a false impression of an organization's financial strength (Suh et al., 2020). Accounting manipulation creates an asymmetry of knowledge for readers of financial statements versus creators of financial statements.

Executives might enter income too early into financial statements. For example, CEO Whittaker at Fuji Xerox in New Zealand launched an aggressive sales practice where clients had to sign new contracts before old contracts expired (Deloitte, 2017). The income from new contracts was immediately registered in financial statements (Hamish, 2016; Henderson, 2016).

The external investigation by auditing firm Ernst & Young (2012) found strong indications that revenues were overstated as a result of many years of manipulations. The fraud examination report suggests that CEO Benulic was the main architect of the fraudulent financial reporting, with the help of other executive members of management. Benulic was one of the founders of Kraft & Kultur and was the chief executive in the company from the beginning. He obviously wanted to perform well in his job, and accounting fraud was a convenient avenue for window dressing.

Accounting is of great importance to any organization. A number of employees record a large number and variety of transactions each day. The appearance should reflect the real financial situation at any time to enable relevant decision-making for internal and external stakeholders. Accounting needs to emerge in accordance with the rules, principles, and standards as well as best practices.

The financial management function at Kraft & Kultur never had a strong position. Benulic had the overall responsibility for financial matters and administration from the start in 2001. In 2003, the company board decided to let Benulic manage all company finances and preparations of management accounting. This responsibility was only supposed to last until professional reporting routines were working. However, Benulic remained in charge of financial reporting (Nødset, 2012).

Corporate investigators draw the following conclusions regarding the opportunity structure for Benulic to commit accounting fraud (Ernst & Young, 2012: 7):

- Despite several comments from Kraft & Kultur's auditor, the situation with partly weak internal control continued, especially until 2008.
- The administration was small and person-dependent, and the chief executive had seemingly much power and influence.
- Financial reporting from the administration and Kraft & Kultur throughout the period has been substandard, with some improvements from 2008.
- The corporation introduced in 2008 a unified corporate reporting, which also included Kraft & Kultur. Despite more visible reporting of outstanding income, which was increasing, and especially since 2009, we cannot see that the board at Kraft & Kultur before the year 2011 implemented special actions to reduce the balance amount.
- Through the years, the chief executive had contact and meetings with auditors concerning all questions related to accounting and financial reporting, including outstanding income.

Board members at Kraft & Kultur had knowledge of the energy industry but no competence in management and financial matters (Ernst & Young, 2012). They claimed that they were unable to uncover the fraud, as they felt being victims of manipulation by Benulic (Nødset, 2012). While board members lacked knowledge of financial matters, Benulic as chief executive had complete control over accounting and auditing. In addition, Benulic was "charismatic, authoritarian, and someone who taught himself the energy business in a very short time" (Ernst & Young, 2012: 28). In many companies, internal controls over financial reporting have no priority (Gao and Zhang, 2019).

Private policing evaluation

On November 11, 2011, a whistleblower detected that revenues, and thus financial results at Kraft & Kultur in Sweden, were unrealistically high for a number of years. As a result, there were items in the balance sheet that were incorrect. The mandate for the fraud investigation by Ernst & Young (2012) included the following issues:

- Decision support for the board at Kraft & Kultur. What kind of information did the auditors provide the board and corporate executives?
- Actions taken by the board at Kraft & Kultur. How did they handle information, and what kind of decision-making did take place?

- Information sharing. What quantity and quality of information arrived at board meetings from corporate management?
- Timing of fraud detection. Are there circumstances indicating that detection should have occurred at an earlier point in time?

Fraud examiners do not answer these questions explicitly in their 31-page report. Concerning the latter issue related to timing of fraud detection, fraud examiners phrase the following question on page 16: "When should the board at Kraft and Kultur have reacted and acted?" However, there is no answer to this question in the report. Rather, there are a number of seemingly unrelated quotes from documents and interviews. Based on this short review, the maturity level of the investigation is at level 2 as indicated in Figure 16.2.

However, one might argue that the corporate investigators helped disclose the opportunity structure as cited above and thus deserve maturity level 3 in the figure. A level 3 assessment can be justified by the perspective of a mandate not relevant for fraud examination, where fraud examiners themselves chose to focus on more important issues than the client had asked for. If we consider the mandate to be less relevant, and the actual examination to be more relevant, then the fraud examination deserves level 3.

Nevertheless, level 2 is more appropriate. It is a messy report with quotes from here and there. To deserve a better classification, examiners would need

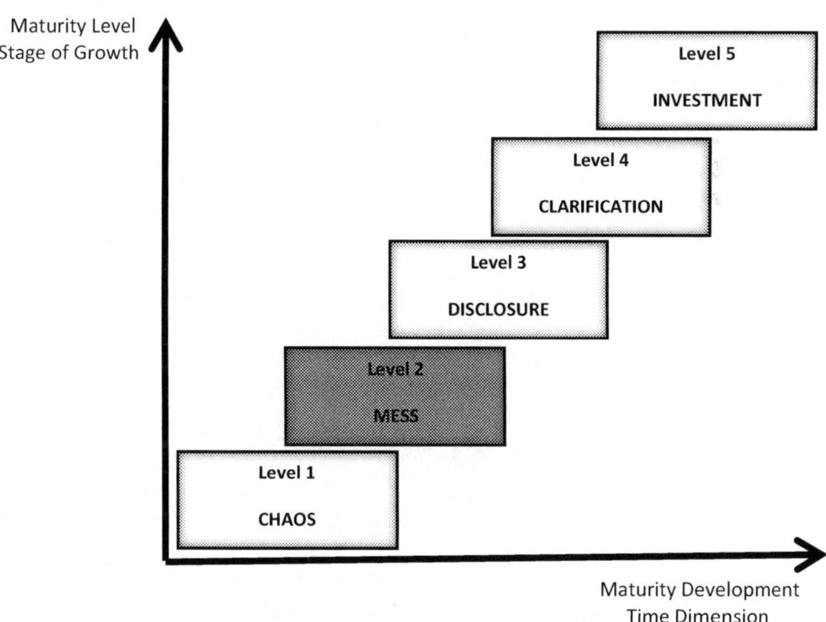

Figure 16.2 Maturity model for internal private investigations applied to Ernst & Young

to structure their investigation in a perspective of reconstructing events and sequences of events in accordance with the mandate. Even though examiners illustrate the opportunity structure, this was no new knowledge anymore when Ernst & Young (2012) presented their report. Troubleshooting teams from the parent company that later resulted in the Nergaard (2013a, 2013b) reports had already identified all the weaknesses that represented the opportunity structure for Benulic.

Bibliography

Baird, J.E. and Zelin, R.C. (2009). An examination of the impact of obedience pressure on perceptions of fraudulent acts and the likelihood of committing occupational fraud, *Journal of Forensic Studies in Accounting and Business*, 1 (1), 1–14.

Benulic, B. (2018). *Inte mitt krig (Not my war)*, Sweden: Cultura Aetatis Publishing.

Deloitte (2013). *Kraft och Kultur i Sverige AB: Utredning av Bolagets revisors arbete i förhållande till god revisionssed i Sverige avseende räkenskapsåren 2007-2017 (Power and Culture in Sweden Limited: Examination of the Company's Auditor's Work in Relation to Good Auditing Practice in Sweden Concerning Accounting Years 2007–2017)*, January 18, Rehnsgatan: Auditing Firm Deloitte.

Deloitte (2017). *Investigation Report*, Independent Investigation Committee, by global auditing firm Deloitte, published June 10, Ito, T., Sato, K. and Nishimura, K., https://www.fujifilmholdings.com/en/pdf/investors/finance/materials/ff_irdata_investigation_001e.pdf.

DN (2014). Denne mannen stolte Troms Kraft 100 prosent på (This man trusted Troms Kraft 100 percent), *Daily Norwegian Business Newspaper Dagens Næringsliv*, www.dn.no, published September 22.

Eberly, M.B., Holley, E.C., Johnson, M.D. and Mitchell, T.R. (2011). Beyond internal and external: A dyadic theory of relational attributions, *Academy of Management Review*, 36 (4), 731–753.

Ernst & Young (2012). *Troms Kraft AS – Gransking av Kraft & Kultur i Sverige AB (Troms Kraft Inc. – Investigation of Kraft & Kultur in Sweden Inc.)*, Oslo: Global Auditing Firm Ernst & Young.

Galvin, B.M., Lange, D. and Ashforth, B.E. (2015). Narcissistic organizational identification: Seeing oneself as central to the organization's identity, *Academy of Management Review*, 40 (2), 163–181.

Gao, P. and Zhang, G. (2019). Accounting manipulation, peer pressure, and internal control, *The Accounting Review*, 94 (1), 127–151.

Hamish, M. (2016). SFO closes Fuji Xerox probe, *The Press*, December 24, https://infoweb.newsbank.com/apps/news/document-view?p=AWNB&t=&sort=YMD_date%3AD&maxresults=20&f=advanced&val-base-0=fuji%20xerox&fld-base-0=alltext&bln-base-2=and&val-base-2=new%20zealand&fld-base-2=alltext&bln-base-3=and&val-base-3=2016&fld-base-3=YMD_date&docref=news/16175F5693A0BFF0.

Henderson, J. (2016). Neil Whittaker exits as local Fuji Xerox MD in shock departure, *ARN Net*, published May 18, https://www.arnnet.com.au/article/600045/shock-departure-neil-whittaker-exits-local-fuji-xerox-md/.

Hollow, M. (2014). Money, morals and motives, *Journal of Financial Crime*, 21 (2), 174–190.

Mo, M.L. (2018). Nå må Boris Benulic sone i fengsel (Now Boris Benulic must be jailed), *Online Newspaper iTromsø*, www.itromso.no, published May 8.

Nergaard, L.L. (2013a). *Sammendrag av Granskingsrapport – Troms Kraft AS (Summary of Investigation Report – Troms Kraft Inc.)*, Norway: Norscan Partners.

Nergaard, L.L. (2013b). *Granskingsrapport Mandat 5: Kraft & Kultur (Investigation Report Mandate 5: Kraft & Kultur)*, Norway: Norscan Partners.

Nichol, J.E. (2019). The effects of contract framing on misconduct and entitlement, *The Accounting Review*, 94 (3), 329–344.

Nødset, I.F. (2012). *Earnings Management Environment with the Case of Troms Kraft*, Master of Science thesis, December 19, Norwegian School of Economics, Bergen.

Suh, I., Sweeny, J.T., Linke, K. and Wall, J.M. (2020). Boiling the frog slowly: The immersion of C-suite financial executives into fraud, *Journal of Business Ethics*, 162, 645–673.

Svea (2017). *Case B 5582–12, Svea hovrätt (Svea Court of Appeals)*, Sweden, November 29.

Södertörn (2015). *Case B 5582–12, Södertörns tingsrätt (Södertörn District Court)*, Sweden, July 8.

Yam, K.C., Christian, M.S., Wei, W., Liao, Z. and Nai, J. (2018). The mixed blessing of leader sense of humor: Examining costs and benefits, *Academy of Management Journal*, 61 (1), 348–369.

Zvi, L. and Elaad, E. (2018). Correlates of narcissism, self-reported lies, and self-assessed abilities to tell and detect lies, tell truths, and believe others, *Journal of Investigative Psychology and Offender Profiling*, 15, 271–286.

17 Private policing costs

Private policing of economic crime by fraud examiners who conduct an internal investigation represents an investment for the client organization. The client organization harmed by a scandal invests in an internal fraud examination conducted by external experts to help solve the crisis. A crisis can be a fundamental threat to an organization often characterized by particular ambiguity of cause, effect, and means of resolution (König et al., 2020). An investment should be profitable in terms of benefits exceeding costs. However, both costs and benefits are hard to establish for private policing. First, disclosure of investigation reports is the exception rather than the rule after private policing (Gottschalk and Tchnerni-Buzzeo, 2017). Next, even in the rare instances of disclosure to the media and the public, leading to case studies as described in this book, an investigation report never includes a figure for the price paid by the client to the examiner. Finally, even when it is possible to detect the price paid as a figure for the costs, the benefits are not at all obvious. One has to speculate what kind of benefits can result from private policing of economic crime. In such a speculation, one needs to have a wide range of options for benefits. For example, a client organization told that they gladly paid the equivalent of US$1 million for an investigation, even though there was nothing new in the report. The benefit for the client was simply that someone outside said in the report, more or less exactly, the same as corporate management had said all along. Having someone externally conduct an independent review and concluding that management is right was worth much more than 1 million dollars, according to the spokesperson for the client organization.

In this chapter, the maturity level of the investigation as a substitute and indication of benefits replace actual unknown benefits. We assume that fraud examinations at level 5 in the maturity model implicitly represent profitable investments where benefits exceed costs.

In some instances, the price for private policing of economic crime becomes a variable. In one case, where Troms Kraft was investigated by Nergaard (2013a, 2013b) in the aftermath of the Kraft & Kultur investigation by Ernst & Young (2012), the client organization refused to reimburse the examiner for all expenses (DN, 2013). In another case, the Oceanteam investigation by Sands (2019a, 2019b), the examiner asked for more funding and got it (Riisnæs, 2018).

This chapter starts by presenting fraud examination reports that business students evaluated in the spring term 2019. Then the chapter moves into the cases presented in this book.

Reviewed policing reports 2019

Business students evaluated some of the reports listed in Appendix A of this book in the previous spring term 2019. Table 17.1 lists reports that students evaluated. Students and faculty were able to find out what clients had paid examiners, even though reports never include such information. The final column lists identified investigation costs in Norwegian kroner, where the exchange rate varies between 7 and 10 kroner for each US dollar. Information on some prices was unobtainable, and those investigations receive an estimate of 1 million kroner in the table, which is an average cost for other reports. The most expensive investigation was at 210 million Norwegian kroner to law firm Bruun Hjejle paid by Danske Bank. The most inexpensive investigation was at 250,000 kroner for Flyktningetjenesten and Tidal. The average for an investigation is 8 million, while the median is 1 million kroner.

Table 17.1 lists the number of student papers on evaluation of each investigation report, the average maturity level suggested in the student papers, and the number of page in each report of investigation. While the sample of 31 investigations is too small for statistical analysis, it is interesting to note that only one of the investigations receives the highest maturity score of 5. In the FilmCamp case, the examination task was simple, and there is only one student paper for this investigation. Nevertheless, the investigation represents an investment as benefits exceeded costs according to the student's evaluation. Most investigations are at the disclosure level (2.5–3.5) and the clarification level (3.5–4.5) with 13 at the disclosure level and 10 at the clarification level.

The most striking result from student evaluations is the fraud examination by law firm Bruun Hjejle at the Danish bank Danske Bank. This investigation was the most frequently reviewed by students with 38 student papers evaluating the work by Bruun Hjejle (2018). The examination was also the most expensive investigation by far, costing 210 million Danish kroner that are approximately US$30 million. While there were variations in student assessments, the average maturity level is only 3.41 in the disclosure level (2.5–3.5), which indicates that the examination had obvious shortcomings. At that level, the costs of the investigation probably exceed the benefits. The benefits expected by Danske Bank seemed not sufficient, which was to clarify facts, implement internal corrective actions, and then close the case of suspected money laundering for Russian oligarchs and other nonresident bank customers (Moscow Times, 2017; Ritzau, 2019). Rather, since the report only supplied indications and no solid evidence, both shareholders and other stakeholders became dissatisfied and decided to sue the bank and the former chief executive officer Thomas Borgen (Högseth, 2019; Lund, 2019). In addition, the serious fraud office in Denmark was dissatisfied with the Bruun Hjejle (2018) report and decided to launch a police

Table 17.1 Prices in Norwegian kroner that clients paid for investigations reviewed in 2019

S. No.	*Private policing at suspicion of economic crime by fraud examiners conducting internal investigations at client organizations*	*Student papers*	*Investigation maturity*	*Pages in the report*	*Price paid for the investigation*
1	Bergensklinikkene *private health clinic.* Ernst & Young *auditing firm 2019. Subsidy fraud*	15	3.71	59	*1,000,000*
2	Bårlidalen *public water waste site.* Svendby *consulting firm 2016. Fraud by overbilling the municipality*	1	3.00	80	**1,100,000**
3	Dale *property development.* Komrev. Rogaland *public audit 2015. Public funds spent on private vacations*	1	4.00	82	*1,000,000*
4	Danske Bank *banking.* Bruun & Hjejle *law firm 2018. Money laundering in Estonian branch*	38	3.41	87	**210,000,000**
5	FilmCamp *public fund for productions.* Komrev. Nord *public audit 2016. Fraud*	1	5.00	90	*1,000,000*
6	Flyktningtjenesten *public refugee funding.* Buunk et al. *internal audit 2015. Embezzlement*	5	4.00	30	**250,000**
7	Fredrikstad *municipality.* PwC *auditing firm 2018. VAT fraud by public company*	1	3.00	78	**1,200,000**

(*Continued*)

Table 17.1 Continued

S. No.	*Private policing at suspicion of economic crime by fraud examiners conducting internal investigations at client organizations*	*Student papers*	*Investigation maturity*	*Pages in the report*	*Price paid for the investigation*
8	Fredrikstad *municipality.* Simonsen *law firm 2018. VAT fraud by public company*	3	3.00	100	**1,200,000**
9	Fyrlykta *foundation childcare.* Deloitte *auditing firm 2017. Fraud of public funds for excessive salaries*	3	3.67	70	**500,000**
10	Fyrlykta *foundation childcare.* Stiftelsestilsynet *public examination 2018. Fraud of public funds*	1	2.00	28	*1,000,000*
11	Helse Nord *hospital.* PwC *auditing firm 2018. Fraud at executive removal from position*	5	4.00	40	**600,000**
12	Jondal *municipality.* SBDL *law firm 2018. Corruption and private enterprise*	1	3.00	36	*1,000,000*
13	Karasjok *municipality.* Vest-Finnmark *public audit 2018. Friends got illegitimate favors*	1	3.00	52	*1,000,000*
14	Klengstua *kinderegarden.* Halden *municipal internal audit 2019. Fraud in subsidies from municipality*	1	2.00	20	*1,000,000*

(*Continued*)

Table 17.1 Continued

S. No.	*Private policing at suspicion of economic crime by fraud examiners conducting internal investigations at client organizations*	*Student papers*	*Investigation maturity*	*Pages in the report*	*Price paid for the investigation*
15	Kvalsund *municipality.* Vest-Finnmark *public audit 2012. Frudulent consulting fees*	1	2.00	101	**750,000**
16	Larvik *municipality.* Komrev. Telemark *public audit 2017. Corruption in container terminal*	1	4.00	92	**1,300,000**
17	Lyoness-Lyconet *gambling enterprise.* Stiftelsestilsynet *public examination 2018. Pyramid scheme*	1	2.00	25	**1,100,000**
18	NDLA *public learning software.* Deloitte *auditing firm 2015. Private abuse of public funds*	1	3.00	57	*1,000,000*
19	Norwegian Poker Team *private gambling.* Aftenposten *media 2018. Money laundering at poker game*	1	3.00	20	**6,500,000**
20	Næringsdepartement *department of industry.* Ernst & Young *auditing firm 2018. Embezzlement by executive*	1	2.00	49	**770,000**
21	Orange *health services provider.* Bergen municipality *audit function 2016. Fraud by executive*	3	2.50	60	*1,000,000*

(*Continued*)

Table 17.1 Continued

S. No.	*Private policing at suspicion of economic crime by fraud examiners conducting internal investigations at client organizations*	*Student papers*	*Investigation maturity*	*Pages in the report*	*Price paid for the investigation*
22	Oslo Boligbygg *municipal housing.* Deloitte *auditing firm 2018. Corruption in public procurement*	3	4.00	593	**13,300,000**
23	Oslo Boligbygg *municipal housing.* Komrev. Oslo *public audit 2018 Corruption at procurement*	1	1.00	88	*1,000,000*
24	Oslo Bymiljø *municipal parks.* Ernst & Young *auditing firm 2019. Fraud by fake invoicing of park works*	1	3.00	28	*1,000,000*
25	Oslo Omsorgsbygg *housing administration.* PwC *auditing firm 2009. Abuse of public funds*	1	3.00	21	**691,000**
26	Re *municipality.* Komrev. Vestfold *public audit 2015. Insurance fraud by putting a building on fire*	1	1.00	81	*1,000,000*
27	Statoil *energy.* Østby et al. *internal controllers 2017. Cost savings in security measures causing accident*	1	4.00	107	*1,000,000*

(*Continued*)

Table 17.1 Continued

S. No.	*Private policing at suspicion of economic crime by fraud examiners conducting internal investigations at client organizations*	*Student papers*	*Investigation maturity*	*Pages in the report*	*Price paid for the investigation*
28	Tidal music *streaming service.* NTNU *research group 2018. Fraudulent manipulation of accounting*	10	2.50	78	**250,000**
29	Tolga *municipality.* Fylkesmann *public examination 2019. Fraudulent diagnoses for retarded inhabitants*	27	2.70	51	**1,600,000**
30	Vestvågøy *municipality.* Komrev. Nord *public audit 2018. Illegal public procurement*	1	4.00	57	*1,000,000*
31	Vistamar *rehabilitation center.* Komrev. Trondheim *public audit 2018. Embezzlement by executive*	2	4.00	92	**1,100,000**

investigation into the matter of money laundering in Danske Bank's Estonian branch (Sivertsen, 2018). Consequently, Danske Bank lost the handle of the matter, and the investigation did not achieve any substantial benefits for the bank as the client of the investigating law firm, according to business school students in the spring term 2019.

Reviewed policing reports 2020

In addition to the price paid to examiners for their work after submission of their reports to the clients, there are internal costs in the client organizations related to the investigations. Executives have to spend time defining a mandate and monitoring internal access provided to examiners. Informants, witnesses, and suspects have to spend time in interviews with examiners. Rumors, accusations, and passivity leading to lower efficiency and effectiveness can also result from the ongoing investigation, which represent extraordinary costs or extraordinary fall in revenues. While such internal costs can be formidable, we have no way of estimating them for each private policing case. Therefore, these internal costs are a relevant topic here, yet they are not part of the discussion in the following.

Focusing on the prices paid by public and private organizations to global auditing firms and local law firms reveals a large spectrum of prices. The cheapest reviewed in 2019 had a price tag of 250,000 kroner, while the most expensive had a price tag of 210 million Norwegian kroner in Table 17.1. The main cost-driving factors seem to be hours and travel.

Our sample the following year has even greater diversity, as listed in Table 17.2. The most expensive one was by far the investigation of money laundering suspicions by Clifford Chance at Swedbank, where the bank paid 1.9 billion Swedish kroner (approximately US$190 million).

The first column in Table 17.2 lists the investigation maturity level suggested in this book. The later column for investigation maturity level is the average of student responses in their term papers in the spring 2020.

The final column in Table 17.2 lists prices paid by client organizations to examination firms. The empty spaces in the column indicate that it was impossible to obtain information on those private policing assignments.

The first column in Table 17.2 lists maturity levels as presented in chapters in this book for each reviewed private policing report. The first policing report was concerned with Caverion suspected of financial crime in terms of substandard wages and long working hours, both representing violations of the Norwegian working environment act. Law firm Wiersholm (2019) wrote the private policing report after their investigation at Caverion. The chapter on Caverion in this book assessed the maturity level at 4, on a stage model from 1 to 5. One student paper evaluated the Wiersholm (2019) investigation and suggested an investigation maturity of three rather than four. This is no major discrepancy since it likely reflects a potential difference in criteria used to assess maturity as well as the implicit importance and weight for applied criteria.

The second policing report was concerned with executives at Ferde suspected of financial crime in terms of abuse of role conflicts. Law firm Kluge (2019) wrote the policing report after their investigation at Ferde. The chapter on Kluge at Ferde in this book assessed the maturity level at 2, on a stage model from 1 to 5. Twenty-five student papers evaluated the Kluge (2019) investigation and suggested an investigation maturity of 2.8 on average. Among the 25 papers, there was level 1 in one paper, level 2 in 9 papers, level 3 in 10 papers, level 4 in 4 papers, and level 5 in 1 paper. This distribution indicates a lack of consistency in terms of definition of maturity levels, lack of consistency in terms of criteria to evaluate maturity levels, and lack of consistency in terms of importance and weight for each criterion. However, the spread of responses also indicates a normal distribution, where the most frequent responses are levels 2 and 3.

Table 17.2 Prices in Norwegian kroner that clients paid for investigations reviewed in 2020

Maturity	*Private policing at suspicion of economic crime by fraud examiners conducting internal investigations at client organizations*	*Student papers*	*Investigation maturity*	*Pages in the report*	*Price paid for the investigation*
4.0	Caverion *subcontractor services.* Wiersholm *law firm 2019. Substandard wages and hours*	1	3.0	53	
2.0	Ferde *toll collection.* Kluge *law firm 2019. Conflict of interest for chief executive at procurement*	25	2.8	40	**1,000,000**
1.0	Ferde *toll collection.* Deloitte *auditing firm 2020. Abuse of position at chaotic mergers*	3	3.0	88	**650,000**
3.0	FIFA *football association.* Garcia *special committee 2014. Corruption at allocation of World Cup*	0	–	359	
4.0	Helgelandssykehuset *public hospital.* KPMG (2019, 2020) *auditing firm. Working environment abuses*	0	–	149	
4.0	Moldova *Banca de Economii Sociala.* Kroll *investigation firm 2015, 2017, 2018a,b,c. Brank fraud by loans transfer*	1	4.0	142	

(*Continued*)

Table 17.2 Continued

Maturity	*Private policing at suspicion of economic crime by fraud examiners conducting internal investigations at client organizations*	*Student papers*	*Investigation maturity*	*Pages in the report*	*Price paid for the investigation*
4.0	Oceanteam *offshore services.* Sands *law firm 2019. Abuse of company money by majority shareholder*	2	2.5	288	**9,000,000**
4.0	Oslo Boligbygg *municipal housing.* Deloitte *auditing firm 2019. Fraud at over-priced procurement*	6	3.3	82	
4.0	Oslo Energigjenvinning *public recycling.* PwC *auditing firm 2019. Fraud by abuse of working hours*	5	3.6	154	**2,100,000**
4.0	Samherji *fishing industries.* Al Jazeera *investigative journalists 2019. Corruption in Namibia*	1	4.0	14	
2.0	Socialstyrelsen *social security.* PwC *auditing firm 2019. Embezzlement by trusted employee*	3	4.3	80	**970,000**
1.0	Socialstyrelsen *social security.* Kammeradvokaten *law firm 2019. Executive lack of guardianship*	0	–	163	

(Continued)

Table 17.2 Continued

Maturity	*Private policing at suspicion of economic crime by fraud examiners conducting internal investigations at client organizations*	*Student papers*	*Investigation maturity*	*Pages in the report*	*Price paid for the investigation*
2.0	Swedbank banking. Clifford Chance *law firm 2020. Money laundering in Baltic states*	4	4.0	218	**1,900,000,000**
2.0	XXL *sports store chain.* DLA Piper *law firm 2020. Price fixing for market manipulation*	56	3.3	41	**2,500,000**
1.0	Forsvaret *military logistics.* PwC *auditing firm 2014. Corruption in military sales unit*	(30)	(3.6)	35	
4.0	Forsvaret *department of defense.* PwC *auditing firm 2015. Illegal profits from sale of vessels*	(30)	(3.6)	50	
2.0	Kraft & Kultur *energy enterprise.* Ernst & Young *auditing firm 2012. Accounting fraud*	0	–	31	

The discrepancy between this book and student papers in terms of maturity assessment becomes visible in the third policing report. While three student papers suggested 2, 3, and 4, respectively, for maturity levels, the relevant chapter in this book suggests maturity level 1. An explanation for the discrepancy is the overall understanding of the investigation. The reviews in this book emphasize whether or not an investigation resulted in new insights and improved understanding of events. This might be an unfair perspective on some investigations. For example, the Deloitte (2020) investigation at Kluge is mainly concerned with procedures, roles, and rules that might improve the situation at Ferde. The investigation was thus less concerned with detection and more concerned with recommendations. Maybe students had this perspective in mind when assessing the maturity level.

When moving down in Table 17.2 to the investigations by PwC (2014, 2015) concerned with the case of navy logistics where commander Bjørn Stavrum later was sentenced to prison for corruption, this book presents maturity assessments of 1 and 4, respectively, for the two investigations. Students did not distinguish between both reports and assigned 3.6 to both of them as an average. Therefore, the numbers have brackets in the table.

Students could choose what investigation to evaluate. Most students chose the investigation of the sports store chain XXL that law firm DLA Piper (2020) investigated. XXL faced the suspicion of fixing pre-prices so that discounted prices emerged with substantial discounts. Among the 56 student papers, there was level 1 in one paper, level 2 in 10 papers, level 3 in 21 papers, level 4 in 20 papers, and level 5 in 4 papers. Again, there is a pattern of normal distribution, this time around levels 3 and 4. The relevant chapter in this book suggests a maturity level of 2 for this investigation.

All reviewed policing reports

In a business perspective, the client can consider private policing by fraud examiners as an investment that should be profitable. Cost-benefit analysis is a way to compare the costs and benefits of an intervention such as private policing of economic crime, where both costs and benefits transform in monetary units. Costs include those monetary consequences of implementing an intervention. Benefits include those monetary consequences resulting from an intervention. An investment in private policing of economic crime by fraud examiners is profitable if the intervention causes more benefits than costs.

Table 17.3 repeats the list of examination reports in Appendix A by focusing on costs and profitability. While costs are limited to the price paid by the client to the examiner, benefits are limited to the monetary equivalent of maturity levels as exemplified in this book, supplemented by other information about benefits in each case study. Profitability is whether benefits exceed costs. Monetary units of benefits are not included in the table because of lacking information. Instead, the table implicitly indicates the benefits by concluding on profitability in each case.

The monetary unit is US$ for all investigations listed in Table 17.3. The exchange rate for Danish, Norwegian, and Swedish kroner varies, but for simplicity it is assumed in the table to be 10 kroner for each dollar for all three kinds of kroner.

The table includes monetary information for those cases where the investigation price was available. Investigation prices that were not available are included in italics. The prices in italics in the cost column represent estimates of the actual

Table 17.3 Costs for private policing in US dollars

Investigated organization	*Investigating organization*	*Costs*	*Profitable*
Bangladesh			
Padakhep Save the Children	Office of the Inspector General	*200,000*	No
Canada			
Niagara municipality	Ombudsman of Ontario	*50,000*	No
Pelham town	KPMG auditing firm	*100,000*	Yes
Denmark			
Danske Bank banking	Bruun & Hjejle law firm	**21,000,000**	No
Region Syddanmark public	Kromann Reumert law firm	*500,000*	Yes
Socialstyrelsen social security	PwC auditing firm	**97,000**	Yes
Socialstyrelsen social security	Kammeradvokaten law firm	*200,000*	No
Ghana			
BioFuel bioenergy production	Kluge law firm	*20,000*	Yes
Iceland			
Samherji fishing industries	Al Jazeera investigative	*200,000*	Yes
Japan			
Olympus digital equipment	Deloitte auditing firm	*300,000*	Yes
Toshiba digital equipment	Deloitte auditing firm	*300,000*	Yes
Moldova			
Moldova Banca de Economii	Kroll investigation firm	*4,000,000*	No
The Netherlands			
Oceanteam offshore services	Sands law firm	**900,000**	Yes
New Zealand			
FujiFilm digital equipment	Deloitte auditing firm	*300,000*	Yes
Nigeria			
Nigerian National Petroleum	PwC auditing firm	*200,000*	No
Norway			
Adecco nursing home	Wiersholm law firm	*100,000*	Yes
Ahus hospital	PwC auditing firm	*50,000*	Yes
Andebu municipality	BDO auditing firm	*50,000*	No
Arendal traffic station	Internal audit function	*50,000*	Yes
Askøy municipality	BDO auditing firm	*50,000*	No
Bergen municipality	Internal control function	*50,000*	No
Bergen havn port authority	Havarikommisjon commission	*50,000*	No

(*Continued*)

Table 17.3 Continued

Investigated organization	*Investigating organization*	*Costs*	*Profitable*
Bergensklinikkene clinic	Ernst & Young auditing firm	*100 000*	Yes
Betanien foundation	BDO auditing firm	*300,000*	Yes
Briskeby public sports arena	Lynx law firm	*200,000*	No
Bærum municipality	G-partner law firm	*100,000*	Yes
Bårlidalen public water waste	Svendby consulting firm	**110,000**	Yes
Caverion subcontractor	Wiersholm law firm	*200,000*	No
Dale property development	Komrev. Rogaland audit	*50,000*	Yes
Demokratene political party	Partirevisjon internal control	*50 000*	No
DNB banking	Hjort law firm	**600,000**	No
Drammen municipality	Deloitte auditing firm	*200,000*	Yes
Eckbo foundations	Thommessen law firm	*300,000*	Yes
Fadderbarna foundation	BDO auditing firm	*300 000*	No
Ferde toll collection	Kluge law firm	**100,000**	No
Ferde toll collection	Deloitte auditing firm	**65,000**	No
FilmCamp public fund	Komrev. Nord public audit	*100,000*	Yes
Fjell municipality	Deloitte auditing firm	*200 000*	No
Flyktningtjenesten public	Buunk et al. internal audit	**25,000**	Yes
Forsvaret military contracts	Dalseide special committee	*100,000*	No
Forsvaret military logistics	PwC auditing firm	*200,000*	No
Forsvaret ministry	PwC auditing firm	*200,000*	No
Fredrikstad municipality	PwC auditing firm	**120,000**	Yes
Fredrikstad municipality	Simonsen law firm	**120 000**	Yes
Fretex Salvation Army	Grette law firm	**200,000**	Yes
Furuheim nursing home	Hald law firm	*90,000*	Yes
Fyrlykta child care	Deloitte auditing firm	**50,000**	Yes
Fyrlykta child care	Stiftelsestilsynet public	*50 000*	No
Gartnerhallen fruits	Wiersholm law firm	*500,000*	Yes
Gassnova public projects	BDO auditing firm	*20,000*	No
Grimstad municipality	BDO auditing firm	*30,000*	No
Grimstad municipality	Hjort law firm	*20,000*	No
Grimstad municipality	Tinia consulting firm	*40,000*	No
Hadeland broadband	PwC auditing firm	*40,000*	No
Hadeland energy supply	PwC auditing firm	*40,000*	No
Halden skating hall	KPMG auditing firm	*50 000*	No
Halden municipality buildings	Hjort law firm	*50,000*	No
Hedmark municipality	Wiersholm law firm	*70,000*	No

(*Continued*)

Table 17.3 Continued

Investigated organization	*Investigating organization*	*Costs*	*Profitable*
Helgelandssykehuset hospital	KPMG auditing firm	*110,000*	Yes
Helse Nord hospital	PwC auditing firm	**60,000**	No
Hordaland police department	Wiersholm law firm	*400,000*	No
Hordaland police department	Stamina consulting firm	*50,000*	No
Jondal municipality	SBDL law firm	*100,000*	No
Karasjok municipality	Vest-Finnmark public audit	*70,000*	No
Kjøpsvik municipality	Komrev. Nord public audit	*50,000*	No
Klengstua kindergarden	Halden municipal audit	*50,000*	No
Kommunaldepartement	BDO auditing firm	*60,000*	No
Kragerø shipping	Deloitte auditing firm	*50,000*	Yes
Kristiansand municipality	Komrev. Agder public audit	*50,000*	No
Kristiansand municipality	Tofte law firm	*100,000*	No
Kvalsund municipality	Vest-Finnmark public audit	**75,000**	No
Kvam Auto car dealer	Wikborg law firm	**200,000**	Yes
Kvinnherad municipality	Deloitte auditing firm	*70,000*	No
Langemyhr building company	PwC auditing firm	*50,000*	No
Larvik havn port authority	Komrev. Telemark audit	*50,000*	No
Larvik municipality	Komrev. Telemark audit	**130,000**	No
Leksvik municipality	Midt-Norge audit	*50,000*	No
Lenvik municipality	KomRev audit	*50,000*	No
Lunde transportation	Vierdal law firm	*200,000*	Yes
Lyoness-Lyconet gambling	Stiftelsestilsynet public	**110,000**	Yes
Moskvaskolen school	Ernst & Young auditing firm	*100,000*	No
NAV social security authority	Wiersholm law firm	*500,000*	Yes
NDLA learning software	Deloitte auditing firm	*100,000*	Yes
NFF players association	Lynx law firm	*70,000*	Yes
NIF sports association	BDO auditing firm	*70,000*	Yes
Norsk Tipping public betting	Deloitte auditing firm	*60,000*	No
Norwegian Poker Team	Aftenposten media	**650,000**	No
Næringsdepartement	PwC auditing firm	*70 000*	No
Næringsdepartement	Ernst & Young auditing firm	77,000	No
Orange health services	Bergen municipality audit	*60,000*	No
Oslo Boligbygg housing	BDO auditing firm	*400,000*	Yes
Oslo Boligbygg housing	Deloitte auditing firm	**1,330,000**	No
Oslo Boligbygg housing	Komrev. Oslo audit	**50,000**	Yes
Oslo Boligbygg housing	Deloitte auditing firm	**115,000**	Yes

(*Continued*)

Table 17.3 Continued

Investigated organization	*Investigating organization*	*Costs*	*Profitable*
Oslo Bymiljø municipal parks	Ernst & Young auditing	*100,000*	Yes
Oslo Energy recovery	PwC auditing firm	**210,000**	No
Oslo Lindeberg nursing home	Kommunerevisjon audit	*50,000*	No
Oslo Omsorgsbygg housing	PwC auditing firm	**69,100**	Yes
Oslo Omsorgsbygg housing	Komrev. Oslo public audit	*50,000*	No
Oslo Omsorgsbygg housing	PwC auditing firm	*300,000*	No
Oslo Renovasjon garbage	Deloitte auditing firm	*1,000,000*	No
Oslo Samferdsel transport	PwC auditing firm	*500,000*	No
Oslo municipal school	Kommunerevisjon audit	*50,000*	No
Oslo municipal school	Kommunerevisjon audit	*50,000*	No
Oslo Unibuss transport	Wiersholm law firm	*300,000*	Yes
Oslo Vei public transport	Kvale law firm	*300,000*	Yes
Politiets utlending police	KPMG auditing firm	*200,000*	No
Rana municipality	PwC auditing firm	*70,000*	No
Re municipality	Komrev. Vestfold audit	*70,000*	No
Romanifolket foundation	Stiftelsestilsynet public	*50,000*	Yes
Romerike Vannverk	Distriktsrevisjon audit	*200,000*	Yes
Sandefjord municipality	Tenden law firm	*30,000*	Yes
Siva state funding	Wikborg law firm	*50,000*	Yes
Skien municipality	BDO auditing firm	*70,000*	No
Skjervøy municipality	KomRev public audit	*50,000*	Yes
Stangeskovene forest	Ernst & Young auditing firm	*2,000,000*	Yes
Statoil energy	Hagen et al. controllers	*100,000*	Yes
Statoil energy	Saure et al. controllers	*100,000*	Yes
Statoil energy	Østby et al. controllers	*100,000*	Yes
Stavanger municipality	PwC auditing firm	*200,000*	No
Sykehusapotekene	Moberg Segrov consulting	*100,000*	No
Sykehusbygg hospital	Kluge law firm	*100,000*	No
Sykehuset Innlandet hospital	Haavind law firm	*100,000*	Yes
Telenor VimpelCom mobile	Deloitte auditing firm	**1,500,000**	No
Tennisforbundet tennis	Lewis et al. consulting firm	*100,000*	No
Tidal music streaming service	NTNU research group	**25,000**	No
Tjøme municipality	BDO auditing firm	*100,000*	No
Tolga municipality	Fylkesmann public	**160,000**	No
Tomter shopping center	Holmen auditing firm	*100,000*	Yes

(*Continued*)

Table 17.3 Continued

Investigated organization	*Investigating organization*	*Costs*	*Profitable*
Transocean oil rig company	Riksadvokaten prosecutor	*100,000*	No
Trendtech investments	Finanstilsynet public audit	*50,000*	No
Troms Kraft energy company	Norscan consulting firm	**4,200,000**	No
Universitetssykehuset Nord	Arbeidsrettsadvokatene	*100,000*	No
Uppsala municipality	KPMG auditing firm	*100,000*	No
Utenriksdepartement ministry	Kontrollenhet internal audit	*50,000*	No
Utenriksdepartement ministry	Kontrollenhet internal audit	*50,000*	No
Utlendingsdirektoratet	Deloitte auditing firm	*200,000*	No
Verdibanken banking	Wiersholm law firm	*100,000*	Yes
Vestre Viken hospital	PwC auditing firm	*200,000*	Yes
Vestvågøy municipality	Komrev. Nord public audit	*100,000*	No
Videoforhandlere series	BDO auditing firm	*100,000*	No
Vistamar rehabilitation center	Komrev. Trondheim audit	**110,000**	No
Vitalegruppen private nursing	BDO auditing firm	*200,000*	No
World Ventures gaming	Stiftelsestilsynet public	*50,000*	No
XXL sports store chain	DLA Piper law firm	**250,000**	No
Zachariasbryggen property	Selmer law firm	*200,000*	No
Sweden			
Karolinska hospital	Setterwalls law firm	*400,000*	Yes
Kraft & Kultur energy	Ernst & Young auditing firm	*200,000*	Yes
Nordea banking	Mannheimer Swartling	*3,000,000*	Yes
Swedbank banking	Clifford Chance law firm	**190,000,000**	No
Switzerland			
FIFA football association	Garcia special committee	*10,000,000*	Yes
The United Kingdom			
Sandstorm bank	PwC auditing firm	*500,000*	No
The United States			
British Petroleum offshore	Freeh special committee	*4,000,000*	Yes
Coatesville school district	BDO auditing firm	*1,000,000*	No
Coatesville school district	Contrad O'Brien law firm	*1,000,000*	No
Chief Technology Officer	Sidely Austin law firm	*1,000,000*	Yes
Enron energy company	Wilmer Cutler Pickering	*500,000*	No
General Motors cars	Jenner Block law firm	*2.000,000*	No
Lehman Brothers bankruptcy	Jenner Block law firm 2010	*2,000,000*	No

(*Continued*)

Table 17.3 Continued

Investigated organization	*Investigating organization*	*Costs*	*Profitable*
Motorola electronic products	SEC Securities and Exchange	*100,000*	Yes
Peregrine financial group	Berkeley research group	*500,000*	No
Philadelphia Police	Pennsylvania Commission	*2,000,000*	Yes
Philadelpia Sheriff's Office	Deloitte auditing firm	*1,000,000*	No
Tax Administration D.C.	Wilmer Cutler Pickering	*1,000,000*	No
Texas university	Hastings law firm	*500,000*	No
Wells Fargo bank	Shearman Sterling law firm	*1,000,000*	Yes
WorldCom communications	Wilmer Cutler Pickering	*500,000*	No
Vietnam			
Utenriksdepartement ministry	Duane Morris law firm	*200,000*	Yes

prices paid by clients to examiners. Estimation basis is an analogy from prices that are known as well as information obtained from each specific case. For example, cost drivers include the number of interviews and the extent of traveling. The number of reviewed documents, however, is seldom a cost driver, since most examiners apply search terms digitally that leave the work to computers doing searches in seconds.

For example, in the first private policing case of an investigation into suspected fraud of Save the Children funding from the United States in Bangladesh, several examiners from the Office of the Inspector General traveled to Bangladesh and stayed there for several weeks. Such traveling is certainly a cost driver. However, despite the travel, examiners failed in getting access to relevant information in Bangladesh. Examiners did not succeed in reconstructing events and sequences of events, which is at the core of any investigation. Therefore, the benefits are modest, leading to negative profitability as indicated in the table with a negative No-conclusion in the column.

Of course, the Profitability column with digital classification into Yes and No is only based on impressions from reviewing reports of investigations, media coverage, and other easily available information sources. Determining a Yes or a No to the question of Profitability is an expert opinion that varies in its foundations. However, since the table includes some confirmed real prices, the reader has a chance to validate whether or not all the estimated prices seem reasonable.

There are 167 private policing reports listed in Table 17.3. A total of 101 investigations are determined to be unprofitable by costs exceeding benefits. Sixty-six investigations are determined to be profitable by benefits exceeding costs. Thus, there are more unprofitable than profitable investigations. The average cost for a profitable investigation was US$500,000, while the average cost for a nonprofitable investigation was US$2,4000,000. While the averages are distinctly different, there is no statistically significant difference between the two numbers as there are large variations in both numbers.

Criminal justice system

Fraud examiners from law firms, auditing firms, and consulting firms conduct private policing when there is suspicion of economic crime. This book has presented a number of case studies of private policing. At the end of their reports of investigations, fraud examiners draw conclusion regarding potential offenses.

Crime in criminology is a phenomenon with two characteristics. First, the action or nonaction is bad, wrong, unethical, and immoral. Second, the action or nonaction deserves a negative reaction. Therefore, crime is behavior that people condemn, and that requires sanctions against the responsible person or entity.

Crime in legal terms is a phenomenon that the penal law covers, where the law defines punishment for the behavior. If there is no law covering the deviant behavior, then it is no crime in a legal sense. Laws vary between jurisdiction, and laws change over time within each jurisdiction. It is the legal definition, rather than the criminological definition, that causes a suspect potentially to face the criminal justice system.

In criminology, deviance is negative behavior that transgresses accepted norms and expectations of other people, organizations, and society. Depending on the penal law coverage, the deviance may or may not be punishable.

Table 17.4 lists the extent of involvement of the criminal justice system following each private policing effort. Where it is blank in the table, this research was unable to find and obtain relevant information. No involvement means that the criminal justice system in the country did not involve itself in the case, neither in the form of public police investigation nor in the form of public prosecution of suspects. Criminal charges mean that the prosecutor is charging defendants in court. Incarceration means that suspects and defendants ended up in prison. Police investigation means that public police has started inquiries into the suspected economic crime, but there was no prosecution, conviction, or incarceration at the time of writing this book. Abandoned by the police means that the police started a public investigation, but they did not find sufficient evidence to pursue the case. Acquitted in court means that the prosecutor argued for conviction of the defendant, but the judge disagreed.

The distribution of responses from the criminal justice system in Table 17.4 has an emphasis on no involvement:

- No involvement: The criminal justice system is reluctant to look into the matter that private examiners have reviewed. A total of 110 cases ended up facing ignorance by the criminal justice system. This is 66% or two-thirds of all cases.
- Abandoned by the police: Public police decides not to pursue the case after reviewing initial information about the matter. The police dismissed 13 cases that represent 8% of all cases.

Table 17.4 The criminal justice system during and after private policing

Investigated organization	*Investigating organization*	*Criminal justice system*
Bangladesh		
Padakhep Save the Children	Office of the Inspector General	No involvement
Canada		
Niagara municipality	Ombudsman of Ontario	No involvement
Pelham town	KPMG auditing firm	No involvement
Denmark		
Danske Bank banking	Bruun & Hjejle law firm	Criminal charges
Region Syddanmark public	Kromann Reumert law firm	No involvement
Socialstyrelsen social security	PwC auditing firm	Incarceration
Socialstyrelsen social security	Kammeradvokaten law firm	Incarceration
Ghana		
BioFuel bioenergy production	Kluge law firm	No involvement
Iceland		
Samherji fishing industries	Al Jazeera investigative	Police investigation
Japan		
Olympus digital equipment	Deloitte auditing firm	Incarceration
Toshiba digital equipment	Deloitte auditing firm	Incarceration
Moldova		
Moldova Banca de Economii	Kroll investigation firm	Criminal charges
The Netherlands		
Oceanteam offshore services	Sands law firm	No involvement
New Zealand		
FujiFilm digital equipment	Deloitte auditing firm	No involvement
Nigeria		
Nigerian National Petroleum	PwC auditing firm	No involvement
Norway		
Adecco nursing home	Wiersholm law firm	No involvement
Ahus hospital	PwC auditing firm	No involvement
Andebu municipality	BDO auditing firm	No involvement
Arendal traffic station	Internal audit function	No involvement
Askøy municipality	BDO auditing firm	No involvement
Bergen municipality	Internal control function	No involvement
Bergen havn port authority	Havarikommisjon commission	No involvement
Bergensklinikkene clinic	Ernst & Young auditing firm	No involvement
Betanien foundation	BDO auditing firm	Incarceration
Briskeby public sports arena	Lynx law firm	Abandoned by the police
Bærum municipality	G-partner law firm	Incarceration
Bårlidalen public water waste	Svendby consulting firm	No involvement
Caverion subcontractor	Wiersholm law firm	No involvement
Dale property development	Komrev. Rogaland audit	No involvement

(*Continued*)

Table 17.4 Continued

Investigated organization	*Investigating organization*	*Criminal justice system*
Demokratene political party	Partirevisjon internal control	Abandoned by the police
DNB banking	Hjort law firm	No involvement
Drammen municipality	Deloitte auditing firm	Incarceration
Eckbo foundations	Thommessen law firm	No involvement
Fadderbarna foundation	BDO auditing firm	Abandoned by the police
Ferde toll collection	Kluge law firm	No involvement
Ferde toll collection	Deloitte auditing firm	No involvement
FilmCamp public fund	Komrev. Nord public audit	Acquitted in court
Fjell municipality	Deloitte auditing firm	No involvement
Flyktningtjenesten public	Buunk et al. internal audit	No involvement
Forsvaret military contracts	Dalseide special committee	Incarceration
Forsvaret military logistics	PwC auditing firm	Incarceration
Forsvaret ministry	PwC auditing firm	Incarceration
Fredrikstad municipality	PwC auditing firm	Abandoned by the police
Fredrikstad municipality	Simonsen law firm	Abandoned by the police
Fretex Salvation Army	Grette law firm	No involvement
Furuheim nursing home	Hald law firm	No involvement
Fyrlykta child care	Deloitte auditing firm	No involvement
Fyrlykta child care	Stiftelsestilsynet public	No involvement
Gartnerhallen fruits	Wiersholm law firm	Criminal charges
Gassnova public projects	BDO auditing firm	No involvement
Grimstad municipality	BDO auditing firm	No involvement
Grimstad municipality	Hjort law firm	No involvement
Grimstad municipality	Tinia consulting firm	No involvement
Hadeland broadband	PwC auditing firm	Incarceration
Hadeland energy supply	PwC auditing firm	Incarceration
Halden skating hall	KPMG auditing firm	No involvement
Halden municipality buildings	Hjort law firm	No involvement
Hedmark municipality	Wiersholm law firm	Abandoned by the police
Helgelandssykehuset hospital	KPMG auditing firm	No involvement
Helse Nord hospital	PwC auditing firm	No involvement
Hordaland police department	Wiersholm law firm	Police internal
Hordaland police department	Stamina consulting firm	Police internal
Jondal municipality	SBDL law firm	No involvement
Karasjok municipality	Vest-Finnmark public audit	No involvement
Kjøpsvik municipality	Komrev. Nord public audit	No involvement

(*Continued*)

Table 17.4 Continued

Investigated organization	*Investigating organization*	*Criminal justice system*
Klengstua kindergarden	Halden municipal audit	No involvement
Kommunaldepartement	BDO auditing firm	No involvement
Kragerø shipping	Deloitte auditing firm	No involvement
Kristiansand municipality	Komrev. Agder public audit	No involvement
Kristiansand municipality	Tofte law firm	No involvement
Kvalsund municipality	Vest-Finnmark public audit	No involvement
Kvam Auto car dealer	Wikborg law firm	No involvement
Kvinnherad municipality	Deloitte auditing firm	No involvement
Langemyhr building company	PwC auditing firm	Acquitted in court
Larvik havn port authority	Komrev. Telemark audit	No involvement
Larvik municipality	Komrev. Telemark audit	No involvement
Leksvik municipality	Midt-Norge audit	No involvement
Lenvik municipality	KomRev audit	No involvement
Lunde transportation	Vierdal law firm	Incarceration
Lyoness-Lyconet gambling	Stiftelsestilsynet public	No involvement
Moskvaskolen school	Ernst & Young auditing firm	Abandoned by the police
NAV social security authority	Wiersholm law firm	No involvement
NDLA learning software	Deloitte auditing firm	No involvement
NFF players association	Lynx law firm	No involvement
NIF sports association	BDO auditing firm	No involvement
Norsk Tipping public betting	Deloitte auditing firm	No involvement
Norwegian Poker Team	Aftenposten media	Abandoned by the police
Næringsdepartement	PwC auditing firm	No involvement
Næringsdepartement	Ernst & Young auditing firm	No involvement
Orange health services	Bergen municipality audit	No involvement
Oslo Boligbygg housing	BDO auditing firm	Criminal charges
Oslo Boligbygg housing	Deloitte auditing firm	Criminal charges
Oslo Boligbygg housing	Komrev. Oslo audit	Criminal charges
Oslo Boligbygg housing	Deloitte auditing firm	Criminal charges
Oslo Bymiljø municipal parks	Ernst & Young auditing	Criminal charges
Oslo Energy recovery	PwC auditing firm	No involvement
Oslo Lindeberg nursing home	Kommunerevisjon audit	No involvement
Oslo Omsorgsbygg housing	PwC auditing firm	No involvement
Oslo Omsorgsbygg housing	Komrev. Oslo public audit	No involvement
Oslo Omsorgsbygg housing	PwC auditing firm	No involvement
Oslo Renovasjon garbage	Deloitte auditing firm	No involvement
Oslo Samferdsel transport	PwC auditing firm	No involvement
Oslo municipal school	Kommunerevisjon audit	Incarceration
Oslo municipal school	Kommunerevisjon audit	Incarceration

(*Continued*)

Table 17.4 Continued

Investigated organization	*Investigating organization*	*Criminal justice system*
Oslo Unibuss transport	Wiersholm law firm	Incarceration
Oslo Vei public transport	Kvale law firm	Abandoned by the police
Politiets utlending police	KPMG auditing firm	Police internal
Rana municipality	PwC auditing firm	No involvement
Re municipality	Komrev. Vestfold audit	No involvement
Romanifolket foundation	Stiftelsestilsynet public	Acquitted in court
Romerike Vannverk	Distriktsrevisjon audit	Incarceration
Sandefjord municipality	Tenden law firm	No involvement
Siva state funding	Wikborg law firm	No involvement
Skien municipality	BDO auditing firm	No involvement
Skjervøy municipality	KomRev public audit	Abandoned by the police
Stangeskovene forest	Ernst & Young auditing firm	No involvement
Statoil energy	Hagen et al. controllers	No involvement
Statoil energy	Saure et al. controllers	No involvement
Statoil energy	Østby et al. controllers	No involvement
Stavanger municipality	PwC auditing firm	No involvement
Sykehusapotekene	Moberg Segrov consulting	No involvement
Sykehusbygg hospital	Kluge law firm	No involvement
Sykehuset Innlandet hospital	Haavind law firm	No involvement
Telenor VimpelCom mobile	Deloitte auditing firm	No involvement
Tennisforbundet tennis	Lewis et al. consulting firm	No involvement
Tidal music streaming service	NTNU research group	Abandoned by the police
Tjøme municipality	BDO auditing firm	Criminal charges
Tolga municipality	Fylkesmann public	No involvement
Tomter shopping center	Holmen auditing firm	No involvement
Transocean oil rig company	Riksadvokaten prosecutor	Acquitted in court
Trendtech investments	Finanstilsynet public audit	No involvement
Troms Kraft energy company	Norscan consulting firm	Incarceration
Universitetssykehuset Nord	Arbeidsrettsadvokatene	No involvement
Uppsala municipality	KPMG auditing firm	No involvement
Utenriksdepartement ministry	Kontrollenhet internal audit	No involvement
Utenriksdepartement ministry	Kontrollenhet internal audit	No involvement
Utlendingsdirektoratet	Deloitte auditing firm	No involvement
Verdibanken banking	Wiersholm law firm	No involvement
Vestre Viken hospital	PwC auditing firm	Criminal charges
Vestvågøy municipality	Komrev. Nord public audit	No involvement
Videoforhandlere series	BDO auditing firm	No involvement
Vistamar rehabilitation center	Komrev. Trondheim audit	No involvement

(*Continued*)

Table 17.4 Continued

Investigated organization	*Investigating organization*	*Criminal justice system*
Vitalegruppen private nursing	BDO auditing firm	No involvement
World Ventures gaming	Stiftelsestilsynet public	Abandoned by the police
XXL sports store chain	DLA Piper law firm	No involvement
Zachariasbryggen property	Selmer law firm	No involvement
Sweden		
Karolinska hospital	Setterwalls law firm	No involvement
Kraft & Kultur energy	Ernst & Young auditing firm	Incarceration
Nordea banking	Mannheimer Swartling	Police investigation
Swedbank banking	Clifford Chance law firm	Police investigation
Switzerland		
Fifa football association	Garcia special committee	No involvement
The United Kingdom		
Sandstorm bank	PwC auditing firm	No involvement
The United States		
British Petroleum offshore	Freeh special committee	Abandoned by the police
Coatesville school district	BDO auditing firm	No involvement
Coatesville school district	Contrad O'Brien law firm	No involvement
Chief Technology Officer	Sidely Austin law firm	Criminal charges
Enron energy company	Wilmer Cutler Pickering	Incarceration
General Motors cars	Jenner Block law firm	No involvement
Lehman Brothers bankruptcy	Jenner Block law firm 2010	No involvement
Motorola electronic products	SEC Securities and Exchange	No involvement
Peregrine financial group	Berkeley research group	No involvement
Philadelphia Police	Pennsylvania Commission	Police internal
Philadelpia Sheriff's Office	Deloitte auditing firm	No involvement
Tax Administration D.C.	Wilmer Cutler Pickering	Incarceration
Texas university	Hastings law firm	No involvement
Wells Fargo bank	Shearman Sterling law firm	No involvement
WorldCom communications	Wilmer Cutler Pickering	Incarceration
Vietnam		
Utenriksdepartement ministry	Duane Morris law firm	No involvement

- Police investigation: Public police decides to conduct an independent inquiry by interrogations, document reviews, and other investigative steps. Three cases were subject to police investigations that represent 2% of all cases.
- Criminal charges: Police detectives hand the matter over to public prosecutors who issue criminal charges. Eleven cases brought criminal charges that represent 7% of all cases.

- Acquitted in court: Public prosecutors fail in providing evidence to convict the defendant. Courts dismissed four cases that represent 2% of all cases.
- Incarceration: The convicted offender ends up in prison. Twenty-two cases resulted in incarcerations that represent 13% of all cases.
- Police internal: Bureaus and agencies for the investigation of police affairs handle wrongdoing by police officers internally in the police force. Four cases were internal that represent 2% of all cases.

Surprisingly often, private policing reports conclude with misconduct but no crime. There is often deviant behavior, there is often wrongdoing, but surprisingly few cases end up in the criminal justice system. There is reason to believe that many private policing assignments are not completely independent and objective. Rather, when a scandal harms a client organization and leads to a crisis, fraud examiners enter into the situation to solve it rather than to escalate it. Fraud examiners tend to focus on measures that can improve the client's situation. Therefore, there are reasons to believe that white-collar offenders often avoid the criminal justice system when fraud examiners successfully have concluded that there was misconduct but no crime.

Without developing a conspiracy theory, evidence here suggests that it is indeed smart to hire fraud examiners to avoid attention from the criminal justice system when a scandal becomes public. Gottschalk and Benson (2020) have illustrated by case studies of fraud examiners how corporate accounts of scandals change over time. If an executive should end up receiving blame so serious that the person ends up in prison, then the organization will distance itself from that person to secure own survival.

Bibiliography

Bruun Hjejle (2018). *Report on the Non-Resident Portfolio at Danske Bank's Estonian Branch*, September 19, Copenhagen: Law Firm Bruun & Hjejle, 87 pages.

Deloitte (2020). *Selskapskontroll. Hordaland, Sogn og Fjordane og Rogald Fylkeskommuner: Ferde AS (Company Control Hordaland, Sogn and Fjordane and Rogaland Municipalities: Ferde Ltd.)*, January, Bergen: Auditing Firm Deloitte.

DLA Piper (2020). *Granskingsrapport XXL ASA (Examination Report XXL Ltd.)*, January, Oslo: Law Firm DLA Piper.

DN (2013). Nekter å betale granskerne mer (Refuses to pay the examiners more), *Daily Norwegian Business Newspaper Dagens Næringsliv*, www.dn.no, published November 13.

Ernst & Young (2012). *Troms Kraft AS – Gransking av Kraft & Kultur i Sverige AB (Troms Kraft Inc. – Investigation of Kraft & Kultur in Sweden Inc.)*, Oslo: Global Auditing Firm Ernst & Young.

Gottschalk, P. and Benson, M.L. (2020). The evolution of corporate accounts of scandals from exposure to investigation, *British Journal of Criminology*, published online https://doi.org/10.1093/bjc/azaa001.

Gottschalk, P. and Tcherni-Buzzeo, M. (2017). Reasons for gaps in crime reporting: The case of white-collar criminals investigated by private fraud examiners in Norway, *Deviant Behavior*, 38 (3), 267–281.

Høgseth, M.H. (2019). Thomas Borgen siktet i hvitvaskingssaken (Thomas Borgen charged in the money laundering case), *Web-Based Norwegian Newspaper E24*, www.e24.no, published May 7.

Kluge (2019). *Vurdering av Forhold i Ferde AS (Assessment of Circumstances at Ferde Ltd.)*, December 4, Bergen: Law Firm Kluge.

König, A., Graf-Vlachy, L., Bundy, J. and Little, L.M. (2020). A blessing and a curse: How CEOs' trait empathy affects their management of organizational crises, *Academy of Management Review*, 45 (1), 130–153.

Lund, K. (2019). Gruppesøksmål mot Danske i hvitvaskingssaken (Group claim against Danske in the money laundering case), *Daily Norwegian Business Newspaper Dagens Næringsliv*, www.dn.no, published March 4.

Moscow Times (2017). Danske Bank under investigation for Russian fraud, *Moscow Times*, published October 16.

Nergaard, L.L. (2013a). *Sammendrag av Granskingsrapport – Troms Kraft AS (Summary of Investigation Report – Troms Kraft Inc.)*, Norway: Norscan Partners.

Nergaard, L.L. (2013b). *Granskingsrapport Mandat 5: Kraft & Kultur (Investigation Report Mandate 5: Kraft & Kultur)*, Norway: Norscan Partners.

PwC (2014). *Forsvarets logistikkorganisasjon: Rapport etter gjennomgang av salg av fartøy (Military Logistic Organization: Report after Review of Sales of Vessels)*, October 31, Oslo: Auditing Firm PricewaterhouseCoopers.

PwC (2015). *Forsvarsdepartementet: Undersøkelse av forhold knyttet til Forsvarets avhending av fartøyer (Ministry of Defense: Examination of Circumstances Relatet to the Military's Sale of Vessels)*, March 20, Oslo: Auditing Firm PricewaterhouseCoopers.

Riisnæs, M.G. (2018). Advokat gransker Oceanteam videre (Attorney continues Oceanteam investigation), *Daily Norwegian Business Newspaper Dagens Næringsliv*, www.dn.no, published September 26.

Ritzau (2019). Danske Bank droppede kulegravning af hvidvask med få timers varsel (Danish Bank dropped digging into money laundering on short notice), *FinansWatch*, www.finanswatch.dk, published June 24.

Sands (2019a). *Factual Report: Oceanteam ASA Investigation of Related Party Transactions*, November 4, Oslo: Law Firm Sands.

Sands (2019b). *Report – Legal Review: Oceanteam ASA Investigation of Related Party Transactions*, November 4, Oslo: Law Firm Sands.

Sivertsen, N.S. (2018). Danske Bank siktet for hvitvasking (Danske Bank charged with money laundering), *Daily Norwegian Financial Newspaper Finansavisen*, November 28.

Wiersholm (2019). *Presentasjon av Granskingsrapport: Lønns- og arbeidsvilkår i Caverion med Utvalgte Underleverandører (Presentation of Investigation Report: Wages and Work Conditions at Caverion with Selected Subcontractors)*, November 18, Oslo: Law Firm Wiersholm.

18 White-collar attorneys

Chapter 17 serves as an introduction to this chapter as it draws attention to the motives and actions of attorneys at work, who conduct a large fraction of private policing investigations. When attorneys are in the role of investigators, they tend to conclude with misconduct but no crime. Thereby the client, who pays for the investigation, receives sufficient blame as a response to stakeholder expectations (Gottschalk and Benson, 2020). At the same time, attorneys help clients avoid the criminal justice system as illustrated by the large fraction of no involvement in the previous chapter.

The research topic of attorneys at work for white-collar offenders is traditionally associated with lawyers who help defendants while they are in the criminal justice system. During police investigation, court prosecution, and incarceration, an attorney can help the client in a subjective defense to limit the sanctions imposed on the client from the criminal justice system. The focus of research is then whether white-collar offenders are less likely to be incarcerated and receive shorter sentences compared to other offenders (Galvin, 2020), whether the special sensitivity hypothesis or the special resilience hypothesis applies to white-collar offenders (Logan et al. 2019), and other research topics related to law enforcement toward this group of offenders.

Criminal justice system avoidance

This book applies a different perspective on attorneys at work for white-collar offenders. Inspired by Mann (1985), researchers have focused on attorneys at work for white-collar offenders who attempt to avoid the criminal justice system for their clients. Their approach is to describe deviance but deny crime. This approach is visible in a number of fraud examination reports, where attorneys have conducted private policing in client organizations. Client organizations hire attorneys from law firms to reconstruct past events and sequences of events that have caused scandals and crisis (Brooks and Button, 2011; Button and Gee, 2013; Button et al., 2007a, 2007b; Gottschalk and Benson, 2020; King, 2020a, 2020b; Schneider, 2006; Williams, 2005). While attorneys conduct their investigations, the criminal justice system typically is reluctant to start public police investigations. When attorneys in their reports of investigations conclude that there was deviance but no crime, the criminal justice system typically remains reluctant to apply investigative resources to such cases (Gottschalk, 2020). Galvin (2020) suggests that the no-crime perspective results from "avoidance of the criminal justice system by institutionally framing 'law breaking' as '(regulatory) rule violations'". This phenomenon has received the label "status advantage".

It is important to emphasize that crime in criminology is a phenomenon with two characteristics. First, the action or nonaction is bad, wrong, unethical, and immoral. Second, the action or nonaction deserves a negative reaction. Therefore, crime is behavior that people condemn, and that requires sanctions against the responsible person or entity.

Crime in legal terms is a phenomenon that penal law covers, where the law defines punishment for the behavior. If there is no law covering the deviant behavior, then it is no crime in a legal sense. Laws vary between jurisdiction, and laws change over time within each jurisdiction. It is the legal definition, rather than the criminological definition, that causes a suspect potentially to face the criminal justice system.

In criminology, deviance is negative behavior that transgresses accepted norms and expectations of other people, organizations, and society. Depending on the penal law coverage, the deviance may or may not be punishable.

Attorneys are knowledge workers who are supposed to be competent in general legal principles and procedures and in the substantive and procedural aspects of the law. They are supposed to have the ability to analyze and provide solutions to legal problems. Attorneys are professionals who have gained knowledge through formal education (explicit) and through learning on the job (implicit). An attorney is a knowledge worker specializing in the development and application of legal knowledge to solve client problems. Attorneys represent their clients in legal matters by presenting evidence and legal arguments as well as providing counsel to clients concerning their rights and obligations.

In white-collar research, there are different kinds of conception and operationalization of the construct of white-collar crime. Even though Sutherland (1939) coined the term more than eight decades ago, white-collar research remains preoccupied with definition. While many still engage in agitation and dispute about the white-collar crime concept, as exemplified by Galvin (2020), this research simply applies the basic characteristics of the offender. These characteristics include hierarchical status, personal respectability, individual trust, admiration by others, and legitimate access to resources, power base, and privileges. This implies that crime is committed in the course of occupational activities where the offender has legitimate access to premises and systems.

Rich and mighty on the shoreline

Status, respectability, trust, social esteem, access to resources, power and privilege can expand beyond occupational activities into private activities for white-collar offenders. Access to attorneys at work can enable privileged individuals to explore and exploit possibilities that other people cannot do. While case studies so far in this book have focused on misconduct and wrongdoing in occupational settings, the following case study focuses on misconduct and wrongdoing in private settings by members of the elite in society.

This case study applies the theory of convenience to white-collar offenses on the shoreline in Norway. The rich and mighty are occupying the most attractive recreational places along the coast with their vacation resorts in the form of summer palaces and private harbors. This case study addresses the abuse of power associated with land development in an extremely attractive resort area in southern Norway. While Norwegian law makes it illegal to construct or expand buildings and other changes in the landscape in the 100-m belt along the coast, white-collar offenders hire architects, attorneys, and others to get what they want and defend what they have done.

Ever since Kenneth Mann published his portrait of attorneys at work (Mann, 1985), prosecutors and criminologists have noticed the special characteristics of defending white-collar wrongdoings. Attorneys do not limit their white-collar work to substance defense. They are also active in symbol defense and information control (Gottschalk, 2014). This chapter presents a case study of attorneys' white-collar work in support of offenders who have caused environmental harm on the shoreline in Norway.

The shoreline is a limited public good that many nations protect and preserve for the recreation and benefit of all its inhabitants and visitors. Privatization of the shoreline, especially in the form of vacation resorts, is thus illegal. Illegal construction in the coastal zone leads to irreversible interference with nature and restricts public access to coastal traffic. The beach zone is an area that is a vulnerable recreation place for the public in general, and an area under great development pressure with the possibility of great financial gain. Environmental crime combines with financial crime. Illegal private activity represents irreversible interventions harming the diversity of nature. Nevertheless, some rich and mighty people are able to violate the law. They build and expand their vacation homes on the shoreline by blasting mountain areas and preventing beach access. With the help of architects, builders, attorneys, and relationships to community planners, they use their resources to get and keep what they want.

While Norway has a very long coastline, the attractive real estates for vacation houses and summer guests are located south of the capital of Oslo. In particular, the island of Tjøme is popular (BDO, 2017; DN, 2019). The theme of environmentally harmful construction and expansion of summerhouses serves as an example in relation to convenience theory. The motive is often to climb Maslow's (1943) hierarchy of needs, the opportunity is typically access to resources (Huisman and Erp, 2013), and the willingness for deviant behavior is dependent on neutralization techniques (Sykes and Matza, 1957), lack of self-control (Craig and Piquero, 2016), and other factors.

This chapter thus applies the theory of convenience to the case study. Convenience theory suggests that there is a motive, an opportunity, and a willingness among white-collar offenders to violate the law (Braaten and Vaughn, 2019; Chan and Gibbs, 2020; Dearden and Gottschalk, 2020; Gottschalk, 2017,

2019; Hansen, 2020; Kireenko et al., 2019; Vasiu and Podgor, 2019). The theory builds on the fraud triangle suggested by Cressey (1972). A white-collar offender is a member of the upper echelon in society who abuses the privileged position for illegitimate benefits (Sutherland, 1939, 1983).

In white-collar research, there are different kinds of conception and operationalization of the construct of white-collar crime. Even though Sutherland (1939) coined the term more than eight decades ago, white-collar research remains preoccupied with definition. While many still engage in agitation and dispute about the white-collar crime concept, as exemplified by Galvin (2020), this research simply applies the basic characteristics of the offender that include status, trust, and access, as discussed previously in this book.

Environmental harm and crime has received increased attention in recent years (Böhm, 2020; Huisman and Erp, 2013; Lynch, 2020). Traditionally, white-collar crime cases have focused on nonviolent financial crime. Recently, with increased environmentalism, researchers have focused on white-collar crime that can impose physical harm on people (Benson and Simpson, 2018: 129):

> These offenses are potentially much more serious in that they can and often do impose physical costs on individuals. This is not to say that the perpetrators deliberately set out to harm other people. They do not. The physical harms that they cause are unintended in the sense that they are not what the offender is trying to achieve. The motivation for the offense is not to impose harm on others but rather to gain a financial advantage.

For example, Wingerde and Lord (2020: 478) argue that the waste industry is a criminogenic industry that is vulnerable to environmental crime:

> First, this concerns the waste product itself. Waste is a product that has a negative value attached to it. ... Second, the industry in itself also has some characteristics that are considered to be criminogenic.

However, few individuals face convictions for environmental crime. For example, after the British Petroleum (BP) Deepwater Horizon oil spill in the Gulf of Mexico in 2010, prosecutors brought criminal charges against four British Petroleum executives, but no one ended up in prison (Fowler, 2014; Freeh, 2013; Thompson, 2017). Greife and Maume (2020) found that:

> Despite recent attention to multi-billion dollar settlements for environmental violations involving high-profile offenders such as BP and VW, criminal sanctioning of individuals and organizations for environmental offenses is uncommon.

Going to prison is a serious matter (Dhami, 2007; Logan et al., 2019; Stadler et al., 2013). One exception is the conviction of both the chief executive officer and the chairperson of the board at Vest Tank in Norway, as well as a chemical advisor to the company, who received prison sentences for a tank explosion caused by dangerous waste (Gormley, 2009; Gulating, 2013, 2015; Nordhordland, 2010; Pedersen, 2017).

The environmental harm in the current case study includes illegal changes in the landscape, pollution from civilization, conquest and privatization of a public good, and prevention of recreational opportunities for people.

Convenient loopholes for mansions

Convenience theory is an emerging approach to integrate well-known perspectives on white-collar crime from criminology, sociology, and management. It is an integrated deductive theory (Chan and Gibbs, 2020; Friedrichs, 2010; Krohn and Eassey, 2014; Liska et al., 1989; Pratt et al., 2019). The choice of convenience theory in this book does not result from a comparison to other perspectives such as power or class. Rather, as an emerging new theoretical perspective on white-collar offenders, it is interesting to explore its empirical application to a case of environmental crime.

Convenience theory suggests that the extent of convenience determines the likelihood of white-collar wrongdoing, which is economic crime committed by privileged individuals with access to resources, who abuse their positions for illegitimate benefits (Sutherland, 1939, 1983; Piquero, 2018). Convenience is the state of being able to proceed with something with little effort or difficulty, avoiding pain and strain (Mai and Olsen, 2016). Convenience is savings in time and effort (Farquhar and Rowley, 2009), as well as avoidance of pain and obstacles (Higgins, 1997). Convenience is a relative concept concerned with efficiency in time and effort as well as reduction in pain and solution to problems (Engdahl, 2015). Convenience is an advantage in favor of a specific action to the detriment of alternative actions. White-collar offenders choose the most convenient path to reach their goals (Wikstrom et al., 2018).

A convenient individual is not necessarily neither bad nor lazy. On the contrary, the person can be seen as smart and rational (Sundström and Radon, 2015). Convenience orientation varies among individuals, as some are more concerned about time saving, effort reduction, and pain avoidance and thus more convenience oriented. For example, Gamache and McNamara (2019: 923) suggest that offenders in the upper echelon who mainly focus on their present time dispositions in their information selection are more inclined to justify their wrongdoing since they have "the proclivity to act impulsively, move quickly with current opportunities, and consider current issues when making decisions".

The theory of convenience defines three dimensions that influence the tendency of white-collar occurrences. First in the motive dimension, if it is possible to avoid threats conveniently, and it is feasible to explore possibilities conveniently, then crime is likely to occur. Examples of threats include falling from position (Piquero, 2012) and bankruptcy (Blickle et al., 2006), while examples of possibilities include climbing in the hierarchy of needs (Agnew, 2014; Maslow, 1943) and satisfying greed (Goldstraw-White, 2012). Greed leads to a need for an increasingly larger home, several chalets and summerhouses, bigger boat, luxurious vacations, and ownership in various enterprises. Greed is a desire among all sorts of people. When there are convenient possibilities for financial gain to enjoy prosperity, then economic crime can be a convenient action. Both Bucy et al. (2008) and Hamilton and Mickletwait (2006) emphasize greed as the most common cause of criminal acts by white-collar offenders.

Acquiring a summer castle on the shoreline is a typical example of climbing in the hierarchy of needs, where only rich and mighty individuals are able to buy or build such vacation resorts (Ytreberg, 2018). Norwegians love the outdoors, and many families have a cabin in the mountains for skiing in the winter, as well as a summerhouse close to the ocean for swimming and boat trips in the summer. The most attractive locations are extremely expensive, and many areas along the shoreline are exclusively for the public in general.

Second, in the opportunity dimension of convenience theory, if it is convenient to commit as well as to conceal illegitimate activity, then wrongdoing is likely to occur. Examples of convenience in committing crime include the too-big-to-fail and too-big-to-fall phenomenon (Pontell et al., 2014) and legitimate access to resources (Benson and Simpson, 2018; Cohen and Felson, 1979; Logan et al., 2019). Examples of convenience in concealing crime include institutional deterioration (Rodriguez et al., 2005), lack of controls (Bosse and Phillips, 2016), and rule complexity preventing compliance (Lehman et al., 2019). A rich and mighty person has legitimate access to architects and builders to plan and construct a summerhouse. The person also has access to attorneys and others who can negotiate and influence municipal officials to get approvals or to avoid refusals because of rule complexity in the legislation (Lehman et al., 2019).

Attorneys do not only provide substance defense for their clients, they often also contribute symbolic defense and information control to manipulate community planners in the municipalities (Gottschalk, 2014). The environmental harm and thus the wrongdoing can disappear from sight, for example, by first removing rock and then building large basements that are not visible to trespassers.

To seek attractive and exclusive homeownership in the most convenient way is not necessarily to choose a new construction or extension in such a modality that would require rich and mighty individuals to hire highly specialized and deviant contractors and attorneys. Rather, the chosen approach is sometimes to find loopholes so that the emerging and expanding mansion at the shoreline seemingly has transgressed no laws or regulations. Laws and regulations tend to be general in their formulations, as the text is supposed to cover all conceivable forms of nonconformity presently and in the future.

Finally, in the willingness dimension, if deviant behavior is a convenient choice where the feeling of justification and innocence is present, then crime is likely to occur. Examples of convenience in choice of crime include deviant identity (Obodaru, 2017; Petrocelli et al., 2003), narcissistic identification with the location (Galvin et al., 2015), perception of benefits exceeding costs (Pratt and Cullen, 2005), and learning from others by differential association (Sutherland, 1983). Examples of convenience by innocence include justification of wrongdoing

(Schnatterly et al., 2018) as well as application of neutralization techniques (Sykes and Matza, 1957). A rich and mighty person building an illegal vacation resort on the shoreline can apply, for example, the neutralization technique of denial of responsibility. The person disclaims responsibility for crime, as the person is not the correct receiver of blame for what happened, since an entrepreneur handled the project. The offender here claims that one or more of the conditions of responsible agency did not occur. The person committing a deviant act defines himself or herself as lacking responsibility for his or her actions. In this technique, the person rationalizes that the action in question is beyond his or her control.

The rich and mighty person claims that architects, builders, and attorneys handled the matter on his or her behalf where agency problems occurred. In the principal-agent perspective, the elite member can claim as the principal that the architect as an agent had a greater risk willingness and a deviant priority compared to the agent, where the agent had no understanding of what was going on because of knowledge asymmetry between principal and agent (Bosse and Phillips, 2016).

Repeated figures in this book have illustrated the structure of white-collar crime convenience. The extent of white-collar convenience manifests itself by motive, opportunity, and willingness. In the motive dimension, wealth might be a goal in itself or an enabler to exploit possibilities and to avoid threats. In the current case study, environmental crime enables climbing in the hierarchy of needs by building or expanding a vacation resort on the shoreline. Generally, it is convenient to exploit possibilities and to avoid threats by financial means (Agnew, 2014; Blickle et al., 2006; Goldstraw-White, 2012; Maslow, 1943; Piquero, 2012, 2018; Vasiu and Podgor, 2019).

In the opportunity dimension, convenience can exist both to commit white-collar crime and to conceal white-collar crime. Offenders have high social status in privileged positions, and they have legitimate access to crime resources. In the current case study, wealthy offenders were able to hire architects, builders, and attorneys to get and keep what they. Generally, disorganized institutional deterioration causes decay, lack of oversight and guardianship causes chaos, and criminal market structures cause collapse (Benson and Simpson, 2018; Cohen and Felson, 1979; Gottschalk, 2017; Pontell et al., 2014; Qiu and Slezak, 2019).

The personal willingness for deviant behavior manifests itself by offender choice and perceived innocence. The choice of crime can be caused by deviant identity, rational consideration, or learning from others. The perceived innocence at crime manifests itself by justification and neutralization. Identity, rationality, learning, justification, and neutralization all contribute to making white-collar wrongdoing a convenient behavior for offenders (Craig and Piquero, 2017; Engdahl, 2015; Pratt and Cullen, 2005; Sutherland, 1983; Sykes and Matza, 1957).

Elite mobilization of top attorneys

This research is concerned with application of convenience theory to the case of rich and mighty white-collar offenders who commit environmental crime by privatizing and harming the shoreline in terms of environmental wrongdoing (Olaussen, 2018). Specifically, this research attempts to explore the opportunity dimension of convenience theory as illustrated repeatedly in this book, where attorneys can help commit and conceal environmental harm. White-collar offenders pay attorneys for their substance defense, symbolic defense, and information control.

This archival research is based on content analysis of newspaper reports (e.g., Aunemo, 2018, 2020; Dugstad and Skaalmo, 2017; Holm, 2019, 2020; Holmøy, 2017, 2018, 2019, 2020a, 2020b, 2020c; Wang, 2018, 2019; Ytreberg, 2018), municipal files (e.g., Tilsynsrapport, 2020), fraud examinations (e.g., BDO, 2017), letters to the municipality of Tjøme from attorneys, and email communication with whistleblowers. Content analysis is any methodology or procedure that works to identify characteristics within texts attempting to make valid inferences (Krippendorff, 1980; Patrucco et al., 2017). Content analysis assumes that language reflects both how people understand their surroundings and their cognitive processes (Bell et al., 2018; Saunders et al., 2007). Therefore, content analysis makes it possible to identify and determine relevant text in a context (McClelland et al., 2010).

In addition to archival material, a whistleblower continued his search for cases and communicated his finding to this research effort. He visited potential crime scenes, took pictures, and continued his dialogue with both politicians and staff in the municipality.

Over a period of three years, a substantial stream of emails and personal communications enabled this research. Thirty-six white-collar cases caused offenders to hire a number of attorneys as listed in Table 18.1 over the three-year period 2017–2020 as the whistleblowers had attracted the attention of politicians and staff in the municipality toward rich and mighty persons on the shoreline (Brevik, 2020).

The elite mobilization of top attorneys was a result of media coverage and municipal wakening about the de facto closing of the shoreline by rich and mighty people who built and expanded their summer palaces along the shoreline. All attorneys started their substance defense, symbol defense, and information control as a consequence of being hired by the rich and wealthy when investigative journalists (Skavhellen and Lien, 2018), whistleblowers, and some left-wing local politicians revealed summerhouse after summerhouse that did not have approval from the relevant authorities. The role of attorneys in these individual scandals is similar to their role in corporate scandals as discussed in this book, where they conclude with misconduct but no crime.

The island of Tjøme in Norway

Our case is concerned with illegally constructed summerhouses and expanded vacation resorts on the beaches and cliffs in the southern part of Norway. Both environmental protection laws and public access laws have made it illegal to build and expand vacation homes in the 100-m wide belt along the coast.

Table 18.1 Identified attorneys in law firms and their white-collar clients

	Attorney	*Law firm*	*White-collar client*
1	Andresen, Ole	Riisa	Ole Andresen
2	Bech, Stig L.	BAHR	Rune Breili
3	Blaauw, Kristine R.	Thommessen	Arnfinn Hafsteen
4	Borge, Ole	Borge	Ole Borge
5	Bruusgaard, Erik	Tenden	Arnfinn Hafsteen
6	Bæra, Vibeke Hein	Hei Bæra	Rune Breili
7	Bæra, Vibeke Hein	Hein Bæra	Werner Osther
8	Eilertsen, Eilert	Byadvokaten	Nanna Fløgstad Sohlberg
9	Gulsvik, Mari Helen	Selmer	Gunnar Fredrik Selvaag
10	Hansson, Nils Petter	Ro Sommernes	Hans Ole Helling
11	Harborg, Henning	Thommessen	Carl Erik Krefting
12	Harborg, Henning	Thommessen	Turid Varner
13	Hauger, Bård Bergem	Advokatene på Jeløy	Hans Petter Abrahamsen
14	Jørgensen, Frode S.	Sandvika advokatkontor	Harald Dybsjord
15	Jørgensen, Frode S.	Sandvika advokatkontor	Sigmund Arnesen
16	Lie, Arne	Haraldsen Bydal Lie	Harald Svendsen
17	Nåmdal, Endre	Riisa	Rune Breili
18	Reusch, Christian H.P.	Simonsen Vogt Wiig	Kristina M. Wilhelmsen
19	Støren, Martin	Schjødt	Lars Hellik Strøm
20	Støren, Martin	Schjødt	Sigmund Arnesen
21	Støren, Martin	Schjødt	Tore Jacobsen
22	Sæveraas, Ingeborg	Lønnum	Øyvind Garner
23	Tellefsen, Anne	Haraldsen Bydal Lie	Fridtjov Botvid Falck
24	Tellefsen, Anne	Haraldsen Bydal Lie	Celestine Clauson
25	Tellefsen, Anne	Haraldsen Bydal Lie	Nanna Fløgstad Sohlberg
26	Tellefsen, Anne	Haraldsen Bydal Lie	Harald Svendsen
27	Tellefsen, Anne	Haraldsen Bydal Lie	77 construction firms
28	Tellefsen, Anne	Haraldsen Bydal Lie	Rune Breili
29	Tellefsen, Anne	Haraldsen Bydal Lie	Svein Homstvedt
30	Tellefsen, Anne	Haraldsen Bydal Lie	Scammer and scammed
31	Tellefsen, Anne	Haraldsen Bydal Lie	Malling og Middelfart
32	Tveten, Mathias	Ro Sommernes	Tom Ragnar Wilhelmsen
33	Waller, Caroline	Simonsen Vogt Wiig	Anders Wilhelmsen
34	Zimmermann, Liv	Hjort	Mette Landgraff
35	Zimmermann, Liv	Hjort	Evy Reimers
36	Zimmermann, Liv	Hjort	Marianne and Ulf Stuge

Nevertheless, rich people have been able to ignore the building ban in the case of municipality of Tjøme (Aunemo, 2018, 2020; Heltne and Klevstrand, 2019; Holm, 2020; Holmøy, 2019; Larssen, 2017; Lien and Brevik, 2020; Wang, 2019). The environmental harm from shoreline violations is twofold. First, illegal privatization reduces and removes public access to attractive recreational areas. Public health suffers harm, and democracy where everyone is equal in front of the law, deteriorates. Second, construction work changes the landscape. Nature and animals suffer harm.

The municipality of Tjøme is located on an island south of the Norwegian capital, Oslo. The island is the most expensive summerhouse resort and may deserve a comparison to Cape Cod in the United States in terms of its attractiveness for people after a cold winter. Tjøme is a summer haven for city dwellers, and it is where Oslo's mercantile elite started building cottages along the shore 100 years ago (Holth and Winge, 2018). The cottages were small and primitive, but were very close to the water. New generations subsequently took over the cottages and wanted to make them more comfortable and much larger (Klevstrand and Randen, 2018).

The social democrats who ruled Norway for several decades decided that the shoreline should be for everybody, not only for privileged and rich people. The original summerhouses, even if they block the shoreline for passing individuals, are legal and remain. Owners may maintain and renew the buildings, but may not carry out expansion work. There is an absolute ban on new summerhouses, cottages, boathouses, and docks in the 100-m belt along the waterfront.

However, as presented by *Dagens Næringsliv* – the Norwegian equivalent of the *Wall Street Journal* or the *Financial Times* – in the autumn of 2017, "cottages" along the coast had increased in size from 50 m^2 and less to 200 m^2 and more (Berglihn, 2019; DN, 2019). A cottage is normally small, while a summerhouse is normally larger: 200 m^2 and more, such as 3,000 ft^2, imply that there are often several bathrooms and many bedrooms. The largest ones can deserve the label of summer palaces almost the size of the Vanderbilt mansion in Newport, Rhode Island, in the United States.

The rich and mighty had builders blast in the mountains and remove rocks (Blix, 2020). They put up fences into the water and created private parks so that nobody would dare to trespass, although it is legal to pass people's houses along the shoreline. In terms of crime signals (Karim and Siegel, 1998), the signal intensity from illegal construction sites was low, except when people observed construction work from boats on the sea. The local population had declining signal alertness, as they knew that no terminations or corrections would occur anyway.

At the center of attention of the illegal construction and expansion of recreational palaces were an architect and a community planner in the municipality of Tjøme (Blix, 2018; Dugstad and Skaalmo, 2017; Holm, 2019; Klevstrand, 2018; Klevstrand et al., 2020; Wang, 2018). The municipal planner had approved absolutely all of the applications from the architect, even those in the 100-m belt, and for a while the community planner found convenient employment in the architectural firm with a nice salary before returning to the municipality. Suspicions of corruption and financial adultery emerged (Holmøy, 2017, 2018). However, in this chapter, we are focusing on the white-collar offenders who hired architects and attorneys listed in Table 18.1 to make their summer cottages develop into summerhouses, summer palaces, and summer mansions along the shoreline (Blix, 2019; Lien and Aunemo, 2019).

Two whistleblowers who live on the island contacted a journalist at *Dagens Næringsliv* in the spring of 2017. They did not only present accusations. They had retrieved documents from the municipality for 60 key summerhouse cases. They presented the cases in a systematic way on a digital platform where journalists could conduct searches. Journalists quickly found names of owners who typically had received public attention before, either because they had inherited large sums of money or because they were self-made rich people. The media published pictures of the newly built summerhouses and summer palaces with pictures of the owners as well.

Local police were reluctant to look at the cases (Klevstrand and Solem, 2020). They probably knew that house owners with almost unlimited resources would do anything to avoid the demolition of their palaces. The house owners might easily be willing to pay fines, but the level of public outrage was high, since rich people had done things that normal people were unable to do. Therefore, the public request was to have all new palaces demolished.

It is interesting to shed some light on rich people's motives, opportunities, and behaviors as defined in the theory of convenience (Gottschalk, 2017, 2019; Vasiu and Podgor, 2019). Their motive in building illegal summerhouses is to climb Maslow's (1943) hierarchy of needs. The Russian-American psychologist Abraham Maslow developed a hierarchy of human needs. This starts at the bottom with physiological needs, need for security, social needs, and need for respect and self-realization. When basic needs such as food and shelter are satisfied, then the person moves up the pyramid to satisfy needs for safety and control over their own life situation. Higher up in the pyramid, the person strives for status, recognition, and self-respect (Blickle et al., 2006). While street crime is often concerned with the lower levels, white-collar crime is often concerned with the upper levels in terms of status and success. Poverty and powerlessness tends to be the cause of street crime, while excessive power and greed is frequently the cause of white-collar crime.

Opportunity for white-collar offenders is concerned with access to resources to both commit and conceal crime (Benson and Simpson, 2018; Cohen and Felson, 1979). An opportunity is attractive as a means of responding to desires, wishes, and ambitions. The resource dimension provides the white-collar criminal with an opportunity to commit financial crime and conceal it in legal activities as a seemingly legitimate enterprise. Building and expanding mansions on the coast increase the value of properties far beyond the material costs. The offense is thus just as much economic crime as environmental crime (Holmøy, 2020a).

Aguilera and Vadera (2008: 434) describe a criminal opportunity as "the presence of a favorable combination of circumstances that renders a possible course of action relevant". Opportunity arises when individuals or groups can engage in illegal and unethical behavior and expect, with a reasonable degree of confidence, to avoid detection and punishment. It is convenient for the offender to conceal crime and give it an appearance of outward acceptability.

The third and final dimension of convenience theory – in addition to motive and opportunity – is willingness for deviant behavior. Most theories concerned with fraud and corruption belong to the behavioral dimension. Researchers have presented numerous suggestions to explain why famous people are willing to commit white-collar crime despite holding privileged positions. Deviant behavior is an individual action that transgresses social norms, including formally enacted rules and informal nonconformity (Aguilera et al., 2018). The most frequently cited theory is neutralization, where offenders apply a number of techniques to rationalize and justify their deviant actions (Sykes and Matza, 1957). The idea of neutralization techniques resulted from work on Sutherland's (1939, 1983) theory of differential association. Criminals apply certain techniques in order to make them feel as though they have not done anything wrong. These guilt removal procedures are neutralization techniques, whereby the feeling of guilt decreases and possibly disappears. One out of several neutralization techniques available to mansion owners was that everyone else did what they do, nicely coordinated by a key architect who had convenient access to corrupt officials in the municipality.

Evidence from attorneys' letters to the municipality as well as newspaper coverage of several cases suggests a number of neutralization techniques applied by homeowners. First, complexity prevented compliance (Lehman et al., 2019). Next, the rich people did not know what architects and construction firms did for them, so they deny responsibility (Sykes and Matza, 1957). Furthermore, some suggest normality of action, and some claim entitlement to action as some rich people think it is just a matter of money to get what you want.

However, in the social democratic tradition in Norway, which is typically to the left on the political spectrum compared to Democrats in the United States, the state and the people are above the corporations and the individuals. The role of the state is to regulate businesses and behaviors. This is in contrast to some other countries, where the state primarily serves the corporate world and the freedom of individuals to do whatever they like, even when they harm the public good.

The theme of illegal construction and expansion of summerhouses thus serves as an example in relation to convenience theory, where the motive is to climb Maslow's hierarchy of needs, the opportunity is access to resources, and the willingness for deviant behavior is dependent on neutralization techniques, lack of self-control, and other enablers of wrongdoing willingness.

Bibliography

Agnew, R. (2014). Social concern and crime: Moving beyond the assumption of simple self-interest, *Criminology*, 52 (1), 1–32.

Aguilera, R.V., Judge, W.Q. and Terjesen, S.A. (2018). Corporate governance deviance, *Academy of Management Review*, 43 (1), 87–109.

Aguilera, R.V. and Vadera, A.K. (2008). The dark side of authority: Antecedents, mechanisms, and outcomes of organizational corruption, *Journal of Business Ethics*, 77, 431–449.

Aunemo, E.W. (2018). Mangemillionær Celestine (21) startet ulovlig bygging av tennisbane, men blir ikke politianmeldt (Multimillionaire Celestine (21) started illegal construction of tennis court, but is not reported to the police), *Daily Local Norwegian Newspaper Tønsbergs Blad*, www.tb.no, published August 29.

Aunemo, E.W. (2020). Advokaten til millionærarving Celestine (22) krever at skattebetalerne skal betale honoraret hennes (The attorney for millionaire heir Celestine (22) requires that the tax payers cover her remuneration), *Daily Local Norwegian Newspaper Tønsbergs Blad*, www.tb.no, published January 19.

BDO (2017). *Tjøme Commune – Gransking (Tjøme Municipality – Investigation)*, Oslo: Auditing Firm BDO, 39 pages.

Bell, E., Bryman, A. and Harley, B. (2018). *Business Research Methods*, 2nd Edition, New York: Oxford University Press.

Benson, M.L. and Simpson, S.S. (2018). *White-Collar Crime: An Opportunity Perspective*, 3rd Edition, New York: Routledge.

Berglihn, H. (2019). Princess-arving dømt til fengsel (Princess heir sentenced to prison), daily Norwegian business newspaper *Dagens Næringsliv*, Friday, September 20, page 4.

Blickle, G., Schlegel, A., Fassbender, P. and Klein, U. (2006). Some personality correlates of business white-collar crime, *Applied Psychology: An International Review*, 55 (2), 220–233.

Blix, N.T. (2018). Hyttemilliardæren har sendt advokatsvar til kommunen. –I den grad det er gjort feil i den tidligere byggesaken, er de ene og alene Tjøme kommunes ansvar (To the extent mistakes have been made in the previous building case, it is Tjøme municipality's responsibility alone), *Local Daily Norwegian Newspaper Tønsbergs Blad*, www.tb.no, published September 21.

Blix, N.T. (2019). Advokaten spurte om søknadsplikt – Sivilombudsmannen vil ikke se på saken (The attorney asked about the application deadline – The civil ombudsman will not look into the matter), *Local Daily Norwegian Newspaper Øyene*, www.oyene.no, published November 17.

Blix, N.T. (2020). Eierne på fritidseiendommen Gryteskjær svarer: -Vi synes det er oppsiktsvekkende og problematisk at Færder kommune nå 10-11 år senere hevder det er ulovlig (The owners on the vacation resort Gryte reefs answer: -We find it surprising and problematic by Færder municipality now 10-11 years later claiming it is illegal), *Local Norwegian Newspaper Øyene*, www.oyene.no, published March 6.

Bosse, D.A. and Phillips, R.A. (2016). Agency theory and bounded self-interest, *Academy of Management Review*, 41 (2), 276–297.

Böhm, M.L. (2020). Criminal business relationships between commodity regions and industrialized countries: The hard road from raw material to new technology, *Journal of White Collar and Corporate Crime*, 1 (1), 34–49.

Braaten, C.N. and Vaughn, M.S. (2019). Convenience theory of cryptocurrency crime: A content analysis of U.S. federal court decisions, *Deviant Behavior*, published online https://doi.org/10.1080/01639625.2019.1706706.

Brevik, H.C. (2020). Så mye har ulovlighetssakene kostet: -Kan argumenteres for at det er selvpåført (So much have the illegality cases costed: -Might argue that it is self inflicted), *Daily Local Norwegian Newspaper Tønsbergs Blad*, www.tb.no, published February 14.

Brooks, G. and Button, M. (2011). The police and fraud investigation and the case for a nationalized solution in the United Kingdom, *The Police Journal*, 84, 305–319.

Bucy, P.H., Formby, E.P., Raspanti, M.S. and Rooney, K.E. (2008). Why do they do it? The motives, mores, and character of white collar criminals, *St. John's Law Review*, 82, 401–571.

Button, M., Frimpong, K., Smith, G. and Johnston, L. (2007a). Professionalizing counter fraud specialists in the UK: Assessing progress and recommendations for reform, *Crime Prevention and Community Safety*, 9, 92–101.

Button, M. and Gee, J. (2013). *Countering Fraud for Competitive Advantage – The Professional Approach to Reducing the Last Great Hidden Cost*, Chichester: John Wiley & Sons.

Button, M., Johnston, L., Frimpong, K. and Smith, G. (2007b). New directions in policing fraud: The emergence of the counter fraud specialists in the United Kingdom, *International Journal of the Sociology of Law*, 35, 192–208.

Chan, F. and Gibbs, C. (2020). Integrated theories of white-collar and corporate crime, in: Rorie, M.L. (editor), *The Handbook of White-Collar Crime*, Hoboken, NJ: Wiley & Sons, chapter 13, pages 191–208.

Cohen, L.E. and Felson, M. (1979). Social change and crime rate trends: A routine activity approach. *American Sociological Review*, 44, 588–608.

Craig, J.M. and Piquero, N.L. (2016). The effects of low self-control and desire-for-control on white-collar offending: A replication, *Deviant Behavior*, 37 (11), 1308–1324.

Craig, J.M. and Piquero, N.L. (2017). Sensational offending: An application of sensation seeking to white-collar and conventional crimes, *Crime & Delinquency*, 63 (11), 1363–1382.

Cressey, D. (1972). *Criminal Organization: Its Elementary Forms*, New York: Harper and Row.

Dearden, T.E. and Gottschalk, P. (2020). Gender and white-collar crime: Convenience in target selection, *Deviant Behavior*, published online https://doi.org/10.1080/01639625.2020.1756428.

Dhami, M.K. (2007). White-collar prisoners' perceptions of audience reaction, *Deviant Behavior*, 28, 57–77.

DN (2019). Ny dom kan skremme pengesterke hytteeiere fra ulovlig bygging – Ny dom gir god hjelp til kommuner som vil stoppe ulovlige byggearbeider i strandsonen (New court sentence might scare money-rich cottage owners from illegal construction building – New court sentence provides good help to municipalities who want to stop illegal construction work in the beach zone), *Daily Norwegian Business Newspaper Dagens Næringsliv*, Saturday, September 21, page 2.

Dugstad, L. and Skaalmo, G. (2017). Slik fikk han de rikes hytter godkjent på Tjøme (This way he got the rich people's huts approved on Tjøme), *Daily Norwegian Business Newspaper Dagens Næringsliv*, www.dn.no, published September 29.

Engdahl, O. (2015). White-collar crime and first-time adult-onset offending: Explorations in the concept of negative life events as turning points, *International Journal of Law, Crime and Justice*, 43 (1), 1–16.

Farquhar, J.D. and Rowley, J. (2009). Convenience: A services perspective, *Marketing Theory*, 9 (4), 425–438.

Fowler, T. (2014). BP's new tactic in oil spill claims: Go after the "special master", *The Wall Street Journal*, www.wsj.com, published January 27.

Freeh, L.J. (2013). *Independent External Investigation of the Deepwater Horizon Court Supervised Settlement Program, Report of Special Master Louis J. Freeh*, www.laed.uscourts.gov, published September 6.

Friedrichs, D.O. (2010). Integrated theories of white-collar crime, in: Cullen, F.T. and Wilcox, P. (editors), *Encyclopedia of Criminological Theory*, Volume 1, Los Angeles, CA: Sage Publications, pages 479–486.

Galvin, M.A. (2020). Substance or semantics? The consequences of definitional ambiguity for white-collar research, *Journal of Research in Crime and Delinquency*, 57 (3), 369–399.

Galvin, B.M., Lange, D. and Ashforth, B.E. (2015). Narcissistic organizational identification: Seeing oneself as central to the organization's identity, *Academy of Management Review*, 40 (2), 163–181.

Gamache, D.L. and McNamara, G. (2019). Responding to bad press: How CEO temporal focus influences the sensitivity to negative media coverage of acquisitions, *Academy of Management Journal*, 62 (3), 918–943.

Goldstraw-White, J. (2012). *White-Collar Crime: Accounts of Offending Behavior*, London: Palgrave Macmillan.

Gormley, T.P. (2009). *Administrative and Criminal Penalties for Illegal Pollution under Pollution Control Act*, September 14, International Law Office, published online https://www.internationallawoffice.com/Newsletters/Environment-Climate-Change/Norway/Arntzen-de-Besche-Advokatfirma-AS/Administrative-and-Criminal-Penalties-for-Illegal-Pollution-under-Pollution-Control-Act.

Gottschalk, P. (2014). *Financial Crime and Knowledge Workers: An Empirical Study of Defense Lawyers and White-Collar Criminals*, New York: Palgrave Macmillan.

Gottschalk, P. (2017). Convenience in white-collar crime: Introducing a core concept, *Deviant Behavior*, 38 (11), 605–619.

Gottschalk, P. (2019). *Convenience Triangle in White-Collar Crime – Case Studies of Fraud Examinations*, Cheltenham: Edward Elgar Publishing.

Gottschalk, P. (2020). Private policing of white-collar crime: Case studies of internal investigations by fraud examiners, *Police Practice and Research*, published online https://doi.org/10.1080/15614263.2020.1789461.

Gottschalk, P. and Benson, M.L. (2020). The evolution of corporate accounts of scandals from exposure to investigation, *British Journal of Criminology*, published online https://doi.org/10.1093/bjc/azaa001.

Greife, M.J. and Maume, M.O. (2020). Do companies pay the price for environmental crimes? Consequences of criminal penalties on corporate offenders, *Crime, Law and Social Change*, 73, 337–356.

Gulating (2013). *Court Case LG-2011-60302 – LG-2012-23847, Gulating lagmannsrett (Gulating Court of Appeals)*, Bergen, March 8.

Gulating (2015). *Court Case 14–039291ASD-GULA/AVD1, Gulating lagmannsrett (Gulating Court of Appeals)*, Bergen, February 16.

Hamilton, S. and Micklethwait, A. (2006). *Greed and Corporate Failure: The Lessons from Recent Disasters*, Basingstoke: Palgrave Macmillan.

Hansen, L.L. (2020). Review of the book "Convenience Triangle in White-Collar Crime: Case Studies of Fraud Examinations", *ChoiceConnect*, 57 (5), Middletown, CT: Association of College and Research Libraries.

Heltne, L. and Klevstrand, A. (2019). Her står Frederik Selvaags hytte ferdig – og ubrukelig. Fredrik Selvaag har fått nei fra Færder kommune til å ta i bruk sin nye Tjøme-hytte. Kommunen ber i stedet om en ny strandsone-søknad for hele hytta

(Here stands Frederik Selvaag's cottage ready – and useless. Fredrik Selvaag has got no from Færder municipality to use his new Tjøme cottage. The municipality asks instead for a new strandzone application for the whole cottage), *Daily Local Norwegian Newspaper Tønsbergs Blad*, www.tb.no, published July 17.

Higgins, E.T. (1997). Beyond pleasure and pain, *American Psychologist*, 52, 1280–1300.

Holm, R.C. (2019). Tjøme-arkitekt sliter etter byggeskandaler (Tjøme architect suffers after building scandals), *Norwegian Public Broadcasting NRK*, www.nrk .no, published June 20.

Holm, R.C. (2020). Har kranglet om 6 kvadratmeter stor bod i to år (Have quarrel about 6 square meters large storage room for two years), *Norwegian Public Broadcasting NRK*, www.nrk.no, published January 5.

Holmøy, E. (2017). Dette er korrupsjon. BDO har misforstått (This is corruption. BDO has misunderstood), *Daily Local Norwegian Newspaper Tønsbergs Blad*, Saturday, September 30, pages 1, 6, and 7.

Holmøy, E. (2018). Byggepolitiker på Tjøme: -Vi stolte både på kompetansen og beslutningene som ble tatt (Building politicians at Tjøme: -We trusted both the competence and the decisions that were made), *Daily Local Norwegian Newspaper Tønsbergs Blad*, www.tb.no, published July 28.

Holmøy, E. (2019). Varsler mulig riving av terrasse hos Turid Varner (Notifies possible demolition of terrace at Turid Varner), *Daily Local Norwegian Newspaper Tønsbergs Blad*, www.tb.no, published April 5.

Holmøy, E. (2020a). Advokaten mener hytteeierens tillatelser er verdt 20 millioner kroner. I dag mistet hun alle (The attorney claims the cottage owner's permit is worth 20 million kroner. Today she lost everything), *Daily Local Norwegian Newspaper Tønsbergs Blad*, www.tb.no, published May 6.

Holmøy, E. (2020b). Tror at også noen hytteeiere blir siktet (Believes that also some cottageowners will be charged), *Daily Local Norwegian Newspaper Tønsbergs Blad*, Thursday, May 14, page 4.

Holmøy, E. (2020c). Advokaten forsøkte å påvirke politikerne: -Jeg opplever dette som et trusselbrev (The attorney attempted to influence the politicians: -I perceive this as a threat letter), *Daily Local Norwegian Newspaper Tønsbergs Blad*, www.tb .no, published May 14.

Holth, F. and Winge, N.K. (2018). Bekymringer etter Tjøme-saken (Concerns after the Tjøme case), *Daily Norwegian Business Newspaper Dagens Næringsliv*, Tuesday, May 22, page 20.

Huisman, W. and Erp, J. (2013). Opportunities for environmental crime, *British Journal of Criminology*, 53, 1178–1200.

Karim, K.E. and Siegel, P.H. (1998). A signal detection theory approach to analyzing the efficiency and effectiveness of auditing to detect management fraud, *Managerial Auditing Journal*, 13 (6), 367–375.

King, M. (2020a). What makes a successful corporate investigator – An exploration of private investigators attributes, *Journal of Financial Crime*, published online https://doi.org/10.1108/JFC-02-2020-0019.

King, M. (2020b). Out of obscurity: The contemporary private investigator in Australia, *International Journal of Police Science and Management*, published online https://doi.org/10.1177/1461355720931887.

Kireenko, A.P., Nevzorova, E.N. and Fedotov, D.Y. (2019). Sector-specific characteristics of tax crime in Russia, *Journal of Tax Reform*, 5 (3), 249–264.

Klevstrand, A. (2018). Nedgraderer Tjøme-arkitekt (Degrades Tjøme architect), *Daily Norwegian Business Newspaper Dagens Næringsliv*, Wednesday, June 20, page 17.

Klevstrand, A. and Randen, M. (2018). Bygget luksushytte på overtid – risikerer riving (Built luxury cottage on overtime – risks demolition), *Daily Norwegian Business Newspaper Dagens Næringsliv*, www.dn.no, published July 23.

Klevstrand, A. and Solem, L.K. (2020). Økokrim undersøker hytteeiere i ny Tjøme-etterforskning (Økokrim examines cottage owners in new Tjøme investigation), *Daily Norwegian Business Newspaper Dagens Næringsliv*, www.dn.no, published May 1.

Klevstrand, A., Solem, L.K., Dugstad, L. and Skaalmo, G. (2020). Tjøme-arkitekt Rune Breili tiltalt for grov korrupsjon – ga arkitekt-råd for 50 000 kr (Tjøme architect Rune Breili charged with serious corruption – gave architect advice for 50 000 kroner), *Daily Norwegian Business Newspaper Dagens Næringsliv*, www.dn.no, published April 30.

Krippendorff, K. (1980). *Content Analysis: An Introduction to its Methodology*, Beverly Hills, CA: Sage.

Krohn, M.D. and Eassey, J.M. (2014). Integrated theories of crime, in: Miller, J.M. (editor), *The Encyclopedia of Theoretical Criminology*, Chichester: John Wiley & Sons, pages 458–463.

Larssen, L.D. (2017). Tjøme kommune svidde av 200.000 kr på kommunikasjonsbyrå (Tjøme municipality spent 200.000 kroner on communication firm), *Daily Local Norwegian Newspaper Tønsbergs Blad*, www.tb.no, published December 19.

Lehman, D.W., Cooil, B. and Ramanujam, R. (2019). The effects of rule complexity on organizational noncompliance and remediation: Evidence from restaurant health inspections, *Journal of Management*, 1–33, published online https://doi.org/10.1177/0149206319842262.

Lien, A.O. and Aunemo, E.W. (2019). Hun får betalt av fleire som er dypt involvert i Tjøme-skandalen. Nå har hun samlet byggebransjen mot kommunen (She gets paid by several who are deeply involved in the Tjøme scandal. Now she has gathered the construction industry against the municipality), *Daily Local Norwegian Newspaper Tønsbergs Blad*, www.tb.no, published May 24.

Lien, A.O. and Brevik, H.C. (2020). Frp-Anders forlot møte i protest: -Det ble rett og slett for drøyt (Right wing party member Anders left the meeting in protest: -It became simply too much), *Daily Local Norwegian Newspaper Tønsbergs Blad*, www.tb.no, published March 9.

Liska, A.E., Krohn, M.D. and Messner, S.F. (1989). Strategies and requisites for theoretical integration in the study of crime and deviance, in: Messner, S.F., Krohn, M.D. and Liska, A.E. (editors), *Theoretical Integration in the Study of Deviance and Crime*, Albany: State University of New York Press, pages 1–20.

Logan, M.W., Morgan, M.A., Benson, M.L. and Cullen, F.T. (2019). Coping with imprisonment: Testing the special sensitivity hypothesis for white-collar offenders, *Justice Quarterly*, 36 (2), 225–254.

Lynch, M.J. (2020). Green criminology and environmental crime: Criminology that matters in the age of global ecological collapse, *Journal of White Collar and Corporate Crime*, 1 (1), 50–61.

Mai, H.T.X. and Olsen, S.O. (2016). Consumer participation in self-production: The role of control mechanisms, convenience orientation, and moral obligation, *Journal of Marketing Theory and Practice*, 24 (2), 209–223.

Mann, K. (1985). *Defending White Collar Crime: A Portrait of Attorneys at Work*, New Haven, CT: Yale University Press.

Maslow, A.H. (1943). A theory of human motivation, *Psychological Review*, 50 (4), 370–396.

McClelland, P.L., Liang, X. and Barker, V.L. (2010). CEO commitment to the status quo: Replication and extension using content analysis, *Journal of Management*, 36 (5), 1251–1277.

Nordhordland (2010). *Court Case 09–098460MED-NOHO, Nordhordland tingrett (Nordhordland District Court)*, Bergen, March 26.

Obodaru, O. (2017). Forgone, but not forgotten: Toward a theory of forgone professional identities, *Academy of Management Journal*, 60 (2), 523–553.

Olaussen, M. (2018). Hvor mye koster det egentlig samfunnet at én privilegert mann bygger ulovlig i strandsonen? (How much does it really cost society that one privileged man builds illegally in the beach zone), *Daily Local Norwegian Newspaper Tønsbergs Blad*, www.tb.no, published May 15.

Patrucco, A.S., Luzzini, D. and Ronchi, S. (2017). Research perspectives on public procurement: Content analysis of 14 years of publications in the Journal of Public Procurement, *Journal of Public Procurement*, 16 (2), 229–269.

Pedersen, N. (2017). "Professoren" sin kamp for å reinvaska seg ("The professor's" struggle to clean himself), *Public Norwegian Broadcasting NRK*, www.nrk.no, published August 19.

Petrocelli, M., Piquero, A.R. and Smith, M.R. (2003). Conflict theory and racial profiling: An empirical analysis of police traffic stop data, *Journal of Criminal Justice*, 31 (1), 1–11.

Piquero, N.L. (2012). The only thing we have to fear is fear itself: Investigating the relationship between fear of falling and white-collar crime, *Crime and Delinquency*, 58 (3), 362–379.

Piquero, N.L. (2018). White-collar crime is crime: Victims hurt just the same, *Criminology & Public Policy*, 17 (3), 595–600.

Pontell, H.N., Black, W.K. and Geis, G. (2014). Too big to fail, too powerful to jail? On the absence of criminal prosecutions after the 2008 financial meltdown, *Crime, Law and Social Change*, 61 (1), 1–13.

Pratt, T.C. and Cullen, F.T. (2005). Assessing macro-level predictors and theories of crime: A meta-analysis, *Crime and Justice*, 32, 373–450.

Pratt, M.G., Kaplan, S. and Whittington, R. (2019). Editorial essay: The tumult over transparency: Decoupling transparency from replication in establishing trustworthy qualitative research, *Administrative Science Quarterly*, 1–19, published online https://doi.org/10.1177/0001839219887663.

Qiu, B. and Slezak, S.L. (2019). The equilibrium relationships between performance-based pay, performance, and the commission and detection of fraudulent misreporting, *The Accounting Review*, 94 (2), 325–356.

Rodriguez, P., Uhlenbruck, K. and Eden, L. (2005). Government corruption and the entry strategies of multinationals, *Academy of Management Review*, 30 (2), 383–396.

Saunders, M., Lewis, P. and Thornhill, A. (2007). *Research Methods for Business Students*, 5th Edition, London: Pearson Education.

Schnatterly, K., Gangloff, K.A. and Tuschke, A. (2018). CEO wrongdoing: A review of pressure, opportunity, and rationalization, *Journal of Management*, 44 (6), 2405–2432.

Schneider, S. (2006). Privatizing economic crime enforcement: Exploring the role of private sector investigative agencies in combating money laundering, *Policing & Society*, 16 (3), 285–312.

Skavhellen, Ø. and Lien, A.Ó. (2018). Tønsbergs Blad vant pris for dekningen av byggeskandalen på Tjøme (Tønsberg Blad won prize for coverage of the building scandal at Tjøme), *Daily Local Norwegian Newspaper Tønsbergs Blad*, www.tb.no, published May 2.

Stadler, W.A., Benson, M.L. and Cullen, E.T. (2013). Revisiting the special sensitivity hypothesis: The prison experience of white-collar inmates, *Justice Quarterly*, 30 (6), 1090–1114.

Sundström, M. and Radon, A. (2015). Utilizing the concept of convenience as a business opportunity in emerging markets, *Organizations and Markets in Emerging Economies*, 6 (2), 7–21.

Sutherland, E.H. (1939). White-collar criminality, *American Sociological Review*, 5 (1), 1–12.

Sutherland, E.H. (1983). *White Collar Crime – The Uncut Version*, New Haven, CT: Yale University Press.

Sykes, G.M. and Matza, D. (1957). Techniques of neutralization: A theory of delinquency, *American Sociological Review*, 22 (6), 664–670.

Thompson, R. (2017). With BP settlement claims winding down, Lafayette lawyer Parick Juneau turns attention to Takata air bag recall, *The Advocate*, www.theadvocate.com, published October 29.

Tilsynsrapport (2020). Gryteskjær fritidsbebyggelse tilsynsrapport (Leisure Building Supervision Report), Færder kommune (Municipality of Færder), reference 19/49893, dated January 17, 4 pages, postmottak@faerder.kommune.no.

Vasiu, V.I. and Podgor, E.S. (2019). Organizational opportunity and deviant behavior: Convenience in white-collar crime, *Criminal Law and Criminal Justice Books*, Rutgers, the State University of New Jersey, July, www.clcjbooks.rutgers.edu.

Wang, M. (2018). Arkitekten i byggesaksskandalen på Tjøme slår tilbake: -Færder kommune somler og bryter reglene (The architect in the building scandal at Tjøme hits back: -Færder municipality grapples and violates the rules), *Daily Local Norwegian Newspaper Tønsbergs Blad*, www.tb.no, published April 28.

Wang, M. (2019). Må søke helt på nytt fordi hytta er flyttet fem meter (Has to apply again because the cottage is moved five meters), *Daily Local Norwegian Newspaper Tønsbergs Blad*, www.tb.no, published June 7.

Wikstrom, P.O.H., Mann, R.P. and Hardie, B. (2018). Young people's differential vulnerability to criminogenic exposure: Bridging the gap between people- and place-oriented approaches in the study of crime causation, *European Journal of Criminology*, 15 (1), 10–31.

Williams, J.W. (2005). Reflections on the private versus public policing of economic crime, *British Journal of Criminology*, 45, 316–339.

Wingerde, K. and Lord, N. (2020). The elusiveness of white-collar and corporate crime in a globalized economy, in: Rorie, M.L. (editor), *The Handbook of White-Collar Crime*, Hoboken, NJ: Wiley & Sons, chapter 29, pages 469–483.

Ytreberg, R. (2018). Rådmannen vil ikke stoppe Selvaags hytte (The councilor will not stop Selvaag's cottage), *Daily Norwegian Business Newspaper Dagens Næringsliv*, Wednesday, May 9, pages 10–11.

19 Attorney defense strategies

Table 19.1 partly repeats Table 18.1 and lists wrongdoing by white-collar clients that their attorneys handle toward public authorities. All these issues came up in the last three years. The task for the attorneys is to prevent any reversal of any permits and to secure new permits to emerge.

Three defense strategies

Three themes are particularly noteworthy when distinguishing white-collar defense strategies from other defense strategies by attorneys. First, the role of white-collar attorneys is radically different from the typical criminal lawyer who defends a person suspected of and charged with street crime. Excessive power and greed is frequently the cause of white-collar crime, while poverty and powerlessness tends to be the cause of street crime. The former defense attorney spends far more time on each case, in terms of both workload and in terms of calendar time. This implies that a white-collar attorney works on fewer cases in parallel. The white-collar attorney gets a case much earlier and is far more likely to succeed in keeping wrongdoing charges away from the client. Second, information control is at the center of the white-collar attorney's work. The attorney is concerned with acquisition of crucial information and keeps damaging information out of the hands of public authorities such as municipalities, police investigators, and public prosecutors. A third theme centers on a major dilemma of these attorneys: How to defend vigorously the client without thereby becoming a party to the criminal act (Gottschalk, 2014).

In line with these themes, three specific strategies applied by white-collar attorneys are typical in defense of rich and mighty clients. First, a substance defense strategy is concerned with when and how an attorney decides to defend the client in a substantive way. Often, the substantive defense starts at a much earlier stage than in a street crime case. Several of the attorneys listed in Table 18.1 went early on into arguments with the municipality that all permits given were legally binding for the municipality.

Second, information control strategy is concerned with how the attorney determines what and how crucial information to control to make it difficult, and sometimes impossible, for public authorities to get the complete picture. Often,

Table 19.1 Identified white-collar clients and their cases of wrongdoing

	White-collar client	*Attorney case*
1	Ole Andresen	Denied swimming pool in Flatås road 109
2	Rune Breili	Architect involved in deviant cases
3	Arnfinn Hafsteen	Serious material competence shortage
4	Ole Borge	Decision to demolish a building
5	Arnfinn Hafsteen	Legality control of new building
6	Rune Breili	Suspected of corruption by the police
7	Werner Osther	Illegal blasting performed by approved company
8	Nanna Fløgstad Sohlberg	Summer house in Langestrand road 71 postponed
9	Gunnar Fredrik Selvaag	Summer house in Nautnes road 129 nonconforming
10	Hans Ole Helling	Demolition of tennis court
11	Carl Erik Krefting	Ottos road 46 liable for replacement
12	Turid Varner	Flekken road 64 with illegal terrace
13	Hans Petter Abrahamsen	Accusation of corruption by receiving bribes
14	Harald Dybsjord	Assessment cannot be reviewed afterward
15	Sigmund Arnesen	Revocation of permission for Mostranda Camping
16	Harald Svendsen	Approval of own building applications
17	Rune Breili	Violation charges for Bukkeliodden 54
18	Kristina M. Wilhelmsen	General permit for Ødekjær road 43 reversed
19	Lars Hellik Strøm	Removal of terrace and splashing walls
20	Sigmund Arnesen	Decision on reversal for Mostranda Camping
21	Tore Jacobsen	Mo road 104 connection to Mostranda Camping
22	Øyvind Garner	Summerhouse moved 5 m
23	Fridtjov Botvid Falck	Removal of stalls and exterior tiles
24	Celestine Clauson	No tennis court or swimming pool
25	Nanna Fløgstad Sohlberg	Postponed of cottage in Langestrand road 71
26	Harald Svendsen	Accusation of illegal construction in Sjøbodsand
27	77 construction firms	Construction industry lacking work
28	Rune Breili	Construction cases since 2010
29	Svein Homstvedt	Case of illegality in Flekken road 96
30	Scammer and scammed	Neholm road 67 fraud of 10 million kroner
31	Malling og Middelfart	Gryte reef blown up and building without permit
32	Tom Ragnar Wilhelmsen	Lilleskag road 89, doubled cottage size
33	Anders C. Wilhelmsen	General permit for Ødekjær road 43 removed
34	Mette Landgraff	Violated property borders
35	Evy Reimers	Illegal boathouses in Dals road 88
36	Marianne and Ulf Stuge	Illegal terrace in Nord harbor 62

information control defense is able to keep secrets and to claim that pieces of information are irrelevant. In municipal control work, there are normally a number of information sources. Controlling and limiting some sources can ensure that municipal control procedures are never successful in solving the wrongdoing puzzle. Several of the attorneys listed in Table 18.1 went early on into the supply of documents in favor of their clients to the municipality, while they denied access to documents in disfavor of their clients.

Third, the symbolic defense strategy addresses all other means that the attorney can apply to divert attention away from legal issues. An example is to use the press or other media to portray the offender as a victim. This was particularly evident when attorney Vibeke Hein Bæra in defense of architect Rune Breili (line 6 in Tables 18.1 and 19.1) portrayed the architect as a victim. His architectural firm had almost collapsed and faced bankruptcy. Breili had bribed nobody in the municipality, but rather helped the head of building permits when that person needed an architect to design his new home (Klevstrand et al., 2020).

Substance defense strategy

The counterpart for an attorney in misconduct and crime cases is the authorities, who decide whether a suspect is required to demolish the summerhouse. To prevent a negative municipal decision, the attorney will try to convince the staff as well as the politicians in the municipality that the client has done nothing that justifies demolition. The strategic issue for the attorney is how to succeed stopping the public authority from advancing the inquiry from suspicion to decisions that harm the client. While very different from other crime cases, an attorney's active defense work often starts in the initial phases of detection, when there are only rumors of wrongdoing that may or may not be relevant for municipal interference (Gottschalk, 2014).

Initially, it does not matter for the attorney whether the client has actually done something wrong that deserves punishment, because rumors so often develop into accusations in the media. In the Tjøme case, the key whistleblower continued to feed the media with information about summerhouses that were not according to permits and landscapes that had changed completely. Investigative journalists got into boats and took pictures of the palaces. Both local media (e.g., Holmøy, 2017, Wang, 2019) and national media (e.g., Dugstad and Skaalmo, 2017; Klevstrand, 2018) published stories with summerhouse pictures and names of owners. Journalists called owners for comments, and the owners transferred the inquiries to their attorneys. In that way, attorneys typically involve themselves long before any potential sanctions are on the agenda in the town hall in the municipality of Tjøme.

If a white-collar attorney were to behave in white-collar cases similar to attorneys in street crime cases, then the attorney would simply wait for the arrival of evidence against the client. Then the attorney would react to the evidence and the potential sanction. The street crime attorney is mainly reactive, while the white-collar attorney is proactive. The street crime attorney waits for formal charges against the client and then makes up an opinion what to do next. Typically, the attorney argues that the evidence is not sufficient to prove wrongdoing or guilt because presented evidence does not document in an adequate and convincing manner that the client has done something wrong that requires sanction. The attorney may argue that the evidence only proves outdated misconduct that cannot lead to sanctions. Uncertainty and doubt should benefit the client, every attorney will argue. It is every attorney's job to interpret laws and regulations in a subjective way, which should lead to a not-guilty conclusion for the client. This is the substance defense strategy. The attorney contributes legal and factual substance to a case handled by a public authority such as a municipality.

White-collar attorneys also contribute substance defense like street crime lawyers, but there are several differences, related to both points in time and magnitude of contribution. A white-collar substance defense starts much earlier in the public agency process, and it may last much longer into all kinds of appeals and retrials. The magnitude of contribution relates to the level of detail and the scope of evidence. Often, financial wrongdoing finds its documentation in detail such as a single bank transaction, a single invoice, or a single procurement of building material. The scope of evidence is often such that a lot of redundant and irrelevant material overflows the case to make sure that the parties overlook nothing of potential relevance. Instead of waiting for a potential sanction from the municipality, such as demolition of parts of the palace or waiting for the criminal case to open in court, the attorney starts substance defense as early as possible potentially to stop the procedure and the client from ever appearing in a municipal case or a court case. It is more the rule than exception that the attorney, in fear of future consequences, is actively on the case already when there are merely suspicion and rumors circulating. More rumors and accusations in the public domain can in fact be helpful to the attorney, as the attorney may argue that the case needs a stronger focus.

For example, in a fraud case in Norway, police investigators accused a family of insider trading in a company where they were involved. National media heavily covered the case. The family was a major owner of a large Norwegian manufacturing company, but there were other shareholders as well. Initially in the case, the police investigated the father and the mother as well as the daughter and son. A defense lawyer for the daughter successfully helped to keep her out of the case, arguing that the police should stay more focused. Despite the fact that the police found an SMS message on her phone saying "papa", which obviously meant her father, police detectives accepted her explanation that she called many older male persons, such as her uncle, for "papa", and the prosecution thus dismissed her case and never prosecuted her in court. The same thing happened to the mother. Only the father and son faced prosecution, and they received convictions to long prison sentences in court.

Similarly, the rich and mighty on the island of Tjøme had attorneys listed in Table 18.1 who argued that their clients did not know how architects, builders, plumbers, carpenters, electricians, landscapers, and other professionals applied for and obtained various permits from the municipality. The attorneys argued that the municipality and potentially the police should focus their cases on those who had submitted misleading applications, and who had deviated in practice from their own applications when doing jobs on elite members' properties on the island. The people who had done the job of creating tennis courts, swimming pools, annexes, park facilities, docks, boathouses, and other surprising elements should be addressed, not to the clients who had hired the people to do the job. It was all about focusing on the relevant offenders, the attorneys argued. This was substance defense in terms of influencing the definition of facts.

Weisburd et al. (1991: 99) formulated in the Yale Series after Mann (1985) how the white-collar defense lawyer is involved at a very early stage:

> From the time there is even a hint that a possible white-collar crime is under investigation by legal authorities, individuals suspected of involvement often begin to retain attorneys and to prepare to defend themselves. Early legal strategies may include negotiations with the agencies involved, the seeking of civil or out-of-court resolution of the case, and the trading of information in return for favorable treatment from the prosecutor's office. Other strategies include defense efforts to limit the scope of the information sought through subpoenaed documents and to curtail the information obtained by the government through search warrants and electronic surveillance.

Bjørn Stordrange, a well-known white-collar lawyer in Norway, defended Acta entrepreneur Fred Anton Ingebrigtsen, who faced accusations of insider trading in the Acta stock by helping family members make illegal profits. Early on, Stordrange expressed in public his frustration with several delays in police investigations (Haakaas, 2009: 2):

> When the charge was out last summer, we were told that the investigation would be completed last fall. The time limit was changed to Easter and then again to October this year. Now we are told that it might be completed by Christmas.

Stordrange's many appearances in the media indicated both active substance defense in the Acta case and symbolic defense, which is a topic later in this chapter. Stordrange was extremely proactive in terms of an organized crime suspicion, where the police wanted to use the Norwegian mafia rule on the case. Stordrange succeeded in convincing the police to drop the organized crime charge against Ingebrigtsen and his crime associates.

Similarly, the rich and mighty on the island of Tjøme who had all used the same architect to make their dreams come true distance themselves from any pattern suggested in the media. While they use the neutralization technique of normality, where everyone else did what they did, they also claim that they did not notice what everyone else did other than what the architects and others told them.

More importantly, in their substance defense, attorneys identified a number of mistakes in procedures in the municipality when handling client cases. There were delays, role conflicts between bureaucrats and politicians, and rule complexity that were impossible to understand for the nonprofessional (Lehman et al., 2019). Attorney Frode S. Jørgensen argued for his client Harald Dybsjord that the municipality simply did not have any relevant legal basis for reviewing previous approvals.

In Norway, white-collar attorneys are typically trying to influence police investigations at Økokrim. Økokrim is the main source of specialist skills for the police and prosecution authorities in their combat against financial and environmental crime (www.okokrim.no). Økokrim is similar to the Serious Fraud Office (SFO) in the United Kingdom. The SFO is an independent government department, operating under the superintendence of the Attorney General. Its purpose is to protect society by investigating and, if appropriate, prosecute those who commit serious or complex fraud, bribery, and corruption and pursuing them and others to recover the proceeds of their crime. For example, on March 11, 2013, the SFO charged three men in a Ponzi-style scheme, and the men appeared at City of London Magistrates Court charged with conspiracy to defraud investors in an alleged investment fraud related to electrical contacts in the hotel sector (www.sfo.gov.uk).

Crime in the legal sense is about the facts and the laws. If the facts do not match the laws, then Økokrim is reluctant to investigate the case. Very often, also in the environmental crime cases on the island of Tjøme, both facts and laws are unclear. The lack of clarity opens up for skilled attorneys to argue that Økokrim should stay away from the cases. The attorneys present client cases early on in such a way that it seems that the cases do not match the statutes. For example, many Norwegian laws have a limitation period where offenses become obsolete. Attorneys thus argue for a date of wrongdoing that causes the obsolescence clause to apply.

Information control strategy

Attorneys tend to take charge of information control at an early stage. Instead of being at the receiving end of documents from public authorities, the attorney is in a position where the attorney can monitor the flow of information. Of particular interest to the attorney is crucial information that can harm the client's case. The flow of harmful facts, insights, and knowledge of causes and effects that might become legal evidence with the public authorities is restricted and with the public authorities is problematic for the client, and therefore the attorney attempts to stop the flow.

An element of information control is control over various parties' explanations. The attorney attempts to keep parties in wrongdoing in line with each other to avoid a blame game between people who had different roles. If the summerhouse owner starts to blame the architect, the architect starts to blame the builder, the builder starts to blame the landscaper, and so on, then information will surface that typically harm all of them. This is in line with the prisoner's dilemma, in which individuals acting in their own self-interests do not produce the optimal outcome. Parties choose to protect themselves at the expense of other participants. As a result, participants find themselves in a worse state than if they had cooperated with each other.

This is exactly what happened in a different shoreline case in Norway, where the rich and mighty Hanne Madsen received a verdict of 45 days in jail by the court. She had bought a property behind her summerhouse, which was within the 100-m belt as well. On the acquired property, she built an illegal tennis court (DN, 2019). She presented herself as a victim of law violations and blamed the carpenter who eventually received a prison sentence as well. Agder (2019: 20) court of appeals wrote in its verdict:

> There is a strong development pressure in the beach zone and people invest very high amounts to gain access to this limited good. Effective enforcement of established rules and guidelines is therefore necessary, and material and serious violations must result in tangible reactions. Often, purely economic reactions will have less deterrent effect.

Strategic substance defense is not necessarily the first defense strategy applied by the attorney in a white-collar case. The defense lawyer's very first goal can be to prevent public authorities from obtaining information and evidence that is harmful to the client and prevent information from application by the criminal justice systems and other authorities to define and justify a formal charge or sanction.

At this stage, not laws and verdicts are of concern to the attorney. All the attorney is worried about is the flow of information that may transform into potential evidence for municipal sanctions and police investigations (Holmøy, 2020b). The attorney's job is all about preventing public authorities – especially the criminal justice system – from acquiring evidence and making it difficult or even impossible for them to understand pieces of information that they have obtained. It is all about stopping the inquiry at an early stage so that the case is closed. This is the defense lawyer's information control strategy (Gottschalk, 2014).

Information control implies that documents can remain confidential and hidden, and that clients and witnesses do not talk to officials in public positions. It may also imply that individuals enjoy protection from the press, so that only the lawyer makes statements about the case. Thereby, avoidance of leaking of unfavorable information is more likely. Summerhouse owners in Table 18.1 paid their attorneys to represent themselves in different contexts, including the media. Attorneys then emphasized information that was in favor of their clients, and denied negative accusations and rumors about their clients. As is evident from the table, one attorney in particular, Anne Tellefsen at local law firm Haraldsen Bydal Lie, represented many rich and mighty wrongdoers. She became an expert in handling different authorities and the media for her clients.

If Tjøme cases would escalate, then some clients are likely to replace local attorneys with nationally reputable attorneys. However, as long as the idea is to portray themselves as hunted innocent individuals suffering from the local municipality's actions, then it may seem smart to pay local attorneys. Clients do not want their cases to escalate. Rather, they would like their cases to close so that the cases move into public memory loss. Therefore, an information control strategy is to tell as little as possible to investigative journalists when they call.

Information control strategy finds application ahead of substance defense strategy whenever a white-collar offender first faces accusations in the media, which then cause initial signal alertness among public authorities. If the lawyer is successful in strategic information control, then raw material for legal argumentation remains hidden from public attention and use. The case for sanctions or prosecution deteriorates because important pieces of information not known to the municipality are missing. If an inquiry represents a puzzle, where all pieces have to be in place to see the picture, then both missing pieces and ill-placed pieces will make it difficult to perceive, understand, and interpret the fragmented picture. Inspectors from the municipality may find themselves with a case that is impossible to solve and thus decide to close it.

If a public agency is aware of information that they so far have not been able to collect, the attorney may argue that the requested information is difficult to retrieve and irrelevant for the case. The attorney may argue that the information is confidential, that it is out of date, or that it links to other problematic information. If the public agency already has gathered the information, the attorney may argue that the information does not apply to the specific case because authorities have collected it in an unethical or inadmissible way, such as pirate copying by other citizens, by trespassing to take pictures, or by violation of data protection laws.

These arguments when performing information control have the purpose of influencing the counterpart, either by convincing the public agency it is not a good idea to press for information or press charges or by obtaining a court ruling stating that information should not be made available or should even be returned to the client or the client's attorney. The attorney communicates procedure rules that support information control to the agency. For example, the attorney may argue that the law prohibits the search for or collection of specific documents. An agency may argue that the law allows it. Nevertheless, public officials must consider whether it is worth the fight with the attorney at this stage.

Strategic information control implies stopping or limiting the flow of information from the client to a public agency, by preventing the public agency access to informants who deny participation in interrogations, by preventing access to other information sources, and by requesting the return of documents not used in the agency (Mann, 1985: 7):

> The defense attorney's aim is to instruct the client or third party holding inculpatory information how to refrain from disclosing it to the government and, if necessary, to persuade or force him to refrain.

Inculpatory, also called incriminating, information is that which shows that a person has been involved in a criminal act. It is self-revealing information by the suspect. Inculpatory information finds application in the criminal justice system as evidence to prove guilt. Exculpatory information helps prove that a person has not been involved in a criminal act. In the information control strategy, the attorney attempts to stimulate the flow of exculpatory information and prevent the flow of inculpatory information.

An attorney's active information control strategy can remain secret to other parties in the case, including the client. Success is often dependent upon the lack of awareness among other parties, including the press.

When an attorney advises a client not to answer certain questions in the next interview and instead answer that he does not know or that he will have to check facts first, the client is subject to information control. The attorney is applying the information control strategy via the client. The public agency knows nothing about it. One result might be that the inquiry suffers from delay and potential termination.

For example, attorney Eilert Eilertsen for client Nanna Fløgstad Sohlberg attempted to delay case handling in the municipality by sending a letter in June 2018:

> The case appears to be very comprehensive and complex. For this reason, I need to have access to some documents in the municipality's possession before I can properly protect the family's interests.

One reason to delay the case might be to make it obsolete after a number of years. Many statutes in Norwegian law define offenses as outdated after some years. Even if a law violation is not yet outdated, an agency will be reluctant to look into a case that soon will become outdated.

A former police officer, now academic at a university on the UK, expressed the following opinion about white-collar solicitors in a personal email communication:

> As an ex-police officer, I anecdotally know that solicitors lie and use all forms of diabolical half-truths to get clients off. They are entrepreneurial in their use of knowledge and of systems to get results. Similar to detectives as entrepreneurs, they are continually working, lurking, and getting results.

Information control does not only occur in white-collar cases. In many other cases, the attorney works to exclude pieces of evidence from agency access and application. The attorney may argue that acquired information in the agency is a result of an illegal manner of information collection, or that information is misleading or irrelevant to the case. What makes white-collar cases so special is that strategic information control is of key importance – it is sometimes the most important activity – successfully to work for the client's best interests. In other kinds of cases, information control is mainly a tactical maneuver to detract attention or delay the case temporarily.

The information control strategy finds support in the attorney-client privilege as well as the work-product privilege. While the attorney-client privilege shields any information communicated to an attorney, the work-product privilege protects information that represents preparation for litigation (Oh, 2004).

Strategic information control is concerned with the flow of damaging information about the client. An attorney will attempt to prevent a public agency from exploring and exploiting various sources of information collection. Strategic information control implies taking control over information sources that are most likely to receive requests from a public agency. A public agency has many information sources when they inquire into a case, and a defense attorney can influence these sources to a varying extent.

Symbolic defense strategy

A symbol is an object or a phrase that represents an idea, a belief, or an action. Symbol defense is the application of symbols that can benefit the client. An example is the symbol of 20 million Norwegian kroner (about US$2 million) that attorney Anne Tellefsen applied to benefit her client Celestine Clauson. Tellefsen claimed that the amount represented what Clauson had paid for expansion rights when she bought the summerhouse (Holmøy, 2020a). Clauson paid 30 million Norwegian kroner for the summerhouse, but it was only worth 10 million Norwegian kroner without the expansion rights. Clauson's attorney claimed that the seller had told Clauson that the municipality had granted expansion rights. The claimed expansion approvals included a swimming pool, a tennis court, a larger basement, as well as changes to the façade of the building. When the whistleblower informed politicians in the municipality that approvals were not according to rules and regulations, the councilor recommended to the politicians to determine permits and approvals as illegitimate and not valid. The reaction from Tellefsen was to send a long letter to the politicians telling that the municipality would be liable for Clauson's loss of 20 million Norwegian kroner. One of the politicians expressed in the media that she perceived the letter as a threat (Holmøy, 2020c). The threat was symbolic, because the municipality said it is never involved in the private transaction of real estate between a seller and a buyer.

Attorney Henning Harborg on behalf of his client Carl Erik Krefting also applied a symbolic defense of threat. The attorney claimed in a letter to the municipality that the municipality would be liable to compensate his client completely for any economic loss that could occur because of the review of Krefting's building matters (Blix, 2018). Harborg was also attorney for the widow Turid Varner, but she decided to tear down the terrace and the park facility that blocked the crawl for people, instead of continuing the quarrel with the municipality.

Symbolic defense is concerned with activities that represent defense, but the activities in themselves are no defense. Symbols take the form of words, sounds, gestures, or visual images. When attorney Vibeke Bæra asked for a picture of herself with her client Rune Breili, the visual image published in the local newspaper signaled a hard-working architect who had done nothing wrong.

Symbolic defense is an alternative and supplement to substance defense. Substance and symbolic defense are different arenas where the white-collar attorney can work actively to try to make the public officials close the case. The purpose of symbolic defense is to communicate information and pseudo-legal opinions by means of symbols. Examples of attorney opinions are concerns about unacceptable delays in public administration, low-quality work by public officials, or other issues related to work at public agencies. Several of the attorneys listed in the table for Tjøme applied this symbolic defense strategy. For example, attorney Stig L. Bech at law firm BAHR wrote a five-page letter to the municipality pointing at all the weaknesses in the local administration. Since the municipality is required to reply to questions phrased in the letter, they had to spend time on their reply rather than on doing casework, which caused a further deterioration in the deadline statistics for the administration.

Complaining about delays in inquiries and administrative work is not substance defense, as the complaint is not expressing a meaning about the wrongdoing and possible sanctioning and punishment. Complaining is a symbolic defense, where the goal is to mobilize sympathy for the white-collar client and to reduce the chances of success for the counterpart.

White-collar attorneys vary in the extent to which they find media coverage a suitable option for symbolic defense. Ideally, each attorney should only have what is best for the client in mind. However, some famous attorneys may have their own media agenda, more or less independent of the current clients they are supposed to help and assist. Irrespective of client and/or attorney agenda, the attorney must be prepared to respond to media inquiries. The client may want to present the story in the press because he or she may believe that press coverage will have a positive impact on personal image as well as proceedings in the public agency and in the criminal justice system. Readers may perceive public agency statements in the press as provocation against the client, who wants to tell a different story.

Two attorneys in Table 18.1 represented themselves, but they presented themselves as attorneys for clients that happened to be themselves. Attorney Ole Andresen complained about the reversal of decision in the municipality. He wanted to have a swimming pool and build an annex, but the municipality had withdrawn the permit. Attorney Ole Borge also represented himself. Tjøme municipality had ordered the removal of his suspension bridge and steel bars. He complained and tried to compare his case with other cases where approvals were still valid.

While the administration in the municipality handled complaints and reviewed permits and withdrawn permits, several attorneys skipped contacting the administration and sent mail to politicians directly instead. Typically, few days before a political body was to meet, the attorney sent a letter as an email attachment to each member of the political body. In that way, the attorney hoped to short-circuit the process in the administration. Tellefsen's letter on behalf of Clauson is an example. Another example is the rich heir Gunnar Fredrik Selvaag who wrote a personal letter to a political committee in the municipality with the help of his attorney Mari Helen Gulsvik.

A frequent theme in the symbolic defense by attorneys was tennis courts and swimming pools. Some cases concerned the denial of permits to build tennis courts and swimming pools. Other cases concerned removal of tennis courts and swimming pools that had not received appropriate permits. Attorney Christian H.P. Reusch was engaged in a former case for summerhouse owner Kristina M. Wilhelmsen, while attorney Nils Hansson was engaged in a latter case for summerhouse owner Hans Ole Helling.

A common approach in symbolic defense is to portray wrongdoing as completely insignificant while the reaction by the public agency is abuse of power. An example is attorney Martin Støren for his client Lars Hellik Strøm. Støren wrote in his letter "the municipality may refrain from prosecuting violations if conditions are of minor importance".

The symbolic defense by attorney Anne Tellefsen on behalf of her client Celestine Clauson was interesting as the summerhouse case evolved in the media. When an investigative journalist interviewed the seller, that is the previous owner, Stein Kittelsen, he denied ever to have applied for permits to have a swimming pool and tennis court (Holmøy, 2020d: 8):

> We sold it, as it is, not with any permits at all. We think the property is worth around 30–35 million kroner, says Kittelsen.

When Celestine Clauson in 2015 bought the summerhouse in Nesholm road 67 on the island of Tjøme from the family Kittelsen, who had owned the place for generations, she was only 18 years old. Her father, Conrad Clauson, was the real owner. He had made a fortune as a broker when he worked for Credit Suisse First Boston in London, where he exploited bank clients for his personal benefit (Ahuja, 2005):

> Credit Suiesse First Boston has started legal proceedings against a former member of staff after he failed to repay a $750,000 loan. CSFB has launched the claim, which was filed in the UK high court in February, against Conrad Clauson, a Norwegian who worked as a private client broker at Donaldson, Lufkin & Jenrette, which became part of Credit Suisse in August 2000.

Clauson had placed his fortune in a trust in the tax haven Virgin Island (Berglihn et al., 2007). In the Tjøme case, he first paid architect Breili to successfully apply for permits in the municipality. Then he paid attorney Tellefsen to fight for the illegal permits by symbolic defense (Holmøy, 2020c).

Bibliography

Agder (2019). *Court Case 18–178766AST-ALAG*, September 16, Agder lagmannsrett (Agder court of appeals), Agder.

Ahuja, V. (2005). CSFB sues former broker over $750,000 loan, *Financial News*, www.fnlondon.com, published August 8.

Berglihn, H. (2019). Princess-arving dømt til fengsel (Princess heir sentenced to prison), daily Norwegian business newspaper *Dagens Næringsliv*, Friday, September 20, page 4.

Blix, N.T. (2018). Hyttemilliardæren har sendt advokatsvar til kommunen. –I den grad det er gjort feil i den tidligere byggesaken, er de ene og alene Tjøme kommunes ansvar (To the extent mistakes have been made in the previous building case, it is Tjøme municipality's responsibility alone), *Local Daily Norwegian Newspaper Tønsbergs Blad*, www.tb.no, published September 21.

DN (2019). Ny dom kan skremme pengesterke hytteeiere fra ulovlig bygging – Ny dom gir god hjelp til kommuner som vil stoppe ulovlige byggearbeider i strandsonen (New court sentence might scare money-rich cottage owners from illegal construction building – New court sentence provides good help to municipalities who want to stop illegal construction work in the beach zone), *Daily Norwegian Business Newspaper Dagens Næringsliv*, Saturday, September 21, page 2.

Dugstad, L. and Skaalmo, G. (2017). Slik fikk han de rikes hytter godkjent på Tjøme (This way he got the rich people's huts approved on Tjøme), *Daily Norwegian Business Newspaper Dagens Næringsliv*, www.dn.no, published September 29.

Gottschalk, P. (2014). *Financial Crime and Knowledge Workers: An Empirical Study of Defense Lawyers and White-Collar Criminals*, New York: Palgrave Macmillan.

Haakaas, E. (2009). Acta-saken kan smuldre bort (The Acta case can mold away), *Daily Norwegian Newspaper Aftenposten*, November 27, Business section, page 2.

Holmøy, E. (2017). Dette er korrupsjon. BDO har misforstått (This is corruption. BDO has misunderstood), *Daily Local Norwegian Newspaper Tønsbergs Blad*, Saturday, September 30, pages 1, 6, and 7.

Holmøy, E. (2020a). Advokaten mener hytteeierens tillatelser er verdt 20 millioner kroner. I dag mistet hun alle (The attorney claims the cottage owner's permit is worth 20 million kroner. Today she lost everything), *Daily Local Norwegian Newspaper Tønsbergs Blad*, www.tb.no, published May 6.

Holmøy, E. (2020b). Tror at også noen hytteeiere blir siktet (Believes that also some cottageowners will be charged), *Daily Local Norwegian Newspaper Tønsbergs Blad*, Thursday, May 14, page 4.

Holmøy, E. (2020c). Advokaten forsøkte å påvirke politikerne: -Jeg opplever dette som et trusselbrev (The attorney attempted to influence the politicians: -I perceive this as a threat letter), *Daily Local Norwegian Newspaper Tønsbergs Blad*, www.tb.no, published May 14.

Holmøy, E. (2020d). De mystiske milliontillatelsene (The mysterious millions permits), *Daily Local Norwegian Newspaper Tønsbergs Blad*, www.tb.no, page 1.

Klevstrand, A. (2018). Nedgraderer Tjøme-arkitekt (Degrades Tjøme architect), *Daily Norwegian Business Newspaper Dagens Næringsliv*, Wednesday, June 20, page 17.

Klevstrand, A., Solem, L.K., Dugstad, L. and Skaalmo, G. (2020). Tjøme-arkitekt Rune Breili tiltalt for grov korrupsjon – ga arkitekt-råd for 50 000 kr (Tjøme architect Rune Breili charged with serious corruption – gave architect advice for 50 000 kroner), *Daily Norwegian Business Newspaper Dagens Næringsliv*, www.dn.no, published April 30.

Lehman, D.W., Cooil, B. and Ramanujam, R. (2019). The effects of rule complexity on organizational noncompliance and remediation: Evidence from restaurant health inspections, *Journal of Management*, published online, pages 1–33, DOI: 10.1177/0149206319842262.

Mann, K. (1985). *Defending White Collar Crime: A Portrait of Attorneys at Work*, New Haven, CT: Yale University Press.

Oh, J.J. (2004). How (Un)ethical are you? Letters to the Editor. *Harvard Business Review*, March, page 122.

Wang, M. (2019). Må søke helt på nytt fordi hytta er flyttet fem meter (Has to apply again because the cottage is moved five meters), *Daily Local Norwegian Newspaper Tønsbergs Blad*, www.tb.no, published June 7.

Weisburd, D., Wheeler, S., Waring, E., and Bode, N. (1991). *Crimes of the Middle Classes*, New Haven, CT: Yale University Press.

20 Private policing outcome

The frequent conclusion in private policing reports is misconduct and wrongdoing, but no offense or crime. This conclusion does not only occur frequently when attorneys from law firms conduct fraud examinations in client organizations. Rather, the conclusion seems valid for all kinds of fraud examiners, including reviewers from auditing firms. This is of concern, as reviewed literature in this chapter indicates that there is a growing gap between public government and private governance when it comes to prevention and detection of misconduct and crime in organizations. This chapter suggests that investigative journalists in the media and fraud examiners in private investigations have the potential of filling some of this gap. Based on the theory of crime signal detection, this chapter finds that investigative journalists are in the position of detecting white-collar crime scandals as they rely on tips and whistleblowing. Empirical evidence from Norway documents that the media disclose a significant fraction of crime stories that later result in prosecution and conviction of white-collar offenders. Empirical evidence from Norway does not document any contribution from fraud examiners in private policing of economic crime, as they typically conclude with misconduct, but no crime, often to the satisfaction of their clients.

White-collar crime magnitude

Gottschalk and Gunnesdal (2018) have estimated a detection rate for white-collar crime of less than 1 out of 12 offenders in Norway, which seems supported by an empirical study of bribery detection in Norway by Andresen and Button (2019). The detection rate in the United States is even lower based on estimates of the magnitude of white-collar crime by the National White-Collar Crime Center (Huff et al., 2010) and the Association of Certified Fraud Examiners (ACFE, 2008, 2014, 2016). Offenders tend to move under the radar (Williams et al., 2019).

However, it is important to note that the term white-collar crime is famously problematic. In the Norwegian estimate, a white-collar offender is a person who abuses the professional position to commit a financial crime to benefit the organization and/or the individual (Gottschalk, 2019). The detection rate of less than 1 out of 12 refers to individuals, not organizations.

Kourula et al. (2019) argue that there is a gap between government and governance, where neither public authorities nor self-regulating bodies involve themselves in the detection of corruption and other forms of financial crime. Actors in the criminal justice system have traditionally a preference toward street criminals rather than white-collar criminals (Galvin and Simpson, 2020; Michel, 2016; Piquero et al., 2008). Actors in auditing and compliance functions in business and public enterprises seem to have a preference toward formal rules and guidelines in the shape of window-dressing rather than detection of potential offenders (Desai, 2020). Alon et al. (2019) argue that accounting and auditing functions have undergone a legitimacy crisis in recent years. At least part of the answer why there is a preference for formal rules and guidelines is the task of confirming rather than questioning figures in financial statements, and conflicts of interest between auditing and the provision of accounting and management consultation.

Kourula et al. (2019: 1109) suggest, "Civil society was perceived to be left to fill the gaps that other sectors did not address", because "growing private regulation often put civil society in the driver's seat in 'policing' business activities" as "privatization of authority" has occurred. Furthermore, Kourula et al. (2019: 1110) suggest, "Governments are losing power", and "Governments lack enforcement capacity to impact multinational companies". Governments are losing oversight power for various reasons, including lack of business knowledge and variations in national jurisdictions. One problem in state cooperation is that different states in their legislation do not agree on what should be legal and illegal activities, as exemplified by Boghossian and Marques (2019).

Eberlein (2019) argues that "globalization opens markets for corporations but outstrip the capacity of states to regulate cross-border business conduct for the public good". Schneider and Scherer (2019: 1147) argue that "the extent to which state authorities can regulate the externalities and the behavior of multinational corporations is limited", and "gaps in governance abound in today's globalized world". Maher et al. (2019) found that governments not just in global business, but also in local business are reluctant to intervene.

Therefore, executives and other privileged individuals in multinational companies tend to have convenient opportunities for tax evasion in high-tax countries, for money laundering in tax havens, and for corruption and other kinds of white-collar crime in transnational operations. There are also complex issues of global versus local auditing and lawyering, making the opportunity structure even more convenient for potential offenders (Gottschalk, 2019). Moreover, some executives are simply too big to fail and too powerful to jail (Pontell et al., 2014). A potential avenue to fill the gap between government and governance might be to strengthen business-government interactions. However, Hamann (2019) found that business-government interactions result in corporate social irresponsibility, where a process of dynamic deterioration leads to passivity in both government and governance.

This chapter suggests that investigative journalists in the media and fraud examiners at global auditing firms and local law firms seem to fill some of the gap between public government and private governance when it comes to detection of white-collar offenders (Button and Gee, 2013; King, 2020a, 2020b; Schneider, 2006; Williams, 2005, 2008, 2014). Press reporters' detection of misconduct and crime "represented an important ingredient of the nineteenth-century newspaper" (Taylor, 2018: 346), and this is certainly also the case so far in the twenty-first-century media in many countries. While the tabloid press dominates the media in some countries, there are still quite a few prominent publishing houses where investigative journalism is the rule rather than the exception.

This chapter raises the question of the contribution of private actors, such as journalists and fraud examiners (Brooks and Button, 2011; Button, 2019; Button et al., 2007a, 2007b; Button and Gee, 2013; Gottschalk and Tcherni-Buzzeo, 2017; King, 2020a, 2020b; Schneider, 2006; Williams, 2005, 2014), in detecting white-collar crime. The role of journalists in exposing white-collar crime seems to be an underdeveloped area of study. In that context, this chapter is an important addition to research.

White-collar crime detection

The theory of crime signal detection is relevant to the study of white-collar crime detection. Signal detection theory is concerned with the ability of individuals to understand pieces of information that can come from various sources. The theory emphasizes individuals' varying signal discrimination processes. Discrimination processes include the sensitivity toward signals in general as well as the separation of real signals from noise signals.

Signal detection theory is a model for how humans detect signals in a background of interference or noise. The theory assumes that the human observer behaves like a rational economic decision-maker, and attempts to balance costs and benefits to arrive at an optimal solution. There are four possibilities in the decision matrix of the observer of potential misconduct and crime (Karim and Siegel, 1998: 368):

- The observer notices a noise when it is a signal (called a miss)
- The observer notices a signal when it is a signal (called a hit)
- The observer notices a noise when it is a noise (called a correct identification)
- The observer notices a signal when it is a noise (called a false alarm)

The observer needs to make a decision concerning the event and classify it either as a signal or as a noise. In an organizational context – where less powerful individuals suspect powerful individuals of wrongdoing – the less powerful will conveniently prefer to think of the event as a noise rather than as a signal.

Signal detection theory may shed some light into why some actors discover and disclose more white-collar crime than other potential observers disclose. Signal detection theory holds that the detection of a stimulus depends on both the intensity of the stimulus and the physical and psychological state of the individual. A detector's ability or likelihood to detect some stimulus is affected by the intensity of the stimulus (e.g., how loud a signal is) and the physical and psychological state of the detector (e.g., how alert the person is). Perceptual sensitivity depends upon the perceptual ability of the observer to detect a signal or target or to discriminate signal from nonsignal events (Szalma and Hancock, 2013).

Furthermore, detecting persons may have varying ability to discern between information-bearing recognition (called pattern) and random patterns that distract from information (called noise).

According to the theory of signal detection, there are a number of determinants of how a person will detect a signal (Huff and Bodner, 2013). In addition to signal intensity, signal alertness, and pattern recognition, there are other factors such as personal competence (including knowledge, skills, and attitude), experience, and expectations. These factors determine the threshold level. Low signal intensity, low signal alertness, and limited pattern recognition, combined with low competence, lack of experience, and lack of expectations, will lead to a high threshold level, meaning the individual will not detect white-collar crime.

Signal alertness is not a stable set of minds over time. Rather, the extent of signal alertness by an observer varies with other concerns that the person may have (Qiu and Slezak, 2019).

Signal detection theory implies that persons make decisions under conditions of uncertainty. The theory assumes that the decision-maker is not a passive receiver of information, but an active decision-maker who makes difficult perceptual judgments under conditions of uncertainty. Whether a stimulus is present or absent, whether a stimulus is perceived or not perceived, and whether an observer ignores a perceived stimulus will influence the decision in terms of detecting or not detecting white-collar crime.

Gomulya and Mishina (2017: 557) introduced the term signal susceptibility since signals may be differently susceptible to potential errors and manipulation:

> This could be due to a variety of possible reasons, including whether the signal is self- or other-reported, whether it is verifiable, or whether it is a "stock" or a "flow" signal. Self-reported signals should on average be more susceptible to manipulations by the focal signaler (i.e., the one who can benefit from a positive signal) compared to signals reported by third parties.

Given this definition, signal susceptibility can be included as an aspect of signal intensity, where signal intensity deteriorates at suspicion of errors and manipulation increases. Similarly, noise in general will reduce signal intensity. Gomulya and Mishina (2017: 555) distinguish between two sources of noise during signaling – noise from the signal itself and noise from the behavior of the signaler.

Another term introduced by Gomulya and Mishina (2017: 55) is signal reliance, where reliance on different types of signals is based on the credibility of the signaler, and "thus a similar signal is likely to have different effects for credible versus less credible" signalers. Given this perspective, signal reliance can be included as an aspect of signal alertness, where less credible signalers cause lower alertness to the signal.

Gomulya and Mishina (2017) discuss pattern recognition in terms of screening theory where the receiver prioritizes among possible types of signals. The focus is on how receivers place differential value on signals that may come from different senders such as documents, accounts, and individuals. Screening theory posits that receivers screen by focusing on signals that they believe are highly correlated with unobservable characteristics of interest.

Signal detection theory characterizes the activity of an individual's discrimination as well as psychological factors that bias his or her judgment. The theory is concerned with the individual's discriminative capacity or sensitivity that is independent of the judgmental bias or decision criterion the individual may have had when the discrimination took place in the head of the observer.

Whistleblowers and informants in general are often important actors in the discovery of white-collar misconduct and crime for both investigative journalists and fraud examiners. Whistleblowing is the disclosure by an individual in an organization or in a society of deviant practices to someone who can do something about it (Bjørkelo et al., 2011). Whistleblowing is the disclosure by organizational members of illegal, immoral, or illegitimate practices under the control of their employers, to persons or organizations that may be able to effect action to terminate such practices (Wells et al., 2020). Whistleblowing is an action by employees who believe that their business or colleague(s) are involved in activities of misconduct and crime, cause unnecessary harm, transgress human rights, or contribute to otherwise immoral offenses (Mpho, 2017). However, one mechanism preventing many potential whistleblowers is the fear of retaliation and reprisals (Miceli and Near, 2013; Rehg et al., 2009). This chapter is not concerned with whistleblowing as such and refers thus only to relevant research on the phenomenon (Alleyne et al., 2013; Andrade, 2015; Culiberg and Mihelic, 2017; Dyck et al., 2010).

This research is concerned with the detection of white-collar criminals. The collection of our Norwegian sample of white-collar offenders below applied the original definition and characteristics of white-collar crime. Our sample thus has the following characteristics: famous individuals in terms of highly exposed social status and respectability, famous companies in terms of major suppliers in their businesses, surprising stories, important events, substantial consequences, matters of principles, and significant public interest. The operational definition of famous is simply that the press has exposed individuals and companies. The two main financial newspapers in Norway are *Dagens Næringsliv* and *Finansavisen*, both of which are conservative-leaning business newspapers. In addition, the business-friendly national daily newspaper *Aftenposten* regularly reports news of white-collar criminals. Left-wing newspapers such as *Klassekampen* very seldom cover specific white-collar criminal cases, although generally report on the white-collar crime phenomenon. The total number of white-collar criminals was 405 reported during 2009–2015. Verification of facts in newspaper accounts took place by obtaining court documents. After registering newspaper accounts as an important indication of white-collar offenders, this research compared the contents of newspaper articles and expanded the notes by court sentences, which typically range from 5 to 50 pages in Norwegian district courts, courts of appeal, and the Supreme Court.

Investigative media journalism

Norwegian courts convicted 405 white-collar offenders to prison from 2009 to 2016. Table 20.1 lists sources of detection for these criminals. We find journalists occupy the top position, followed by crime victims, bankruptcy lawyers, internal auditors, tax authority clerks, bank employees, external auditors, and police officers.

A real example of the contribution of an investigative journalist to uncover white-collar crime in Norway is relevant to provide here. Seven decommissioned Norwegian naval vessels ended up in the hands of a warlord in Nigeria. The 2012 sale took a surprising turn when an investigative journalist in a Norwegian daily newspaper (Egeberg, 2014, 2015) revealed that the vessels were serving, two years later, in the private flotilla of a former Nigerian rebel (Evans, 2017; Tufts, 2018). Nigeria is rich in oil resources where the rebels fight for control (Ezeonu, 2020; PwC, 2015; Reporter, 2013). The news about the six demilitarized missile torpedo boats and one naval support vessel triggered both an internal fraud examination by PwC (2014, 2015) for the Ministry of Defense in Norway and a police investigation by Økokrim (Norwegian national authority for investigation and prosecution of economic and environmental crime).

The police investigation led to the conviction in May 2017 of one Norwegian official on bribery charges and the revelation of the role played by a UK intermediary, CAS-Global Ltd. The firm applied for export licenses in Norway and for a re-export license for the naval support vessel from the UK, telling the Norwegians that the ships would support an official West African mission, and the British that the ships should serve the Nigerian government (Tufts, 2018).

The Norwegian official appealed the conviction in a district court in Norway in May 2017 via a court of appeals and further to the Supreme Court (Oslo tingrett,

Table 20.1 Detection of white-collar crime in Norway

S.No.	*Crime detection source*	*Sum*	*%*
1	Journalists investigating tips from readers	101	25%
2	Crime victims suffering financial loss	52	13%
3	Bankruptcy lawyers identifying misconduct	45	11%
4	Internal auditors controlling transactions	45	11%
5	Tax authority clerks carrying out controls	25	6%
6	Bank employees controlling accounts	18	4%
7	External auditors controlling clients	18	4%
8	Police officers investigating financial crime	9	2%
9	Stock exchange clerks controlling	4	1%
10	Other knowledge workers as detection sources	88	23%
	Total	405	100%

2017; NTB, 2019). The Supreme Court confirmed in May 2019 the sentence in Borgarting court of appeals from October 2018 of 4 years and 3 years in prison for the former commander Bjørn Stavrum in the Norwegian navy (Borgarting, 2018; Eriksen, 2019; Høyesterett, 2019).

Table 20.2 presents an exploratory attempt to describe signal detection features of observers who have noticed and discovered white-collar crime. Signal intensity, signal alertness, pattern recognition, and personal experience from signal detection theory are characteristics of detection ability.

Pattern recognition is a matter of sense-making and contextualization. Contextualization captures the ongoing process of understanding and explaining relationships between information elements. High gives a score of 3, medium a score of 2, and low a score of 1.

We argue that signal intensity for tips to journalists normally is high, as whistleblowers tend to be upset and want to get attention (Andresen and Button, 2019). Furthermore, we suggest that signal alertness is high among journalists, as they are dependent on tips in their daily work to cover news stories. The issue of pattern recognition is not obvious for journalists, since they often present fragments on a publishing basis, rather than a complete and consistent story of events. Personal experience will vary among journalists who may or may not have been writing about white-collar crime before, depending on the extent of specialization among journalists in the newspaper.

The idea of Table 20.2 is to apply four characteristics of signal detection theory to detection of white-collar crime. At this stage, the items and values represent exploratory research that need further study to be trustworthy. Selection of characteristics as well as judgment along these characteristics for each crime detection source requires multiple raters to enable inter-rater reliability in future research.

One reason for the high signal alertness among journalists is their complete dependence on external tips to produce news stories. Journalists always need

Table 20.2 Characteristics of stimulus in detection of white-collar crime

S.No.	*Crime detection*	*Signal intensity*	*Signal alertness*	*Pattern recognition*	*Personal knowledge*	*Score*
1	Media journalists	High	High	Low	Medium	9
2	Crime victims	High	Low	Medium	Low	7
3	Bankruptcy lawyers	Low	Low	Medium	Medium	6
4	Internal auditors	Low	Medium	Medium	Medium	7
5	Tax clerks authority	Low	Medium	Low	Medium	6
6	Bank employees	Low	Medium	Low	Low	5
7	External auditors	Low	Medium	Medium	Low	6
8	Police officers	Low	Medium	High	Low	7
9	Stock clerks	Low	Low	Medium	Low	5
10	Other sources	–	–	–	–	–

sources to which they have no access unless the sources cooperate with the media. By being polite and receptive, journalists increase the likelihood that whistle-blowers and others will contact the media when they learn of potential misconduct and crime (Andresen and Button, 2019). There seems to be a lot to learn from investigative media and their journalists. Rather than formal procedures often applied on a routine basis by auditors and internal controllers, information sources in terms of persons in networks seem to be a more fruitful approach to detection of white-collar crime.

It is beyond the scope of this chapter to speculate about the extent that journalists have the top position in relation to exposing white-collar crime. However, there might be reasons to believe that it is peculiar in Scandinavia where the media has a strong position in any public rating of trustworthiness. Especially in Norway, where the publicly funded broadcasting corporation (NRK) has a strong position, combined with state subsidies to a number of newspapers to keep a large spectrum of publications, the role of investigative journalism is important.

Similar to the signal detection theory consisting of intensity-alertness-recog nition-knowledge is the awareness-motivation-capability framework by Downing et al. (2012).

Private economic crime policing

Fraud examiners at global auditing firms and local law firms are in the business of reconstructing past events and sequences of events when there is suspicion of white-collar crime in client organizations. They contribute to the detection of offenders. Table 17.3 listed 167 reports of investigations, mainly from Norway, which were available for research. The investigated organization is the client for the examination, such as nursing home Adecco, hospital Ahus, municipality Andebu, and traffic station Arendal. The investigating firm is the fraud examiner, such as local law firm Wiersholm, auditing firm PwC, auditing firm BDO, and an internal audit function. The suspected white-collar crime included fraud, corruption, embezzlement, etc. as listed in Appendix A with suspects in Appendix B.

Twenty-two cases resulted in incarcerations that represent 13% of the cases. The most frequent detection source was a whistleblower to an investigative journalist in the media. Fraud examinations then followed in the aftermath. Private policing as presented in this book detected only 2 of the 22 incarcerated individuals in the list of cases in Table 17.3.

This result is in itself interesting for two main reasons. First, fraud examiners hired by client organizations tend to deliver what clients expect in terms of descriptions of misconduct and suggestions for preventive actions in the future. Clients prefer fraud examiners to avoid indications of crime in terms of law violations (Gottschalk and Tcherni-Buzzeo, 2017). Second, injustice is extremely important to avoid at all costs in the Norwegian culture (Holmes et al., 2020). If there is any doubt at all, a suspected offender must never face prosecutuion, let alone suffer incarceration. Therefore, a large number of guilty persons are never on trial to avoid that an innocent person ever ends up on trial. If Norway would have the same incarceration rate as the United States relative to the national population, Norway would have 38.000 individuals rather than the current 3.800 individuals in prison. There is thus a ten times difference, which is explained by a number of factors, including the fear of miscarriage of justice.

While Table 17.3 lists a total of 167 fraud investigation reports, which is a large sample, we have no way of telling whether the sample is in any way representative of all fraud examination reports in Norway and the rest of the world. As emphasized by Gottschalk and Tcherni-Buzzeo (2017), most reports remain secret and never disclosed to neither the public nor the police. Our sample may thus have a bias in some unknown direction.

It is beyond the scope of this chapter to compare Norway with other countries. However, over the years, this research has been able to collect some fraud examination reports from other countries as listed in Table 17.3. Attorneys who conducted private policing were from law firms Clifford Chance, Conrad O'Brian, Duane Morris, Hastings, Jenner Block, Shearman Sterling, Sidely Austin, and Wilmer Cutler Pickering in the United States. In Denmark, law firms Bruun & Hjejle, Kromann Reumert, and Kammeradvokaten conducted investigations. In Sweden, law firms Mannheimer Swartling and Setterwalls conducted investigations.

One of the main problems with detecting many forms of white-collar crime is that they are not obvious. Indeed, the perpetrators often deliberately design the offenses so that they appear to be legitimate business practices. Thus, unlike most ordinary forms of street crime, outsiders do not often recognize white-collar offenses, at least not for some time. Poverty and powerlessness tends to be the cause of street crime, while excessive power and greed is frequently the cause of white-collar crime. Piecing together evidence that a white-collar crime has actually occurred is always much more difficult than it is for other types of offenses. This means that detecting and interpreting signals of a white-collar offense is indeed a problem, and perhaps signal detection theory can find a useful application in this context.

This chapter first reviewed some literature on public government versus private governance in regulating business conduct in organizations. Next, the theory of signal detection illustrated factors that influence detection of white-collar crime signals. Two empirical studies from Norway followed, where one is a sample of convicted white-collar offenders in Table 19.2, and the other is a sample of investigations by fraud examiners in Table 17.3. While investigative journalists disclose a significant fraction of crime stories that later result in prosecution and conviction of white-collar offenders, few fraud examiners make similar contributions to fill the gap between government and governance.

While miscarriage of justice is a top priority in Norwegian society with less than 6 million inhabitants, crime detection and evidence development seem more at the core of investigative journalism compared to fraud examination. An avenue for future research is to study mandates in fraud examinations and competence of fraud examiners. Maybe auditing and legal knowledge are less relevant compared to competence in psychology, sociology, and management to improve the ability of crime signal detection.

This chapter confirms a long-standing finding that businesses generally prefer the handling of misconduct, broadly defined, internally. In addition, the avoidance of injustice at all costs within the Norwegian culture is an important factor.

Bibliography

ACFE (2008). *2008 Report to the Nation – On Occupational Fraud & Abuse*, Austin, TX: Association of Certified Fraud Examiners.

ACFE (2014). *Report to the Nations on Occupational Fraud and Abuse, 2014 Global Fraud Study*, Austin, TX: Association of Certified Fraud Examiners.

ACFE (2016). *CFE Code of Professional Standard*, Association of Certified Fraud Examiners, www.acfe.com/standards/.

Alleyne, P., Huldai, M. and Pike, R. (2013). Towards a conceptual model of whistle-blowing intentions among external auditors, *The British Accounting Review*, 45 (1), 10–23.

Alon, A., Mencken, A. and Mencken, A. (2019). Dynamics and limits of regulatory privatization: Reorganizing audit oversight in Russia, *Organization Studies*, 40 (8), 1217–1240.

Andrade, J. (2015). Reconceptualizing whistleblowing in a complex world, *Journal of Business Ethics*, 128 (2), 321–335.

Andresen, M.S. and Button, M. (2019). The profile and detection of bribery in Norway and England & Wales: A comparative study, *European Journal of Criminology*, 16 (1), 18–40.

Bjarke, B., Einar Sen, S., Nielsen, M.B. and Matthiessen, S.B. (2011). Silence is golden? Characteristics and experiences of self-reported whistleblowers, *European Journal of Work and Organizational Psychology*, 20 (2), 206–238.

Boghossian, J. and Marques, J.C. (2019). Saving the Canadian fur industry's hide: Government's strategic use of private authority to constrain radical activism, *Organization Studies*, 40 (8), 1241–1268.

Borating (2018). *Case Number 17-108216AST-BORG/02, Borating lagmannsrett (Borating Court of Appeals)*, Oslo, October 10.

Brooks, G. and Button, M. (2011). The police and fraud investigation and the case for a nationalized solution in the United Kingdom, *The Police Journal*, 84, 305–319.

Button, M. (2019). The "new" private security industry, the private policing of cyberspace and the regulatory questions, *Journal of Contemporary Criminal Justice*, 1–17, published online https://doi.org/101177/1043986219890194.

Button, M. and Gee, J. (2013). *Countering Fraud for Competitive Advantage – The Professional Approach to Reducing the Last Great Hidden Cost*, Chichester: John Wiley & Sons.

Button, M., Frimpong, K., Smith, G. and Johnston, L. (2007a). Professionalizing counter fraud specialists in the UK: Assessing progress and recommendations for reform, *Crime Prevention and Community Safety*, 9, 92–101.

Button, M., Johnston, L., Frimpong, K. and Smith, G. (2007b). New directions in policing fraud: The emergence of the counter fraud specialists in the United Kingdom, *International Journal of the Sociology of Law*, 35, 192–208.

Caliber, B. and Mihalik, K.K. (2017). The evolution of whistleblowing studies: A critical review and research agenda, *Journal of Business Ethics*, 146 (4), 787–803.

Desai, N. (2020). Understanding the theoretical underpinnings of corporate fraud, *VIKALPA The Journal for Decision Makers*, 1–7, https://doi.org/10.1177/0256090920917789.

Downing, S.T., Kang, J.S. and Markman, G.D. (2012). What you don't see can hurt you: Awareness cues to profile indirect competitors, *Academy of Management Journal*, 62 (6), 1872–1900.

Dyck, A., Morse, A. and Zingales, L. (2010). Who blows the whistle on corporate fraud? *The Journal of Finance*, 65 (6), 2213–2253.

Eberlein, B. (2019). Who fills the global governance gap? Rethinking the roles of business and government in global governance, *Organization Studies*, 40 (8), 1125–1146.

Segeberg, K. (2014). Norske kingship haven't i Nigeria – Lang i fra have som var avialan, sire Forsvaret (Norwegian warships ended up in Nigeria – Far from what was the agreement, the Military Defense says), *Daily Norwegian Newspaper Dagbladet*, www.dagbladet.no, published June 14.

Segeberg, K. (2015). *Nigeria-butene: Matterport til Suppression 2014 (The Nigeria Boats: Methods Report to the Scup Prize 2014)*, Oslo: Dagbladet.

Eriksen, N. (2019). Reattracting Reattracting i Nigeriabåt-saken (Enforceable corruption verdict in Nigeria boat case), *Daily Norwegian Newspaper Dagbladet*, www.dagbladet.no, published May 15.

Evans, R. (2017). Anti-corruption police investigate UK firm over ex-Nigerian warlord deal, *The Guardian*, www.theguardian.com, published May 14.

Ezeonu, I. (2020). Market criminology: A critical engagement with primitive accumulation in the petroleum extraction industry in Africa, in: Rorie, M.L. (editor), *The Handbook of White-Collar Crime*, Hoboken, NJ: Wiley & Sons, chapter 25, pages 398–417.

Galvin, M.A. and Simpson, S.S. (2020). Prosecuting and sentencing white-collar crime in US federal courts: Revisiting the Yale findings, in: Rorie, M.L. (editor), *The Handbook of White-Collar Crime*, Hoboken, NJ: Wiley & Sons, chapter 24, pages 381–397.

Gomulya, D. and Mishina, Y. (2017). Signaler credibility, signal susceptibility, and relative reliance on signals: How stakeholders change their evaluative processes after violation of expectations and rehabilitative efforts, *Academy of Management Journal*, 60 (2), 554–583.

Gottschalk, P. (2019). *Convenience Triangle in White-Collar Crime – Case Studies of Fraud Examinations*, Cheltenham: Edward Elgar Publishing.

Gottschalk, P. and Gunnesdal, L. (2018). *White-Collar Crime in the Shadow Economy: Lack of Detection, Investigation, and Conviction Compared to Social Security Fraud*, London: Palgrave Pivot, Palgrave Macmillan, Springer Publishing.

Gottschalk, P. and Tcherni-Buzzeo, M. (2017). Reasons for gaps in crime reporting: The case of white-collar criminals investigated by private fraud examiners in Norway, *Deviant Behavior*, 38 (3), 267–281.

Hamann, R. (2019). Dynamic de-responsibilization in business-government interactions, *Organization Studies*, 40 (8), 1193–1216.

Holmes, M.C.S., Huuse, C.F., Engen, R.V. and Kristiansen, T. (2020). Kallmyr i NAV høring: En annen type justismord (Kallmyr in NAV hearing: Another kind of miscarriage of justice), *Daily Norwegian Newspaper VG*, www.vg.no, published January 13.

Huff, M.J. and Bodner, G.E. (2013). When does memory monitoring succeed versus fail? Comparing item-specific and relational encoding in the DRM paradigm, *Journal of Experimental Psychology: Learning, Memory, and Cognition*, 39 (4), 1246–1256.

Huff, R., Desilets, K. and Kane, J. (2010). *The National Public Survey on White Collar Crime*, Fairmont: National White Collar Crime Center, www.nw3c.org.

Høyesterett (2019). Dom avsagt 13. mai 2019i anke over Borgarting lagmannsretts dom 23. oktober 2018 (Verdict announced May 13, 2019 regarding appeal for Borgarting court's verdict October 23, 2018), *Høyesterett* (Norwegian Supreme Court), Oslo.

Karim, K.E. and Siegel, P.H. (1998). A signal detection theory approach to analyzing the efficiency and effectiveness of auditing to detect management fraud, *Managerial Auditing Journal*, 13 (6), 367–375.

King, M. (2020a). What makes a successful corporate investigator – An exploration of private investigators attributes, *Journal of Financial Crime*, published online https://doi.org/10.1108/JFC-02-2020-0019.

King, M. (2020b). Out of obscurity: The contemporary private investigator in Australia, *International Journal of Police Science and Management*, published online https://doi.org/10.1177/1461355720931887.

Kourula, A., Moon, J., Salles-Djelic, M.L. and Wicker, C. (2019). New roles of government in the governance of business conduct: Implications for management and organizational research, *Organization Studies*, 40 (8), 1101–1123.

Maher, R., Valenzuela, F. and Böhm, S. (2019). The enduring state: An analysis of governance-making in three mining conflicts, *Organization Studies*, 40 (8), 1169–1192.

Miceli, M.P. and Near, J.P. (2013). An international comparison of the incidence of public sector whistle-blowing and the prediction of retaliation: Australia, Norway, and the US, *Australian Journal of Public Administration*, 72 (4), 433–446.

Michel, C. (2016). Violent street crime versus harmful white-collar crime: A comparison of perceived seriousness and punitiveness, *Critical Criminology*, 24, 127–143.

Mpho, B. (2017). Whistleblowing: What do contemporary ethical theories say? *Studies in Business and Economics*, 12 (1), 19–28.

NTB (2019). En del av Nigeriabåt-saken opp i Høyesterett (Part of the Nigerian boat case in the Supreme Court), *Daily Norwegian Newspaper Dagbladet*, www.dagbladet.no, published May 1.

Oslo tingrett (2017). Verdict 16–110357MED-OTIR/04, judge Lise Bogen Behrens, *Oslo Tingrett* (Oslo District Court), May 16.

Piquero, N.L., Carmichael, S. and Piquero, A.R. (2008). Assessing the perceived seriousness of white-collar and street crimes, *Crime and Delinquency*, 54, 291–312.

Pontell, H.N., Black, W.K. and Geis, G. (2014). Too big to fail, too powerful to jail? On the absence of criminal prosecutions after the 2008 financial meltdown, *Crime, Law and Social Change*, 61 (1), 1–13.

PwC (2014). *Forsvarets logistikkorganisasjon: Rapport etter gjennomgang av salg av fartøy (Military Logistic Organization: Report after Review of Sales of Vessels)*, October 31, Oslo: Auditing Firm PricewaterhouseCoopers.

PwC (2015). *Forsvarsdepartementet: Undersøkelse av forhold knyttet til Forsvarets avhending av fartøyer (Ministry of Defense: Examination of Circumstances*

Relatet to the Military's Sale of Vessels), March 20, Oslo: Auditing Firm PricewaterhouseCoopers.

Qiu, B. and Slezak, S.L. (2019). The equilibrium relationships between performance-based pay, performance, and the commission and detection of fraudulent misreporting, *The Accounting Review*, 94 (2), 325–356.

Rehg, M.T., Miceli, M.P., Near, J.P. and Scotter, J.R.V (2009). Antecedents and outcomes of retaliation against whistleblowers: Gender differences and power relationships, *Organization Science*, 19 (2), 221–240.

Reporter (2013). Nigerians yawn over missing billions, *The Sun*, December 31, published online https://infoweb.newsbank.com/apps/news/document-view?p=AWNB&t=&sort=YMD_date%3AD&maxresults=20&f=advanced&val-base-0=NNPC&fld-base-0=alltext&bln-base-1=and&val-base-1=oil%20revenues&fld-base-1=alltext&bln-base-2=and&val-base-2=2013&fld-base-2=YMD_date&docref=news/14C0EF3456A37C88, retrieved November 3, 2018.

Schneider, S. (2006). Privatizing economic crime enforcement: Exploring the role of private sector investigative agencies in combating money laundering, *Policing & Society*, 16 (3), 285–312.

Schneider, A. and Scherer, A.G. (2019). State governance beyond the 'shadow of hierarchy': A social mechanisms perspective on governmental CSR policies, *Organization Studies*, 40 (8), 1147–1168.

Szalma, J.L. and Hancock, P.A. (2013). A signal improvement to signal detection analysis: Fuzzy SDT on the ROCs, *Journal of Experimental Psychology: Human Perception and Performance*, 39 (6), 1741–1762.

Taylor, J. (2018). White-collar crime and the law in nineteenth-century Britain, *Business History*, 60 (3), 343–360.

Tufts (2018). *CAS-Global Ltd. and the Private Nigerian Coast Guard Fleet*, Compendium of Arms Trade Corruption, World Peace Foundation, The Fletcher School, Tufts University, www.sites.tufts.edu/corruptarmsdeals/.

Wells, J.B., Minor, K.I., Lambert, E.G. and Reeves, A. (2020). An exploratory study of possible correlates of individual whistleblowing propensity among sworn staff in a city jail, *Criminal Justice Policy Review*, 1–29, published online https://doi.org/10.1177/0887403420919478.

Williams, J.W. (2005). Reflections on the private versus public policing of economic crime, *British Journal of Criminology*, 45, 316–339.

Williams, J.W. (2008). The lessons of Enron: Media accounts, corporate crimes, and financial markets, *Theoretical Criminology*, 12 (4), 471–499.

Williams, J.W. (2014). The private eyes of corporate culture: The forensic accounting and corporate investigation industry and the production of corporate financial security, in: Walby, K. and Lippert, R.K. (editors), *Corporate Security in the 21st Century – Theory and Practice in International Perspective*, Hampshire: Palgrave Macmillan, pages 56–77.

Williams, M.L., Levi, M., Burnap, P. and Gundur, R.V. (2019). Under the corporate radar: Examining insider business cybercrime victimization through an application of routine activities theory, *Deviant Behavior*, 40 (9), 1119–1131.

21 Social security injustices

Private policing of economic crime can take on many forms as illustrated in this book. The case study of internal investigation by fraud examiners in this chapter is concerned with public administration's abuse of power financially to hurt entitled social security recipients and legally to cause incarceration of several social security recipients for alleged fraud. The case study illustrates what the outcome can be when institutions that are supposed to ensure that public authorities do not cause injustices to individuals do not have the competence required to do so and do not react or communicate adequately. In the perspective of convenience theory, blame game, institutional deterioration, and neutralization techniques are some of the convenience themes that can explain the deviant practice in Norwegian social security.

When the deviant behavior by the social security agency in Norway was detected, the Norwegian government appointed a committee to conduct an internal investigation by examining why benefit receivers were harmed by the agency. The report of investigation was published in the form of an official government publication NOU (2020). This chapter evaluates the maturity of the investigation report.

Social security scandal

White-collar offenders and social security fraudsters are two groups that commit financial crime. In a perspective of critical criminology, white-collar offenders belong to the elite in society with certain mechanisms of protection and often privileged treatment in the criminal justice system, while social security offenders are treated like street criminals with less protection and almost automated treatment in the criminal justice system. When miscarriage of justice occurs, a white-collar convict can receive a large financial compensation from the government. This chapter presents the case of miscarriage of justice against 36 individuals who were wrongfully convicted of social security fraud and incarcerated. The case is discussed in the perspectives of social conflict theory, blame game hypothesis, and executive destiny from organizational accounts.

A scandal is a publicized instance of transgression that runs counter to social norms, typically resulting in condemnation and discredit and other consequences such as bad press, disengagement of key constituencies, the severance of network ties, and decrease in key performance indicators (Piazza and Jordan, 2018). Slyke and Bales (2012) suggest that individuals with high social status and privileged positions – such as chief executives – cannot avoid detection and blame. Executives might lose in the blame game (Eberly et al., 2011; Lehman et al., 2019: Schnatterly et al., 2018). On the other hand, Pontell et al. (2014) suggest that the accused might simply be too powerful to blame. Depending on how accounts of a scandal evolve over time, shifts in attribution of blame and scapegoating might occur (Lee and Robinson, 2000; Resodihardjo et al., 2015; Xie and Keh, 2016). The blamed individual will typically deny responsibility based on the neutralization technique of disclaiming wrongdoing (Sykes and Matza, 1957).

This chapter presents the case study also to illustrate chief executive destiny caused by changing accounts of events and changing attributions of blame. This research is important as the chief executives are in a principal-agent relationship (Khanna et al., 2015; Zahra et al., 2005; Williams, 2008), where opportunistic behavior is motivated by individual utility maximization (Bosse and Phillips, 2016; Pillay and Kluvers, 2014).

The scandal in this case is concerned with wrongful prosecution and conviction of individuals who received social security benefits (Meldalen and Lofstad, 2019; NTB, 2019). The case is concerned with miscarriage of justice. Misleading interpretations of laws caused conviction and incarceration of innocent individuals for social security fraud (Larsen, 2019; Loftstad, 2019). The scandal is particularly interesting in the social conflict perspective, where white-collar offenders may feel entitled to violate and then modify the law, while social security fraudsters are at the bottom of social status and have to accept whatever happens to them (Petrocelli et al., 2003; Schwendinger and Schwendinger, 2014).

The Norwegian Labor and Welfare Administration (NAV) was embroiled in a controversy after it incorrectly interpreted rules from the European Union (EU). While not being a member of EU, Norway is part of the European Economic Area (EEA) that cooperates with the EU on legal and other matters. The controversy quickly developed into a serious scandal with demands made for the authority's chief executive, Sigrun Vågeng, to resign. Politicians were also quickly critical, with left-wing Red party leader Bjørnar Moxnes calling for the case of a scandal where the minister in charge of labor and social issues in the Norwegian government, Anniken Hauglie, should resign. Socialist party leader Audun Lysbakken described it as a catastrophe, while Prime Minister Erna Solberg said that it was incredibly unfair and should not happen in Norway (NTB, 2019). State prosecutor Tor-Aksel Busch asked all law enforcement agencies to review recent social security fraud cases (Meldalen and Loftstad, 2019).

NAV is responsible for around a third of Norway's state budget. The authority administers social security programs, including unemployment benefits, pensions, and child benefits. Compared to other countries, the welfare benefits in Norway are quite good. For example, sickness leave and unemployment only cause minimal reductions in income and thus marginal reductions in standard of living for the benefit receivers.

On Monday, October 29, 2019, the authority admitted it had made comprehensive errors in its interpretation of sickness benefits, which is support for people who need medical treatment or other activities to help them get back to work. Sickness benefits are called work assessment allowances in Norway, which also include support for people who are unable to work due to a sick child's care needs. At least 48 individuals had been wrongly convicted of social security fraud, out of which 36 individuals had served time in jail (Lofstad, 2019).

The issue specifically affected people who received benefits while living in Norway but staying temporarily in another EEA country. NAV practiced rules for being on work assessment allowances or other care benefits incorrectly. NAV thought that benefit receivers had to stay in Norway when on benefits. However, as an EEA country, not only the flow of capital, but also the flow of people is encouraged within Europe. EU regulations made this explicit for social security in 2012, when it was documented that receivers of social security benefits could travel and stay wherever they like within EEA.

Thirty-six receivers of social security benefits were not just in a difficult situation in their lives, they were denied further benefits, they had to pay back received money, and they had to serve time in jail, because they had stayed temporarily abroad. They were victims of miscarriage of justice, which is considered extremely serious in Norway. When people are asked how many guilty persons should be free to avoid incarcerating an innocent person, people tend to say at least 100. In the Norwegian culture, it is extremely serious wrongdoing to punish innocent persons (Larsen, 2019).

Sigrun Vågeng was born in 1950 and is thus entitled to retire in 2020 at the age of 70. She holds a master of business administration (MBA) degree and became a chief executive at NAV in 2015. Four years later, the social security scandal became public. Then she said she would retire anyway next year.

Both government minister Hauglie and chief executive Vågeng promised to conduct independent investigations of the scandal. They would hire fraud examiners from local law firms or global auditing firms to conduct internal investigations. Research has shown that it can be a smart move to be the client for a fraud examination as fraud examiners can help move attention away from the client.

Welfare administration

Over the course of many years, the NAV has applied the requirement of stay in Norway under the Norwegian National Insurance Act for recipients of social security benefits such as sickness compensation, attendance allowance, and work assessment allowance in a manner contrary to and in conflict with European commitments. Within Europe, Norwegians are allowed to move freely independent of their status. Employees at NAV as well as ministry officials, police investigators, state prosecutors, defense lawyers, judges at criminal courts, officers at correctional institutions, academic researchers, and law professors have all ignored or misunderstood the European social security regulation. While not a member of the European Union, Norway has signed a number of treaties requiring the country to align with most EU regulations.

The result of ignorance and misunderstanding has been that a number of social security recipients were prosecuted, convicted, and incarcerated when NAV detected that they had been abroad in Europe while receiving social security benefits. The politicians in Norway do not like what they call befits export, where Norwegians receive substantial social benefits and spend the money elsewhere, often in countries where they get much more value for their money. The governments in Norway – both left-wing and right-wing governments in recent decades – want to prevent export of social benefits. The purpose is to make it less attractive to become benefit receivers and to make it more attractive to be workers paying tax.

EEA law applies to Norwegian legislation, but the incorporation of EEA social security regulation into Norwegian law was ignored by application of the Norwegian National Insurance Act instead. The ignorance was in line with the perspective of rule complexity, where public agencies can claim that the complexity of having both EEA laws and local Norwegian laws that were never aligned made it difficult to be compliant. While EEA commitments are supposed to overrule local Norwegian laws, rule complexity prevented compliance.

As suggested by Lehman et al. (2019), rule complexity can create a situation where nobody is able to tell whether an action represents a violation of the law. It is thus impossible to understand what is right and what is wrong. Some laws, rules, and regulations are so complex that compliance becomes random, where compliance is the action of complying with laws, rules, and regulations. The regulatory legal environment is supposed to define the boundaries of appropriate agency conduct. However, legal complexity is often so extreme that even specialist compliance officers struggle to understand what to recommend to executives in organizations. Then regulatory inspection does not work for compliance (Braithwaite, 2020). Agency executives can thus find the large gray zone in legal matters a convenient space for misconduct and offenses based on political signals from ministers and other politicians. This is especially so when operating internationally and globally where states do not agree on what should be legal and illegal activities (Boghossian and Marques, 2019; Eberlein, 2019; Maher et al., 2019; Pontell et al., 2020).

The reluctance of an agency to follow EEA rules becomes stronger when the rules are both complicated and in conflict with political priorities. This is anomie in the sense of low commitment to rules that do not fit (Schoepfer and Piquero, 2006). Trying to follow the law may result in inefficient business practices that depress organizational results and hurt careers of organizational members. Noncompliance might allow the agency to be more successful in the eyes of the government. Rule complexity combined with rule inappropriateness encourages deviant behavior (Kroneberg and Schultz, 2018). The situational action perspective addresses how environments shape opportunities for deviant behavior and, subsequently, how modifications in environments can increase deviant opportunities (Huisman and Erp, 2013). When the situational action perspective by Wikstrom et al. (2018) distinguishes between three stages – (1) perception of action alternatives (legal alternatives, illegal alternatives), (2) process of choice (habit, rational deliberation), and (3) action – then Kroneberg and Schultz (2018) conceptualize lack of self-control as well as lack of deterrence on the axis from (2) to (3). The latter items belong in the willingness dimension of convenience. The situational action perspective aims to integrate personal and environmental explanatory perspectives within the framework of a situation.

NOU (2020: 26) argues that a major cause of the misapplication of the requirement of stay in Norway has been a failure to align the provisions of the National Insurance Act correctly with the rules under EEA law:

> The attention of successive governments has been directed at efficient social security administration, combating social security fraud and reduction of export of benefits. Rather less attention has been directed at considerations of safeguarding the rights of individuals.

In draft legislative amendments, the Ministry of Labor and Social Affairs has not had a tradition of explaining the limitations placed by EEA law on the application of the National Insurance Act rules imposing a requirement of stay in Norway. It is claimed that there is solid knowledge of the relevant EEA law in the ministry, but that knowledge has not resulted in legislative texts or clear preparatory documents. When the new social security regulation was implemented by the national regulation of June 1, 2012, that implementation was not accompanied by preparatory documents or other guidance as to how the rules were to be interpreted, and it was not spelled out in the act that the rules imposing a requirement of stay in Norway had to be waived in a number of practical situations. The ministry proceeded on the basis that the social security regulation from EEA law did not entail any significant changes. NAV was still to ensure correct practice through circulars. The problem was that NAV was misinterpreting EEA law in its circulars, even though NAV interpretations were questioned from time to time (NOU: 2020: 26):

> Through the years questions have arisen on a number of occasions, both within and outside NAV, about various aspects of practices relating to the requirement of stay in Norway and the relationship to EEA law. One reason why the error nevertheless was not discovered earlier is that all previous sources of discussion about the EEA rules – internally in NAV, with the Ministry and with the EFTA Surveillance Authority (ESA) – have been treated and written off as individual cases. No one, apparently, has lifted their gaze or taken the initiative to undertake any kind of systematic review in order to ensure uniform, correct practice. In the absence of critical review, officials handling cases in NAV have continued to base themselves on existing circulars, thereby continuing to misapply the rules.

The interpretation of the law as expressed in the circulars was not challenged by researchers or others writing or lecturing on the rules governing the benefits in question. The EEA law implications for the application of the requirement of a stay in Norway were consistently not flagged up as an issue. Neither defense lawyers nor academic researchers seemed interested in challenging the practice at NAV, which is in line with the social conflict perspective, where the ruling class tends to ignore misconduct suffered by the ruled class (Petrocelli et al., 2003). According to the social conflict perspective, the justice system is biased and designed to protect the wealthy and powerful (Arrigo and Bernard, 1997; Schoultz and Flyghed, 2019). It is not designed to protect the poor and powerless. The losers in society are to be taken care of in a way determined by the winners (Michel, 2016). If the losers deviate from arrangements determined by the winners, then they are quickly sanctioned in countries such as Norway (Gottschalk and Gunnesdal, 2018).

Weak management culture

NOU (2020: 26) suggests that NAV has been characterized by a management culture with clear weaknesses:

> There has been no tradition of asking questions about established truths or making pronouncements about issues not falling within one's own sphere of responsibility. The agency has had some case-handling officials with solid competence in EEA matters, but they have not worked with the specific rules relating to the benefits in question; few have viewed the rules in their overall context. A number of case-handling officials have told the Committee of substantive uncertainty, particularly in relation to EEA law issues. In the Labor and Welfare Directorate, the quality control of new elements in circulars dealing with the EEA rules has, in some cases, such as the introduction of the new social security regulation in 2012, consisted in referring the circular to a case-handling official in the Directorate having broad but general knowledge of EEA law. The circulars contain no indication of any uncertainty about the interpretation of the provisions of the EU regulation. The Directorate assumed that the interpretation would be challenged if it was incorrect and that NAV Appeals or the National Insurance Court would, if necessary, correct the interpretation in the circular.

This did not happen, however. Instead, NAV overturned decisions in individual cases in which the interpretation was challenged, but the interpretation of the rules on which the overturning was based did not result in changes in the circulars.

The tradition of not asking questions about established truths might be explained by both organizational conditions and individual attitudes. In some public agencies, executives use language that people do not understand (Ferraro et al., 2005). Some public sector agencies are involved in the blame game by misleading attribution to others (Eberly et al., 2011) without any sense of responsibility for deviance. The NOU (2020) report of investigation is yet another example of blame game, where all are to blame. By sharing blame with a number of other actors in public administration and the criminal justice system, nobody will ultimately feel especially responsible for having incarcerated innocent social security recipients. There was institutional deterioration based on legitimacy (Rodriguez et al., 2005), inability to control because of social disorganization between various parts of the public sector (Hoffmann, 2002), and interference and noise in signals of wrongdoing (Karim and Siegel, 1998). There was lack of control in principal-agent relationships (Bosse and Phillips, 2016), where police investigators trusted examiners at NAV, while defense attorneys and court judges trusted police investigators.

The practice of reporting innocent individuals to the police might be explained by learning from others because of differential association (Sutherland, 1983), where the action is according to authority as obedience (Baird and Zelin, 2009). NAV had a collectivist value orientation (Bussmann et al., 2018) where a peer pressure (Gao and Zhang, 2019) led to individual application of neutralization techniques (Sykes and Matza, 1957).

NOU (2020: 27) investigators found a few examples of case-handling officials in NAV having expressed uncertainty about the interpretation in the circulars through informal internal channels:

> No answers were given to those questions of interpretation and nor were they raised through formal channels. The Committee has not received any documentation indicating that employees warned that the rules were being applied incorrectly.
>
> The practical work of implementing the social security regulations in the agency seems to have been characterized by a lack of competence, capacity, communication and critical thinking. Nor has sufficient attention been paid to general EEA law in the work on the rules, circulars and practical management of benefits. This has led to people being refused benefits they ought to have had, or losing benefits they were entitled to receive. Many have been served with wrongful claims for repayment. A number of people have also served prison terms to which they should not have been sentenced.

The NAV circulars are intended to ensure correct, uniform practice by having front line case-handling officials familiarize themselves and be trained to apply rules that put the requirements of the law into practice, without a need to interpret and apply the law directly by front line employees. This approach aims to simplify the case-handling procedure and ensure equal treatment for similar beneficiaries and legal certainty. The approach is, however, vulnerable to error, especially when the set of rules in question is virtually invisible to the average benefits recipient, as EEA law was in this case (NOU, 2020: 27):

> It becomes particularly serious when the consequence of an incorrect interpretation of the rules by NAV may be baseless criminal proceedings brought

> against individuals. Viewed in the light of the importance of the circulars, the Committee takes the view that the processes employed by the Directorate for the implementation of the new EU/EEA social security regulation were inadequate and undeniably blameworthy.
>
> It has been claimed from a number of quarters that, over time, the Directorate's substantive competence has been weakened by several rounds of reorganizations and staffing reductions.

Weakened competence tends to cause institutional deterioration. Institutional deterioration can occur conveniently as a result of external legitimacy where deviance is the norm (Rodriguez et al., 2005). Institutional deterioration often occurs at the same time as social disorganization, which further improves the opportunity structure for deviance without notice. The disorganization perspective argues that structural conditions lead to higher levels of social disorganization – especially of weak social controls – in organizations and between organizations, which in turn results in higher rates of deviance (Pratt and Cullen, 2005). While the objective of NAV's distribution processes has been described as a "lean and strategic" directorate that leads and coordinates a line organization in which the substantive competence in the agency is close to the users, the Directorate nevertheless has the same formal substantive responsibility as previously without being able to exercise that responsibility in a principal-agent perspective (Bosse and Phillips, 2016).

NOU (2020) investigators found that the question whether the Directorate has the necessary capacity and competence to manage the substantive responsibility imposed on it had not been raised to the level of a formal discussion within the ministry, although it had been a topic of discussion in more informal fora. The investigators express no view on whether it has been expedient to "slim down" the Directorate, but note that the efficiency measures that had been implemented have led to a situation in which the Directorate seems to lack the competence – and resource-related prerequisites for safeguarding the substantive responsibility imposed on it in a sound manner (NOU, 2020: 27):

> The Directorate has not managed to coordinate the different result areas in NAV. This is worrying. For those Ministry employees who did know what the EU/EEA social security regulations entailed, the interpretation it is now known was relied on by NAV was shocking. The Ministry was not aware of NAV's long-standing practice in the area, however. That, and the fact that the Ministry has lacked systems to ensure better knowledge of NAV's practice is, in the Committee's view, worrisome.

The principal-agent challenge was thus not only a problem in the decentralization and distribution of competence within NAV, but also a problem in the relationship between the ministry and the NAV Directorate.

The requirement of a stay in Norway laid down in the National Insurance Act has remained in place through several legislative amendments and has not been the subject of much debate, since corrective EEA regulations were ignored. There was and is broad political agreement that benefit recipients should be followed closely by NAV in order to get them back to work as quickly as possible. For many recipients, it has been practically feasible to stay abroad and at the same time comply with planned follow-up measures. Many have nevertheless been refused benefits, because NAV has worked based on the assumption that prior permission is required for a stay abroad, and that permission may be given only for up to four weeks per year, corresponding to statutory holiday. Yet many were not on holiday; they were exercising their right under the EU/EEA social security regulation to stay elsewhere in the EEA – such as with their own family if they are of foreign origin, such as Poles working in Norway. NAV did not recognize or acknowledge this fact of wrongfully denying benefits and punishing recipients.

No critical defense

An important part of the agency's mission is to prevent and detect benefits fraud and other misuses of social security schemes. Travel abroad has been relatively easy to spot, particularly since NAV has acquired technological tools enabling tracking of IP addresses. In a number of cases, stays in the EEA elsewhere than in Norway have formed the sole basis for decisions to stop or claim repayment of benefits, without further consideration of whether the stay abroad has impeded follow-up in the individual case. NAV employees fell into the trap of sense-making of actions without understanding those actions in a relevant context (Bernburg et al., 2006; Hamann, 2019; Holt and Cornelissen, 2014; Weick, 1995; Weick et al., 2005). Since travel abroad was easy to spot, the perceived crime signal was a real noise signal called false alarm in the signal detection perspective (Karim and Siegel, 1998; Rooij and Fine, 2020; Szalma and Hancock, 2013).

The cases were not viewed as particularly complicated, and the legal issues relating to EEA law were not identified when NAV adopted decisions to report cases to the police. Similarly, prosecutors and judges viewed cases from NAV as obvious and straightforward to handle in the criminal justice system. Nobody questioned the misrepresentation in the criminal justice system, where defense lawyers spent little time and effort on each case. Low-level defendants receive far less support compared to high-level defendants. While street crime is often concerned with the lower levels, white-collar crime is often concerned with the upper levels in terms of status and success (Logan et al., 2019; Piquero, 2018). Poverty and powerlessness tend to be the cause of street crime, while excessive power and greed are often the cause of white-collar crime (Galvin, 2020).

Three themes are particularly noteworthy when distinguishing white-collar defense strategies from other defense strategies by attorneys. First, the role of white-collar attorneys is radically different from the typical criminal lawyer who defends a person suspected of and charged with street crime. For instance, the former spends far more time on each case, both in terms of workload and in terms of calendar time. This implies that a white-collar attorney works on fewer cases in parallel. The white-collar attorney gets a case much earlier and is far more likely to succeed in keeping wrongdoing charges away from the client (Weisburd et al., 1991). Second, information control is at the center of the white-collar attorney's work. The attorney is concerned with acquisition of crucial information and keeps damaging information out of the hands of public authorities such as municipalities, police investigators, and public prosecutors. A third theme centers on a major dilemma of these attorneys: how to defend vigorously the client without thereby becoming a party to the criminal act (Gottschalk, 2014; Mann, 1985).

The only ground for conviction and incarceration of social benefits receivers was that they had been abroad without NAV's permission. Where the benefits recipient had traveled outside Norway without notifying, or had notified that he or she was still in Norway, NAV generally reported the person for fraud to the police. The threshold for reporting was the equivalent of only US$10,000 in Norwegian kroner. This amount can be compared to the average amount involved in white-collar crime in Norway, which is the equivalent of US$4 million in Norwegian kroner (Gottschalk and Gunnesdal, 2018).

Both the Norwegian prosecuting authority and the courts have largely relied on NAV's determinations, without examining the question whether or not the person in question was actually entitled to the benefit during the stay abroad. The interpretation of the law that has formed the basis for the decisions in the administrative cases has thus scarcely been tested in connection with criminal cases in the ordinary courts of law. While white-collar crime cases in Norwegian courts tend to last for several months, where defendants have ample opportunity to present various witnesses and documents, street crime cases, including NAV cases, tend to last for a few days.

NOU (2020: 28) suggests that an error that strikes in this way can easily "slip under the radar":

> The State's opponent in this area is not strong or organized and, where benefits recipients have had access to legal counsel, it has seldom been of assistance. Very few of the lawyers who have been involved in the cases, whether it be in connection with an appeal or proceedings before the National Insurance Court or the ordinary courts of law, have realized the EEA law issue involved. When a lawyer in a criminal case raised the point of EEA law, the submission was rejected on the ground that the accused was under a duty to abide by "Norwegian rules".
>
> Nor did the Supreme Court of Norway see any problem with sentencing a person to a prison term for having had stays in another EEA country without permission from NAV during periods when there was no follow-up in which to participate. The Supreme Court based itself solely on the wording of the National Insurance Act, even though the Main Part of the EEA Agreement has been Norwegian law since 1994, and the social security regulations have been implemented in Norway through national regulations since 1994, with primacy over the requirements of the National Insurance Act. A reading of the general exceptions laid down in the National Insurance Act, to which no reference is made in the provisions on requirement of stay in Norway, together

> with the Norwegian regulation implementing the social security regulation and Article 21 of the regulation, shows – on a correct interpretation – that the requirement of stay in Norway cannot be applied as per the wording of the National Insurance Act. The Supreme Court undertook no such reading.

The role of the National Insurance Court in Norway is to evaluate administrative decisions in individual cases for benefits receivers. This specialist court body did not consider the EEA law issue specifically until 2017, when members of the court emphasized that NAV's circulars did not convey a correct interpretation of the regulation, and that NAV was requiring a stay in Norway in situations where there was no basis for such a requirement. Subsequently, a number of cases raising the same issue came before the National Insurance Court, but not all court members understood what their colleagues had realized a few months earlier, which is that NAV was failing to consider EEA law in cases involving stays abroad for persons who were registered as residents in Norway. Thus, for a while the court was failing to convey a clear and consistent – and correct – interpretation of the law and was instead reaching decisions in individual cases without reference to the relevant EEA rules.

The vast majority of court members who finally found that the EU/EEA regulation was applicable started to apply the same interpretation of it. Nevertheless, NAV case workers considered the returned cases from the court as exceptions rather than the result of a new practice aligned with EEA rules. The chair of the National Insurance Court may decide that more than two members are to take part in a case if the decision may become "determinative for practice". This was not done. It took one and a half years from the time the court delivered the first principle-setting ruling until the Norwegian Labor and Welfare Directorate contacted the Ministry of Labor and Social Affairs to get the practice changed. Active and competent defense lawyers were completely absent in this process, since their clients were similar to street criminals rather than rich and influential white-collar criminals (Galvin, 2020; Gottschalk, 2014; Logan et al., 2019; Mann, 1985; Piquero, 2018).

It took NAV two years after the first ruling before publishing internal notices of amended practice, and six months later the extent of the error became known (NOU, 2020: 28):

> The Committee takes the view that NAV, the Ministry and the National Insurance Court all share responsibility for its having taken such a long time before the practice was rectified. In the Committee's view, one reason is that the National Insurance Court has viewed itself too much as a court of law that communicates only through rulings in individual cases. It seems that the body has lost sight of the fact that the National Insurance Court is intended to be a hybrid between an appeal body and a court, an institution with a particular responsibility for ensuring legal certainty for ordinary people finding themselves in demanding situations and up against a powerful opponent – the State.

The absence of critical thinking, apt organization and conduct in keeping with the responsibility the bodies have, has led to a situation in which the importance of EEA law has been a blind spot for virtually everyone involved. The result has been that certain individuals have wrongfully had their payments stopped, received claims for repayment of social security benefits, been labeled as social security fraudsters and also been sentenced to prison terms on incorrect grounds.

The case illustrates what the outcome can be when the institutions that are supposed to ensure that public authorities do not cause injustices to individuals do not have the resources required to do so, are not substantively up to date and do not react or communicate adequately.

Social conflict theory

Both social security fraud and white-collar offenses represent serious forms of financial crime causing harm to victims in society. The police have limited resources to investigate economic crime and have to prioritize their resources by dropping a large portion of cases (Brooks and Button, 2011). The two types of cases are in many ways two extremes on the scale of economic criminals (Gottschalk and Gunnesdal, 2018). While social security fraud is committed by people who basically need financial help from the community to live decent lives, white-collar crime is committed by individuals in the upper echelons of society, who abuse their positions to enrich themselves or the organizations they are associated with.

A number of situations are viewed as social security fraud, including misuse of benefits, making false statements on claims, and buying or selling social security cards. Concealing information that affects eligibility for benefits is also considered to be fraud. People who represent social security recipients commit fraud if they misuse the benefits they are entrusted with (Lensvelt-Mulders et al., 2006). It is considered fraud when people knowingly provide inaccurate information when they apply for social security benefits. Anyone receiving social security disability benefits must inform the social security administration if they also receive workers' compensation benefits from their organizations where they are or were employed.

The social conflict theory suggests that the powerful and wealthy in the upper class of society define what is right and what is wrong. The rich and mighty can behave like "robber barons" because they make the laws. Therefore, the ruling class does not consider a white-collar offense as a regular crime, and certainly not one similar to street crime or social security fraud (Michel, 2016).

Social conflict theory holds that laws and law enforcement are used by dominant groups in society to minimize threats to their interests posed by those whom they perceive as dangerous and greedy (Petrocelli et al., 2003). Crime is defined by legal codes and sanctioned by institutions of criminal justice to secure order in society. The ruling class secures order in the ruled class by means of laws and law enforcement. Conflicts and clashes between interest groups are restrained and stabilized by law enforcement.

In addition, particularly in Scandinavian countries, conflicts and clashes are restrained also by the minimum standard of living provided by social security benefits. Sick people, disabled people, refugees, and others suffering from negative life events are very well taken care of in terms of a reasonable standard of living. However, when there is suspicion of benefit abuse, NAV quickly report cases to the police, the police quickly deliver cases to the prosecution, prosecutors quickly show up in court, and judges quickly sentence offenders to jail. The defendants are incapable of defending themselves effectively with the help of second-rate attorneys. The criminal justice system seems to work almost automatically in social security cases (Gottschalk and Gunnesdal, 2018). The best attorneys work for white-collar defendants.

According to the social conflict theory, the justice system is biased and designed to protect the wealthy and powerful (Arrigo and Bernard, 1997; Schoultz and Flyghed, 2019). It is not designed to protect the poor and powerless.

Blame game hypothesis

Internally at NAV, a blame game started. The first looser in the blame game was announced on December 4, 2019, which was one month after the scandal became public. One of the senior executives reporting to Vågeng resigned from her position. The media reported (Ruud and Spence, 2019):

> Kjersti Monland will be the first to step down as a result of the social security scandal. She will quit her job Monday, December 9.

NAV published a press release about Monland's resignation:

> Over the past few weeks, Nav has received heavy criticism for its handling of the EEA regulations related to cash benefits. Confidence in Nav is greatly weakened and many Nav employees have a difficult working day.
>
> I have respect and understanding for Kjersti's decision, but I am also happy that she will continue to use her expertise and capacity to the best of our organization's development work. Kjersti is also available to contribute clarification and knowledge about the coming work on the EEA case, says Sigrun Vågeng.
>
> I have come to the conclusion that it is both necessary and appropriate to appoint a new leader who can continue this important work, as well as strengthen the power of the department in this critical phase. All tasks in the department and the line must be able to be filled satisfactorily, both in relation to government ministries, the management of Nav and the outside world says benefits director Kjersti Monland.

Kjersti Monland became an obvious scapegoat as many commented in the Norwegian media after the announcement of her resignation from the position of benefits director. Scapegoating is a form of denial of responsibility accompanied with placement of blame on an individual or group of individuals (Lee and Robinson, 2000; Resodihardjo et al., 2015; Xie and Keh, 2016).

Moland's resignation occurred less than a week before an internal audit report was due. Vågeng had asked the internal audit function at Nav to conduct a review as the scandal broke. Being the client for the audit review, Vågeng decided on the mandate. This is in line with many famous internal reviews, where being the client for the review can protect the client from negative attention.

As the social security scandal reached the headlines in all media in December 2019, the blame game expanded from the social security service Nav to a number of other actors in the criminal justice system. The police received blame for simply trusting cases from NAV without conducting independent criminal investigations. The prosecution received blame for simply trusting cases from the police without conducting independent evaluation of presented evidence and application of the law. District courts received blame for simply trusting the prosecution and not helping defendants tell their stories. Judges received blame for sentencing defendants to jail even when the amount was only the equivalent of US$10,000.

This blame game caused a fear "in the top legal expertise to be drawn into the scandal" (Spence and Ruud, 2019). While all actors in the criminal justice system were attacked by blame attribution, each actor could point at the other actors to reduce own blameworthiness.

After more than a month of public attention, most suspected actors in the scandal had successfully distributed blame in the media, where confusion occurred among politicians and others about who to really blame.

By successfully playing the blame game, the offender will attribute blame for wrongdoing to someone else (DeScioli and Bokemper, 2014; Eberly et al., 2011; Hurrell, 2016; Keaveney, 2008; Lee and Robinson, 2000, Sonnier et al., 2015), thereby reducing the perceived violation of trust.

Essentially, in blame game hypothesis, all involved persons attempt to pass the blame on, absolving themselves of the responsibility for the negative event. Lack of causal accounts increases disapproval ratings of the harm carried out by placing the blame of harmful acts on others. For example, by attributing corruption to an executive in the organization as a rotten apple, the suspect will feel betrayed by other executives who, in their opinion, belong to a rotten apple basket in terms of a criminogenic business culture.

External attribution is obviously the preference by most to avoid internal attribution. External attributions place the cause of a negative event on external factors, absolving executives from personal responsibility. However, unstable attributions suggest that the cause of a negative event is unlikely to persist over time, and as such mitigate the severity of the predicament. Uncontrollable attributions suggest that the cause of the event is not within the control of the attributor, further removing any blame or responsibility for unjust act from the account giver (Lee and Robinson, 2000).

Self-blame is rare and often nonexistent. Nobody will blame oneself for a negative event. Self-blame is attributing a negative event to one's behavior or disposition (Lee and Robinson, 2000).

Some are too powerful to blame. Pontell et al. (2014) found that the financial crisis obviously had its cause in mismanagement in the financial sector, but all in the financial sector avoided serious blame. The investigation of the collapse at Lehman Brothers is a typical example (Jenner Block, 2010). Status-related factors such as influential positions, upper-class family ties, and community roles often preclude perceptions of blameworthiness (Slyke and Bales, 2012).

Chief executive destiny

In attempting to respond to and manage scandals, private and public organizations and their executives develop and publicize explanations (Bundy and Pfarrer, 2015; Whyte, 2016) as accounts of events (Albrecht, 1996; Hearit, 2006), since media coverage is critical in shaping opinions (Gamache and McNamara, 2019). Accounts are statements made by an actor to explain unanticipated or untoward behavior that is subject to some sort of evaluative inquiry by other actors (Scott and Lyman, 1968). Initial accounts are typically supportive of top management by claiming that mistakes and deviant behavior occurred in various functions in the organization.

Chief executive Vågeng received such a message from the first internal report, where chief auditor Klepp (2019: 4) claimed in the executive summary of the report that "responsibilities and tasks for arrangements abroad are spread across several units both in-line and between-lines".

However, as a scandal evolves, a key part of the evolution of accounts seems to be the divergence of interests between the organizational entity and individual top leaders (Bandura, 1999; Schoultz and Flyghed, 2019; Schnatterly et al., 2018). The interests of the organization diverge from those of the individuals who first responded to the crisis.

Reports of investigations by fraud examiners are an important source of information regarding executive destiny in organizations. Unfortunately, most client organizations keep reports secret and are not willing to make them available for research (Gottschalk and Tcherni-Buzzeo, 2017). It was possible to find and retrieve 13 reports from Canada, Denmark, Japan, New Zealand, Nigeria, Norway, Sweden, and most from the United States:

> In the reports, we searched for corporate accounts as communicated excuses and justifications for wrongdoings. We found that denial of knowledge and denial of responsibility are frequent corporate excuses, while claiming higher loyalties and claiming entitlement to action are frequent justifications. We were also interested in the destiny of executives who received blame for deviance. Seven out of thirteen executives received blame in investigation reports and received termination from their companies. Three executives found themselves terminated since the companies went bankrupt.

More and more commentators in the media, professors in academics, politicians in parliament, and others called for the resignation of chief executive Vågeng and government minister Hauglie. But they did not resign. Vågeng replied to her critics that she would restore trust in NAV before she retired the following year. Hauglie replied to her critics that an investigation committee appointed by the government would present its report in the following year. However, in January 2020, both governmental minister Hauglie and chief executive Vågeng were forced to announce their resignations.

The case study supports the social conflict theory, where miscarriage of justice against social security fraudsters is less serious than miscarriage of justice against white-collar fraudsters. The case study also supports the blame game hypothesis where nobody is willing to take on the blame for the scandal, but instead is willing to attribute blame to others. As a consequence, executive destiny became less traumatic or nonexistent.

White-collar convenience

As illustrated in Figure 21.1, the motive for NAV was to follow political signals to avoid payments to social security clients who traveled abroad. The crime against

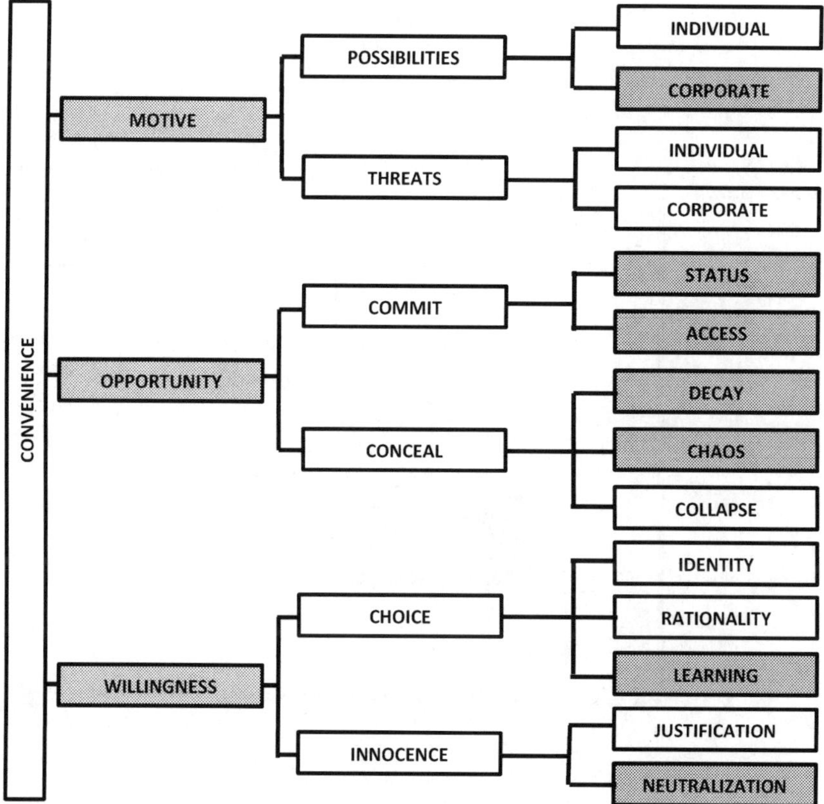

Figure 21.1 Convenience themes in the case of NAV

clients was possible because of the status of government agencies compared to the rights of low-level clients. The social security agency and the criminal justice system had access to resources to ignore signals of deviance. There were elements of decay and chaos as well in the Norwegian public administration regarding the country's legal commitments in Europe. Wrongdoing among employees at NAV was the result of learning and neutralization.

Private policing evaluation

NOU (2020) does not contribute to any clarification compared to what was already known in advance. The report does not reconstruct events and sequences of events, and it does not contribute to insights into what happened, when it happened, and who did what to make it happen or not happen. Rather, the report is mainly an assessment of what was already known. Therefore, the investigation cannot achieve a higher score than level 2 (Figure 21.2).

> One reason for lack of new insights was the procedure for selection of interviewees and the conduct of interviews. Examiners only interviewed people recommended to them, and they conducted interviews as a communication event rather than as a goal-oriented procedure.

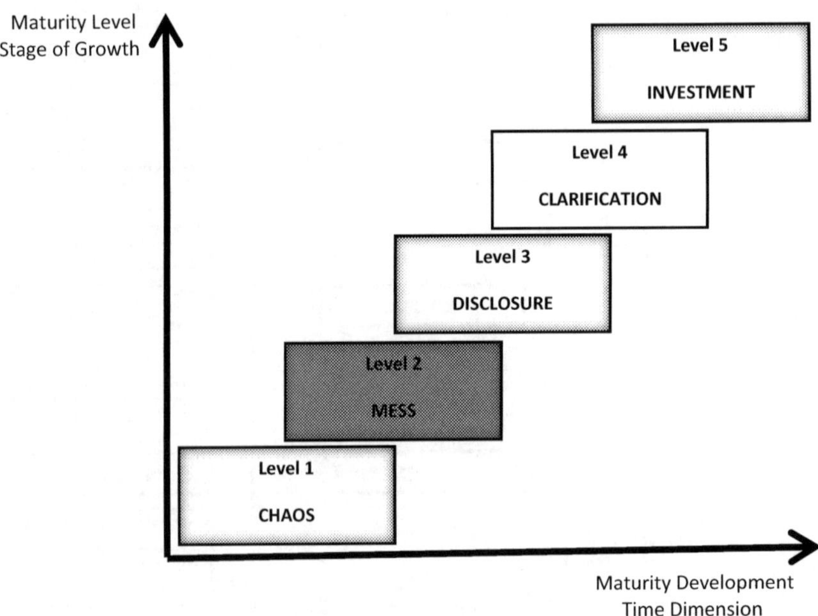

Figure 21.2 Maturity model for internal private investigation applied to the NOU

Bibliography

Albrecht, S. (1996). *Crisis Management for Corporate Self-Defense: How to Protect Your Organization in a Crisis– How to Stop a Crisis before it Starts*, New York: American Management Association.

Arrigo, B.A. and Bernard, T.J. (1997). Postmodern criminology in relation to radical and conflict criminology, *Critical Criminology*, 8 (2), 39–60.

Baird, J.E. and Zelin, R.C. (2009). An examination of the impact of obedience pressure on perceptions of fraudulent acts and the likelihood of committing occupational fraud, *Journal of Forensic Studies in Accounting and Business*, 1 (1), 1–14.

Bandura, A. (1999). Moral disengagement in the perpetration of inhumanities, *Personality and Social Psychology Review*, 3 (3), 193-209.Bao, D., Kim, Y., Mian, G.M. and Su, L. 2019. Do managers disclose or withhold bad news? Evidence from short interest, *The Accounting Review*, 94 (3), 1–26.

Bernburg, J.G., Krohn, M.D. and Rivera, C.J. (2006). Official labeling, criminal embeddedness, and subsequent delinquency, *Journal of Research in Crime and Delinquency*, 43 (1), 67–88.

Boghossian, J. and Marques, J.C. (2019). Saving the Canadian fur industry's hide: Government's strategic use of private authority to constrain radical activism, *Organization Studies*, 40 (8), 1241–1268.

Bosse, D.A. and Phillips, R.A. (2016). Agency theory and bounded self-interest, *Academy of Management Review*, 41 (2), 276–297.

Braithwaite, J. (2020). Regulatory mix, collective efficacy, and crimes of the powerful, *Journal of White Collar and Corporate Crime*, 1 (1), 62–71.

Brooks, G. and Button, M. (2011). The police and fraud investigation and the case for a nationalized solution in the United Kingdom, *The Police Journal*, 84, 305–319.

Bundy, J. and Pfarrer, M.D. (2015). A burden of responsibility: The role of social approval at the onset of a crisis, *Academy of Management Review*, 40 (3), 345–369.

Bussmann, K.D., Niemeczek, A. and Vockrodt, M. (2018). Company culture and prevention of corruption in Germany, China and Russia, *European Journal of Criminology*, 15 (3), 255–277.

DeScioli, P. and Bokemper, S. (2014). Voting as a counter-strategy in the blame game, *Psychological Inquiry*, 25, 206–214.

Eberlein, B. (2019). Who fills the global governance gap? Rethinking the roles of business and government in global governance, *Organization Studies*, 40 (8), 1125–1146.

Eberly, M.B., Holley, E.C., Johnson, M.D. and Mitchell, T.R. (2011). Beyond internal and external: A dyadic theory of relational attributions, *Academy of Management Review*, 36 (4), 731–753.

Ferraro, F., Pfeffer, J. and Sutton, R.I. (2005). Economics language and assumptions: How theories can become self-fulfilling, *Academy of Management Review*, 30 (1), 8–24.

Galvin, M.A. (2020). Substance or semantics? The consequences of definitional ambiguity for white-collar research, *Journal of Research in Crime and Delinquency*, 57 (3), 369–399.

Gamache, D.L. and McNamara, G. (2019). Responding to bad press: How CEO temporal focus influences the sensitivity to negative media coverage of acquisitions, *Academy of Management Journal*, 62 (3), 918–943.

Gao, P. and Zhang, G. (2019). Accounting manipulation, peer pressure, and internal control, *The Accounting Review*, 94 (1), 127–151.

Gottschalk, P. (2014). *Financial Crime and Knowledge Workers: An Empirical Study of Defense Lawyers and White-Collar Criminals*, New York: Palgrave Macmillan.

Gottschalk, P. and Gunnesdal, L. (2018). *White-Collar Crime in the Shadow Economy: Lack of Detection, Investigation, and Conviction Compared to Social Security Fraud*, London: Palgrave Pivot, Palgrave Macmillan, Springer Publishing.

Gottschalk, P. and Tcherni-Buzzeo, M. (2017). Reasons for gaps in crime reporting: The case of white-collar criminals investigated by private fraud examiners in Norway, *Deviant Behavior*, 38 (3), 267–281.

Hamann, R. (2019). Dynamic de-responsibilization in business-government interactions, *Organization Studies*, 40 (8), 1193–1216.

Hearit, K.M. (2006). *Crisis Management by Apology: Corporate Responses to Allegations of Wrongdoing*, Mahwah, NJ: Lawrence Erlbaum Associates.

Hoffmann, J.P. (2002). A contextual analysis of differential association, social control, and strain theories of delinquency, *Social Forces*, 81 (3), 753–785.

Holt, R. and Cornelissen, J. (2014). Sensemaking revisited, *Management Learning*, 45 (5), 525–539.

Huisman, W. and Erp, J. (2013). Opportunities for environmental crime, *British Journal of Criminology*, 53, 1178–1200.

Hurrell, S.A. (2016). Rethinking the soft skills deficit blame game: Employers, skills withdrawal and the reporting of soft skills gaps, *Human Relations*, 69 (3), 605–628.

Jenner Block (2010). *In Regard Lehman Brothers Holdings Inc. to United States Bankruptcy Court in Southern District of New York*, Law Firm Jenner & Block, A.R. Valukas, published online https://jenner.com/lehman/VOLUME%203.pdf, downloaded September 23, 2018.

Karim, K.E. and Siegel, P.H. (1998). A signal detection theory approach to analyzing the efficiency and effectiveness of auditing to detect management fraud, *Managerial Auditing Journal*, 13 (6), 367–375.

Keaveney, S.M. (2008). The blame game: An attribution theory approach to marketer-engineer conflict in high-technology companies, *Industrial Marketing Management*, 37, 653–663.

Khanna, V., Kim, E.H. and Lu, Y. (2015). CEO connectedness and corporate fraud, *The Journal of Finance*, 70, 1203–1252.

Klepp, T. (2019). *Spesialoppdrag – D2019-10. Kartlegging av fakta i EØS-saken. Internrevisjon (Special Assignment – D2019-10. Documentation of Facts in the EEA Case)*, Arbeids- og velferdsetaten (Norwegian Labor and Welfare Administration), December 11, 74 pages.

Kroneberg, C. and Schulz, S. (2018). Revisiting the role of self-control in situational action theory, *European Journal of Criminology*, 15 (1), 56–76.

Larsen, M.H. (2019). NAV-svindel straffes hardere enn hvitsnippforbrytelser (NAV fraud punished harder than white-collar crime), *Daily Norwegian Newspaper Aftenposten*, www.aftenposten.no, published November 1.

Lee, F. and Robinson, R.J. (2000). An attributional analysis of social accounts: Implications of playing the blame game, *Journal of Applied Social Psychology*, 30 (9), 1853–1879.

Lehman, D.W., Cooil, B. and Ramanujam, R. (2019). The effects of rule complexity on organizational noncompliance and remediation: Evidence from restaurant health inspections, *Journal of Management*, 1–33, published online https://doi.org/10.1177/0149206319842262.

Lensvelt-Mulders, G.J.L.M., Heijden, P.G.M. and Laudy, O. (2006). A validation of a computer-assisted randomized response survey to estimate the prevalence of fraud in social security, *Journal of the Royal Statistical Society*, 69, 305–318.

Lofstad, R. (2019). Hentet ut av fengsel etter ni dager (Brought out of jai lafter nine days), *Daily Norwegian Newspaper Dagbladet*, www.dagbladet.no, published October 30.

Logan, M.W., Morgan, M.A., Benson, M.L. and Cullen, F.T. (2019). Coping with imprisonment: Testing the special sensitivity hypothesis for white-collar offenders, *Justice Quarterly*, 36 (2), 225–254.

Maher, R., Valenzuela, F. and Böhm, S. (2019). The enduring state: An analysis of governance-making in three mining conflicts, *Organization Studies*, 40 (8), 1169–1192.

Mann, K. (1985). *Defending White Collar Crime: A Portrait of Attorneys at Work*, New Haven, CT: Yale University Press.

Meldalen, S.G. and Lofstad, R. (2019). Måtte selje leilighet etter feilaktig NAV-dom (Had to sell apartment after incorrect NAV judgment, *Daily Norwegian Newspaper Dagbladet*, www.dagbladet.no, published October 30.

Michel, C. (2016). Violent street crime versus harmful white-collar crime: A comparison of perceived seriousness and punitiveness, *Critical Criminology*, 24, 127–143.

NOU (2020). *Blindsonen: Gransking av feilpraktiseringen av folketrygdlovens oppholdskrav ved reiser i EØS-området (The Blind Spot: Investigation of the Incorrect Practice of the National Insurance Act's Residence Requirements When Traveling in the EEA Area)*, Norges offentlige utredninger (Norway's public inquiries) 2020:9, 328 pages, Oslo.

NTB (2019). SV og Rødt vurderer mistillit – krever klare NAV-svar fra Hauglie (SV and Red assess distrust – require clear NAV answers from Hauglie, *Daily Norwegian Business Newspaper Dagens Næringsliv*, www.dn.no, published November 4.

Petrocelli, M., Piquero, A.R. and Smith, M.R. (2003). Conflict theory and racial profiling: An empirical analysis of police traffic stop data, *Journal of Criminal Justice*, 31 (1), 1–11.

Piazza, A. and Jourdan, J. (2018). When the dust settles: The consequences of scandals for organizational competition, *Academy of Management Journal*, 61 (1), 165–190.

Pillay, S. and Kluvers, R. (2014). An institutional theory perspective on corruption: The case of a developing democracy, *Financial Accountability & Management*, 30 (1), 95–119.

Piquero, N.L. (2018). White-collar crime is crime: Victims hurt just the same, *Criminology & Public Policy*, 17 (3), 595–600.

Pontell, H.N., Black, W.K. and Geis, G. (2014). Too big to fail, too powerful to jail? On the absence of criminal prosecutions after the 2008 financial meltdown, *Crime, Law and Social Change*, 61 (1), 1–13.

Pontell, H.N., Ghazi-Tehrani, A.K. and Burton, B. (2020). White-collar and corporate crime in China, in: Rorie, M.L. (editor), *The Handbook of White-Collar Crime*, Hoboken, NJ: Wiley & Sons, chapter 22, pages 347–362.

Pratt, T.C. and Cullen, F.T. (2005). Assessing macro-level predictors and theories of crime: A meta-analysis, *Crime and Justice*, 32, 373–450.

Resodihardjo, S.L., Carroll, B.J., Eijk, C.J.A. and Maris, S. (2015). Why traditional responses to blame games fail: The importance of context, rituals, and sub-blame games in the face of raves gone wrong, *Public Administration*, 94 (2), 350–363.

Rodriguez, P., Uhlenbruck, K. and Eden, L. (2005). Government corruption and the entry strategies of multinationals, *Academy of Management Review*, 30 (2), 383–396.

Rooij, B. and Fine, A.D. (2020). Preventing corporate crime from within: Compliance management, whistleblowing, and internal monitoring, in: Rorie, M.L. (editor), *The Handbook of White-Collar Crime*, Hoboken, NJ: Wiley & Sons, chapter 15, pages 229–245.

Ruud, S. and Spence, T. (2019). Kjersti Monland går av som ytelsesdirektør i Nav (Kjerti Monland resigns as benefits director at Nav), *Daily Norwegian Newspaper Aftenposten*, www.aftenposten.no, published December 4.

Schnatterly, K., Gangloff, K.A. and Tuschke, A. (2018). CEO wrongdoing: A review of pressure, opportunity, and rationalization, *Journal of Management*, 44 (6), 2405–2432.

Schoepfer, A. and Piquero, N.L. (2006). Exploring white-collar crime and the American dream: A partial test of institutional anomie theory, *Journal of Criminal Justice*, 34 (3), 227–235.

Schoultz, I. and Flyghed, J. (2019). From "we didn't do it" to "we've learned our lesson": Development of a typology of neutralizations of corporate crime, *Critical Criminology*, published online https://doi.org/10.1007/s10612-019-09483-3.

Schwendinger, H. and Schwendinger, J. (2014). Defenders of order or guardians of human rights? *Social Justice*, 40 (1/2), 87–117.

Scott, M.B and Lyman, S.M. (1968). Accounts, *American Sociological Review*, 33 (1), 46–62.

Slyke, S.V. and Bales, W.D. (2012). A contemporary study of the decision to incarcerate white-collar and street property offenders, *Punishment & Society*, 14 (2), 217–246.

Sonnier, B.M., Lassar, W.M. and Lassar, S.S. (2015). The influence of source credibility and attribution of blame on juror evaluation of liability of industry specialist auditors, *Journal of Forensic & Investigative Accounting*, 7 (1), 1–37.

Spence, T. and Ruud, S. (2019). Jusprofessor ber Stortinget nedsette egen granskingskommisjon av trygdeskandalen (Law professor asks the parliament to establish its own investigation committee for the social security scandal), *Daily Norwegian Newspaper Aftenposten*, www.aftenposten.no, published December 28.

Sutherland, E.H. (1983). *White Collar Crime – The Uncut Version*, New Haven, CT: Yale University Press.

Sykes, G.M. and Matza, D. (1957). Techniques of neutralization: A theory of delinquency, *American Sociological Review*, 22 (6), 664–670.

Szalma, J.L. and Hancock, P.A. (2013) A signal improvement to signal detection analysis: Fuzzy SDT on the ROCs, *Journal of Experimental Psychology: Human Perception and Performance*, 39 (6), 1741–1762.

Weick, K.E. (1995). What theory is not, theorizing is. *Administrative Science Quarterly*, *40*, 385–390.

Weick, K.E., Sutcliffe, K.M. and Obstfeld, D. (2005). Organizing and the process of sensemaking, *Organization Science*, 16 (4), 409–421.

Weisburd, D., Wheeler, S., Waring, E. and Bode, N. (1991). *Crimes of the Middle Classes*, New Haven, CT: Yale University Press.

Whyte, D. (2016). It's common sense, stupid! Corporate crime and techniques of neutralization in the automobile industry, *Crime, Law and Social Change*, 66 (2), 165–181.

Wikstrom, P.O.H., Mann, R.P. and Hardie, B. (2018). Young people's differential vulnerability to criminogenic exposure: Bridging the gap between people- and place-oriented approaches in the study of crime causation, *European Journal of Criminology*, 15 (1), 10–31.

Williams, J.W. (2008). The lessons of Enron: Media accounts, corporate crimes, and financial markets, *Theoretical Criminology*, 12 (4), 471–499.

Xie, Y. and Keh, H.T. (2016). Taming the blame game: Using promotion programs to counter product-Hhrm crises, *Journal of Advertising*, 45 (2), 211–226.

Zahra, S.A., Priem, R.L. and Rasheed, A.A. (2005). The antecedents and consequences of top management fraud, *Journal of Management*, 31, 803–828.

22 Norfund digital by PwC

Norfund is the Norwegian government's investment fund for developing countries. The mission is to create jobs and to improve lives by investing in businesses that drive sustainable development. Norfund is owned and funded by the Norwegian government and is the government's most important vehicle for strengthening the private sector in developing countries and for reducing poverty. Norfund had total commitments of US$2.5 billion in 2019 in various developing countries.

Norfund reported on May 13, 2020, that the fund had been exposed to a serious case of fraud through a data breach. Two months earlier, on March 16, Norfund transferred US$9,888,055 to a bank account in Banco Mercantil del Norte, Mexico, which Norfund believed belonged to its client, the Cambodian financial institution LOLC. In fact, the bank account was controlled by a so-called threat actor, who managed to compromise an email account belonging to an employee at Norfund, to register fake domains and to impersonate Norfund's and LOLC's employees in the conversation (Solgård, 2020; Speed, 2020; Stave, 2020).

In their press release on May 13, 2020, Norfund (2020) claimed to be a victim of "a serious case of fraud through an advanced data breach". The term "advanced" is interesting as it sometimes indicates and reflects lack of knowledge about the digitalization, applications of information technology, and digital forensics. Norfund hired PwC (2020) to investigate the matter.

White-collar convenience

The assumption in the following is that the so-called threat actor committing so-called advanced data breach is a criminal organization that found it convenient to defraud Norfund based on the criminal business's financial motive, organizational opportunity, and willingness for deviant behavior. A business founded on crime will follow the same business phases and logic in its operation and development as any legal or legitimate business venture. The main difference between a legal and illegal business is one of legislation not one of development (Dean et al., 2010). Both types of business organizations need entrepreneurialism to survive and succeed, where entrepreneurship is the practice of starting new organizations or revitalizing mature organizations, particularly new businesses generally in response to identified opportunities. Entrepreneurial activity is substantially different from operational activity as it is mainly concerned with creativity and innovation. Just like digitalization by application of information technology created new business models and value configurations for legitimate business ventures, so did the communication and technology revolution create new business opportunities for criminal organizations. Criminal organizations – like noncriminal organizations – develop opportunities by entrepreneurship. Criminal organizations – like noncriminal organizations – can organize their businesses in hierarchies, networks, or other forms of structures (Gottschalk and Smith, 2011; McElwee and Smith, 2015; Ramoglou and Tsang, 2016; Smith, 2009; Tonoyan et al., 2010; Welter et al., 2017).

Figure 22.1 illustrates convenience themes for the criminal organization Threat Actor when targeting Norfund. First of all, the financial motive for the criminal organization is the possibility of corporate economic gain. Maybe members of the organization want to climb the hierarchy of needs for status and success (Goldstraw-White, 2012; Maslow, 1943) and suffer from the American

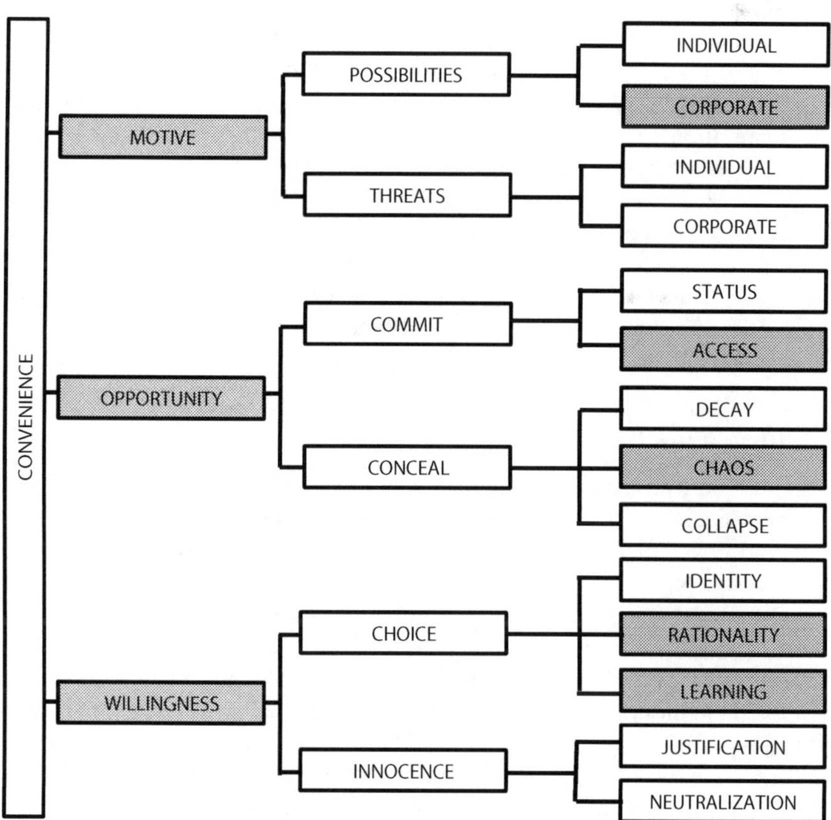

Figure 22.1 Convenience themes for the criminal organization against Norfund

dream of prosperity (Cullen, 2010; Schoepfer and Piquero, 2006). The choice of crime might also derive from sensation seeking. Craig and Piquero (2017) suggest that the willingness to commit financial crime by some white-collar offenders has to do with their inclination for adventure and excitement. Offenders are not only seeking new, intense, and complicated experiences and sensations, as well as exciting adventures, they are also accepting the legal, physical, financial, and social risks associated with these adventures. They attempt to avoid boredom by replacing repetitive activities such as regular meetings with thrill and adventures. They search risky and exciting activities and have distaste for monotonous situations.

In the opportunity dimension of convenience theory, most criminals have no status in society (Pontell et al., 2014), but they have access to tools and vehicles to compromise email accounts and register fake domains and impersonate employees involved in financial transactions (Benson and Simpson, 2018; Ramoglou and Tsang, 2016). Concealing crime in the digital financial world is also a matter of access to resources to quickly move money away from the Mexican account while deleting all traces (Adler and Kwon, 2002). An important opportunity theme is also the lack of digital knowledge in the victim organization Norfund and in police forces in Norway and globally that is indicated by chaos in Figure 22.1, where participation in crime networks (Nielsen, 2003) and markets with crime forces (Chang et al., 2005) represents convenient business practice for the criminal organization.

In the willingness dimension of convenience theory, the choice of crime is a rational choice by the criminal organization. The criminals have a perception of benefits exceeding costs (Pratt and Cullen, 2005). If successful, the criminals can experience behavioral reinforcement of deviance over time (Benartzi et al., 2017). The choice of crime is strengthened by learning from other criminals by differential association (Sutherland, 1983) and collectivist value orientations in the criminal organization (Bussmann et al., 2018).

Fraud examination outcome

Norfund (2020) hired fraud examiners from PwC (2020) to assess existing internal controls and routines regarding payments. They were not hired to investigate the fraud case, but they nevertheless provide a description of the sequence of events as follows.

Prior to the fraud on March 16, 2020, the criminal organization Threat Actor comprised an email account belonging to an employee at Norfund on September 27, 2019. The Threat Actor then monitored Norfund's communication for seven months. On March 9, 2020, the criminal actor intercepted email correspondence between Norfund and LOLC about the forthcoming transaction. LOLC is located in Sri Lanka, and the money was destined for Cambodia. Threat Actor managed to change bank account details in the disbursement notice and convinced Norfund that a Mexican bank was used to avoid several bank intermediaries in the transaction. Threat Actor used the Corona virus as a factor to convince LOLC that the bank transfer was delayed. At the same time, the criminals sent emails to Norfund confirming that the funds were received by LOLC to prevent immediate suspicion and potential review by Norfund management.

On April 24, 2020, Threat Actor tried to manipulate a transaction with another Norfund client in Cambodia, First Finance, and asked to change the bank account details to Banco Mercantil del Norte. Norfund's investment manager requested First Finance to confirm the change of banking details. In the meantime, Norfund received an email on April 30 from LOLC stating that the bank account details in the transfer on March 16 were incorrect. Following the discovery of the fraud and fraud attempt, Norfund started reviewing the incident in cooperation with their Norwegian bank DNB, their IT service provider Visolit, as well as reporting the incident to the police.

Police attorney Eivind Kluge at Oslo police district contacted Interpol in France about the case. The Norwegian ministry of foreign affairs contacted Mexican authorities through the Norwegian embassy in Mexico City. However, the police expressed early on that they believed that they would never be able to capture the criminals or retrieve the money stolen (Speed, 2020). Rather than admitting the police force's potential lack of competence and insights into digital fraud locally and globally, the police argued that the criminals were very sophisticated by an "advanced data breach". Key persons at Norfund, such as chairperson Olaug Svarva, chief executive officer Tellef Thorleifsson, and communications executive Per Kristian Sbertoli, communicated a similar message that was supported by PwC's (2020) fraud examiners (Solgård, 2020b; Stave, 2020).

However, examiners at PwC (2020: 5) identified the approach used by Threat Actor to defraud Norfund as the well-known technique of Business Email Compromise (BEC):

> In this type of scam, a criminal threat actor uses email to impersonate a business executive or other employees to request fraudulent payments. In Norfund's case, the threat actor leveraged relatively simple techniques in terms of circumventing existing IT security controls. PwC found no signs of malicious software being used.

Norfund had no appropriate IT security controls that could have helped detect the breach, and they had no competent technology expert internally. By intercepting Norfund's email system, Threat Actor had acquired knowledge of Norfund's operations generally and money transfers particularly. Threat Actor was successfully able to manipulate communication between Norfund and its clients. The combination of Threat Actor's technical capabilities, digital experience, and understanding of Norfund's communication with clients made the fraud convenient for the criminal organization. Convenience was also caused by Norfund's inability to detect fraud and the Norfund employee's ignorance and naivety, which examiners phrase politely (PwC, 2020: 5):

It's PwC's assessment that the risk management framework could be further developed and improved to ensure Norfund's operational resilience.

The BEC scam that was used against Norfund is quite a common technique (Bakarich and Baranek, 2020: A1):

> Business email compromise (BEC) is a sophisticated email scam targeting companies that frequently work with foreign suppliers or businesses and utilize wire transfers as their regular method of transferring funds. These scams usually involve the compromise of legitimate business email accounts to conduct unauthorized transfers of funds, although other variations include requesting personally identifiable information.

Criminal organizations may use insiders in victim organizations to leak relevant information, bank clerks to open legitimate bank accounts, attorneys to keep secrets because of the attorney-client privilege, police officers to look another way, and various other helpers who the criminals pay off or threaten. When fraud is completed, then money laundering of proceeds from the criminal activity is important.

PwC (2020: 14) identified no singular control failure as the root cause of the incident at Norfund, but rather institutional deterioration that they label "unanticipated interaction of multiple failures in a complex system":

> In hindsight, the reasons why such accidents occur may be obvious. However, they are challenging to predict due to the number of actions and pathways that may lead up to them.

Examiners at PwC (2020) conclude that "a chain of unfortunate events, insufficient controls, and human error, all contributed to the incident".

Money laundering

Money laundering means securing of the proceeds of the criminal act. The proceeds must be integrated into the legal economy before the perpetrators can use it. The purpose of laundering is to make it appear as if the proceeds were acquired legally as well as disguising its illegal origins. Money laundering takes place within all types of profit-motivated crime, such as embezzlement, fraud, misappropriation, corruption, robbery, distribution of narcotic drugs, and trafficking human beings.

Money laundering has often been characterized as a three-stage process that requires (1) moving the funds from direct association with the crime, (2) disguising the trail to foil pursuit, and (3) making them available to the criminal organization once again with their occupational and geographic origins hidden from view. The first stage is often the most risky one for the criminals because money from crime is introduced into the financial system. In the Norfund case, the money was already in the financial system. Stage 1 is often called the placement stage. Stage 2 is often called the layering stage, in which money is moved in order to disguise or remove direct links to the offense committed. The money may be channeled through several transactions, which could involve a number of accounts, financial institutions, companies, and funds as well as the use of professionals such as lawyers, brokers, and consultants as intermediaries. Stage 3 is often called the integration stage, in which a legitimate basis for asset origin has been created. The money is made available to the criminal organization and can be used freely for regular expenditures and investments in legal businesses (Menon and Siew, 2012; Naheem, 2018).

PwC (2020) suggests that banks located in China, Hong Kong, United Kingdom, and Mexico often are involved in fraudulent transfers. Recent money laundering by criminal organizations in Russia involved Danske Bank in Denmark (Bruun Hjejle, 2018) and Swedbank in Sweden (Clifford Chance, 2020).

According to Joyce (2005), criminal money is frequently removed from the country in which the crime occurred to be cycled through the international payment system to obscure any audit trial. The third stage of money laundering is done in different ways. For example, a credit card might be issued by offshore banks, casino "winnings" can be cashed out, capital gains on option or stock trading might occur, and real estate sale might cause profit. When crime generates significant proceeds, the perpetrators need to find a way to control the assets without attracting attention to themselves or the offense committed. Thus, the money laundering process is decisive in order to enjoy the proceeds without arousing suspicion.

The proceeds of crime find their ways into different sectors of the economy. A survey in Canada indicates that deposit institutions are the single largest recipient, having been identified in 114 of the 149 proceeds of crime cases (Schneider, 2006). While the insurance sector was implicated in almost 65% of all cases, in the vast majority, the offender did not explicitly seek out the insurance sector as a laundering device. Instead, because motor vehicles, homes, companies, and marine vessels were purchased with the proceeds of crime, it was often necessary to purchase insurance for the assets.

Transnational criminals

Transnational criminals such as Threat Actor represent a challenge to societies all over the world. Transnational crime encompasses illegal activities that are carried out across national borders, which includes the planning and execution of illegal activities. Globalization has quickly facilitated the spread of these criminal activities. Transnational criminal organizations are organizations that conduct and carry out criminal operations across international borders. A transnational criminal organization may plan a crime in one country, carry it out in another, escape to a third, and keep the proceeds in a fourth country (Gottschalk and Markovic, 2016). Transnational crime has three broad objectives: provision of illicit goods, provision of illicit services, and the infiltration of business and government operations (Albanese, 2012). The Norfund fraud is an example of the latter, where Threat Actor infiltrated Norwegian government operations to steal $10 million. Transnational criminal organizations include mafia organizations such as La Cosa Nostra based in Italy, Los Zetas based in Mexico, and Hells Angels Motorcycle Club headquartered in the United States. Such organizations vary in their structure, culture, and fields of activity (Paraschiv, 2013). Some organizations recruit members based on ethnicity, while others recruit criminals based on competence and network. To join Threat Actor, computer skills and finance knowledge are probably required.

Traditional crime generally concerns personal or property offenses that law enforcement has continued to combat for centuries. Cybercrime is characterized by being technologically different; it can occur almost instantaneously and it is difficult to observe and detect by traditional investigative methods. Cybercrime is sometimes easy to track, as digital detectives can follow electronic traces. While the crime scene in terms of computers involved may be easy to track, the criminals as actors are more difficult to find and prosecute. The problem of offender identification occurs because of the relative anonymity afforded by the Internet as well as the transcendence of geographical and physical limitations in cyberspace. Also, decentralized peer-to-peer networks may prevent material from being tracked to a specific location, and sophisticated encryption lets criminals keep online chats private from those policing the web.

Transnational cybercrime encompasses illegal activities carried out across national borders using information technology. Criminals are able to take advantage of a virtually limitless pool of potential victims. This is the case, for example, in online grooming where pedophile offenders find child victims across borders. Similarly, transnational music piracy is committed through a multitude of modus operandi. Also, financial crime in terms of, for example, electronic money laundering is frequently transnational between banking sectors with different legislations and secrecy practices.

Transnational CEO fraud

BEC fraud is often associated with CEO fraud. Chief executive officers (CEOs) typically enjoy substantial individual freedom in their professions with little or no control. The CEO is the only person at that hierarchical level in the organization. Below the CEO, there are a number of executives at the same hierarchical level. Above the CEO, there are a number of board members at the same hierarchical level. But the CEO is alone at his or her level. The CEO is supposed to be controlled by the board, but the board only meets once in a while to discuss business cases. Executives below the CEO are typically appointed by the CEO and tend to be loyal to the CEO. Therefore, power, influence, and freedom are characteristics of CEOs.

CEO power and influence can be illustrated by what is labeled CEO fraud in law enforcement. CEO fraud is not fraud by CEOs. Rather, CEO fraud is fraud committed by someone claiming to be the CEO. If someone claims to be the CEO, most people in the organization will do what they are told. As long as they believe that the message stems from the real CEO, they are completely obedient and do as they are told by the fake CEO. The U.S. Federal Bureau of Investigation (FBI) warned in 2016 about a dramatic increase in CEO fraud, email scams in which the attacker spoofs a message from the boss and tricks someone at the organization into wiring funds to the fraudsters. The FBI estimates these scams cost organizations in the United States more than $1 billion per year. Organizations that are victimized by CEO fraud can be characterized by a combination of CEO power and obedience culture.

Some of the surprises for new CEOs arise from time and knowledge limitations – there is so much to do in complex new areas, with imperfect information and never enough time. Others stem from unexpected and unfamiliar new roles and altered professional relationships. Still others occur because of the frequent paradox that the more power you have, the harder it is to use it. While several of the challenges may appear familiar, Porter et al. (2004) discovered that nothing in a leader's background, even running a large business within his or her company, fully prepares them to be CEO. Given the required struggle for CEOs to succeed under such circumstances, their subordinates have to cope with initiatives and decisions that may seem random without any clear pattern. After a while with a new CEO, little will surprise those who have to execute CEO decisions. This opens up for CEO fraud, where external criminals can take advantage of an institutional climate where every decision by a CEO is expected to be executed, whether or not the decision makes sense.

CEOs have long been recognized as the principal architects of corporate strategy and major catalysts of organizational change, and the extent to which CEOs can effect change in corporate strategy is thought to be determined largely by the power they possess, and how they decide to apply it (Hambrick and Lovelace, 2018). Thus, CEO fraud is enabled by change initiatives, where CEO behavior itself changes in ways so that there is no suspicion when deviant requests for money transfers occur.

While strategy development as well as organizational change may be at the center of CEO work, many CEOs spend much more time on other – and more minor – matters and issues. Conflicts between individuals in the organization take time to resolve and sudden media attention can steal even more time – and sometimes sleep – from important strategic thinking. Trivial matters tend to occupy much of CEO time. Given an understanding for a stressful situation among employees, CEO fraud is enabled based on the lack of formal rules guiding CEO decision-making and implementation.

Many CEOs discover that they are alone, particularly in difficult times. They have nobody on their side at the same organizational level with whom they can openly discuss how to get out of a crisis situation. Rather, others in an organization may speculate whether or not the CEO will survive in the position and act accordingly to rescue their own future in the organization. Therefore, employees who receive strange requests from an alleged CEO will be reluctant to contact the real CEO to check whether or not they should execute money transfer as requested.

Problem-solving is at the core of CEO work. Mindsets are conceived as distinct cognitive operations that facilitate problem-solving. The concept dates back to the end of the nineteenth century and the experimental psychologist Oswald Külpe, who showed that most of human thinking happens without images (imageless thoughts) and that most of it also occurs outside of our awareness. The resulting term, "Bewusstseinslage", literally a "state of mind", was later translated into the concept of mindsets, "Einstellung". Subordinates tend to spend time speculating in the mindset of the CEO and thus feel distant from communicating with the CEO.

Külpe showed that subjects would single out the features related to their tasks, while unimportant or irrelevant features were rejected from their attention. For example, faced with the task of observing the number of letters presented to them, subjects may be totally unable to recall the color and may even deny that color has been experienced at all. This is the original meaning of the term "mindset": the brain is "set" to perceive the world according to predefined criteria. In the course of his research, it was observed that, while given tasks were conscious initially, after a few repetitions the tasks would gradually disappear from consciousness. Upon increased practice, conscious awareness concerning the task waned, although the task could be completed even if there was no awareness of it. Subjects had no phenomenological awareness of inner speech at the time of study, i.e., there was no longer conscious reflection about the tasks. The original purpose is duly forgotten and appearance of the stimulus automatically activated the prescribed conduct. In our perspective of speculation with lack of communication, subordinates can be fearful of the possible response by the CEO if they contact the person concerning a requested money transfer. Again, this phenomenon is an enabler of CEO fraud.

The word "set" in "mindset" describes how the actor is perceptually prepared or "set" to detect and respond to a given situation, a cognitive recognition pattern that is automatically evoked when scanning the environment. The core aspect is that mindsets are (a) caused by repetitive tasks; (b) automatic behaviors set in play with little or no awareness; and (c) replace personality-based dispositions with mindset content. Mindsets can be extremely effective in terms of seizing business opportunities, but are in themselves neither lawful nor unlawful since the ethical implications may not be a part of the mindset. Instead, they may be seen as automated recognition of opportunity with instrumental value as profit maximizing in a competitive setting.

Bigley and Wiersema (2002) argue that CEOs' cognitive orientation should influence how they wield their power to affect corporate strategy. On the other hand, predictions about a CEO's use of power require an understanding of the CEO's cognitive orientation toward his or her firm's strategy, because power is simply the ability to bring about a preferred or intended effect. Hypothesized association between a CEO's cognitive orientation and corporate strategy presupposes that the CEO has sufficient power to bring about the preferred or intended effects.

At the core of a CEO's mindset, we sometimes find himself or herself. Being alone at the top with rivaling executives as main contacts, the CEO has to enter the role of team player without really believing that it will work. There is no top management team and the CEO is alone. Over time, a CEO may focus more and more on managing the role rather than managing the company.

Not all CEOs work for change. Some are more committed to status quo – particularly to their organization's current strategy and leadership profile – than others. Hambrick et al. (2018) found that many organizations do not adapt effectively to changes in their environments because of CEO commitment to status quo. Organizational inertia can thus be caused by the CEO, making the organization unable to change at the same rate as its environment. McClelland et al. (2010) found that CEO commitment to status quo is influenced by variables at the individual, firm, and industry levels. Increasing CEO age and tenure are associated with greater status quo commitment. CEOs in firms with financial slack view change more favorably. In contrast, CEOs at firms with liquidity problems may be more committed to the status quo out of necessity.

CEOs' mindsets and strategic beliefs are likely to be instantiated to a significant degree in their firms' current strategies. When a top executive seeking advice confirms and/or restores his or her confidence in the correctness of strategic beliefs, the CEO will be less inclined to alter firm strategy. The mindsets of CEOs are expected to cause them to be the principal architects of corporate strategy and major catalysts of organizational change. Belonging to their mindsets is how to use power and secrecy, building alliances with some people and keeping others in the dark about their dispositions, as shown by Bigley and Wiersma (2002). McDonald and Westphal (2003) theorized that relatively poor firm performance can prompt CEOs to seek more advice from executives of other firms who are their friends or similar to them and less advice from acquaintances or dissimilar others and suggest how and why this pattern of advice seeking could reduce firms' propensity to change corporate strategy in response to poor performance.

Similarly, CEOs can have a tendency to listen more to executives in their top management teams who confirm rather than disconfirm their beliefs. Differential association theory postulates that CEO learning occurs in association with those who find their behavior and thinking favorable and in isolation from those who find it unfavorable. Differential association is the process whereby one is exposed to normative definitions favorable or unfavorable to illegal or law-abiding behavior. Whether CEOs engage in white-collar crime is largely based on their socialization within certain peer groups (Holtfreter, 2015).

McDonald and Westphal (2003) tested their hypothesis that relatively poor firm performance can prompt CEOs to seek self-confirming advice. The results from a large sample confirm their hypothesis and show that executives' social network ties can influence firms' responses to economic adversity, in particular by inhibiting strategic change in response to relatively poor organizational performance. Additional findings indicate that CEOs' advice seeking in response to low performance may ultimately have negative consequences for subsequent performance, suggesting how CEOs' social network ties could play an indirect role in organizational decline and downward spirals in form performance.

Private policing evaluation

Similar to Norfund who used the term "advanced data breach", PwC (2020: 14) claims that "the fraud was carried out by a resourceful and highly motivated threat actor who had an in-depth knowledge of financial transactions, and access to a global payment infrastructure." Such statements seem to be in contrast to PwC's (2020: 5) claim earlier in their report that the technique used is common and "relatively simple":

> In the past few years, the cyber threat landscape has undergone significant changes. Tools, techniques and capabilities that were previously exclusively available to highly resourceful threat actors have not only become easily accessible to less-skilled threat actors, but have also become easier to use. While substantial in terms of the financial losses incurred by Norfund, the LOLC incident was by no means exceptional.

In addition to the seemingly helpless approach to understanding digital fraud, criminal organizations, and identity of potential offenders, the PwC (2020) report seems like a biased work to satisfy the client. The report creates an impression that the main purpose of the review was to confirm that Norfund does what they can to prevent future fraud, for example (PwC, 2020: 27):

> PwC's assessment is that Norfund has a strong commitment to change and sets an appropriate "tone at the top". It is PwC's opinion that following the Alios incident, Norfund conducted a thorough assessment and identified appropriate measures to improve IT security.

In the summer of 2018, one of Norfund's borrowers, Alios, suffered an incident which appears similar to the LOLC incident (PwC, 2020: 26):

> In this incident, a threat actor infiltrated the communication between Alios and Norfund, and manipulated Alios to make a payment to an account under the threat actor's control. Following the incident, Norfund conducted an internal investigation in cooperation with third parties.

PwC (2020) argues that Norfund learned from the episode, while examiners at the same time present excuses for the LOLC incident that happened less than two years later. The client Norfund is probably happy with the PwC report that seems less critical and more client-friendly than is expected of work by objective and independent examiners. Therefore, the investigation only reaches level 2 in its maturity as illustrated in Figure 22.2.

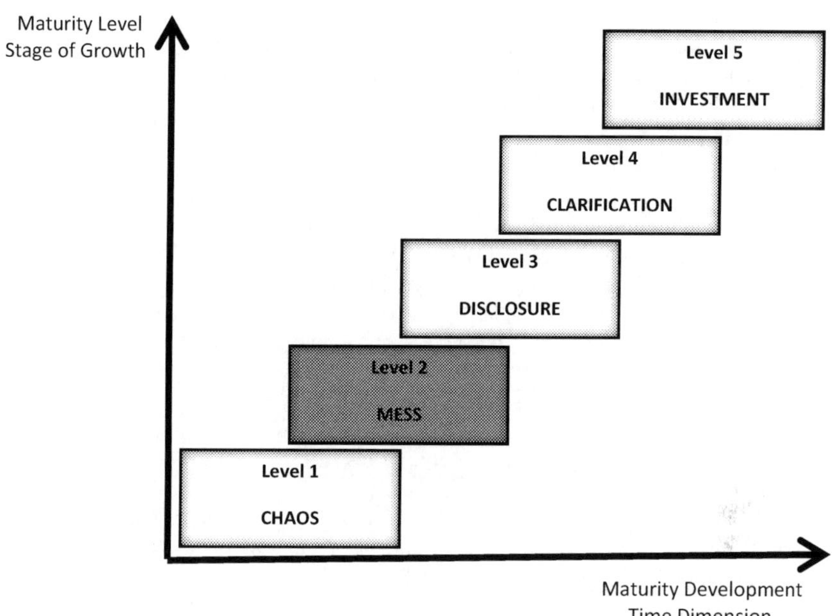

Figure 22.2 Maturity model for internal private investigations applied to PwC

Bibliography

Adler, P.S. and Kwon, S.W. (2002). Social capital: Prospects for a new concept, *Academy of Management Review*, 27 (1), 17–40.

Albanese, J.S. (2012). Deciphering the linkages between organized crime and transnational crime, *Journal of International Affairs*, 66 (1), 1–16.

Bakarich, K.M. and Baranek, D. (2020). Something phish-y is going on here: A teaching case on business email compromise, *Current Issues in Auditing*, 14 (1), A1–A9.

Benartzi, S., Beshears, J., Milkman, K.L., Sunstein, C.R., Thaler, R.H., Shankar, M., Tucker-Ray, W., Congdon, W.J. and Galing, S. (2017). Should governments invest more in nudging? *Psychological Science*, 28 (8), 1041–1055.

Benson, M.L. and Simpson, S.S. (2018). *White-Collar Crime: An Opportunity Perspective*, 3rd Edition, New York: Routledge.

Bigley, G.A. and Wiersma, M.F. (2002). New CEOs and corporate strategic refocusing: How experience as heir apparent influences the use of power, *Administrative Science Quarterly*, 47, 707–727.

Bruun Hjejle (2018). *Report on the Non-Resident Portfolio at Danske Bank's Estonian Branch*, September 19, Copenhagen: Law Firm Bruun & Hjejle, 87 pages.

Bussmann, K.D., Niemeczek, A. and Vockrodt, M. (2018). Company culture and prevention of corruption in Germany, China and Russia, *European Journal of Criminology*, 15 (3), 255–277.

Chang, J.J., Lu, H.C. and M. Chen (2005). Organized crime or individual crime? Endogeneous size of a criminal organization and the optimal law enforcement, *Economic Inquiry*, 43 (3), 661–675.

Clifford Chance (2020). *Report of Investigation on Swedbank*, March 23, Washington, DC: Law Firm Clifford Chance.

Craig, J.M. and Piquero, N.L. (2017). Sensational offending: An application of sensation seeking to white-collar and conventional crimes, *Crime & Delinquency*, 63 (11), 1363–1382.

Cullen, F.T. (2010). Cloward, Richard A., and Lloyd E. Ohlin: Delinquency and opportunity, in: Cullen, F.T. and Wilcox, P. (editors), *Encyclopedia of Criminological Theory*, Volume 1, Los Angeles, CA: Sage Publications, pages 170–174.

Dean, G., Fahsing, I. and Gottschalk, P. (2010). *Organized Crime – Policing Illegal Business Entrepreneurialism*, Oxford: Oxford University Press.

Goldstraw-White, J. (2012). *White-Collar Crime: Accounts of Offending Behavior*, London: Palgrave Macmillan.

Gottschalk, P. and Markovic, V. (2016). Transnational criminal organizations (TCOs): The case of combating criminal biker gangs, *International Journal of Criminal Justice Sciences*, June-December, 30–44.

Gottschalk, P. and Smith, R. (2011). Criminal entrepreneurship, white-collar criminality, and neutralization theory, *Journal of Enterprising Communities: People and Places in the Global Economy*, 5(4), 300–308.

Hambrick, D.C. and Lovelace, J.B. (2018). The role of executive symbolism in advancing new strategic themes in organization: A social influence perspective, *Academy of Management Review*, 43 (1), 110–131.

Holtfreter, K. (2015). General theory, gender-specific theory, and white-collar crime, *Journal of Financial Crime*, 22 (4), 422–431.

Joyce, E. (2005). Expanding the international regime on money laundering in response to transnational organized crime, terrorism, and corruption, in: P. Reichel (editor), *Handbook of Transnational Crime and Justice*, London: Sage publications, pages 79–97.

Maslow, A.H. (1943). A theory of human motivation, *Psychological Review*, 50 (4), 370–396.

McClelland, P.L., Liang, X. and Barker, V.L. (2010). CEO commitment to the status quo: Replication and extension using content analysis, *Journal of Management*, 36 (5), 1251–1277.

McDonald, M.L. and Westphal, J.D. (2003). Getting by with the advice of their friends: CEOs' advice networks using content analysis, *Administrative Science Quarterly*, 48 (1), 1–32.

McElwee, G. and Smith, R. (2015). Towards a nuanced typology of illegal entrepreneurship: A theoretical and conceptual overview, in: McElwee, G. and Smith, R. (editors), *Exploring Criminal and Illegal Enterprise: New Perspectives on Research, Policy & Practice: Contemporary Issues in Entrepreneurship Research Volume 5*, Bingley: Emerald.

Menon, S. and Siew, T.G. (2012). Key challenges in tackling economic and cybercrimes – Creating a multilateral platform for international co-operation, *Journal of Money Laundering Control*, 15 (3), 243–256.

Naheem, M.A. (2018). Fifa – highlighting the links between global banking and international money laundering, *Journal of Money Laundering Control*, 21 (4), 498–512.

Nielsen, R.P. (2003). Corruption networks and implications for ethical corruption reform, *Journal of Business Ethics*, 42 (2), 125–149.

Norfund (2020). *Norfund er utsatt for alvorlig svindel (Norfund is Exposed to Serious Fraud)*, Norfund, www.norfund.no, published May 15.

Paraschiv, G. (2013). Conceptualizing transnational organized crime, *Economics, Management, and Financial Markets*, 8 (2), 173–178.

Pontell, H.N., Black, W.K. and Geis, G. (2014). Too big to fail, too powerful to jail? On the absence of criminal prosecutions after the 2008 financial meltdown, *Crime, Law and Social Change*, 61 (1), 1–13.

Porter, M.E., Lorsch, J.W. and Nohria, N. (2004). Seven surprises for new CEOs, *Harvard Business Review*, October, 62.

Pratt, T.C. and Cullen, F.T. (2005). Assessing macro-level predictors and theories of crime: A meta-analysis, *Crime and Justice*, 32, 373–450.

PwC (2020). *Independent Assessment of the LOLC Incident: Report Developed for Norfund, Report of Investigation*, Oslo: PricewaterhouseCoopers, 34 pages.

Ramoglou, S. and Tsang, E.W.K. (2016). A realist perspective of entrepreneurship: Opportunities as propensities, *Academy of Management Review*, 41, 410–434.

Schneider, S. (2006). Privatizing economic crime enforcement: Exploring the role of private sector investigative agencies in combating money laundering, *Policing & Society*, 16 (3), 285–312.

Schoepfer, A. and Piquero, N.L. (2006). Exploring white-collar crime and the American dream: A partial test of institutional anomie theory, *Journal of Criminal Justice*, 34 (3), 227–235.

Smith, R. (2009). Understanding entrepreneurial behavior in organized criminals, *Journal of Enterprising Communities: People and Places in the Global Economy*, 3 (3), 256–268.

Solgård, J. (2020). Norfund ble svindlet for 100 millioner: -Vi har gjort mye, men ikke raskt nok for å styrke våre rutiner og systemer (Norfund was defrauded for 100 million: -We have done a lot, but not fast enough to strengthen our routines and systems), *Daily Norwegian Business Newspaper Dagens Næringsliv*, www.dn.no, published July 9.

Speed, J. (2020). Politiet: Lite trolig at Nordfun får igjen svindelpenger (The police: It is unlikely that Norfund will get back fraud money), *Foreign Aid Magazine BistandsAktuelt*, www.bistandsaktuelt.no, published May 15.

Stave, T.K. (2020). Norfund tar selvkritikk etter gigantsvindel (Norfund takes self-criticism after giant fraud), *Daily Norwegian Newspaper Aftenposten*, www.e24.no, published July 9.

Sutherland, E.H. (1983). *White Collar Crime – The Uncut Version*, New Haven, CT: Yale University Press.

Tonoyan, V., Strohmeyer, R., Habib, M. and Perlitz, M. (2010). Corruption and entrepreneurship: How formal and informal institutions shape small firm behavior in transition and mature market economies, *Entrepreneurship: Theory & Practice*, 34 (5), 803–831.

Welter, F., Baker, T., Audretsch, D.B. and Gartner, W.B. (2017). Everyday entrepreneurship: A call for entrepreneurship research to embrace entrepreneurial diversity, *Entrepreneurship: Theory and Practice*, 41 (3), 323–347.

Conclusion

White-collar crime is a global problem of enormous magnitude. Fraud, manipulation, embezzlement, and corruption incidents occur to varying degrees in every economy and society in the world. The fraudulent schemes and corporate corruption scandals of the past two decades have confirmed once again the continuing relevance of white-collar crime as a significant threat to the economic and social health of nations across the globe as well as an important area of criminological research. For criminologists, the importance of white-collar crime lies in part in its seeming differences from other forms of crime along several perspectives. Among the most important of these perspectives are the sociodemographic backgrounds of the individuals who commit these types of offenses, in particular class and gender, as well as the link between white-collar crime and legitimate occupational, organizational, and economic activities.

When there is suspicion of economic crime by white-collar offenders in organizations, the organizations tend to hire fraud examiners to conduct private policing by internal investigations in the organizations. The affected organizations become clients of law firms and auditing firms who reconstruct past events and sequences of events to determine the extent of misconduct and crime. "Corporate clients can effectively choose to sidestep the criminal justice system and not report matters to authorities, propagating debate on the treatment of white-collar criminals compared to others" (King, 2020b: 9).

This book has presented a number of relevant case studies to illustrate the extent of convenience in white-collar crime and the level of maturity in fraud examinations. Overall, most internal investigators have a long way to go before their work deserves the classification of an investment for the clients. Failing interviews, lack of relevant knowledge, and conclusions without reliable evidence are some of the shortcomings identified in the case studies. As pointed out in previous research (e.g., Brooks and Button, 2011; Button and Gee, 2013; Button et al., 2007a, 2007b; Gottschalk, 2020; King, 2020a, 2020b; Schneider, 2006; Williams, 2005), many fraud examiners have a long way to go before they can deserve the label of professional investigators.

The extent of convenience is an interesting topic in itself that I have covered in a previous book (Gottschalk, 2019). A remaining question is whether suspected misconduct at Caverion, Ferde, FIFA, Helgeland hospital, Moldova banks,

Oceanteam, Oslo housing, Oslo recycling, Samherji, Social security, Swedbank, and XXL represent single scandals, or do they illustrate organizations where economic scandals have occurred before or will occur again in the future. Recidivism is a research topic within criminology (Chen and Shapiro, 2007; Skardhamar and Telle, 2012), and recidivism in corporate and occupational economic crime is no exception (Barnard, 2008; Henning, 2015; Murphy and Harris, 2007; Listwan et al., 2010; Piquero and Weisburd, 2009; Podgor, 2007; Slawotsky, 2015).

According to Collins et al. (2017), recidivism is the behavior of a person or persons repeating an illegal act after having experienced negative penal consequences of a previous offense. In our perspective concerned with white-collar offenders, convicted criminals need to return to elite positions before they have an opportunity for recidivism (Henning, 2015: 1):

> There was virtually no chance he would be trusted again, so there is no likelihood of recidivism; nor did he pose any future physical danger to society.

Among all those white-collar offenders who return to trusted positions with access to resources to commit and conceal misconduct and crime, recidivism is indeed possible. Slawotsky (2015: 280) found that:

> Some financial institutions have become serial lawbreakters, violating not only civil, but also criminal laws. Many of the institutions are subject to multiple investigations, and some of them previously assured prosecutors and regulators that criminal activity would not be repeated after they were involved in what was widely considered a historic settlement. Financial corporations' systemic violation of the law reveals that financial institutional misconduct is widespread, deeply embedded, and broad based.

Harbinson et al. (2019) suggest that elite members with narcissistic and neurotic traits are more likely to recidivate. They report that an appreciable proportion of the people convicted of white-collar offenses (about 30%) recidivated and some did repeatedly. Those who were recidivists could be distinguished from nonrecidivists on the basis of certain personal and social characteristics.

In the Norwegian sample of white-collar convicts presented by Gottschalk (2019), 7% reoffended, faced prosecution, and returned to prison. About 7% was also the case for a comparison group who did not commit economic crime. According to Gottschalk and Gunnesdal (2018), the detection rate for white-collar offenders in Norway is 1 out of 11 criminals. The actual recidivism is thus much higher than 7%.

In a sample of white-collar offenders in the United States, Listwan et al. (2010) found that half of the individuals in the sample suffered rearrests. However, new arrests of the individuals often occurred because of a variety of charges such as system violations that include offenses such as failure to appear and failure to adhere to conditions. Nevertheless, there was a substantial fraction of recidivism in terms of repeated and detected financial crime by white-collar offenders.

The recidivism exemplified from Norway and the United States is interesting, because the suspected misconduct or crime investigated by fraud examiners is not necessarily the first time or the last time for offenders. While convicted companies suffer financial loss in the form of fines by the state, individual offenders suffer incarceration after failing defense in court. The implication for private policing is that fraud examiners might expand their perspective historically and into the future. They do sometimes the latter by recommending measures that serve to prevent future occurrences. For example, sanctioning deviant individuals, including shaming (Murphy and Harris, 2007), has a deterrent effect, while a material appreciation to whistleblowers has a detecting effect. Ethical guidelines and formal auditing routines, however, have probably little or no effect.

Private policing remains a controversial issue that is worth further studies. The parameters, limits, and standards of private policing are varying and unclear in different jurisdictions. There are no legal or ethical standards that must be followed when conducting fraud investigations, since the growing business of internal investigations is unregulated in all known jurisdictions. Rule of law, due process, presumptions of innocence, collection and use of admissible evidence, victims, witnesses, whistleblower protection, suspect management, data protection, and other fundamental rights are observed in private policing to the extent necessary and relevant for investigation business success.

Bibliography

Barnard, J.W. (2008). Securities fraud, recidivism, and deterrence, *Penn State Law Review*, 113 (1), 189–228.

Brooks, G. and Button, M. (2011). The police and fraud investigation and the case for a nationalized solution in the United Kingdom, *The Police Journal*, 84, 305–319.

Button, M., Frimpong, K., Smith, G. and Johnston, L. (2007a). Professionalizing counter fraud specialists in the UK: Assessing progress and recommendations for reform, *Crime Prevention and Community Safety*, 9, 92–101.

Button, M. and Gee, J. (2013). *Countering Fraud for Competitive Advantage – The Professional Approach to Reducing the Last Great Hidden Cost*, Chichester: John Wiley & Sons.

Button, M., Johnston, L., Frimpong, K. and Smith, G. (2007b). New directions in policing fraud: The emergence of the counter fraud specialists in the United Kingdom, *International Journal of the Sociology of Law*, 35, 192–208.

Chen, M.K. and Shapiro, J.M. (2007). Do harsher prison conditions reduce recidivism? A discontinuity-based approach, *American Law and Economics Review*, 9 (1), 1–29.

Collins, S.E., Lonczak, H.S. and Clifasefi, S.L. (2017). Seattle's law enforcement assisted diversion (LEAD): Program effects on recidivism outcomes, *Evaluation and Program Planning*, 64, 49–56.

Gottschalk, P. (2019). *Convenience Triangle in White-Collar Crime – Case Studies of Fraud Examinations*, Cheltenham: Edward Elgar Publishing.

Gottschalk, P. (2020). Private policing of white-collar crime: Case studies of internal investigations by fraud examiners, *Police Practice and Research*, published online https://doi.org/10.1080/15614263.2020.1789461.

Gottschalk, P. and Gunnesdal, L. (2018). *White-Collar Crime in the Shadow Economy: Lack of Detection, Investigation, and Conviction Compared to Social Security Fraud*, London: Palgrave Pivot, Palgrave Macmillan, Springer Publishing.

Harbinson, E., Benson, M.L. and Latessa, E.J. (2019). Assessing risk among white-collar offenders under federal supervision in the community, *Criminal Justice and Behavior*, 46 (2), 261–279.

Henning, P.J. (2015). Is deterrence relevant in sentencing white-collar criminals? Law Faculty Research Publications, Wayne State University, 1-1-2015, *Wayne Law Review*, 61 (27), 1–34.

King, M. (2020a). What makes a successful corporate investigator – An exploration of private investigators attributes, *Journal of Financial Crime*, published online https://doi.org/10.1108/JFC-02-2020-0019.

King, M. (2020b). Out of obscurity: The contemporary private investigator in Australia, *International Journal of Police Science and Management*, published online https://doi.org/10.1177/1461355720931887.

Listwan, S.J., Piquero, N.L. and Voorhis, P. (2010). Recidivism among a white-collar sample: Does personality matter? *Australian & New Zealand Journal of Criminology*, 43 (1), 156–174.

Murphy, K. and Harris, N. (2007). Shaming, shame and recidivism: A test of reintegrative shaming theory in the white-collar crime context, *British Journal of Criminology*, 47 (6), 900–917.

Piquero, N.L. and Weisburd, D. (2009). Developmental trajectories of white-collar crime, in: Simpson, S. and Weisburd, D. (editors), *The Criminology of White-Collar Crime*, York: Springer, pages 153–171.

Podgor, E.S. (2007). The challenge of white collar sentencing, *Journal of Law and Criminology*, 97 (3), 731–760.

Schneider, S. (2006). Privatizing economic crime enforcement: Exploring the role of private sector investigative agencies in combating money laundering, *Policing & Society*, 16 (3), 285–312.

Skardhamar, T. and Telle, K. (2012). Post-release employment and recidivism in Norway, *Journal of Quantitative Criminology*, 28 (4), 629–649.

Slawotsky, J. (2015). Reining in recidivist financial institutions, *Delaware Journal of Corporate Law*, 40 (1), 280–352.

Williams, J.W. (2005). Reflections on the private versus public policing of economic crime, *British Journal of Criminology*, 45, 316–339.

Appendix A

Over the years, this research into private policing of economic crime in terms of case studies of internal investigations by fraud examiners has resulted in a database with fraud examination reports from all over the world. In this appendix, the table lists the complete set of reports retrieved so far. The list includes the presented 16 cases in this book. By networking with scholars and by student assignments in Norway and the United States, the database has grown into a large number of cases. It is a significant number of cases given corporate investigators' and client organizatons' efforts to keep reports secret to avoid disclosure to the media, the police, and to the public in general (Gottschalk and Tcherni-Buzzeo, 2017). "Typically, corporations tend to take their own measures to resolve instances of fraud without resorting to the police" (King, 2020: 1). As is evident from Table A.1, most private policing reports are from Norway, since the base for this research is the Norwegian Business School in Oslo.

My previous books discuss many of the private policing reports listed in the table. Examples include British Petroleum investigated by Freeh, FujiFilm investigated by Deloitte, Nigerian National Petroleum Corporation investigated by PwC, Olympus investigated by Deloitte, Pelham investigated by KPMG, Philadelphia Sheriff's Office investigated by Deloitte, Toshiba investigated by Deloitte, and Wells Fargo investigated by Shearman Sterling.

Table A.1 Characteristics of fraud examinations at suspicion of white-collar crime

Investigated client organization	*Investigating examination firm*	*Suspicion of white-collar crime investigated*
Bangladesh		
Padakhep Save the Children *NGO*	Office of the Inspector General *U.S. 2012*	*Embezzlement of funds to fight disease*
Canada		
Niagara *municipality*	Ombudsman of Ontario	*Improper hiring of chief administrative officer*
Pelham *town*	KPMG *auditing firm 2017*	*Development project manipulation*
Denmark		
Danske Bank *banking*	Bruun & Hjejle *law firm 2018*	*Money laundering in Estonian branch*
Region Syddanmark *public authority*	Kromann Reumert *law firm 2015*	*Fraud by abuse of public position*
Socialstyrelsen *social security*	PwC *auditing firm 2019*	*Embezzlement by trusted employee*
Socialstyrelsen *social security*	Kammeradvokaten *law firm 2019*	*Executive lack of guardianship*
Ghana		
BioFuel *bioenergy production*	Kluge *law firm 2009*	*Corruption in Ghana to obtain licenses*
Iceland		
Samherji *fishing industries*	Al Jazeera *investigative journalists 2019*	*Corruption for fishing rights in Namibia*
Japan		
Olympus *digital equipment provider*	Deloitte *auditing firm 2011*	*Accounting manipulation and fraud*
Toshiba *digital equipment provider*	Deloitte *auditing firm 2015*	*Accounting manipulation and fraud*
Moldova		
Moldova Banca de Economii Sociala	Kroll *investigation firm 2015, 2017, 2018a,b,c*	*Bank fraud by loans transferred abroad for money laundering*
The Netherlands		
Oceanteam *offshore services*	Sands *law firm 2019*	*Abuse of company money by majority shareholder*
New Zealand		
FujiFilm *digital equipment leasing*	Deloitte *auditing firm 2017*	*Accounting fraud*

(*Continued*)

Table A.1 Continued

Investigated client organization	*Investigating examination firm*	*Suspicion of white-collar crime investigated*
Nigeria		
Nigerian National Petroleum Corporation	PwC *auditing firm 2015*	*Embezzlement and corruption in oil exploration*
Norway		
Adecco *nursing home*	Wiersholm *law firm 2011*	*Fraud in employment contracts for hourly rates*
Ahus *hospital*	PwC *auditing firm 2013*	*Fraud when charging mapping services*
Andebu *municipality*	BDO *auditing firm 2014*	*Abuse of mayor position in procurement*
Arendal *traffic station*	*Internal audit function 2017*	*Corruption for illegal vehicle permits*
Askøy *municipality*	BDO *auditing firm2018*	*Public procurement from family members*
Bergen *municipality*	*Internal control function 2018*	*Building permit to friends without control*
Bergen havn *port authority*	Havarikommisjon *commission 2019*	*Accident from maintenance cost savings*
Bergensklinikkene *private health clinic*	Ernst & Young *auditing firm 2019*	*Subsidy fraud by false number of addicts*
Betanien *foundation*	BDO *auditing firm2014*	*Embezzlement by chief executive (CEO)*
Briskeby *public sports arena*	Lynx *law firm 2011*	*Fraud in public construction funds*
Bærum *municipality*	G-partner *law firm 2007*	*Corruption at public procurement among family members*
Bårlidalen *public water waste site*	Svendby *consulting firm 2016*	*Fraud by overbilling the municipality*
Caverion *subcontractor services*	Wiersholm *law firm 2019*	*Substandard wages and working hours*
Dale *property development*	Komrev. Rogaland *public audit 2015*	*Public funds spent on private vacations*
Demokratene *political party*	Partirevisjon *internal control function 2016*	*Illegitimate government subsidy*
DNB *banking*	Hjort *law firm 2016*	*Tax evasion in wealth management revealed by Panama Papers*

(*Continued*)

Table A.1 Continued

Investigated client organization	*Investigating examination firm*	*Suspicion of white-collar crime investigated*
Drammen *municipality*	Deloitte *auditing firm 2017*	*Corruption in building permits*
Eckbo *foundations*	Thommessen *law firm 2009*	*Chairperson fraud in foundation funds*
Fadderbarna *foundation*	BDO *auditing firm 2011*	*Fake documents hiding fraud abroad*
Ferde *toll collection*	Kluge *law firm 2019*	*Conflict of interest for chief executive at procurement*
Ferde *toll collection*	Deloitte *auditing firm 2020*	*Abuse of position at mergers*
FilmCamp *public fund for productions*	Komrev. Nord *public audit 2016*	*Fraud by abuse of public funding*
Fjell *municipality*	Deloitte *auditing firm 2017*	*Corruption in construction permits*
Flyktningtjenesten *public refugee funding*	Buunk et al. *internal audit 2015*	*Embezzlement by refugee services manager*
Forsvaret *military contracts*	Dalseide *special committee 2006*	*Corruption in military computer contracts*
Forsvaret *military logistics*	PwC *auditing firm 2014*	*Corruption in military sales unit*
Forsvaret *department of defense routines*	PwC *auditing firm 2015*	*Illegal profits from sale of discarded equipment*
Fredrikstad *municipality*	PwC *auditing firm 2018*	*VAT fraud by public company*
Fredrikstad *municipality*	Simonsen *law firm 2018*	*VAT fraud by public company*
Fretex *Salvation Army*	Grette *law firm 2017*	*Financial targets to remove executive*
Furuheim *foundation nursing home*	Hald *law firm 2006*	*Fraud in foundation construction*
Fyrlykta *foundation child care*	Deloitte *auditing firm 2017*	*Fraud of public funds for excessive salaries*
Fyrlykta *foundation child care*	Stiftelsestilsynet *public examination 2018*	*Fraud of public funds for excessive salaries*
Gartnerhallen *fruits and vegetables*	Wiersholm *law firm 2018*	*Fraud by farmers demanding repay*
Gassnova *public projects*	BDO *auditing firm 2013*	*Corruption in public procurement*
Grimstad *municipality*	BDO *auditing firm 2016*	*Manipulation and corruption in public procurement*

(*Continued*)

Table A.1 Continued

Investigated client organization	*Investigating examination firm*	*Suspicion of white-collar crime investigated*
Grimstad *municipality*	Hjort *law firm 2018*	*Manipulation and corruption in public procurement*
Grimstad *municipality*	Tinia *consulting firm 2018*	*Fraud against caretaker of handicapped person*
Hadeland *broadband mobile company*	PwC *auditing firm 2014*	*Embezzlement by chief financial officer (CFO)*
Hadeland *energy supply company*	PwC *auditing firm 2014*	*Embezzlement by chief financial officer (CFO)*
Halden *municipality skating hall*	KPMG *auditing firm 2012*	*Fraud in construction project*
Halden *municipality buildings*	Hjort *law firm 2013*	*Corruption in building permits*
Hedmark *municipality*	Wiersholm *law firm 2007*	*Illegal benefits for executives in positions*
Helgelandssykehuset *public hospital*	KPMG (2019, 2020) *auditing firm*	*Working environment abuses*
Helse Nord *hospital*	PwC *auditing firm 2018*	*Fraud at executive removal from position*
Hordaland *police department*	Wiersholm *law firm 2015*	*Whistleblower financial retaliation*
Hordaland *police department*	Stamina *consulting firm 2019*	*Corruption in public procurement*
Jondal *municipality*	SBDL *law firm 2018*	*Corruption and private enterprise*
Karasjok *municipality*	Vest-Finnmark *public audit 2018*	*Friends got illegitimate favors*
Kjøpsvik *municipality*	Komrev. Nord *public audit 2015*	*Fraud by property developer*
Klengstua *kindergarden*	Halden *municipal internal audit 2019*	*Fraud in subsidies from municipality*
Kommunaldepartement *department of interior*	BDO *auditing firm 2018*	*Fraud in subsidies for kindergartens*
Kragerø *shipping*	Deloitte *auditing firm 2012*	*Compensation for leader without contract*
Kristiansand *municipality*	Komrev. Agder *public audit 2016*	*Private property developer abused political position*

(*Continued*)

Table A.1 Continued

Investigated client organization	*Investigating examination firm*	*Suspicion of white-collar crime investigated*
Kristiansand *municipality*	Tofte *law firm 2018*	*Harassment for financial benefit*
Kvalsund *municipality*	Vest-Finnmark *public audit 2012*	*Fraudulent consulting fees*
Kvam Auto *car dealer*	Wikborg *law firm 2015*	*Majority shareholder fraudulent behavior*
Kvinnherad *municipality*	Deloitte *auditing firm 2019*	*Fraud in chief executive retirement compensation*
Langemyhr *building company*	PwC *auditing firm 2008*	*Fraudulent working hours invoicing*
Larvik havn *port authority*	Komrev. Telemark *public audit 2018*	*Corruption in container terminal*
Larvik *municipality*	Komrev. Telemark *public audit 2017*	*Corruption in building permits*
Leksvik *municipality*	Midt-Norge *audit organization 2017*	*Illegal benefits to chief executive*
Lenvik *municipality*	KomRev *audit organization 2018*	*Fraud by executive*
Lunde *transportation company*	Vierdal *law firm 2012*	*Bankruptcy fraud*
Lyoness-Lyconet *gambling enterprise*	Stiftelsestilsynet *public examination 2018*	*Pyramid play similar to Ponzi scheme*
Moskvaskolen *school in Moscow*	Ernst & Young *auditing firm 2013*	*Paid teachers without teaching*
NAV *social security authority*	Wiersholm *law firm 2016*	*Employees illegal abuse of information for gain*
NDLA *public learning software*	Deloitte *auditing firm 2015*	*Private abuse of public funds*
NFF *football players association*	Lynx *law firm 2012*	*Fraud in player transfers*
NIF *sports association*	BDO *auditing firm 2014*	*Association president bribed*
Norsk Tipping *public betting*	Deloitte *auditing firm 2010*	*CEO private property served*
Norwegian Poker Team *private gambling*	Aftenposten *media investigation 2018*	*Money laundering at poker game*
Næringsdepartement *department of industry*	PwC *auditing firm 2016*	*Corruption in state-owned enterprises*
Næringsdepartement *department of industry*	Ernst & Young *auditing firm 2018*	*Embezzlement by executive in aid program*

(*Continued*)

Table A.1 Continued

Investigated client organization	*Investigating examination firm*	*Suspicion of white-collar crime investigated*
Orange *health services provider*	Bergen *municipality audit function 2016*	*Fraud by executive compensation*
Oslo Boligbygg *municipal housing*	BDO *auditing firm 2017*	*Corruption in public procurement*
Oslo Boligbygg *municipal housing*	Deloitte *auditing firm 2018*	*Corruption in public procurement*
Oslo Boligbygg *municipal housing*	Komrev. Oslo *public audit 2018*	*Corruption at procurement of facilities*
Oslo Boligbygg *municipal housing*	Deloitte *auditing firm 2019*	*Fraud at over-priced procurement*
Oslo Bymiljø *municipal parks*	Ernst & Young *auditing firm 2019*	*Fraud by fake invoicing of park works*
Oslo Energigjenvinning *public recycling*	PwC *auditing firm 2019*	*Fraud by abuse of working hours*
Oslo Lindeberg *nursing home*	Kommunerevisjon *public audit 2013*	*Fraud in employment contracts*
Oslo Omsorgsbygg *housing administration*	PwC *auditing firm 2009*	*Abuse of Norwegian public funds in Spain*
Oslo Omsorgsbygg *housing administration*	Komrev. Oslo *public audit 2018*	*Chief executive employed family members*
Oslo Omsorgsbygg *housing administration*	PwC *auditing firm 2019*	*Chief executive employed family members*
Oslo Renovasjon *public garbage collection*	Deloitte *auditing firm 2017*	*Fraud in employment contracts*
Oslo Samferdsel *public transportation*	PwC *auditing firm 2007*	*Corruption in public procurement*
Oslo *municipal school buildings*	Kommunerevisjon *public audit 2006*	*Project manager bribed in corruption*
Oslo *municipal school buildings*	Kommunerevisjon *public audit 2006*	*Property manager bribed in corruption*
Oslo Unibuss *public transportation*	Wiersholm *law firm 2012*	*Corruption in public procurement*
Oslo Vei *public transportation firm*	Kvale *law firm 2013*	*Bankruptcy fraud*
Politiets utlending *police department*	KPMG *auditing firm 2016*	*Executive abuse of overtime compensation*
Rana *municipality*	PwC *auditing firm 2008*	*Corruption in public investment fund*
Re *municipality*	Komrev. Vestfold *public audit 2015*	*Insurance fraud by putting a building on fire*

(*Continued*)

Table A.1 Continued

Investigated client organization	*Investigating examination firm*	*Suspicion of white-collar crime investigated*
Romanifolket *foundation*	Stiftelsestilsynet *public examination 2017*	*Fraud in abuse of public subsidies*
Romerike Vannverk *public waterworks*	Distriktsrevisjon *public audit 2007*	*Fraud in privatization of public property*
Sandefjord *municipality*	Tenden *law firm 2017*	*Abuse of executive position for family benefit*
Siva *state funding of industries*	Wikborg *law firm 2018*	*Chief executive funded his own company*
Skien *municipality*	BDO *auditing firm 2017*	*Fraudulent removal of sand from public property*
Skjervøy *municipality*	KomRev *public audit 2015*	*Public funds allocated to personal property*
Stangeskovene *forest company*	Ernst & Young *auditing firm 2013*	*Private stock exchange excluding bidders*
Statoil *energy*	Hagen et al. *internal controllers 2013*	*Cost savings in security measures causing accident*
Statoil *energy*	Saure et al. *internal controllers 2016*	*Cost savings in security measures causing accident*
Statoil *energy*	Østby et al. *internal controllers 2017*	*Cost savings in security measures causing accident*
Stavanger *municipality*	PwC *auditing firm 2013*	*Kidnapping fraud in public child care*
Sykehusapotekene *hospital pharmacies*	Moberg Segrov *consulting firm 2019*	*Harassment for corporate profits*
Sykehusbygg *hospital buildings*	Kluge *law firm 2017*	*Executive benefit from harassment of subordinate*
Sykehuset Innlandet *hospital*	Haavind *law firm 2011*	*Fraudulent abuse of chief executive position*
Telenor *VimpelCom mobile company*	Deloitte *auditing firm 2016*	*Corruption to obtain licenses in Uzbekistan*
Tennisforbundet *tennis association*	Lewis et al. *consulting firm 2018*	*Fraudulent arrangements of game results*
Tidal *music streaming service*	NTNU *research group 2018*	*Fraudulent manipulation of streaming accounting*

(*Continued*)

Table A.1 Continued

Investigated client organization	*Investigating examination firm*	*Suspicion of white-collar crime investigated*
Tjøme *municipality*	BDO *auditing firm 2017*	*Corruption in building permits at the seaside*
Tolga *municipality*	Fylkesmann *public examination 2019*	*Fraudulent diagnoses for retarded inhabitants*
Tomter *shopping center association*	Holmen *auditing firm 2014*	*Fraud in deregulation of shopping area*
Transocean *oil rig company*	Riksadvokaten *public prosecutor 2017*	*Tax evasion*
Trendtech *investment securities*	Finanstilsynet *public audit 2016*	*Misrepresentation of investor figures*
Troms Kraft *energy company*	Norscan *consulting firm 2013*	*Fraudulent abuse of company funds*
Universitetssykehuset Nord *hospital*	Arbeidsrettsadvokatene *law firm 2015*	*Economic exploitation of work force*
Uppsala *municipality*	KPMG *auditing firm 2018*	*Manipulation of audited numbers*
Utenriksdepartement *state department*	Kontrollenhet *internal audit 2016*	*Fraud in financing of development project*
Utenriksdepartement *state department*	Kontrollenhet *internal audit 2017*	*Fraud in financing of development project*
Utlendingsdirektoratet *foreign affairs*	Deloitte *auditing firm 2016*	*Subsidy fraud at return of refugees*
Verdibanken *religious banking*	Wiersholm *law firm 2012*	*Insider trading in bank shares*
Vestre Viken *hospital*	PwC *auditing firm 2018*	*Fraudulent diagnoses to obtain more state funding*
Vestvågøy *municipality*	Komrev. Nord *public audit 2018*	*Illegal procurement*
Videoforhandlere *series production*	BDO *auditing firm 2013*	*Abuse of state subsidies*
Vistamar *rehabilitation center*	Komrev. Trondheim *public audit 2018*	*Embezzlement by chief executive*
Vitalegruppen *private nursing*	BDO *auditing firm 2017*	*Fraud in municipal subsidies*
World Ventures *gaming company*	Stiftelsestilsynet *public examination 2014*	*Illegal pyramid of Ponzi scheme*
XXL *sports store chain*	DLA Piper *law firm 2020*	*Price fixing for market manipulation*
Zachariasbryggen *property development*	Selmer *law firm 2014*	*Fraud in transfer of property rights*

(*Continued*)

Table A.1 Continued

Investigated client organization	*Investigating examination firm*	*Suspicion of white-collar crime investigated*
Sweden		
Karolinska *hospital*	Setterwalls *law firm 2018*	*Public procurement of consulting without tender*
Kraft & Kultur *energy enterprise*	Ernst & Young *auditing firm 2012*	*Accounting fraud by misrepresentation*
Nordea *banking*	Mannheimer Swartling *law firm 2016*	*Tax evasion in wealth management*
Swedbank *banking*	Clifford Chance *law firm 2020*	*Money laundering in Baltic states*
Switzerland		
Fifa *football association*	Garcia *special committee 2014*	*Corruption at allocation of world cup*
The United Kingdom		
Sandstorm *bank*	PwC *auditing firm 1991*	*Manipulation of loans and deposit accounts*
The United States		
British Petroleum *offshore oil*	Freeh *special committee 2013*	*Fraud in settlement program after deepwater accident*
Coatesville *school district*	BDO *auditing firm 2014*	*Embezzlement of income from athletic activities*
Coatesville *school district*	Contrad O'Brien *law firm 2015*	*Embezzlement of income from athletic activities*
Chief Technology Officer *D.C.*	Sidely Austin *law firm 2010*	*Corruption in software procurement*
Enron *energy company*	Wilmer Cutler Pickering *law firm 2002*	*Accounting fraud*
General Motors *car manufacturer*	Jenner Block *law firm 2014*	*Ignition switch failure fraud*
Lehman Brothers *bankruptcy*	Jenner Block *law firm 2010*	*Executive deviance in securities*
Motorola *electronic products*	SEC *Securities and Exch. Commission 2002*	*Selectively disclosed information for insider trading*
Peregrine *financial group*	Berkeley *research group 2013*	*Ignorance of concerns for reverse repurchasing*
Philadelphia Police Department	Pennsylvania Crime Commission *1974*	*Police corruption in drugs, gambling, and prostitution*
Philadelpia Sheriff's Office	Deloitte *auditing firm 2011*	*Contracts with vendors not in compliance*

(*Continued*)

Table A.1 Continued

Investigated client organization	*Investigating examination firm*	*Suspicion of white-collar crime investigated*
Tax Administration *D.C.*	Wilmer Cutler Pickering *law firm 2008*	*Embezzlement of property tax refunds*
Texas university	Hastings *law firm 2012*	*Abuse of university funds for private travel*
Wells Fargo's Community bank	Shearman Sterling *law firm 2017*	*Deviant sales practices*
WorldCom *communications*	Wilmer Cutler Pickering *law firm 2003*	*Fraudulent accounting influencing share prices*
Vietnam		
Utenriksdepartement *state department*	Duane Morris *law firm 2016*	*Fraud in housing rental for diplomats*

Bibliography

Gottschalk, P. and Tcherni-Buzzeo, M. (2017). Reasons for gaps in crime reporting: The case of white-collar criminals investigated by private fraud examiners in Norway, *Deviant Behavior*, 38 (3), 267–281.

King, M. (2020). What makes a successful corporate investigator – An exploration of private investigators attributes, *Journal of Financial Crime*, published online https://doi.org/10.1108/JFC-02-2020-0019.

Appendix B

The list of private policing reports in this appendix is reduced compared to the list in Appendix A. The list here in Appendix B only includes investigation reports where a white-collar suspect could be identified. Table B.1 lists a total of 80 reports from Norway, while Table B.2 lists a total of 23 reports from other parts of the world. The first column tells the name of the organizations where suspected wrongdoing occurred. Some organizations are public organizations such as municipalities in Norway. Other organizations are banks and business enterprises. The second column shows fraud examiner firms such as global audit firms and local law firms. The bibliography for all reports in this appendix is included at the end of the appendix.

The lists in this appendix do not include reports that are shorter than 30 pages, as less than 30 pages make it hard to identify convenience themes and maturity levels. However, for some investigations, it was possible to access additional information elsewhere, such as verdicts, media reports, and several examination reports about the same case. Those are included in the lists.

The last names of the suspects are listed in the fourth column. The purpose of listing names is to enable readers easily to find case stories in the media. As listed in the fifth and final column, most suspects were innocent based on the presumptions of innocence in democratic nations. When brackets are applied in the final column, then it is the repetition of the above. For example, PwC (2014b) and PwC (2014c) are concerned with Hadeland broadband and Hadeland energy, respectively, where both investigations focus on Brorson as the suspect.

In Norway, 18 out of 80 individuals were sentenced to prison and incarcerated, which represents a conviction rate of 23% among those investigated by private fraud examiners. The convictions were not necessarily a result of work by fraud examiners. Convictions occurred in some cases before fraud examinations, while other convictions occurred during or after fraud examinations were completed.

Eight out of 23 suspects investigated in other parts of the world were convicted to prison, which represents a conviction rate of 35% among those investigated by fraud examiners.

Table B.1 Characteristics of fraud examinations with white-collar suspects in Norway

Organization	*Examiner*	*Pages*	*Suspect*	*Verdict*
Askøy municipality	BDO (2018)	39	Ådlandsvik	None
Bergensklinikkene health	Ernst & Young (2019a)	59	Lossius	None
Betanien foundation	BDO (2014)	10+verdict	Blomhoff	Prison
Breili architects	BDO (2017a)	39	Breili	None
Briskeby sports stadium	Lynx (2011)	267	Stensrud	None
Bærum municipality	G-partner (2007)	43	Ramstad	Prison
City Taxi	PwC (2007)	88	Clausen	Prison
DNB bank	Hjort (2016)	18+media	Bjerke	None
Drammen municipality	Deloitte (2017a)	53	Cranner	Prison
Eckbo foundation	Thommessen (2009)	119	Eckbo	None
Ferde toll collection	Deloitte (2020)	88	Juvik	None
Ferde toll collection	Kluge (2019)	40	Juvik	None
Fjell municipality	Deloitte (2017b)	33	Bjørndal	None
Forsvaret military logistics	PwC (2014a)	35	Stavrum	Prison
Forsvaret military routines	PwC (2015a)	50	Stavrum	(Prison)
Fredrikstad municipality	PwC (2018a)	78	Finess	None
Fredrikstad municipality	Simonsen (2018)	100	Finess	(None)
Fretex salvation army	Grette (2017)	132	Vestre	None
Furuheim foundation	Hald (2006)	164	Walle	Prison
Fyrlykta foundation	Deloitte (2017c)	70	Sahlström	None
Gartnerhallen fruits	Wiersholm (2018)	32	Hansen	Prison
Grimstad municipality	BDO (2016)	64	Lyngstad	None
Hadeland broadband	PwC (2014b)	32	Brorson	Prison
Hadeland energy	PwC (2014c)	25+broad	Brorson	(Prison)
Halden ice hall	KPMG (2012)	121	Montelius	None

(*Continued*)

Table B.1 Continued

Organization	*Examiner*	*Pages*	*Suspect*	*Verdict*
Halden municipality	Hjort (2013)	46	Montelius	(None)
Helse Nord hospital	PwC (2018b)	40	Ingebrigtsen	None
Jondal municipality	SBDL (2018)	71	Isdal	None
Kraft & Kultur energy	Deloitte (2013)	136	Benulic	Prison
Kraft & Kultur energy	Ernst & Young (2012)	31	Benulic	(Prison)
Kragerø fjord boats	Deloitte (2011a)	109	Rognli	None
Kristiansand municipality	Kommunerevisjon (2016)	25+media	Ugland	None
Kvam Auto cars	Wikborg Rein (2015)	93	Vikør	None
Kvinnherad municipality	Deloitte (2019a)	86	Øvregård	None
Langemyhr construction	PwC (2008a)	27+dismissal	Langemyhr	None
Leksvik municipality	Kommunerevisjon (2017)	36	Dretvik	None
Lenvik municipality	Kommunerevisjon (2018a)	104	Hagerupsen	None
Lunde Group transport	Vierdal (2012)	86	Lunde	Prison
Moscow school	Ernst & Young (2013a)	52	Grahn	None
NDLA learning arena	Deloitte (2015a)	57	Høines	None
NFF player transfers	Lynx (2012)	50	Haakonsen	None
Norsk Tipping betting	Deloitte (2010)	61	Nordby	None
Nærings ministry	Ernst & Young (2018)	49	Williams	None
Oceanteam offshore	Sands (2019)	256	Halbesma	None
Orange health	Bergen kommune (2016)	60	Paulsen	None
Oslo housing	BDO (2017b)	79	Fredriksen	None
Oslo housing	Deloitte (2018)	593	Fredriksen	(None)
Oslo housing	Deloitte (2019b)	82	Fredriksen	(None)
Oslo urban environment	Ernst & Young (2019b)	28+verdict	Skjaker	Prison
Oslo energy recycling	PwC (2019a)	154	Kristiansen	None
Oslo care buildings	PwC (2009)	92	Clausen	None

Oslo care buildings	PwC (2019b)	21+media	Johansen	None
Oslo renovation	Deloitte (2017d)	93	Enger	Prison
Oslo educational buildings	Kommunerevisjon (2006a)	44	Murud	Prison
Oslo educational buildings	Kommunerevisjon (2006b)	30	Nettli	Prison
Oslo unibuss transportation	Wiersholm (2012)	23+verdicts	Leite	Prison
Oslo road construction	Kvale (2013)	53	Staff	None
Politiets police unit	KPMG (2016)	74	Kvigne	None
Rana municipality	PwC (2008b)	52	Reithaug	None
Revac garbage recycling	Kommunerevisjon (2015a)	81	Aas	Prison
Romerike water works	Distriktsrevisjon (2007)	555	Henriksen	Prison
Siemens technology	Dalseide (2006)	184	Moestue	Fine
Siva industrial growth	Wikborg Rein (2018)	74	Susegg	None
Skjervøy fisheries	Kommunerevisjon (2015b)	138	Waage	None
Stangeskovene forests	Ernst & Young (2013b)	103	Schweigaard	None
Stavanger municipality	PwC (2013)	14+media	Thune	None
Taters association	Stiftelsestilsyn (2017)	36	Gustavsen	None
Telenor VimpelCom	Deloitte (2016)	54	Espen	None
Tidal streaming	NTNU (2018)	78	Sanders	None
TrendTech brokerage	Finanstilsynet (2016)	29+media	Jensen	None
Troms Kraft energy	Nergaard (2013)	38	Schei	None
Tromsø municipality	Kommunerevisjon (2015c)	30	Engdahl	Prison
Utenriks ministry	Duane Morris (2016)	172	Trang	None
Utenriks ministry	Kontrollenhet (2016)	23+25	Nystuen	None
Utenriks ministry	Kontrollenhet (2017)	25+23	Nystuen	(None)
Vestre Viken hospital	PwC (2018c)	30	Jacobsen	None
Vistamar nursing home	Kommunerevisjon (2018b)	92	Ruiz	None
XXL sports stores	DLA Piper (2019)	41	Grøterud	None
Vitale Group health	BDO (2017c)	50	Andersson	None
Zachariasbryggen property	Selmer (2014)	52	Hauge	None

Table B.2 Characteristics of fraud examinations with white-collar suspects globally

Organization	*Country*	*Examiner*	*Pages*	*Suspect*	*Verdict*
BP Deepwater Horizon	USA	Freeh (2013)	93	Sutton	None
Coatesville school district	USA	BDO (2015)	54	Como	None
CTO Washington	USA	Sidley Austin (2010)	60	Acar	Prison
Danske Bank	Denmark	Bruun Hjejle (2018)	87	Borgen	None
Enron energy	USA	Wilmer Cutler Pickering (2002)	218	Lay	Prison
FIFA World Cup 2018/2022	Switzerland	Garcia (2014)	359	Blatter	None
FujiFilm technology	New Zealand	Deloitte (2017e)	89	Whittaker	Prison
General Motors	USA	Jenner Block (2014)	325	Barra	None
Lehman Brothers bank	USA	Jenner Block (2010)	239	Fuld	None
Moldova banking sector	Moldova	Kroll (2017)	58	Shor	Prison
NNPC petroleum	Nigeria	PwC (2015b)	199	Kachikwu	None
Nordea bank	Sweden	Mannheimer Swartling (2016)	42	Wærsted	None
Olympus technology	Japan	Deloitte (2011b)	243	Kikukawa	Prison
Pelham public project	Canada	KPMG (2017)	100	Pupo	None
Social security	Denmark	Kammeradvokaten (2019)	163	Nielsen	Prison
Social security Socialstyrelsen	Denmark	PwC (2019c)	80	Nielsen	(Prison)
Swedbank offshore clients	Sweden	Clifford Chance (2020)	218	Bonnesen	None
Syddanmark region	Denmark	Kromann Reumert (2015)	27+media	Holst	None
Tax Washington	USA	Wilmer Cutler Pickering (2008)	126	Walters	Prison
Texas University	USA	Hastings (2012)	365	Wildenthal	None
Toshiba technology	Japan	Deloitte (2015b)	90	Tanaka	Prison
Wells Fargo bank	USA	Shearman Sterling (2017)	113	Tolstedt	None
WorldCom technology	USA	Wilmer Cutler Pickering (2003)	345	Ebbers	Prison

Bibliography

BDO (2014). *Anonymisert og revidert sammendrag (Anonymized and revised summary), Betanien Foundation*, report of investigation, 10 pages, Oslo: Audit Firm BDO.

BDO (2015). Coatesville Area School District: Investigative Report, report of investigation, 54 pages, report to attorney Matthew H. Haverstick at law firm Conrad O'Brien by audit firm BDO, Philadelphia.

BDO (2016). Rapport til kontrollutvalget: Undersøkelse om kjøp av helsetjenester i Grimstad kommune (Report to the control committee: Investigation of procurement of health care services in Grimstad municipality), report of investigation, 64 pages, Oslo: Audit Firm BDO.

BDO (2017a). *Rapport Tjøme kommune 17/6008 Gransking (Report Tjøme municipality 17/6008 Investigation)*, Breili architects, report of investigation, 39 pages, Oslo: Audit Firm BDO.

BDO (2017b). Rapport om risikokartlegging for Boligbygg Oslo (Report on risk assessment for Housing Oslo), report of investigation, 79 pages, Oslo: Audit Firm BDO.

BDO (2017c). *Rapport: Leverandørkontroll Vitalegruppen (Report: Supplier control Vitale Group), Vitale Group health services*, report of investigation, 50 pages, Oslo: Audit Firm BDO.

BDO (2018). Rapport om undersøkelser: Levering av tjenester til teknisk avdeling i Askøy kommune i perioden 2009–2017 (Report of examination: Delivery of services to technical department at Askøy municipality in the period 2009–2017), report of investigation, 39 pages, Oslo: Audit Firm BDO.

Bergen kommune (2016). *Kontroll med lønns- og arbeidsvilkår hos Orange Helse (Control of salary and working conditions at Orange Health)*, report of investigation, 60 pages, Bergen: Procurement section at Bergen Municipality.

Bruun Hjejle (2018). Report on the Non-Resident Portfolio at Danske Bank's Estonian *Branch*, report of investigation, 87 pages, Copenhagen: Law Firm Bruun Hjejle.

Clifford Chance (2020). Report of Investigation on Swedbank, report of investigation, 218 pages, Washington, DC: Law Firm Clifford Chance.

Dalseide (2006). Rapport fra Granskingsutvalget for IKT-kontrakter i Forsvaret oppnevnt av Kongen i statsråd 6. januar 2006 (Report from the Investigation committee for ICT contracts in the Defense appointed by the King in ministry January 6, 2006), report of investigation, 184 pages, Oslo: Department of Defense.

Deloitte (2010). Norsk Tipping – Granskingsrapport (Norwegian Betting – Investigation Report), report of investigation, 61 pages, Oslo: Audit Firm Deloitte.

Deloitte (2011a). Rapport Kragerø Fjordbåtselskap – Gransking (Report Kragerø Fjord Boat Company – Investigation), report of investigation, 109 pages, Oslo: Audit Firm Deloitte.

Deloitte (2011b). Investigation Report, Olympus Corporation, Third Party Committee, report of investigation, 243 pages, Tokyo: Audit Firm Deloitte Touche Tomatsu.

Deloitte (2013). Kraft och Kultur i Sverige: Utredning av Bolagets revisors arbete i förhållande til god revisionssed i Sverige avseende räkenskapsåren 2007-2010 (Kraft and Kultur in Sweden: Examination of the Company auditor's work in relation to good auditing practice in Sweden regarding accounting years 2007–2010), report of investigation, 136 pages, Stockholm: Audit Firm Deloitte.

Deloitte (2015a). Forvaltningsrevisjon Hordaland fylkeskommune, Nasjonal digital læringsarena (Management audit Hordaland county council, National digital learning arena), report of investigation, 57 pages, Oslo: Audit Firm Deloitte.

Deloitte (2015b). *Investigation Report, Summary Version, Independent Investigation Committee for Toshiba Corporation*, report of investigation, Tokyo: Audit Firm Deloitte Tohmatsu.

Deloitte (2016). Review – Ownership VimpelCom Telenor, report of investigation, 54 pages, Oslo: Audit Firm Deloitte.

Deloitte (2017a). Gransking Byggesaksavdelingen Drammen kommune (Investigation Construction Case Department Drammen municipality), report of investigation, 53 pages, Oslo: Audit Firm Deloitte.

Deloitte (2017b). *Undersøkelse av varsel, Fjell kommune (Examination of whistleblowing, Fjell municipality)*, report of investigation, 33 pages, Bergen: Audit Firm Deloitte.

Deloitte (2017c). Økonomisk analyse av Stiftelsen Fyrlykta (Economic analysis of the Foundation Fyrlykta), report of investigation, 70 pages, Bergen: Audit Firm Deloitte.

Deloitte (2017d). Renovasjonsetaten, Oslo kommune, Gjennomgang av anskaffelsesprosess og kontraktsoppfølging i Renovasjonsetaten (Renovation agency, Oslo municipality, Review of procurement process and contract management in the Renovation agency), report of investigation, 93 pages, Oslo: Audit Firm Deloitte.

Deloitte (2017e). FujiFilm Holdings Corporation: Independent Investigation Committee's Investigation Report and Future Measures in New Zealand, report of investigation, 89 pages, Tokyo: Audit Firm Deloitte Tohmatsu.

Deloitte (2018). Eiendomstransaksjoner, Boligbygg Oslo (Property transactions, Housing contruction Oslo), report of investigation, 593 pages, Oslo: Audit Firm Deloitte.

Deloitte (2019a). Forvaltningsrevisjon, Kvinnherad kommune, Forvaltning av kraftfondet (Management audit, Kvinnherad municipality, Management of energy fund), report of investigation, 86 pages, Oslo: Audit Firm Deloitte.

Deloitte (2019b). Lilleakerveien 39 A, Boligbygg Oslo, Gransking (Lilleaker road 39 A, Housing Buildings Oslo), report of investigation, 82 pages, Oslo: Audit Firm Deloitte.

Deloitte (2020). *Selskapskontroll, Hordaland, Sogn og Fjordane og Rogaland fylkeskommunar, Ferde (Corporate control, Hordaland, Sogn and Fjordane and Rogaland county municipalities, Ferde)*, Ferde toll collection company, report of investigation, 88 pages.

Distriktsrevisjon (2007). Rapport etter granskingsoppdrag fra styrene i Nedre Romerike Vannverk og Sentralrenseanlegget (Report after investigation assignment from the boards at Nedre Romerike Water Works and the Central Cleaning Plant), report of investigation, 555 pages, Lillestrøm: District Audit Agency Distriktsrevisjonen.

DLA Piper (2019). Granskingsrapport XXL (Investigation report XXL), XXL sports stores, report of investigation, 41 pages, Oslo: Law Firm DLA Piper.

Duane Morris (2016). Project House – report, conclusions and notes from interviews with selected landlords, real estate agents and locally engaged employees of the Royal Norwegian Embassy in Hanoi, report of investigation, 172 pages, Hanoi.

Ernst & Young (2012). Troms Kraft: Gransking av Kraft & Kultur i Sverige (Troms Energy: Investigation of Energy & Culture in Sweden), report of investigation, 31 pages, Stockholm: Audit Firm Ernst & Young.

Ernst & Young (2013a). *Gransking – NRVS (Investigation – NRVS)*, Moscow school run by Norwegian educational institution, report of investigation, 52 pages, Oslo: Audit Firm Ernst & Young.

Ernst & Young (2013b). Stangeskovene granskingsberetning (Stange forests investigation report), report of investigation, 103 pages, Oslo: Audit Firm Ernst & Young.

Ernst & Young (2018). *Vurdering av dagens praksis og forslag til endring av regelverk og rutiner for håndtering av bistandsprosjekter (Assessment of current practice and suggestions for change of regulations and routines for handling of development assistance projects)*, government ministry of industries, report of investigation, 49 pages, Oslo: Audit Firm Ernst & Young.

Ernst & Young (2019a). *Rapport Stiftelsen Bergensklinikkene (Report Foundation Bergen Clinics)*, health care services, report of investigation, 59 pages, Bergen: Audit Firm Ernst & Young.

Ernst & Young (2019b). Rapport Bymiljøetaten i Oslo kommune (Report Urban Environment Agency in Oslo municipality), report of investigation, 28 pages, Oslo: Audit Firm Ernst & Young.

Finanstilsynet (2016). Tilbakekall av tillatelser til å yte investeringstjenester (Revocation of authorizations to provide investment services), report of investigation, 29 pages, Oslo: The Financial Supervisory Authority of Norway.

Freeh (2013). *Independent External Investigation of the Deepwater Horizon Court Supervised Settlement Program*, British Petroleum, report of investigation, 93 pages, report by Special Master Louis J. Freeh, Wilmington: Freeh Group International Solutions.

Garcia (2014). Report on the Inquiry into the 2018/2022 Fifa World Cup Bidding Process, report of investigation, 359 pages, Zürich: Investigatory Chamber, Fifa Ethics Committee.

G-partner (2007). *Gransking av eiendomsforvaltningen i Bærum kommune (Investigation of property management in Bærum municipality)*, report of investigation, 43 pages, Oslo: Law Firm G-partner.

Grette (2017). *Granskingsrapport til Fretex Norge fra advokatfirmaet Grette (Investigation report to Fretex Norway from law firm Grette)*, Fretex as part of the Salvation Army in Norway, report of investigation, 132 pages, Oslo: Law Firm Grette.

Hald (2006). Granskingsrapporten (The Investigation Report), submitted to the Norwegian Gaming and Foundation Authority from Øyestad health care housing foundation Furuheim, report of investigation, 164 pages, Arendal: Law Firm Hald Dalane Heimvik.

Hastings (2012). Special Investigative Report regarding Allegations of Impropriety by Dr. C. Kern Wildenthal relating to Travel and Entertainment Expenses paid for by University of Texas Southwestern Medical Center, report of investigation, 365 pages, Houston, TX: Law Firm Paul Hastings.

Hjort (2013). Gransking i Halden kommune, enhet for plan, byggesak og geodata (Investigation in Halden municipality, unit for plan, building matters, and geo data), report of investigation, 46 pages, Oslo: Law Firm Hjort.

Hjort (2016). Rapport til styret i DNB (report to the board at DNB), bank mentioned in the Panama Papers, report of investigation, 18 pages, Oslo: Law Firm Hjort.

Jenner Block (2010). *United States Bankruptcy Court, Southern District of New York: Lehman Brothers Holdings*, report of investigation, 239 pages, Chicago, IL: Law Firm Jenner Block.

Jenner Block (2014). Report to the Board of Directors of General Motors Company regarding Ignition Switch Recalls, report of investigation, 325 pages, Chicago, IL: Law Firm Jenner Block.

Kammeradvokaten (2019). Ansvarsvurdering vedrørende sagen om svindel med tilskudsmidler – Offentlig rapport (Assessment of liability regarding the case of fraud with benefit funds – Public report), report of investigation, 163 pages, Copenhagen: Law Firm Kammeradvokaten Poul Schmith.

Kluge (2019). *Vurdering av forhold i Ferde (Assessment of conditions at Ferde)*, Ferde toll collection company, report of investigation, 40 pages, Bergen: Law Firm Kluge.

Kommunerevisjon (2006a). Granskingsrapport 2 Undervisningsbygg Oslo (Investigation report 2 Educational buildings Oslo), report of investigation, 44 pages, Oslo: Internal Audit Function in the Municipality.

Kommunerevisjon (2006b). Granskingsrapport Undervisningsbygg Oslo (Investigation report Educational buildings Oslo), report of investigation, 30 pages, Oslo: Internal Audit Function in the Municipality.

Kommunerevisjon (2015a). Granskning av hendelsen på Linnestad næringsområde (Investigation of the event at Linnestad industrial area), report of investigation, 81 pages, Tønsberg: Vestfold County Auditing.

Kommunerevisjon (2015b). Undersøkelse i Skjervøy fiskeriutvikling (Investigation of fisheries development), report of investigation, 138 pages, Tromsø: County Auditing KomRev Nord.

Kommunerevisjon (2015c). Rapport om Flyktningtjenesten i Tromsø kommune (Report on the Refugee service in Tromsø municipality), report of investigation, 30 pages, Tromsø: Audit Group at Tromsø Municipality.

Kommunerevisjon (2016). Undersøkelse av Bjarne Uglands roller i forbindelse med vedtak om utbygging av parkeringsanlegg under Torvet (Investigation of Bjarne Ugland's role in connection with the decision to develop a parking facility under the Square), report of investigation, 25 pages, Kristiansand: Agder County Auditing.

Kommunerevisjon (2017). *Gransking: Rådmannens avtaler (Investigation: The councillor's contract), Leksvik municipality*, report of investigation, 36 pages, Trondheim: Midt-Norge Public Audit.

Kommunerevisjon (2018a). Forvaltningsrevisjon: *Anskaffelse av helse- og omsorgstjenester (Agency audit: Procurement of health and nursing services)*, Lenvik kommune (Lenvik municipality), report of investigation, Tromsø: KomrevNord, 104 pages.

Kommunerevisjon (2018b). *Utvidet selskapskontroll av Vistamar (Expanded corporate review of Vistamar)*, report of investigation, Trondheim: Trondheim municipality's auditing office, 92 pages.

Kontrollenhet (2016). Gjennomgang av Utenriksdepartementets tildeling og forvaltning av tilskudd til ILPI gjennom prosjektet QZA-11/0341 Nuclear Weapons Project (Review of the Ministry of Foreign Affair's allocation and management of grants to ILPI through the QZA-11/0341 Nuclear Weapons

Project), report of investigation, 23 pages, Oslo: Central Control Unit at the Ministry of Foreign Affairs.

Kontrollenhet (2017). Gjennomgang av Utenrikstjenestens forvaltning av samarbeidet med ILPI 2009–2016 (Review of the Foreign Service's management of the corporation with ILPI 2009–2016), report of investigation, 25 pages, Oslo: Central Control Unit at the Ministry of Foreign Affairs.

KPMG (2012). Halden kommune: Gransking av disposisjoner i Halden Ishall og Halden Ishall Eiendom (Halden municipality: Examination of dispositions at Halden Ice Hall and Halden Ice Hall Property), report of investigation, 121 pages, Oslo: Audit Firm KPMG.

KPMG (2016). Politiets utlendingsenhet: Faktaundersøkelse og vurdering (The police immigration unit: Facts finding and review), report of investigation, 74 pages, Oslo: Audit Firm KPMG.

KPMG (2017). The Corporation of the Town of Pelham: Forensic Review of Certain Concerns Regarding the East Fonthill Development Project, report of investigation, 100 pages, Canada: Audit Firm KPMG.

Kroll (2017). *Project Tenor II, Summary Report, Report Prepared for The National Bank of Moldova*, report of investigation, 58 pages, London: Audit Firm Kroll. (2016: Project Tenor – Scoping Phase, 84 pages. 2018: Project Tenor II, Confidential Working Papers Part I to the Detailed Report, Detailed tracing analysis, 60 pages. 2018: Project Tenor II – Confidential working papers – Part II, Evidence Packs – Funds traced to: Ilan Shor, Alexandr Macloivici and Olga Bondarciuc. 2018: Project Tenor II – Detailed Report, Report Prepared for The National Bank of Moldova, 154 pages).

Kromann Reumert (2015). Region Syddanmark: Undersøgelse af hændelsesforløbet vedrørende tilretning og ændring af fakturatekst fra ekstern leverandør (Region South Denmark: Investigation of the course of events regarding adjustment and change of invoice text from external vendor), report of investigation, 27 pages, Copenhagen: Law Firm Kromann Reumert.

Kvale (2013). Oslo Vei, dets konkursbo (Oslo Road, its bankruptcy), report of investigation, 53 pages, Oslo: Law Firm Kvale.

Lynx (2011). *Briskebyrapporten (The Briskeby report), Briskeby sports stadium in the city of Hamar*, report of investigation, 267 pages, Oslo: Law Firm Lynx.

Lynx (2012). *1192-rapporten: Gransking av internasjonale spilleroverganger 2007–2011 (The 1192 Report: Investigation of international player transfers), Norwegian soccer association*, report of investigation, 50 pages, Oslo: Law Firm Lynx.

Mannheimer Swartling (2016). Report on Investigation of Nordea Private Banking in Relation to Offshore Structures*)*, report of investigation, 42 pages, Stockholm: Law Firm Mannheimer Swartling.

Nergaard (2013). Sammendrag av granskingsrapport – Troms Kraft (Summary of investigation report – Troms Energy), report of investigation, 38 pages, investigator Leiv L. Nergaard at Norscan Partners in association with law firm Grette, Oslo.

NTNU (2018). Digital Forensics Report for Dagens Næringsliv, by Jan William Johnsen and Katrin Franke, Norwegian University of Science and Technology, NTNU Digital Forensics Group, An examination of Tidal streaming accounts, Gjøvik.

PwC (2007). Granskingsrapport, Samferdselsetaten, Undersøkelser foretatt på oppdrag fra Oslo kommune, Byrådslederens avdeling v/Seksjon for internrevisjon (Investigation report, Transport agency, Examination commissioned by Oslo municipality, the City Council leader's department at Section for internal audit), report of investigation, 88 pages, Oslo: Audit Firm PricewaterhouseCoopers.

PwC (2008a). Granskingsrapport, Undersøkelse foretatt på oppdrag fra Oslo kommune, byrådslederens avdeling v/Seksjon for internrevisjon (Investigation report, Examination commissioned by Oslo municipality, City Council leader's department by Section for internal audit), report of investigation, 27 pages, Oslo: Audit Firm PricewaterhouseCoopers.

PwC (2008b). Granskingsrapport, Terra-saken i Rana kommune (Investigation report, The Terra case in Rana municipality), report of investigation, 52 pages, Oslo: Audit Firm PricewaterhouseCoopers.

PwC (2009). Gransking av Spania-prosjektet i Oslo kommune (Examination of the Spain project in Oslo municipality), report of investigation, 92 pages, Oslo: Audit Firm PricewaterhouseCoopers.

PwC (2013). Kontrollutvalget i Stavanger v/Rogaland Kontrollutvalgssekretariat: Undersøkelse/gransking knyttet til Stavanger kommunes utbetaling av á-kontobeløp i forbindelse med den såkalte Tyrkia-saken (The control committee in Stavanger by Rogaland control committee secretariat: Examination/investigation related to Stavanger municipality's payment in part in connection with the so-called Turkey case), report of investigation, 14 pages, Oslo: Audit Firm PricewaterhouseCoopers.

PwC (2014a). Forsvarets logistikkorganisasjon: Rapport etter gjennomgang av salg av fartøy (The Defense's logistics organization: Report after review of sales of vessels), report of investigation, 35 pages, Oslo: Audit Firm PricewaterhouseCoopers.

PwC (2014b). *Hadeland og Ringerike bredbånd: Rapport Gransking (Hadeland and Ringerike broadband: Report investigation)*, report of investigation, 32 pages, Oslo: Audit Firm PricewaterhouseCoopers.

PwC (2014c). *Hadeland energy: Rapport gransking (Hadeland energy: Report investigation)*, 25 pages, Oslo: Audit Firm PricewaterhouseCoopers.

PwC (2015a). *Forsvarsdepartementet: Undersøkelse av forhold knyttet til Forsvarets avhending av fartøyer (Defense ministry: Investigation of matters related to the Armed Forces' disposal of vessels)*, report of investigation, 50 pages, Oslo: Audit Firm PricewaterhouseCoopers.

PwC (2015b). *Auditor-General for the Federation: Investigative Forensic Audit into the Allegations of Unremitted Funds into the Federation Accounts by the NNPC, Nigerian National Petroleum Corporation*, report of investigation, 199 pages, Lagos: Audit firm PricewaterhouseCoopers.

PwC (2018a). Fredrikstad kommune: Rapport fra undersøkelse (Fredrikstad municipality: Report from investigation), report of investigation, 78 pages, Oslo: Audit Firm PricewaterhouseCoopers.

PwC (2018b). Helse Nord og Universitetssykehuset Nord-Norge: Rapport fra ekstern undersøkelse av hendelsesforløp (Health North and University hospital North Norway: Report from external investigation of sequence of events), report of investigation, 40 pages, Oslo: Audit Firm PricewaterhouseCoopers.

PwC (2018c). *Vestre Viken: Rapport fra ekstern undersøkelse av takstbruk ved Avdeling for Klinisk Patologi (Vestre Viken: Report from external examination of fees applied in the Department for Clinical Pathology)*, 30 pages, Oslo: Audit Firm PricewaterhouseCoopers.

PwC (2019a). Undersøkelse av Energigjenvinningsetaten i Oslo kommune (Examination of the Energy recovery agency in Oslo municipality), report of investigation, 154 pages, Oslo: Audit Firm PricewaterhouseCoopers.

PwC (2019b). Gjennomgang av ansettelsesprosesser i Omsorgsbygg Oslo (Review of hiring processes at Care Housing Oslo), report of investigation, 21 pages, Oslo: Audit Firm PricewaterhouseCoopers.

PwC (2019c). Ekstern undersøgelse af tilskudsadministrationen 1977-2018: Udarbejdet for Socialstyrelsen (External investigation of benefits administration 1977–2018: Provided to the Social security administration), report of investigation, 80 pages, Copenhagen: Audit Firm PricewaterhouseCoopers.

Sands (2019). Factual report Oceanteam: Investigation of related party transactions, report of investigation, 256 pages, Oslo: Law Firm Sands.

SBDL (2018). Rapport: Undersøkelse etter påstander om korrupsjon og privatpraksis (Report: Investigation after accusations of corruption and private praxis), Jondal municipality, report of investigation*)*, 71 pages, Oslo: Law Firm Storeng Beck Due-Lund.

Selmer (2014). Granskingsrapport Zachariasbryggen, dets konkursbo (Investigation report Zacharias harbor, its bankruptcy), report of investigation, 52 pages, Oslo: Law Firm Selmer.

Shearman Sterling (2017). *Independent Directors of the Board of Wells Fargo & Company: Sales Practices Investigation Report*, Community Bank, report of investigation, 113 pages, San Francisco, CA: Law Firm Shearman Sterling.

Sidley Austin (2010). Report of Investigation regarding Procurement Practices at the Office of the Chief Technology Officer of the District of Columbia, report of investigation, 60 pages, Washington, DC: Law Firm Sidley Austin.

Simonsen (2018). Rapport til Fredrikstad kommune (Report to Fredrikstad municipality), report of investigation, 100 pages, Oslo: Law Firm Simonsen Vogt Wiig.

Stiftelsestilsyn (2017). Stiftelsen romanifolkets / taternes kulturfond (The foundation romani people / taters' culture fund), report of investigation, 36 pages, Førde: Norwegian Gaming and Foundation Authority.

Thommessen (2009). Uavhengig undersøkelse av Eckbos legater (Independent investigation of Eckbo's Legacies), report of investigation, 119 pages, Oslo: Law Firm Thommessen.

Vierdal (2012). Rapport til Stavanger tingrett: Lunde Gruppen konkursbo (Report to Stavanger district court: Lunde Group bankruptcy), report of investigation, 86 pages, Stavanger: Law Firm Vierdal.

Wiersholm (2012). Rapport til styret i Unibuss (Report to the board at Unibuss), report of investigation, 23 pages, Oslo: Law Firm Wiersholm.

Wiersholm (2018). Rapport til landsstyret i Gartnerhallen (Report to the national board at Gartnerhallen), report of investigation, 32 pages, Oslo: Law Firm Wiersholm.

Wikborg Rein (2015). *Granskingsrapport (Investigation report)*, Kvam Auto, report of investigation, 93 pages, Bergen: Law Firm Wikborg Rein.

Wikborg Rein (2018). *Granskning i Siva (Investigation at Siva)*, Siva industrial development, report of investigation, 74 pages, Oslo: Law Firm Wikborg Rein.

Wilmer Cutler Pickering (2002). Report of Investigation by the Special Investigative Committee of the Board of Directors of Enron Corp., report of investigation, 218 pages, Washington, DC: Law Firm Wilmer Cutler Pickering.

Wilmer Cutler Pickering (2003). Report of Investigation by the Special Investigative Committee of the Board of Directors of WorldCom, report of investigation, 345 pages, Washington, DC: Law Firm Wilmer Cutler Pickering.

Wilmer Cutler Pickering (2008). *Report of Investigation submitted by the Council of the District of Columbia, Office of Tax and Revenue Investigation Special Committee, Chairman Vincent C. Gray, Councilmember Jack Evans*, report of investigation, 126 pages, Washington, DC: Law Firm Wilmer Cutler Pickering.

Index

Page numbers in **bold** reference tables; Page numbers in *italics* reference figures.

Printed in the United States
By Bookmasters